Library of
Davidson College

The Fortunes of German Writers in America

The Fortunes of German Writers in America: Studies in Literary Reception

Edited by

Wolfgang Elfe, James Hardin, and Gunther Holst

University of South Carolina Press

Copyright © 1992 University of South Carolina Press

Published in Columbia, South Carolina, by the
University of South Carolina Press

Printed in Canada

Library of Congress Cataloging-in-Publication Data

The Fortunes of German writers in America : studies in literary
  reception / edited by Wolfgang Elfe, James Hardin, and Günther
  Holst.
      p.   cm.
    Expanded and rev. versions of papers presented at a conference
  held Apr. 5–7, 1990 at the University of South Carolina, sponsored
  by the Dept. of Germanic, Slavic, and Oriental Languages and
  Literatures.
    Includes bibliographical references and index.
    ISBN 0-87249-786-0 (alk. paper)
    1. German literature–Appreciation–United States. 2. German
  literature–History and criticism. I. Elfe, Wolfgang. II. Hardin,
  James N. III. Holst, Günther. IV. University of South Carolina.
  Dept. of Germanic, Slavic, and Oriental Languages and Literatures.
  PT123. U6F65 1991
  830.9–dc20   91-23815

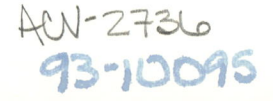

Contents

Introduction	vii
The Reception of German Literature in South Carolina, 1795–1861 BETTINA COTHRAN	1
The Bostonian Cult of Classicism: The Reception of Goethe and Schiller in the Literary Reviews of the *North American Review*, *Christian Examiner*, and the *Dial* (1817–1865) THOMAS L. BUCKLEY	27
In the Freedom Stall Where the Boors Live Equally: Heine in America JEFFREY L. SAMMONS	41
The Fame of Theodor Storm in America in the Late Nineteenth and Early Twentieth Centuries CLIFFORD ALBRECHT BERND	69
Lifting the Cultural Blockade: The American Discovery of a New German Literature after World War I — Ten Years of Critical Commentary in the *Nation* and the *New Republic* WULF KOEPKE	81
Gerhart Hauptmann in the United States WARREN R. MAURER	99
Kafka in America: His Growing Reputation during the Forties JÜRGEN BORN	121

Hoover's Mann: Gleanings from the FBI's Secret File
on Thomas Mann
HANS RUDOLF VAGET						131

The Reception of Arthur Schnitzler in the United States
DONALD G. DAVIAU						145

From Austria to America via London: Tom Stoppard's
Adaptations of Nestroy and Schnitzler
GUY STERN							167

Franz Werfel: Waiting for His Time to Come
TERRY REISCH							185

The Novels of Erich Maria Remarque
in American Reviews
HANS WAGENER							211

"Brecht, Motherhood, and Justice": The Reception of
The Caucasian Chalk Circle in the United States
SIEGFRIED MEWS							231

Making It in the Big Apple: Heinrich Böll
in the New York Press, 1954–1988
RALPH LEY							249

A Different Drummer: The American Reception
of Günter Grass
PATRICK O'NEILL							277

The Economics of Literature: More Thoughts on the
Reception of German Literature in the *New York Times*
VOLKMAR SANDER						287

Introduction

FROM APRIL 5 TO April 7, 1990, the Department of Germanic, Slavic and Oriental Languages and Literatures at the University of South Carolina sponsored a conference, The Fame of German Writers in America. The essays contained in this volume are expanded and revised versions of the conference papers, incorporating, where appropriate, the results of the lively and stimulating discussion during the conference.

The word *German* in the conference title refers to writers from Germany and the other German-speaking countries. The word *Fame* is used in the older meaning of that term, meaning "fate" or "repute," but also in the modern sense. We wished to concentrate on German writers who at a certain time achieved or are still experiencing fame in North America. For this reason the majority of articles in the volume is devoted to specific authors who fit this description: Johann Wolfgang von Goethe (1749–1832), Friedrich von Schiller (1759–1805), Heinrich Heine (1797–1856), Theodor Storm (1817–1888), Arthur Schnitzler (1862–1931), Gerhart Hauptmann (1862–1946), Thomas Mann (1875–1955), Franz Kafka (1883–1924), Franz Werfel (1890–1945), Bertolt Brecht (1898–1956), Erich Maria Remarque (1898–1970), Heinrich Böll (1917–1985), and Günter Grass (1927–). Specialists in the field of German literature will notice lacunae in our list of authors covered; for example, Hermann Hesse (1877–1962), Lion Feuchtwanger (1884–1958) and Friedrich Dürrenmatt (1921–1990), and others certainly fulfill the criteria stated. But the time limitations of a three-day conference and the space limitations of a conference volume make a selection unavoidable, and we believe that the essays found in this volume, taken as a whole, provide a representative overview of the fortunes of German writers in North America during a period of almost two hundred years. The largely chronological arrangement of the essays in the volume is designed to facilitate that overview.

Encouraged by the editors, the contributors to this volume have made sure not to burden their essays with too much theory in order not to lose the spontaneity of their presentations. The essays use a variety of methodological approaches, and they not only summarize known facts but also provide new information.

The first essay is devoted to the reception of German literature in South Carolina in the first half of the nineteenth century. Basing her results on a study of neglected primary sources, Bettina Cothran shows that German literature played an important role in the rich cultural life of Charleston. Plays by German writers, notably August von Kotzebue (1761–1819), Goethe, and Schiller, were performed extensively — mostly in English translation — and German literature was reviewed in the leading cultural and literary journals of the Southeast. Interest in German literature was nourished not only by the sizeable German community in Charleston but also by native-born Americans, especially students returning from study in Germany.

High esteem for German literature was part of an increasing respect for German scholarship in arts and sciences at that time. Thomas L. Buckley writes about another cultural center in nineteenth-century America, Boston, and shows how several important literary journals, the *North American Review*, the *Christian Examiner*, and the *Dial*, played a pioneering role in disseminating information about German authors and their works, especially on Goethe and Schiller. He concludes that "in nineteenth-century America literary reviews on German authors were one reflection of the developing discourse concerning German language and culture in general. They accompanied and reinforced the increased appreciation of German literary and scholarly accomplishments." Buckley notes in particular that the German educational system was used as a paradigm for higher education in America in the nineteenth century and that German — first introduced in America as an academic discipline in 1824 at the University of Virginia — "had become an integral part of the American educational system."

Jeffrey Sammons deals with the author Heinrich Heine, who in the nineteenth century received considerable popular and critical attention in America. Sammons sees this substantial discourse on Heine "embedded in the general interest in German literature and culture that governed American intellectual life for much of the century and up to World War I." Just as Cothran and Buckley observe the application of aesthetic as well as moral — chiefly Christian puritanical — categories in the American discussion of Goethe and Schiller, Sammons also notes "the puritanical streak that long survived in American intellectual discourse" in his analysis of the American Heine discussion. Heine's fame in nineteenth-century America stands in marked contrast to the present lack of interest in Heine outside the colleges and universities. In Sammons's view this is "a symptom of the total lack in our culture of interest in the German literary tradition of the past."

In the Heine reception in nineteenth-century America Sammons distinguishes among three groups: (1) German-Americans (the largest group), (2) educated Americans who read German literature in the original, and (3) Americans without knowledge of German who read German literature in translations. In his essay on Theodor Storm Clifford Bernd makes a similar distinction and focuses on the significance of the massive German immigration in making German the most widely studied foreign language in the United States between the Civil War and the American entry into World War I and also in helping to bring about an efflorescence of the study of German literature in America. Judging from the listings in the *National Union Catalogue*, Schiller's drama *Wilhelm Tell* and Storm's novella *Immensee* were the most published German literary texts in the second half of the nineteenth century and up to World War I. Bernd attributes this fact to the massive numbers of refugees from Germany following the failed revolution of 1848 who saw their political ideals expressed in Schiller's drama and who chose Storm's novella less for its content and more for the exemplary political biography of its author. The widespread reception of these two works among German-Americans, notably the Forty-Eighters, also resulted in numerous English translations, bringing these two works into the mainstream of American culture.

As is pointed out in several papers, World War I brought about a significant change in the reception of German literature in America. Wulf Koepke documents the negative impact on the study of German language and literature resulting from the cultural blockade against Germany following America's entry into the war. Even though this blockade was over by 1925, it continued to have a lasting adverse effect. When some interest in German literature was revived in the 1920s, the German novel fared better than the drama. As Koepke explains, "The exploration of new areas of psychology, social life, and history in the German novels had a decidedly liberating effect in America, a country ruled by isolationism, moral censorship, prohibition, and a defensive attitude toward the world." Thomas Mann, who became a Nobel laureate in 1929, played a special role in this process because — according to Koepke — he "not only provided the ultimate proof for the validity of the new German culture, but he also legitimized the novel as more than distraction and entertainment." But World War I may not have been the only reason for the aversion towards Germany and German culture. As Koepke explains, the affinity of many German intellectuals to socialist ideals was a contributing factor, given the antisocialist mentality in the United States.

Warren Maurer's essay on Gerhart Hauptmann is another interesting case study. In the beginning several Hauptmann plays ran into censorship problems in America for moral or for political reasons. In addition, the American theater audience was unprepared for the nontraditional, innovative works of a foreign playwright. The enormous success of Hauptmann in Germany, his international acclaim — he won the Nobel Prize for Literature in 1912 — and the efforts of American Germanists finally aided the reception of Hauptmann in the United States in a significant way. But whereas Hauptmann enjoys the status of a modern classic in present-day Germany, "he has been largely relegated to the obscurity of the academy" in the United States.

Jürgen Born deals with a writer who — unlike Hauptmann — is considered a modern classic in Germany as well as in America: Franz Kafka. In his analysis of the Kafka discussion of the 1940s Born points out the impact of the philosophical and ideological conflict among intellectuals in the United States. While a Marxist-materialist view of Kafka's work prevailed in one group, a metaphysically oriented religious view dominated the Kafka criticism of another group. In spite of those differences Born credits the American Kafka critics of the 1940s — American-born and -educated critics as well as central European exiles in the United States — with keeping the interest in Kafka alive during the turmoil of fascism and war in Europe. As a result, Kafka was paradoxically reintroduced to Germany and Austria after World War II via America.

That the study of the reception of German literature in America says as much about America — namely its political, social, and ideological realities — as it does about German literature becomes particularly evident in Hans Vaget's essay. Vaget points out that exiled writers, artists, and scientists who had fled Germany after Hitler's rise to power, including the internationally famous and respected writer Thomas Mann, "were the target of elaborate clandestine surveillance conducted by the United States Bureau of Investigation." Since — according to Vaget — fascism was viewed by the right-wing Establishment as a bulwark against communism, the antifascism of these exiles was viewed as premature and potentially subversive before America's entry into the war. Even though Thomas Mann was not in any danger and unaware that he was under surveillance, the public political harassment he experienced in this country especially after the outbreak of the Cold War — FBI-inspired harassment in Vaget's view — may have been an important factor in his decision to leave the United States and to return to Europe.

It is not always apparent what exactly causes the ups and downs in the reception of an author. In the case of Arthur Schnitzler, whose fortune in the United States is documented in detail by Donald Daviau, the continued reception in the popular as well as in the academic sphere "is proof of the universality of the characters and situations in his writings." Interest in Schnitzler and also in Johann Nestroy (1801–1862) has been aided by Tom Stoppard's adaptations, as Guy Stern demonstrates in his essay "From Austria to America via London: Tom Stoppard's Adaptations of Nestroy and Schnitzler." Stern points out that Stoppard's translations and/or adaptations "are often treated on a par with his original plays."

The writer Franz Werfel already had an American reputation before coming here in 1941. His life story, especially his dramatic escape from

France in World War II, may have contributed to the enormous success of his novel *The Song of Bernadette* (1941). But Terry Reisch, in his article on Werfel, also points to the perfect timing of the publication of this work: the interest in spiritual and religious books at that particular time of World War II clearly helped the book sales; the war was seen as a fight between good and evil, and the spirituality and the glorification of the human being in this book was linked to the war effort in the early, difficult phase of the war. Conversely, the failure of Werfel's *Star of the Unborn* (1945) in America can, in part, be attributed to the mood of the country after the period of uncertainty and worry about the future had ended.

Hans Wagener deals with the author Erich Maria Remarque, whose antiwar novel *All Quiet on the Western Front* became a worldwide success. Wagener, who provides a detailed analysis of newspaper reviews, comes to the conclusion that Remarque was more favorably treated by American than by German critics. While German critics essentially categorize him as a one-book author of questionable aesthetic and intellectual caliber, American critics rank him alongside great American as well as German writers of the twentieth century. Thus, the Remarque reception indicates that German literary critics often find it difficult to detect artistic and intellectual merit in a work that enjoys wide popular success.

Whereas Remarque's fame in America may have been greater than in Germany, Bertolt Brecht's fame in America did not come until after his American exile. As Siegfried Mews shows in his essay on the reception of Brecht's drama *The Caucasian Chalk Circle* in the United States, Brecht now enjoys the stature of one of the major playwrights of the twentieth century. In the American reception of *The Caucasian Chalk Circle* by American critics and audiences Mews observes a greater understanding and appreciation of Brecht the dramatist and a lesser of Brecht the philosopher, Marxist, and literary theorist.

Two essays in the volume are devoted to two authors who established their literary reputation after World War II: Heinrich Böll and Günter Grass. Ralph Ley deals with the reception of Böll in the New York press — he considers the New York press representative for the entire cultural scene in America — and concludes that Böll's works have been reviewed more often than those of any other author writing in the

German language and published in America since the end of World War II. Böll, who reached the height of critical acclaim in the U.S. shortly after being awarded the Nobel Prize for Literature in 1972, had more books translated into English and sold in America than any other German-writing author since 1945. In terms of quality, the reception of Böll has been mixed, however. While Grass does not yet equal Böll in the number of translations and the number of copies sold in America, he is — in the judgment of Patrick O'Neill — the best-known contemporary German writer in North America. As O'Neill states, "He is certainly the only German writer ever to have been awarded what is probably the ultimate accolade of North American popular criticism, a cover story in *Time* magazine." O'Neill observes a similarity in the Grass reception in Germany and in America, namely "a very noticeable polarization of opinion." But he also detects differences: while in Germany there is outrage on the political Right and the extreme Left on one side and enthusiastic support elsewhere, one can detect in America outright indifference, if not boredom, on one side and even more lavish praise on the other. The highly political aspect of Grass's work was less clearly seen or appreciated in America, where Grass was "very quickly elevated to the essentially depoliticized status of a 'world author.'"

Grass's and Böll's relative success in America notwithstanding, the general prospect for German literature in present-day America is bleak. In his essay on the most recent reception of German literature in the *New York Times*, "the most influential source of ... information for the general public," Volkmar Sander provides the statistical proof that there is very limited coverage. The absolute number of reviews of foreign books in general is decreasing, and cross-cultural knowledge and foreign language expertise are lacking in the book market. Sander also points out a major impediment to a reception of German literature, namely, the unavailability of a body of core texts. English translations of German literary texts are usually published in small editions and, as a rule, are available for only three years.

Finally, we want to emphasize again that the reception of literature is never an exclusively literary phenomenon. Rather, it is embedded in a broader political, social, economic, and cultural context. Thus, this volume is as much a history of German-American literary relations as it is a cultural history of the United States.

We should like to take this opportunity to express our gratitude to the staff of the University of South Carolina Press for its guidance and cooperation in publishing this book. Thanks are also due to Dr. Renate Wilson for editorial assistance and Miss Christine Batrla who prepared the index.

Wolfgang Elfe
James Hardin
Gunther Holst

The Reception of German Literature in South Carolina, 1795–1861

BETTINA COTHRAN

AMERICAN CULTURE IN THE nineteenth century is characterized by a strong eccentricity, the absence of a natural center, a phenomenon common in cultures in the process of their definition. Newborn forms of culture are still looking for authenticity and definitions based on the contributions of the Old World. Types of reception may include the reading and the discussion of texts and ideas of foreign authors as well as productive types of reception such as translations and imitation. A text such as *The American Scholar* by Ralph Waldo Emerson (1837) shows the characteristics of this kind of a search in the spiritual history of a country. This explains why so many professionals and students, scholars, philosophers and politicians legitimate their search through the European peregrination and sojourn as well as their attendance at German, French, and English universities, libraries, and centers of culture.

It may be of interest to the scholar of American-German relations to know that Philip Tidyman of Charleston, South Carolina, was the first American to receive a degree from a German university. He took his degree in medicine from the University of Göttingen in 1800, and, once back at home, he was instrumental in furthering the German cause. For example, he supported the German Friendly Society of Charleston through extensive and repeated gifts of German books such as the "eighteen volumes of the works of Goethe, in the original,"[1] given in 1829. Thomas Caute Reynolds studied law in Munich and then in Heidelberg, where he received his doctorate in 1842. While in Germany, he visited August Wilhelm Schlegel and Ottilie von Goethe, with whom he corresponded upon his return.

The most illustrious son of South Carolina who was a great admirer of German thought was probably Hugh Swinton Legaré. An attorney and prominent public figure, he represented the United States as chargé d'affaires in Brussels from 1832 to 1836. During this time he also studied German so that he could read Goethe in the original. He wrote to his sister, "I began yesterday (for it is quite an epoch in my life) to read Goethe's *Faust* in the original, and am happy to find it less difficult than I was led to expect. It is now eleven months since I first began to learn German...."[2] During his travels through Germany, recorded in his book *Travels on the Rhine*, he also paid A. W. Schlegel a visit of several days. His discussions on subjects ranging from the educational system and the religious tolerance of Prussia to Greek tragedy and "the picturesque and the beautiful" attest to Legaré's interest in literary matters. Legaré was also one of the editors of the noted *Southern Review*, which devoted considerable space to the discussion of things German.

To talk about Charleston as a major cultural and intellectual center may not be convincing at first glance. It may come as a surprise to hear that Charleston in 1775 had one hundred thousand citizens and was the fourth largest metropolis in the American colonies. As an important port city, especially before the advent of steamships and during the war with England, when ships sailed to Charleston rather than New York, it had direct connections to the Old World. Its wealth — based on cotton, rice, and indigo — provided the basis for elegant and cultured living. Society had a decidedly feudal structure; the aristocracy, the wealthy planters and merchants, chose Charleston as their cultural center. City life in the "season" with its balls, concerts, theater productions, private clubs, and societies was probably quite similar to elegant

---

[1] George Gongaware, *The History of the German Friendly Society of Charleston, South Carolina, 1766–1918* (Richmond: Garrett & Massie, 1935), 105.

[2] Hugh Swinton Legaré, *Writings* (Charleston: Burges & James, 1845), 1:237.

living in the capitals of the Old World. Josiah Quincy of Massachusetts, visiting Charleston in the year 1773, was enraptured by the sight. "Charleston makes a most beautiful appearance as you come up to it, and in many respects a magnificent one.... I can only say that in splendor of building, decorations, equipages, commerce, shipping etc. it far surpasses all I ever saw or even expected to see in America!"[3] Legaré wrote of the concomitant standard of education, "Before and just after the revolution, ... most of our youth of the opulent families, were educated at English schools and universities. There can be no doubt that their attainments in polite literature were far superior to those of their contemporaries at the North, and the standard of scholarship in Charleston was, consequently, much higher than in any other city on the continent."[4] This position of eminence slowly waned in the 1820s and 1830s, when the economic situation became more tenuous as the cotton trade became less profitable and Charleston's harbor declined in importance relative to New York's. The political differences over abolition and nullification increasingly strained relations between North and South, ultimately pushing the South into an isolated and defensive position.

Charleston society was composed of various elements with roots in the cultures of the Old World. Even though the French element played a dominant role in Charleston, it has been said of the German element: "In commerce, in civic affairs, in religion and in music their part has been particularly significant. German is the only language other than English which has ever had a wide usage in Charleston."[5] Prominent Charleston residents of German origin did their share to introduce German culture to the city. More important, however, was the reception of German thought by the intellectuals. For a study of reception, this critical echo is of particular interest.

The term *reception* is of relatively recent origin. Introduced in the late sixties by Hans Robert Jauss and Wolfgang Iser, it supplanted concepts such as "influence" (*Einfluß*) and "response" (*Wirkung*) with

---

[3] Josiah Quincy, quoted in "Antebellum Charleston," *Southern Bivouac* 1 (September 1885): 3.

[4] Legaré, *Writings* 2:71.

[5] Gongaware, xv.

the theory of reception. Its major characteristic is the emphasis on the reader. Roman Ingarden's discussion of the reading process and the cognition of literary works yields the useful distinction between the literary work itself and its concretizations, which come about through the reader's — or viewer's — response. Ingarden distinguishes between "unequivocal and universally determined" objects, i.e., real objects, and objects represented in a literary work, which exhibit "points" or "places" of indeterminacy (*Unbestimmtheitsstellen*). In Wolfgang Iser's concept of text-reader communication, this phenomenon is referred to as *blanks* (*Leerstellen*). By filling in these indeterminate places, readers take an active part in concretizing the literary work by imaginational experience, or, in the case of a play, by perceptual experience.[6] The outcome of the concretization may vary not only from reader to reader, but also with successive readings by the same reader, depending on his present mood or viewpoints. It follows then that the concretization of a literary work is influenced by the general atmosphere of the cultural epoch in which it is read or performed. Ingarden refers to the "life" of a literary work as it develops in a historical process constituting the identity of the work in question.[7] This concretization, however, must remain within the "directives" of the literary work, or else the critic does not arrive at an appropriate reaction. If his own experiences or his world view are very different from the literary work he is reading, it is possible that he "sees" nothing of the represented objects and loses contact with the represented world. Felix Vodicka expands on Ingarden's theory of concretization, insisting that the structure of the entire work takes on a new character when the circumstances involving time, place, or social

---

[6] See Wolfgang Iser, "Die Apellstruktur der Texte," in *Rezeptionsästhetik*, ed. Rainer Warning (Munich: Wilhelm Fink, 1979), 228–52.

[7] Roman Ingarden, "Konkretisation und Rekonstruktion," in *Rezeptionsästhetik*, 47–49. This theory is also reminiscent of T. S. Eliot's position expressed in the essay "Tradition and the Individual Talent." "What happens when a new work of art is created is something that happens simultaneously to all the works of art which preceded it. The existing monuments form an ideal order among themselves, which is modified by the introduction of the new (the really new) work of art among them. The existing order is complete before the new work arrives; for order to persist after the supervention of the novelty, the *whole* existing order must be, if ever so slightly, altered; and so the relations, proportions, values of each work of art toward the whole are readjusted; and this is conformity between the old and the new." In *Selected Prose of T. S. Eliot* (New York: Harcourt, Brace, Jovanovich, 1975), 38, 39.

conditions are altered. He calls attention to the differentiation of various strata of readers, which may be guided by different norms. He places particular emphasis on the literary critic as indicator of a predominant literary taste. He also stresses the difficulty of determining the reception of a literary work in the environment of a foreign country; not only are literary norms different from those in which the work of art was written, but the very act of translation constitutes an act of concretization, which in turn may influence the critical echo.[8] The approach of "reception" postulates thus at least a cursory glance at what may be termed the social environment (*Umfeld*) as well as a reconstruction of the literary norms of the place and time under consideration.

Of a total of 93,000 inhabitants of South Carolina in 1755, 15,000 had come from Germany.[9] Many of them were farmers or skilled craftsmen, of which Charleston as the port city received its fair share.[10] By the beginning of the nineteenth century the Germans in Charleston had become one of the most active civic forces in the city. Many of them joined the German Friendly Society, founded in 1766 by Michael Kalteisen, as well as the German Fusileers, established in 1775.

John A. Wagener, who arrived in 1833 from a small city near Bremen, was particularly active in the political and civic arena. Among other projects he founded a German Fire-extinguishing Company, (an important public institution for a city threatened and occasionally devastated by fires) and was instrumental in establishing a German language newspaper *Der Teutone*. It was governed by the motto: "Immer vorwärts ein löbliches Ziel zu erreichen, Und Treu' ohne Furcht im Herzen verwahrt; Kühn und edel, vom Pfad der Pflicht nicht verweichen, Thatkräftig, das ist Deutscher Sinn und Deutsche Art" (March on to reach your worthy goal; and keep a loyal and fearless heart; with courage and a noble mind, never waver from the path of

---

[8] Felix V. Vodicka, "Rezeptionsgeschichte literarischer Werke," in *Rezeptionsästhetik*, 73–74.

[9] Albert Bernhardt Faust, *The German Element in the United States* (New York: The Steuben Society of America, 1927), 285.

[10] For a detailed description, see Gotthard D. Bernheim, *History of the German Settlements and the Lutheran Church in North and South Carolina* (Philadelphia: Lutheran Book Store, 1872), 89.

duty; never idle: that is a German's mind and character).[11] In this spirit, he also founded an athletic club (*Turnverein*) in 1846 and a rifle association (*Schützengesellschaft*) in 1855. One of his lasting projects was the founding of a community, Walhalla, in the South Carolina piedmont. In the years after the Civil War he even briefly held the position of mayor of Charleston.

John Bachmann, pastor of St. John's Lutheran Church, was another prominent member of the community. Born in New York, his family had preserved the German language and tradition. He was not only an outstanding shepherd of his congregation, but also an ardent scientist who gained fame as the collaborator of John Audubon, particularly for *The Viviparous Quadrupeds of North America*. (The friendly relations went even beyond the professional scope when Bachmann became the father-in-law of John Audubon.) In 1838 he visited Wilhelm von Humboldt in Berlin and was awarded an honorary doctorate.[12]

The musical life of the city profited from the efforts of the son of the famous Johann Pachelbel, Carl Theodor Pachelbel, who was music director at a local church and had also established a "singing school" for young ladies. Charles Gilfert was the German-born director of the Charleston Theatre from 1817 until 1825 and responsible for bringing such talented actors as Thomas Cooper and Brutus Booth to Charleston.[13]

One important measure of the reception of German literature in Charleston is the success of German drama on Charleston's stages. Charlestonians were fond of the diversion the theater offered, supporting two theater companies over much of the period under consider-

---

[11] Gertha Reinert, "Aus dem Leben des Auswanderers Johann Sievers Wagener," *Jahrbuch der Männer vom Morgenstern*, Heimatbund an Elb– und Wesermündung (Bremerhaven: Ditzen, 1981), 123ff.

[12] This and other events are related in the travel logs of his young companion. Claude Henry Neuffer, ed., *The Christopher Happoldt Journals* (Charleston: The Charleston Museum, 1960), 156ff.

[13] "Perhaps no man did more for the advancement of the theatrical art in the city than he.... With theatrical interests in Charleston, Savannah, Richmond and elsewhere, he did much to further the profession in the South." W. Stanley Hoole, *The Ante-Bellum Charleston Theatre* (Tuscaloosa: The University of Alabama Press, 1946), 21ff.

ation. The epilogue to one of the first productions indicates an open-mindedness and joy of life unhampered by puritanical blinders.

> Nor real virtue blames the pleasing strife,
> To blend amusement with the shades of life;
> Wise, innocent, serene, she smiles at ease
> Nor hanging witches, nor abjuring plays.[14]

Almost 400 productions between 1795 and 1861 are attributable to German origins. The German theater on Charleston's stages had an auspicious beginning with the performance of Lessing's *Minna von Barnhelm* on 18 February 1795 under the title of *The Disbanded Officer or the Baroness of Bruchsal*, thus preceding New York and Philadelphia in being the first American stage to produce a German drama in translation.[15]

The most popular author was August von Kotzebue. "Kotzebue's works in English constitute more than half the plays of German origin staged in the English language in the Carolina town. Accounts of as many as four hundred performances of German plays in English translation have been found.... Two hundred and sixteen were from the pen of Kotzebue."[16] Friedrich Schiller ranked a distant second with approximately twenty performances each of *William Tell, or the Swiss Patriot*, and *The Robbers*. Also popular were Heinrich Zschokke with *Abaellino, or the Great Bandit* and Friedrich Halm with *Ingomar, or the Son of the Wilderness*.

Although the number of performances justify certain broad conclusions about the popular taste of the Charleston public, we have a much more accurately measurable response in the critical reviews of Stephen Cullen Carpenter, an Irishman who had come to Charleston from London, where he had been theater critic of the Royal Theatres.

---

[14] Thomas Wertenbaker, *The Golden Age of Colonial Culture* (New York: New York UP, 1949), 146.

[15] Arthur Hobson Quinn, *A History of the American Drama: From the Beginning to the Civil War*, 2nd ed. (New York: F. S. Crofts, 1946), 12.

[16] Arthur H. Moehlenbrock, "Kotzebue on the Charleston Stage," *Furman Studies* 34, no. 4 (Winter 1951): 3.

Even though he was an expatriate, Carpenter represented one particular critical standard of his adopted home town. From 1803 to 1806 he published critical reviews in the *Charleston Courier*. The first copy of this newspaper announces to the public the moral standards guiding this publication: "... to maintain the federal Constitution inviolate, pure and uncorrupted, generally; to defend, as far as they can, the cause of Christianity, order and good government, and to oppose every attempt that may be made, to pervert the sound principles, or contaminate the morals of the community." Kotzebue was a man to Carpenter's liking. First, Kotzebue's dramas were very effective stage pieces. *Pizarro, or the Death of Rolla* (*Die Spanier in Peru*) and its sequel, *The Virgin of the Sun* (*Die Sonnenjungfrau*) were the most popular German dramas, which justified, among other extravagances, a seventeen-piece orchestra as well as various dance numbers performed by the Peruvians and processions of the priest and virgins of the sun. A viewer's reaction indicates the general norms of reception. He notes "... the liberality of expense and the uncommon exertion with which they have brought forward the elegant entertainment of *Pizarro* as a criterion for public taste." He adds, "The citizens of Charleston are indebted their best support of productions of this description."[17] Secondly, there was nothing censurable about Kotzebue from a critic's point of view. On the contrary, next to the Bible, there could not have been a better illustration of the Christian principles of repentance and forgiveness than in *The Stranger* (*Menschenhaß und Reue*). Carpenter can say, "... for the spiritual guidance of man, [one] could hardly have imagined a case superior to that offered by Kotzebue in *The Stranger*.... They must indeed be destitute of all noble feeling, who have not a tear of sorrow to shed over the misfortunes, and another of joy over the reconciliation of the 'Stranger' and his wife."[18] An incident several years later proved Carpenter right in his judgment that Mrs. Haller gave an excellent example "to admonish and deter" when a lady fainted during a performance. The actress representing Mrs. Haller noted in her diary with satisfaction that she had been "instrumental in saving at least one

---

[17] *Gazette*, 16 November 1808.

[18] *Charleston Courier*, 28 December 1803.

frail being from becoming 'like stars that fall to rise no more.'"[19] Of particular interest to Charlestonians was the drama *False Shame, or: The American Orphan in Germany* (*Falsche Scham*). Part of the action centers on the siege of Charleston during the Revolution and the saving of an orphan from the flames by a young Hessian officer, who returns with the child to his native country. The *Gazette and Daily Advertiser* praised it as one of Kotzebue's "chastest dramas," with the character of the American orphan being "one of the sweetest sketches of his inimitable pen."[20]

If Charlestonians reveled in the "chaste and sweet" productions of Kotzebue, how would they react to something like Schiller's *The Robbers*? From its first performance on 11 May 1796 it was the subject of much discussion. A preview in the *Daily Courier* pointed to two specific obstacles to reception:

> ... a very celebrated drama in five acts, called "The Robbers," — Altered from the German of Schiller, by Mr. Hodgkinson and compressed into the usual compass of plays on the English and American Theatres. The public are respectfully informed that an alteration in the catastrophe of this great and celebrated Drama has been made, and will be submitted in the performance, this evening, to their judgement and approbation.[21]

It seems plausible that a happy ending was substituted; this may at least be conjectured from the a critical review by Carpenter of 26 December 1803, in which he suggests a change "by which the catastrophe would be infinitely more pathetic and affecting, and much of its present ... absurdities cleared away. One by which the monster of the play should be made to receive before the audience exemplary punishment; and the rest disposed of in a manner suitable to their characters and commensu

---

[19] Anna Cora Mowatt, *Autobiography of an Actress, or Eight Years on the Stage* (Boston: Ticknor, Reed, and Fields, 1854), 248.

[20] *Gazette*, 18 March 1800.

[21] In addition to the announcement in the *Daily Courier*, William Dunlap makes the following reference to these changes: "... and the *Robbers* is so mutilated and mangled as to give no adequate idea of the great German poet." William Dunlap, *History of the American Theatre* (New York: Burt Franklin, 1797; reprinted 1963), 2:104.

rate with their crimes.... Amelia ought certainly to be spared." Even though Amelia is definitely in Carpenter's "good" category, she does not quite fit in with his conception of the delicate Charleston ladies. Carpenter notes with indignation that she exhibits behavior "too coarse for our notions of female heroism and virtue." The fact that in her rage she is persuaded to call Franz Moor a few names "detract from our esteem for her. ... what ever it may be considered in Franconia, would be looked down upon as downright masculine vulgarity in England."[22]

An anonymous reviewer in the *City Gazette* writes of the various possibilities of critical reception, "Of this most extraordinary production, ... different opinions may be formed by the Critics, according to those various standards."[23] In Carpenter's critical canon, however, the *The Robbers* must find strict censure as a play that leaves doubt in the spectator's mind about the moral character of the heroes and heroines; in Carpenter's words, "He who attempts to reconcile vice with virtue flies in the face of nature and God."[24] Schiller's genius seems to have been strong enough, however, to cause Carpenter's critical principles to waver.

> Never has the human fancy teemed with so strange a production — never did it weave into the compass of a five act play such a variegated issue of contrasted qualities — of vigorous thought and frightful paradox — of vivid genius and terrific gloom — of so much to agitate and rouse the feelings, interest the heart, to swell the imagination, to attract and rivet attention, to set curiosity on fire, and at the same time of so much to appall the soul, to send it back sickened with horror, to make it start with fright from a spectacle on which, even while it retires from it, it casts back a lingering look, wishing, yet fearing again to behold it.[25]

---

[22] *Charleston Courier*, 22 December 1803.

[23] *City Gazette*, 4 March 1807.

[24] *Charleston Courier*, 26 December 1803.

[25] *Charleston Courier*, 20 December 1803.

Carpenter cannot decide whether to be for or against "Charles de Moor"; although he feels he has to make just that distinction based on his role as arbiter of taste and mores. On a humorous note, his ambivalence is expressed by giving extensive quotes from scenes that the actor "to the credit of his good taste and judgement" had omitted from the performance but that obviously fascinate Carpenter so much that he has to dwell on them; among them is Charles's boastful listing of those princes, public officials, and priests who misused their power and the public trust. Carpenter quickly clarifies his stance, however, and concludes:

> ... let it not be imagined that we argue in defence of a play which so triumphantly tramples upon critical laws; we only mean to say that notwithstanding all its defects, there is such a portion of genius infused into it, that we could not help yielding up our hearts for the time to the necromantic art of the poet....[26]

Having been caught once off guard, he now seems to be searching for anything not living up to his strict moral norms and finally finds another topic deserving of severe censure: Charles's offer to an old, penniless soldier to make use of the bounty set for his capture. This adds the proverbial last straw, "... to stain a noble soldier with the office of a mercenary informer. Abominable!"[27] In his last review for the *Charleston Courier* Carpenter's summary judgment of all German authors is less than admiring. Carpenter participates

> in the prosecution against this general conspiracy against religion in favor of atheism.... To this general work of wickedness, the German dramatists have given their hands and heads, and all their thought.... It is the object, and it is the duty of true criticism, to omit no opportunity that occurs, of admonishing ... against the pernicious principles now allowed.[28]

---

[26] Ibid.

[27] It does not escape Carpenter's attention that the robbers, numbering only eighty, were victorious over sixty hussars, ninety-six dragoons, and forty light horses, in all two hundred!

[28] *Charleston Courier*, 16 February 1804.

Carpenter's attack indicates that he was in congruence with what William Charvat has termed "certain common denominators" of critical thought in the beginning of the nineteenth century and which he has subsumed under the following six maxims: 1. The critic thought of himself as the watchdog of society; 2. Literature must not condone rebellion of any kind against the existing social and economic order; 3. Literature must not contain anything implicitly or explicitly derogatory to religious ideals and moral standards; 4. Literature should be optimistic; it should not condone philosophical pessimism or skepticism; 5. Literature should deal with the intelligible, not the mystical or obscure; 6. Literature should be social in point of view, not egocentric.[29] Given this critical canon, it is understandable that the American critic did not appreciate Schiller's drama. Aside from some reactions typical for the American context, such as the sensibility to proper female behavior, there are some parallels to the contemporary German reception. Oellers documents that Schiller's popularity with the average theatergoer rested primarily on a predilection for the "heartrending and sentimental elements, as well as a love for glittering and pompous productions."[30] A sentiment strikingly similar to the Charlestonians' reaction to *Pizarro* is recorded for the Berlin production of *The Maid of Orleans*. Oellers relates that the public adored the extravagant coronation procession to such an extent that August Wilhelm Iffland is supposed to have entertained plans for a full-length production of the march only, without the rest of the drama.[31] It is furthermore interesting to note that in Berlin Schiller's dramas ranked in popularity behind those of other popular writers, such as Kotzebue and Iffland.

The tenets of the Scottish "school of common sense" certainly constituted one of the major norms for literary production of the time in question. However, they were not the only postulates influencing the critical taste, as is apparent in the critical reviews of the time.

---

[29] William Charvat, *The Origins of American Critical Thought* (New York: A. S. Barnes, 1961), 7–27.

[30] Norbert Oellers, *Schiller: Geschichte seiner Wirkung bis zu Goethes Tod, 1805–1832* (Bonn: H. Bouvier, 1967), 330, 331.

[31] Ibid., 327.

Charleston could boast over seventy magazines serving various interests published between 1795 and 1861. For the purposes of this discussion the five most interesting ones are the *Southern Review* (1828–1832), the *Rose Bud*, later called the *Southern Rose* (1832–1839), the *Southern Quarterly Review* (1842–1857), *Russell's* (1857–1860) and the *Southern Literary Messenger* (1834–1864), published in Richmond, Virginia, which, however, was widely read in Charleston and also had contributors from Charleston.

Whereas some journals such as the *Southern Rose* were aimed at entertainment and instruction, thus interspersing longer articles with shorter observations on a variety of topics as well as printing poems or serial novels, the "serious" reviews such as the *Southern Review* or the *Southern Quarterly Review* contained only review articles "of the quarterly type, long, substantial, learned and — for the modern reader — heavy and often tedious."[32] Following the generally accepted principles of universality, these journals regarded it their mission to inform their readers speedily about new developments and ideas in a spectrum of fields. Thus they were in appearance quite similar to journals such as the *Edinburgh Review* or the *Revue des Deux Mondes*. A cursory study of the hundred and forty-one articles of the *Southern Review* reveals that forty-eight articles are devoted to literature, twenty-seven to history, twenty-six to legal and economic issues; twenty-five concern themselves with natural sciences, eleven with travelogues, and four with pedagogical issues. The time frame extended from classical antiquity to the future. The qualifications of the contributors corresponded to this concept; they were generally well-educated men of the world — lawyers, bankers, scientists, as well as professors — who were living examples of Emerson's vision of the American scholar, a statesman-philosopher. Recently published books usually served as the points of departure. Often they were printed abroad or translations of foreign works. Judging the worth of these publications and evaluating their usefulness for the American context was the task of the critic. The frequent mention of the word *Southern* in the title calls attention to the fact that the South — like other regions of the United States — saw

---

[32] Jay Hubbell, *The South in American Literature, 1607–1900* (Durham: Duke UP, 1954), 269.

itself as an independent region with its own concerns and a right to contributions to the nation as a whole, for which these publications served as a forum. A regional pride, possibly a certain defensive competitiveness increasing towards 1861, can also be discerned. The prospectus of the *Southern Review*, as published in various reviews of a similar character, defines its raison d'être in 1828 as follows:

> It shall be among our first objects to vindicate the rights and privileges, the character of the Southern States, to arrest, if possible, the current which has been directed so steadily against our country generally, and the South in particular; and to offer to our fellow citizens one Journal which they may read without finding themselves the objects of perpetual sarcasm, or of affected commiseration.

In an article entitled "Our Literature; Its Character and Condition in the South," published in the *Magnolia*, Southern literature is described as different from Northern literature. Alluding to different national literatures on the continent based on the distinct national characteristics of the countries, the author draws the conclusion that the differences here "are such as grow out of the different regions, tempered, perhaps, by the influence of climate."[33]

In the quest for an emerging national literature, the South wanted to have a voice. The topic of creating a national identity and a national literature, separate and distinct from the colonial motherland, whose bond was felt to be oppressive, was the subject of numerous articles. The thought of creating a new world, infinitely superior to the old one, imbued the idealistic critic with the loftiest visions of a new Golden Age.

> ... a nation has arisen, European in language and descent, which has laid the foundation of a literature broader and deeper than ever [any] nation did before, — in the nature of man, in the character of universal society, in the principles of social order, in

---

[33] "Our Literature; Its Character and Condition in the South," *Magnolia* 1 (1840): 215.

popular rights and popular government, in the welfare and education of the people.[34]

Realistic observers conceded that "... we are as ready as other people to boast of the talent of some of our native artists.... But certainly as a nation, we have scarcely made any progress in such things."[35] This insight leads to a search for appropriate models, resulting in the understanding that "no nation can be imagined beyond the reach of improvement from foreign sources."[36] Aside from the English and Scottish, whose natural affinity could not be denied, the French and Germans presented themselves as worthy models too.

The evaluation of the contributions of foreign nations was frequently not based on the works under consideration but on preconceived notions. One recalls the characterization of the Germans and French in Madame de Staël's *De l'Allemagne*, published in English translation in 1814, "The Germans often run into the error of introducing into conversation that which is fit only for books; the French sometimes commit the contrary fault, of inserting in books that which is pardonable only in conversation."[37] Dr. Robert Henry may have just that in mind when he prefaces his discussion "Romances of the Baron de la Motte Fouqué" with an observation about

> ... the indignation which has frequently seized upon us whilst considering the extremely iniquitous judgements which are passed ... on what are called FOREIGN works of genius. Many of these criticisms appear to have no other merit than the alliterative language in which they are couched. Accordingly, if a performance be Dutch, it is, by prescription, dull; if French, flimsy; if German, grave.[38]

---

[34] *Southern Review* 1 (1828): 5.

[35] *Southern Review* 2 (1829): 73.

[36] *Southern Quarterly Review* 11 (October 1847): 306.

[37] Anne Louise Germaine Baronne de Staël, *De l'Allemagne* (London: J. Murray, 1814), 5.

[38] *Southern Review* 3 (February & May 1829): 35.

16 The Fortunes of German Writers in America

The Germans generally had the good fortune to be considered "profound and original," as opposed to the French, on whom the reviewer bestows the epithet "the flippant ignorance of the Parisian wits."[39] Interestingly enough, the image of the Germans as the more accurate and precise scholars as compared to the French gave way to another perception about 1840, when the Romantic poets entered the picture. Notably the *Southern Literary Messenger* gives a very unfavorable characterization of "the strange and dreamy style of German literature,"[40] a fault which is later extended to all intellectual productions of German origin.

> Instead of that admirable distinctness, and that lucid order which enchant us in nearly all the scientific works of France, we meet everywhere on crossing the Rhine, with a despairing vagueness of thought and awkwardness of method ... a radical want of clearness of conception; and this fault consequently appears as well in science, in philology and law, as in the imaginative portion of German literature. Leibnitz and Gauss, K. O. Muller and Niebuhr, Hugo and Savigny — the greatest names of Germany — are as truly chargeable with this clumsiness of arrangement and indistinctness as Jean Paul himself.[41]

Mostly, however, the hegemony of the Germans in the areas of science and classical studies is undisputed. Of Schleiermacher's translation of *Plato* we read, "... we can hardly hope to see any translation in our own language, equal to the ... one ... of Schleiermacher in the German."[42] And: "The fact cannot be disguised that we no longer repair for information on these topics to Oxford and Cambridge, to London and Edinburgh. We must go to Berlin, Göttingen, Heidelberg and

---

[39] *Southern Review* 3 (February & May 1829): 194.

[40] *Southern Literary Messenger* 5 (1839): 851.

[41] *Southern Literary Messenger* 12 (1846): 65.

[42] *Southern Quarterly Review* 29 (1856): 415.

Halle."[43] In a later edition of the same review this judgment includes literature.

> ... Germany's poets, historians, moralists and authors in every department of elegant letters and philosophy, ... are exerting at the present moment, a controlling and ennobling influence upon the whole empire of mind, throughout both Europe and America.[44]

A list of all references to German thought in the Charleston publications contains about four hundred items, including short notices (for example information about the number of volumes in German libraries), announcements of book publications (usually accompanied by brief commentaries), thorough review articles about specific works, and finally examples of productive reception, poems or stories in translation as well as stories in imitation of the German and poems "in the German style." The wide spectrum of German works covered and the currency and intensity of discussion bespeak a wide-ranging interest in German thought by the Charleston public.

Even though German literature of earlier periods was not totally unknown to Charlestonians, it is fair to say that marked interest began with the discussion of the works by Goethe and Schiller. Referring to the slow recovery of German culture after the Thirty Years' War and possibly to the relatively recent recognition of German as a language capable of literary expression, Dr. Robert Henry states in the *Southern Review*, "In Schiller and Goethe, champions have arisen, whose success has fairly removed every barrier, whether native or foreign, which opposed itself to the literary renown of their country."[45] The famous speech by George Calvert, first given before the Athenaeum Society in Baltimore in 1836 and reprinted in numerous literary magazines such as the *Southern Literary Messenger*, was instrumental in highlighting the new achievements of German literature. He divides German literature

---

[43] *Southern Quarterly Review* 5 (1844): 353.

[44] *Southern Quarterly Review* 7 (1845): 197.

[45] *Southern Review* 3 (February & May 1829): 37.

into three major epochs, of which "Goethe represents the third," after the epochs of the "Nibelungenlied" and of "Luther," respectively.[46]

The spirit of the time postulated an interest in the person of the artist as well as in his work. The number of biographies and descriptions of the "life and works" of a particular artist attest that one sought illumination by grasping that which was particular about the person of the artist, especially in his personal habits or eccentricities. Often consideration of the person overshadowed the artist's work, as one may gather from Carlyle's remarks prefacing his book *The Life of Friedrich Schiller*, "... to gather from his life and works some picture of himself."[47] It is easy to see that gossip was frequently the result of these inquisitions. Furthermore, an artist with a "reprehensible" lifestyle had often little chance to win the critics' favor. A case in point is Goethe.

An all-encompassing interest in Goethe's person is reflected in news about his personal habits. At one point we hear about the strict daily regimen Goethe observed, about his disciplined work habits, but also about his appreciation of a good bottle of wine, "... what will the total-abstinence people say to that picture of his taste and habits?"[48] His independent nature was faulted for his violating codes of friendship, a serious offence. Even critics well disposed towards him felt forced to admit, "... he seems a little too calm, too cold." The two reproaches, however, deserving greatest censure are identified in an article published in the *Southern Literary Messenger* in 1856 entitled "Moral Tendency of Goethe's Writings."

> Our charges against him are two:
> 1. The poison of atheistic infidelity is diffused through his works, dissolved in a menstruum of intoxicating poetry and attractive fiction.

---

[46] George H. Calvert, "German Literature," *Southern Literary Messenger* 2 (1836): 373–80.

[47] An example is Carlyle's discussion of Schiller in his book *The Life of Schiller*, published in 1825 in London and in 1830 in Frankfurt in German translation. Carlyle appreciates the works of Schiller on the background of the "ideal man" Schiller strove to be throughout his life. See Norbert Oellers, *Schiller: Geschichte seiner Wirkung bis zu Goethes Tod, 1805–1832*, 144ff.

[48] *Russell's* 1 (1857): 268.

2. His views of life are material and sensuous. Professing to study Humanity as an artist, he excludes from the realm of Art the highest attributes, Conscience, Religion, Immortality.[49]

Surprisingly, only few of Goethe's poems were printed in the journals and magazines. Aside from "Erlkönig," variously rendered as "The Erlking" or "The Elfking," only two poems received wide recognition, "Gretchen am Spinnrad," in various translations, occasionally homespun, under the title of "The Song of Margaret" (or "Margaret and Faust") and "Der König in Thule," most frequently rendered as "The Monarch's Goblet." One exceptional venture by a dedicated professor of foreign languages was the publication of a monthly journal devoted to modern languages, the *Polyglott*. During its short life — it was published monthly from March to August 1844 — it also printed four Goethe poems that otherwise might not have received public exposure: "Das Göttliche," "Harzreise im Winter," "Gesang der Geister über den Wassern," and "Der Gott und die Bajadere."

Goethe's novels *The Elective Affinities* and *Wilhelm Meister* posed the greatest challenge to the reviewers. A review of *Wilhelm Meister's Apprenticeship and Travels* in the *Southern Literary Messenger* turns sternly against this "Pantheistic bible," which is characterized mainly as a description of loosely connected love affairs on the lowest level. "No feeling, no affection, no scene which Goethe describes is free from a tinge of the licentious colouring in which his imagination seems to revel.... Jarno ... is in fact a libertine of the worst kind, being governed in his amours by a spirit of cold sensuality, unredeemed by a single passionate impulse; a man after Goethe's own heart; in fact, such a man as was Goethe himself."[50]

The reviewer feels provoked to sum up all the prejudices that an American could have towards Goethe.

... when Religion required an advocate, when Freedom needed a protector, when Truth demanded a champion, — why, during this long period of strife and peril, Goethe wrote no line, uttered

---

[49] *Southern Literary Messenger* 22 (1855): 180.

[50] *Southern Literary Messenger* 17 (1851): 441.

no word suited to the times.... The same apathetic spectator ab extra — passionless, yet observant, semi-sensuous, yet semi-philosophical spirit, which dictated this interrogatory as to the nature of patriotism, pervades all his later writings, but in none it is so visible as in *Faust* and *Meister*.[51]

It appears that the *Southern Literary Messenger* was in the forefront of anti-Goethe sentiment. In Charleston, on the other hand, several critics formed a more positive opinion of his works.

In a review of *Wilhelm Meister* in the *Southern Review*, the charge is addressed that "Meister, like Werther, has been accused of immoral tendency"; but the charge is immediately put into perspective: "chiefly, however, by a class of philosophers who can descry no safe-guard for virtue except in an absolute ignorance of all temptation."[52] The scope of critical reception, ranging from belligerent rejection on the one hand to enthusiastic acceptance on the other, was even more evident in the case of Goethe's *Faust*, then judged to be his most important contribution to literature. For example, we read in a review of 1845 that "in *Faust* ... Goethe obfuscates his readers ... unless he doesn't even know himself what he wants to say."[53] But a discussion of *Faust* printed in *Russell's* in 1859 proclaims that "it is now universally acknowledged, that Goethe is by far the greatest poetical genius that modern Germany has produced, and it is no less generally admitted that his *Faust* is the most important, as well as the most perfect, of the many works which he has left to posterity."[54]

In Germany too, Goethe's writings were controversial, most notably *The Elective Affinities* and *Wilhelm Meister*. The various movements and critical leagues against Goethe have been well documented. They included representatives of the Enlightenment, such as Nicolai and Kotzebue, and especially spokesmen for the nascent Romanticism led by among others the brothers Schlegel. These attacked Goethe

---

[51] Ibid., 431.

[52] *Southern Review* 3 (1830): 379.

[53] *Southern and Western Monthly Magazine and Review* 1 (1845): 432.

[54] *Russell's* 4 (1859): 481.

primarily for his "classical" definition of art as an autonomous ideal that lacked a realistic, political dimension. Among his most vociferous opponents was Wolfgang Menzel, who vilified Goethe in his literary history *Die deutsche Literatur*. Representatives of the movement Junges Deutschland joined the chorus of anti-Goethean sentiments, charging him and his followers with an aloofness characteristic of people who, to speak with Heine, "view art as an independent second world, which they put on such a lofty pedestal that all human concerns, morals and religion, ever changing, remain far below it."[55]

Many of the issues raised by the German readers and critics can be found in the American context as well. Against the background of a rather narrow-minded puritanical moral code much of what Goethe wrote was questionable. In a newly founded democracy where the courageous fight for freedom was very much in everyone's memory, a writer perceived as decidedly "apolitical" could not well be heroic. The Anglo-Saxon mind, being by and large of a practical, down-to-earth nature, resisted the speculative nature inherent in many German writings, Goethe not excepted. Goethe occasionally expressed displeasure with the mundane tastes of an uneducated German audience; one might expect an even less refined general reader in a country where colonization had only recently ended and high culture was a rather recent acquisition. In addition, the reception of Goethe — like that of any other foreign writer — was complicated by the most immediate problem of transplanting a work of literary art from one culture to another one: that of obtaining an adequate translation. Taking all that into account, it is astonishing to find in Charleston an elite group of readers and critics who appreciated in Goethe the poet and philosopher who could help shape their definition of taste and be a beacon in guiding the fledgling native muse.

As in Germany, contrasting Schiller and Goethe was a topos also taken up by the Southern magazines. If Goethe's life-style gave reason

---

[55] "... jene Gruppe, die von Heine in seiner *Romantischen Schule* als 'Goetheaner' bezeichnet wurde und die nach ihm 'die Kunst als eine unabhängige zweite Welt [betrachten], die sie so hoch stellen, daß alles Treiben der Menschen, ihre Religion und ihre Moral, wechselnd und wandelbar unter ihr hin sich bewegt.'" Karl Robert Mandelkow, ed., *Goethe im Urteil seiner Kritiker: Dokumente zur Wirkungsgeschichte Goethes in Deutschland. Teil I, 1773–1832* (Munich: C. H. Beck, 1975), xxx.

for complaint, Schiller's life called for the highest encomiums. "The individual characteristic of Schiller is elevation. The predominant tendency of his mind is ever upwards. Open his volumes anywhere and in a few moments the reader feels himself lifted up into an ideal region."[56] Another distinction between the two authors is the rather naive division between classic and romantic. "Schiller warms Goethe with his passion and romance, while receiving from the other his highest concepts of classical art and analysis."[57] In 1839 Elizabeth F. Ellet of Charleston published a book *The Characters of Schiller*, which was the source of several excerpts published in the Charleston journals. In this way she probably contributed to the popularity of the author, although it is questionable how much she did for a fitting aesthetic reception. As Carpenter has done earlier, she also made a careful distinction between the spheres of "good and bad." In spite of her general praise of the author she criticizes a perceived lack of immediacy. "His philosophy was undoubtedly erroneous; the true poet is always philosophical, but his knowledge of nature is intuitive, not derived from his studies of theoretical rules."[58] Her critical evaluation may also derive intuitively from Wolfgang Menzel, from which she quotes. "It is — to use the language of Menzel in speaking of other creations of Schiller — the tone of heavenly flute amid wild discordant music, the blue of ether amid a storm, a Paradise on the edge of a crater."[59] Even if clouded by her own "romantic" viewpoint, Mrs. Ellet did mention Schiller's status as a critic as well as a poet. She also furthered knowledge of Schiller by translating various poems which were published in the Charleston magazines. However, the critics found Schiller the dramatist most accessible. "Schiller's great reputation rests, and will ever rest, unshaken, on his dramas."[60] This is George Calvert's evaluation as expressed in his speech "German Literature," printed in 1836 in the *Southern Literary Messenger*. In spite of popular success of *The Robbers*,

---

[56] *Southern Literary Messenger* 2 (1836): 378.

[57] *Southern and Western Monthly Magazine and Review* 1 (1845): 432.

[58] Elizabeth F. Ellet, *The Characters of Schiller* (Boston: Otis, Broaders, 1839), 14.

[59] Elizabeth E. Ellet, "Schiller's Thekla," *Southern Rose* 6 (April 1828): 273.

[60] *Southern Literary Messenger* 2 (1836): 378.

critics referred mostly to Schiller's first three dramatic productions, *The Robbers*, *Fiesco*, and *Love and Intrigue* (sometimes also entitled *The Harper's Daughter*) as "preparatory studies to his dramatic career."[61] Only the later productions evincing the "adoption of legitimate and classical standards" received positive reviews.[62] Proper length, however, also appears to be a matter of personal, or national, preference. *Don Carlos* was judged to be entirely too long and therefore unfit for stage production. "His *Don Carlos* would probably keep us all night; and there is no such passion for theatricals among our people ... in fact it is difficult to believe that the passion for theatricals, even with the best pieces, survives a certain period in youth...."[63] It may be attributable to this quality that discussion of Schiller's dramas is frequently reduced to summary evaluations such as "he has left finished tragedies, viz. — *Don Carlos*, *The Maid of Orleans*, *Wallenstein*, *Mary Stuart*, *The Bride of Messina*, and *William Tell* — works, in whose conception and execution the highest principles of art control with plastic power the glowing materials of a rich, deep, fervent mind."[64] The novel fragment *Der Geisterseher* (The Spiritualist) in a local translation appeared in serial form in 1841 in the *Magnolia*. Based on the impression of Schiller "as pure, and simple, and noble, as a man, as he is powerful and beautiful as a poet,"[65] his fame grew as "the most widely popular ... of all Teutonic writers."[66]

This synopsis gives an indication of the reception of German authors in Charleston. The various reactions, synchronic as well as diachronic, show the many obstacles a literary work encounters in a foreign setting. Frequently misunderstandings arose from faulty translations, or at least a full appreciation was hampered by stylistic problems, such as a too literal translation, reflecting even German word order. The most challenging hurdle to overcome was that of a differing *Lebensanschau-*

---

[61] Ibid., 379.

[62] *Southern Quarterly Review*, n.s. 5 (April 1852): 429.

[63] Ibid., 433.

[64] *Southern Literary Messenger* 2 (1836): 378.

[65] Ibid., 379.

[66] *Southern Literary Messenger* 15 (1849): 109.

ung (view of life) expressed in the literary work as it clashed with the local canon of taste. The new views may either be rejected on the basis of the existing moral or artistic code, or they may be perceived as avant-garde and, upon reflection, may even cause a shift in the accepted norm itself. Exponents of the aesthetics of reception have termed this a change in the horizon of expectation. This study points to evidence that Charleston's intellectual climate was congenial to a reception of German literature, a trend that was not evident in, for instance, the *Southern Literary Messenger*. During the time between 1795 and 1861 Charleston reviews show a change in the critical norms. The question of taste is discussed time and again in the context of works of German literature and philosophy. The pivotal role of the critic is perceived as on the one hand monitoring prevailing taste, on the other hand influencing, through a change in the artistic norm, artistic production.

> In spite of the general laws which have been laid down by eminent writers, we find its canons ever varying with the varying character of different ages.... For criticism is but the expression of taste; and taste, though not creative, has a reflex influence on art.[67]

And especially on literature, we may add. In 1806 the critical stance of Stephen Cullen Carpenter proceeding from the strictly moralistic-utilitarian notions of the Scottish school may be seen as a point of departure. His role of arbiter was "... to defend the cause of Christianity, order and good government, and to oppose every attempt that may be made, to pervert the sound principles, or contaminate the morals of the community."[68] It does not surprise that he could not see beyond the "general work of wickedness [to which] the German dramatists have given their head and hand." The reviewer of Schlegel's work in 1855 condemns "that rigid sect of narrow-minded moralists, who despise all

---

[67] *Southern Quarterly Review* 27 (1855): 398, 404.

[68] William L. King, *The Newspaper Press of Charleston, South Carolina* (Charleston: Edward Perry, 1872), 97.

culture excepting that which promotes that bitter zeal of misconceived duty which they suppose to be religion."[69]

In the development of critical norms, the Charleston intellectuals and literati carefully examined what German poets and thinkers had to say. It is a fitting tribute to that country's thought when our reviewer quotes Goethe in pleading for a critical canon based on aesthetics, which, in his words, "alone can be the measure of culture, and consequently of [the] progress in refinement and the higher walks of civilization."[70]

---

[69] *Southern Quarterly Review* 27 (1855): 413, 414.

[70] Ibid., 412.

The Bostonian Cult of Classicism: The Reception of Goethe and Schiller in the Literary Reviews of the *North American Review*, *Christian Examiner*, and the *Dial*, 1817–1865

THOMAS L. BUCKLEY

Introduction

LITERARY REVIEWS CONSTITUTE ONE important mode of disseminating information about authors and their works. In nineteenth-century America literary reviews on German authors were one reflection of the developing discourse concerning German language and culture in general. They accompanied and reinforced the increased appreciation of German literary and scholarly accomplishments. The sometimes lengthy essays not only provided a critique of a work under review, but also served to inform the reading public about the authors, often through extended excerpts from the work. At the beginning of the nineteenth century, most knowledge of German literature was based upon translations and articles from British sources. There was little firsthand knowledge.[1] This trend was altered when American students began to study at German universities in the second decade of the

[1] Scott Holland Goodnight, *German Literature in American Magazines Prior to 1846*, Bulletin of the University of Wisconsin, Philology and Literature Series no. 188 (Madison, 1907), 33.

century and a major influx of German immigrants commenced in the 1820s (over 1 million between 1820 and 1860).[2] Now the stage was set for a more serious and nonderivative view of German literature. The study of the German language was introduced first at the University of Virginia under Georg Blättermann in 1824, soon to be followed by the appointment of Carl Follen at Harvard in 1825. The German educational system was used as a paradigm for the American system, which further cemented the reputation of the study of German culture.[3] By the end of the period under consideration, that is around 1870, German had become an integral part of the American educational system.[4] A review from the *Christian Examiner* of 1869 corroborated this view. The author noted that the book being reviewed — a book in German entitled *Abriß der deutschen Literaturgeschichte* (Outline of German Literary History) — would have gone "almost without notice" some forty years ago. "Now," he stated, "such a book interests a public numbered by millions, and will be sent to all parts of the land."[5] He continued further down, "In one generation a marvelous change has come. The German language has been brought into the very front rank of ordinary studies" (3). The fifty-year period from approximately 1817 to 1865 represented an important transitional stage toward the firm establishment of the study of the German language and literature. It was during this period that an initial familiarity with German literature was developed among a large educated audience.

This pioneering exposure to German literature was nurtured by some literary journals that, in certain instances, made the task a veritable crusade. Boston was the major center of the new interest in everything German. Three of the journals that were most enthusiastic about German literature were the *North American Review*, the *Christian*

---

[2] Richard Spuler, *"Germanistik" in America: The Reception of German Classicism, 1870–1905* (Stuttgart: Hans-Dieter Heinz, 1982), 43.

[3] See John A. Walz, *German Influence in American Education and Culture* (Philadelphia: Carl Schurz Memorial Foundation, 1936).

[4] Spuler, *"Germanistik" in America*, 44.

[5] C. H. Brigham, "On the Study of German in America," *Christian Examiner* 87 (1869): 1–20. All references to journal articles will receive one complete citation in a footnote. However, the appropriate page number from a journal article for a particular reference or quotation will be provided in the text itself.

Examiner, and the *Dial*.[6] The *North American Review*, one of the most influential journals of the period, was particularly important in the earlier phase of the American reception of German literature due to the ground-breaking nature of its undertaking. The *Christian Examiner*, a Unitarian-affiliated journal, was not as uniformly enthusiastic about German literature and culture yet on the whole represented it in a favorable light. The *Dial*, the journalistic mouthpiece of New England Transcendentalism, though short-lived (1840–1844), espoused a very pro-German stance. What united all three journals was their consistent preoccupation with Goethe and Schiller. The literary reviews from all three journals serve as an indicator of the interest in Goethe and Schiller during this period.

The background of the individuals who wrote about these writers' lives and their works is also of special interest because it was so homogeneous. In all instances they had a close affiliation with Harvard College, either as graduates or faculty or both. In addition, most enjoyed ties to the Unitarian church or its "radical" offshoot, Transcendentalism.[7] Some had also studied in Germany (usually at Göttingen), which made them favorably disposed toward German culture. They returned to America already converts to the cause, so to speak, due to their favorable exposure to both authors abroad.

The Literary Reception of Goethe and Schiller

For the period under consideration Goethe and Schiller were the best-known German authors. One-third of all periodical items dealt

---

[6] *Christian Examiner and General Review*, 1824–1869 (preceded by *Christian Disciple*, 1814–1823), *Dial: A Magazine for Literature, Philosophy, and Religion*, 1840–1844 (repr. New York: Russell and Russell, 1961); *North American Review*, 1815–1935. All three reviews were published in Boston. For more information about these journals, see Frank Luther Mott, *A History of American Magazines* (Cambridge: Harvard University Press, 1957).

[7] The term *Transcendentalism* does have its origins in the writings of Kant. It is used, however, only in its most general and superficial meaning, that is, referring to what is beyond sensual experience. There is a wealth of literature about New England Transcendentalism. See in particular the annotated bibliography: Joel Myerson, ed., *The Transcendentalists: A Review of Research and Criticism* (New York: MLA, 1984), which provides a good discussion of primary and secondary sources.

with the works and the lives of these two authors.[8] The reviews themselves did not endeavor to undertake an in-depth analysis of the works of Goethe and Schiller; instead, many were marked by a paucity of knowledge about both authors, and relied on secondary sources and their own incomplete knowledge of German literature. The reviews betrayed a decided predilection for the personal qualities of Goethe and Schiller. In other words, the criticism of both authors was often based upon their own personal attributes rather than upon their literary accomplishments. Those reviewers who had studied in Germany, however, tended to defend Goethe and Schiller on the basis of their aesthetic achievements. The reviews, therefore, fluctuated between unabashed and uncritical praise on the one hand and on the other hand unsubstantiated condemnation of the works that was based on the author's personal life, especially in the case of Goethe.

Edward Everett's landmark review of the first three volumes of Goethe's autobiographical work, *Aus meinem Leben — Dichtung und Wahrheit*, in the *North American Review* of 1817 ushered in the new era of interest in German literature.[9] Everett, a Harvard professor who was a member of the first wave of Americans to have studied in Germany and therefore to have gained firsthand knowledge of German culture, composed the article while still studying in Göttingen. As could be expected, Goethe was enthusiastically reviewed. *Werther* was praised for its "rhetorical purity" and "moral power." The work was seen as an "original inspiration of Genius." *Faust* was deemed his greatest work. Everett complained, though, that not enough was known about Goethe and that the only source of information, the French author Madame de Staël (1766–1817), whose work *De l'Allemagne* had appeared in English translation in 1814, was inadequate. He expressed the hope that he had "succeeded in increasing the interest our readers feel in him [Goethe]." This interest, however, was still slow in coming.

In the 1820s, with a genuine German craze sweeping Boston intellectual circles, more attention was paid to both authors in the *North*

---

[8] Henry A. Pochmann, *German Culture in America: Philosophical and Literary Influences 1600–1900* (Madison: University of Wisconsin, 1957), 329. This third was the share in all journals from the period, not just the three journals discussed here.

[9] Edward Everett, review of *Aus meinem Leben — Dichtung und Wahrheit*, by J. W. von Goethe, *North American Review* 4 (1817): 217–62.

American Review. In a review from 1822 concerning the comedies of Aristophanes, the reviewer, remarking favorably about German scholarship, placed Goethe above Aristophanes.[10] Nathaniel L. Frothingham, a Unitarian minister, in a review of the nineteenth-century Austrian dramatist Franz Grillparzer's *The Golden Fleece* (*Das goldene Vließ*) from 1823, commented that the genius of Goethe was "the pride of Germany."[11] In the same year two reviews appeared in the *North American Review* about Schiller. The first was by the brother of Edward Everett, Alexander Hill Everett, who had also studied in Germany.[12] He reviewed a biography of Schiller, which he found "indifferent" and of "no great merit" (398). For Schiller, though, he had great words of praise. *The Robbers* (*Die Räuber*) was characterized as a "true sign of real genius" (401), though he did question the possible adverse moral influence of such a work of art; the portrayal of highway robbers as heroic could cause confusion among the readers. Nevertheless, Schiller withstood a comparison with Shakespeare and could still be termed a great writer in his own right. As is the case with all favorable reviews of Schiller, it was the dramatist's irreproachable moral standpoint that won over any doubters. "All his writings are distinguished by a pure morality, and an elevated tone of thought and feeling" (424). Goethe and Wieland, Everett noted, were not as "pure" as Schiller. This criticism of Goethe was a first indication of a discussion that persisted throughout the period concerning Goethe's questionable morals. In the very same year, George Bancroft, who also had studied in Göttingen (1818–1820), wrote a review of Schiller's poems.[13] He praised the genius of Schiller, his nobility, virtuousness, and "chaste character."

---

[10] Review of *The Comedies of Aristophanes*, by T. Mitchell, *North American Review* 14 (1822): 273–96.

[11] Nathaniel L. Frothingham, review of *Das goldene Vließ*, by Franz Grillparzer, *North American Review* 16 (1823): 283–99.

[12] Alexander Hill Everett, review of *Friedrich von Schillers Leben*, by Heinrich Doering, *North American Review* 16 (1823): 397–425.

[13] George Bancroft, "Friedrich von Schiller's *Gedichte* — Schiller's Minor Poems," *North American Review* 17 (1823): 268–87.

In the following year George Bancroft composed an essay on the works of Goethe, also published in the *North American Review*.[14] He labeled Goethe the most national, representative, and popular of all German authors, and though opinions were divided about him, "it is too late to dispute his genius" (306). His popularity was a reflection of his poetic excellence. *Faust*, though, was "not of a purely moral tendency" (311); it was too extravagant and daring, yet *Iphigenia* and *Tasso* were great monuments to his genius. The reviewer admitted that he was avoiding the unpleasant and unworthy passions, which were treated in some of Goethe's works, and concentrating on that which was excellent. It was possible, however, to draw instruction of a practical moral nature from Goethe's works, according to Bancroft, though this dramatist was not a religious man. Goethe's writings, in general "promote a love for the arts, for activity, for truth" (325).

The *Christian Examiner* printed its first literary review of Goethe in the year 1830.[15] The reviewer was Cornelius C. Felton, Harvard professor and later member of the Transcendentalist Club. He reviewed Goethe's *Iphigenia* and all his other works in glowing terms. He spoke of Goethe's succession of great works, each one having strengthened the impression of his genius. Now at the end of his life, he was the last of the giants — the others being Schiller, Wieland and Klopstock — who remained.

> Of that constellation, one star only, but that the brightest of all, yet remains; shining on with a pure and steady lustre, amidst the flood of softened and reflected light that still lingers over the horizon where those kindred stars have set. (188)

This bombastic praise communicates the tone of the review, which went on to acclaim Goethe's great versatility, universal knowledge, tremendous appeal, and his mastery of the language. In the drama *Iphigenia* Goethe had captured "the essential spirit" (200) of the Greeks.

---

[14] George Bancroft, "The Works of Goethe," *North American Review* 19 (1824): 303–25.

[15] Cornelius C. Felton, review of *Goethe's Werke. Iphigenie auf Tauris: Ein Schauspiel*, *Christian Examiner* 8 (1830): 187–200.

In 1834 both the *North American Review* and the *Christian Examiner* published reviews of a biography of Friedrich Schiller. George H. Calvert, a student in Göttingen in 1824–25, authored the review in the *North American Review*.[16] At the beginning of this article he discussed poetical genius and its "intense sensibility to the beautiful" (2), obviously referring to Schiller. Schiller possessed a "rich intellect and pure heart" (20). Calvert considered *Wallenstein* to be Schiller's masterpiece and the greatest drama of the age. Frederic H. Hedge, a member of the Transcendentalist circle educated chiefly in Germany, discussed the work in the *Christian Examiner*.[17] Hedge applauded the biographer for a job well done. He was particularly impressed by Schiller's *The Robbers*, which he felt overshadowed Goethe's *Werther* and *Götz*, and was better than Schiller's later plays. His praise for Schiller was not unqualified, however. Though his writings were full of "beautiful thoughts" and "noble sentiments" (387), he was "deficient in poetic feeling" (381), even if this did not prevent him from being high on the list of great poets. Even more surprisingly, Hedge did not consider Schiller's morality irreproachable; his works were neither immoral nor particularly moral. Notwithstanding all these misgivings, Schiller still belonged to those immortal writers who had made Germany great, though he did not rank higher than Goethe. This critique of Schiller's moral character represented an exception to the otherwise positive Schiller reception.

Two translated works of Goethe's and Schiller's were reviewed in the *Christian Examiner* in 1839. The first, Schiller's *Wilhelm Tell*, was hailed as one of his "most admired dramatic pieces" (385), which was a "living work of Art" with "the integrity of Nature" (390).[18] The second article, a review of translated poems by Goethe and Schiller, was

---

[16] George H. Calvert, review of *Life of Schiller*, *North American Review* 39 (1834): 1–30.

[17] Frederic H. Hedge, review of *The Life of Schiller, comprehending an Examination of his works*, *Christian Examiner* 16 (1834): 365–92.

[18] John S. Dwight, review of *William Tell; a Drama, in five Acts.* by Schiller, trans. Rev. C. T. Brooks, *Christian Examiner* 25 (1839): 385–91.

of greater significance due to its very harsh criticism of Goethe.[19] The reviewer was William Ware, at the time the editor of the *Christian Examiner* and a Unitarian minister. His primary objections to Goethe were his lack of scruple and his subservience to power and authority. Goethe was viewed as being inferior to Voltaire in genius, but even more so in morality. *The Elective Affinities* illustrated his lack of morals. Ware's searing condemnation of Goethe's works culminated in the observation "Twaddle will not long pass for wisdom," yet on the very same page he maintained, "In the art of writing German he has no superior" (367). This paradox, to a certain extent, took the sting out of Ware's criticism. On the subject of Schiller, however, he was unambiguous. Schiller was "a purer writer and a nobler man" (373). Ware described Schiller's character as

> high tragic and moral interest and dignity. His tastes were exalted; his love of humanity a consuming passion; his ardor for freedom and social progress, an absorbing feeling.... His genius was kindled with the divine light. (373)

Ware was obviously much more concerned about the moral and spiritual aspects of these two authors. On the basis of such a comparison, Schiller "triumphed" over Goethe, yet it was grudgingly admitted that the latter was a master craftsman of the German language.

The *Dial* commenced publication in 1840, and it was in this Transcendentalist journal, edited by the author and early feminist Margaret Fuller (1810–1850) and then the philosopher and poet Ralph Waldo Emerson (1803–1882), that the life and works of Goethe were given much attention and praise, although none of it was unqualified. Schiller, surprisingly, was not treated at all. The articles about Goethe were prime examples of Transcendentalist literary criticism, which

---

[19] William Ware, "*Specimens of Foreign Standard Literature. Vol. III containing Select Minor Poems of Goethe and Schiller*," *Christian Examiner* 26 (1839): 360–78. Translations of works from the German were on the increase starting in the 1830s. For example, the work here under review is one book in the above-named series, which was edited by George Ripley, a Unitarian minister and Transcendentalist. Fourteen volumes were published between 1838 and 1842, ten of which are German works. Notable American translators from this same Harvard-affiliated circle are: Charles T. Brooks, Frederic H. Hedge, Margaret Fuller and John S. Dwight.

unequivocally spelled out their creed. In the editors' note in the first volume Emerson spoke about the "progress of a revolution" (2), that is the Transcendentalist movement, but conceded that the ideals of this movement had not yet been rendered in the form of literature. "In literature, this influence appears not yet in new books so much as in the higher tone of criticism" (3).[20] It was in the literary reviews that the new thinking must be sought.

In the second volume of the *Dial* from the same year, Emerson expounded upon how this new literature ought to be in an article entitled "Thoughts on Modern Literature."[21] According to Emerson, literature was God-inspired; it emanated from thought. The highest class of books were those with a "moral element." These were followed by works of the imagination and then by works of science. The great immortal works were contingent upon their spirit.

> In the spirit in which they were written is the date of their duration, and never in the magnitude of the facts. Everything lasts in proportion to its beauty. In proportion as it was not polluted by any wilfulness of the writer, but flowed from his mind after the divine order of cause and effect, it was not his but nature's, and shared the sublimity of the sea and sky. (138)

Great works led to metaphysical nature and to moral abstractions, which were the "essence and soul" of nature (147). Judged upon these attributes, Goethe fell woefully short, according to Emerson. Goethe was lauded, however, as a many-sided Universalist, who reflected the characteristics of his age. He was a realist, who tried to discern the meaning of every object. His analyses always resulted in wholes. But in Goethe Emerson detected "the absence of the moral sentiment" (154). Nature was moral and this morality could only be seen by the moral mind. Nature was the ideal, but Goethe depicted merely the actual, which was ephemeral (155). He was the poet of the actual, as was clear in *Wilhelm Meister*, which was the actual and nothing more. Unfortunately for Goethe, his moral faculty was not as developed as his other

---

[20] Ralph Waldo Emerson, "The Editors to the Reader," *Dial* 1 (1840): 1–4.

[21] Ibid., "Thoughts on Modern Literature," *Dial* 1 (1840): 137–58.

powers. For this reason Goethe could not be a "Redeemer of the human mind," but instead "drop[ped] ... into the common history of genius" (156).

In 1841 there were three articles in the *Dial* regarding Goethe that are worthy of note. The first need only be mentioned in passing. It was an article by Theodore Parker, another Transcendentalist, that discussed German literature and celebrated it as being the best literature of modern times.[22] He went on to consider a recent translation of a work on German literature by Wolfgang Menzel (1798–1873), the famous German literary historian, stating that it was much too prejudiced, especially against Goethe. Although Parker admitted that Goethe was by no means perfect, particularly from a moral standpoint, he was nevertheless a great author. It was precisely Menzel's view on Goethe that prompted Margaret Fuller to write an essay rebutting his position.[23] She determined that Menzel, though possessing a "brilliant mind," approached Goethe from the perspective of a philistine, who was incapable of understanding genius. Though clearly a great admirer of Goethe's, Fuller questioned whether he lived up to the "standard of ideal manhood" (344). She found that he could have been a priest, but instead he was only a sage. Though his intellectual abilities were astounding, he did not reach the highest development; he was incomplete, even if he did rise to "Ulyssean stature" (347). These thoughts were continued in a longer article from the same year.[24] In this second article the critique was reminiscent of Emerson's. According to Fuller, Goethe's intellect was more developed than his moral nature; he possessed a deep mind but a shallow heart. He was much too worldly, having wasted his time at the court in Weimar. Goethe spent too much time nurturing his own nature and abilities and thus lost sight of higher aims. He did not become a prophet poet, though he was a "poetic artist" (21). Fuller considered *Faust* to be Goethe's greatest work, even if he did not attain with it what he could have. The article was replete with such "almost" statements, indicating Goethe's failure to live up to his potential. Yet Fuller wavered towards the end of the

---

[22] Theodore Parker, "German Literature," *Dial* 1 (1841): 315–39.

[23] Margaret Fuller, "Menzel's View of Goethe," *Dial* 1 (1841): 340–47.

[24] Ibid., "Goethe," *Dial* 2 (1841): 1–41.

article, heaping great praise upon works such as *The Elective Affinities* and *Iphigenia* and wondering if she had not been too critical of Goethe's genius.

The vacillation on the part of Margaret Fuller befitted a movement which was unclear about its own aims. Both Emerson and Fuller seemed to praise Goethe, on the one hand, but on the other hand they negated their own tribute to his genius. The exacting moral standards applied to him could hardly be lived up to by any author. This position was in keeping with the forward-looking nature of the movement, the sense of not yet having arrived in a better future world. The Transcendentalists hoped for "the Genius of the time," as Emerson put it, who "will write in a higher spirit, and a wider knowledge, and with a grander practical aim, than ever yet guided the pen of poet."[25] It was this genius who was yet to come.

The subsequent reviews in the two remaining journals — the *Dial* ceased publication in 1844 — concentrated for the most part on Goethe. He still was plagued by some criticism of his morality, though everyone took it as a given that he was a genius. Witness Cornelius Felton's turnabout (he had praised Goethe in an earlier review) when he labeled *The Elective Affinities* "the most licentious and detestable book of modern literature" in a *Christian Examiner* review.[26] And an unknown reviewer of a translation of Goethe's *Egmont* in the *North American Review* of 1843 was appalled that Goethe had turned a noble historical figure into a licentious seducer.[27] For this reason the drama had "moral faults," and was not a good specimen of Goethe's genius. J. M. Mackie, a journalist and admirer of Emerson and Parker, though no real Transcendentalist himself, had no second thoughts about either

---

[25] Emerson, "Modern Literature," *Dial* 1 (1840): 158.

[26] Cornelius C. Felton, review of *History of Speculative Philosophy*, by Francis Bowen, *Christian Examiner* 32 (1842): 398. The review contains remarks about Goethe's novels.

[27] Review of *Egmont; a Tragedy in Five Acts*, by Goethe, *North American Review* 54 (1843): 250–52.

Schiller or Goethe and labeled their works "the restoration of ancient classical beauty" (103).[28]

Andrew Preston Peabody, a Unitarian minister, reviewed Hedge's *Prose Writers of Germany* and again returned to the moral issue in the *North American Review* of 1848.[29] At the beginning he acknowledged the unduly severe criticism that was meted out to German language and literature and found the assessment unfounded. He then went on to review Hedge's work, noting that a large amount of space had been reserved for Goethe. Though himself not an ardent admirer, he did admit that Goethe was "the most accomplished man of his age," yet he "appear[ed] to have committed moral suicide" (479). Goethe's name tended to elicit such responses, especially among the Unitarian clergy.

A very interesting comparison was drawn between Goethe and George Washington in a review from the *Christian Examiner* of 1856, and once again it was Goethe's character that was questioned.[30] Washington was praised as a man of good character, a patriot, who fought unselfishly for a just cause. Goethe, on the other hand, though a great man of letters, a genius even, could not be regarded as highly as Washington, for his character was not as great as his intellect. Goethe remained only a sayer, while Washington was a doer; "the genius of character ... transcends the genius of intellect" (324). Frederic H. Hedge, the selfsame translator of Goethe and a Transcendentalist, tried to defend Goethe's morality in a review of Lewes's *The Life and Works of Goethe* of the same year in the *North American Review*.[31] He admitted to being a great admirer of Goethe's and expounded upon his

---

[28] John Milton Mackie, review of *Geschichte der Poetischen National-Literatur der Deutschen von G. G. Gervinus, North American Review* 58 (1844): 79–109. Also reviewed is Gervinus's *Neuere Geschichte*.

[29] Andrew Preston Peabody, review of *Prose Writers of Germany*, by Frederic H. Hedge, *North American Review* 67 (1848): 464–85.

[30] C. A. B., "Washington and Goethe," *Christian Examiner* 60 (1856): 317–26. The reviewer could be Cyrus Augustus Bartol, a Harvard Divinity School graduate, liberal theologian, and a great admirer of German literature. This review, however, is not in keeping with an essay of his from 1885, in which Goethe is praised and staunchly defended, also on moral grounds.

[31] Frederic H. Hedge, review of *The Life and Works of Goethe*, by G. H. Lewes, *North American Review* 82 (1856): 564–68.

accomplishments in various fields. Hedge was particularly grateful to Lewes for bringing up the moral issue and placing it in a more positive light, but he feared that it would not convince those of the current generation, who perceived Goethe as heartless and selfish. Only at a later date would Goethe's works be appreciated on their own merit without the distraction of his personal life. In this instance Hedge was trying to separate the aesthetic from the personal in order to make Goethe's works more palatable to a morally conservative audience. One last article from the decade of the 1850s, which should be mentioned in passing, was a review of a translation of Goethe's *Faust Part I* in the *Christian Examiner* of 1857.[32] It hailed the drama as "a tragedy of every-day life whose sweetness and pathos have never been surpassed" (8).

The last three reviews to be considered, all from the year 1865, were equally favorable and did not treat the moral question regarding Goethe. Instead, they concentrated on the works themselves — in this case *Wilhelm Meister* and *Faustus: The Second Part* (both translations) — and viewed both works very positively, though the second part of Faust was thought to be too idealistic and to have been an almost impossible undertaking.[33] The final review fittingly treated Schiller and revered him as a "reformer and prophet" of his people (143).[34]

Conclusion

The reviews from all three journals testify to an avid interest in Goethe and Schiller. The high praise for both authors remained consistent throughout the whole period, yet there were many voices in this discourse that did not express unqualified enthusiasm for them. The criticism, as we have seen, revolved around their personal attributes and moral stance. Schiller received high marks from most reviewers in both

---

[32] Review of Brooks's *Faust*, *Christian Examiner* 63 (1857): 1–18.

[33] Henry James, Jr., review of *Wilhelm Meister's Apprenticeship and Travels*, by J. W. von Goethe, trans. Thomas Carlyle, *North American Review* 101 (1865): 281–85; "Review of Current Literature," *Christian Examiner* 78 (1865): 141–44 (contains a review of *Faustus: The Second Part*).

[34] "Review of Current Literature," *Christian Examiner* 79 (1865): 143–46. Part of this article, "Criticism," contains remarks about Schiller.

categories. Goethe's morality and personal life, on the other hand, were scrutinized and often condemned. But he was rarely criticized on aesthetic grounds. The origin of this criticism lay clearly in the strong Unitarian and Transcendental emphasis on morality, which was undoubtedly a legacy of the Puritan past.

The Transcendentalist vacillation concerning Goethe and the stature of his genius signaled a first step toward uncoupling moral certitude from aesthetic merit. Margaret Fuller was certainly an enthusiastic admirer of Goethe's, but she could not see past her own moral vantage point and therefore articulated only qualified praise for him. Frederic H. Hedge openly confronted this issue and strove for an assessment of Goethe based solely on aesthetic criteria. It was his viewpoint that was destined to win out. The last three reviews from the year 1865, which concentrated only on the works themselves, could be viewed as a step in this direction.

The preoccupation with Goethe and Schiller in these literary reviews was one important reflection of the discourse on German culture that was developing in nineteenth-century America. This interest, which initially had been championed by students returning from Germany, took on a life of its own as the century progressed. Though the number of reviews treating both authors actually decreased towards the end of the period under consideration, that is in the 1850s and 1860s, this trend was by no means an indication of a decline in interest in both authors, but rather that the reputation of Goethe and Schiller had now become established.

In the Freedom Stall Where the Boors Live Equally: Heine in America

JEFFREY L. SAMMONS

THE TOPIC OF HEINE in America, like, I assume, several others to be discussed at this conference, is a matter of three distinguishable if overlapping constituencies: immigrants and their descendants whose mother tongue is German; educated Americans whose mother tongue is English but who are well acquainted with German language and literature; and Americans deprived of these benefits for whom German writers must be mediated in English. Of these three constituencies, the first may well have been the largest, but it is also the least researched. A good many years ago the Heine authorities in Düsseldorf asked me whether I would be kind enough to locate the commentary on Heine in German-American periodicals. Since it was my understanding that there are some eight hundred German-language newspapers and magazines scattered in broken sets around the country, I declined the honor. I have still not done it, nor has anyone else. Whether it would be more than donkey work that would contribute further to our understanding of the German-Americans or of Heine is a good question. From what we do know we can make out the lineaments of the situation fairly clearly: Heine was a lively presence among German-Americans and the attitude toward him tended to run along the ideological fault lines of the German-American community.

The one study that has been made of literary materials in German-American periodicals, concerning nineteenth-century newspapers in St. Louis, suggests that an exhaustive search would yield an unmanageable quantity of material. In those papers Heine was discussed more than any other German author except Goethe and Schiller; many of his poems appeared, along with thirteen parodies, more than of any other poet. There are passages from his memoirs and from contemporary studies of Heine, anecdotes and gossip about his personal life. The quarrel about erecting a monument to him in Germany is closely followed, and the plan to erect the Heine Fountain in New York instead is noted.[1] Heine's works were sold in America at least from the 1830s.[2] In 1843 Heine was informed that Baron Wilhelm von Eichthal, who was editing a newspaper in New York, the *German Express for European Conditions, Public and Social Life of Germany* (*Deutsche Schnellpost für Europäische Zustände, öffentliches und sociales Leben Deutschlands*), wished to have contributions from him, though nothing came of it.[3] Two unauthorized back-translations of the French version of *The Gods in Exile* (*Die Götter im Exil*) came out in New York and Philadelphia in 1833.[4] In 1855 a Philadelphia publisher put out an edition of the *Travel Pictures* (*Reisebilder*).[5] This led to one of the spectacular episodes in the early history of Heine's international reception: a Philadelphia pirate, John Weik, decided to put out a collected edition of Heine's works. Heine and his publisher had long discussed a collected edition but had not been able to come to an agreement, so that when the Weik edition was completed, it was the

---

[1] Erich P. Hofacker, *German Literature as Reflected in the German-Language Press of St. Louis Prior to 1898* (St. Louis: Washington University, 1946), 53–62.

[2] See Robert E. Cazden, *A Social History of the German Book Trade in America to the Civil War* (Columbia, SC: Camden House, 1984), 85.

[3] Gustav Kolb to Heine, mid-May 1843, *Heinrich Heine Säkularausgabe*, ed. Nationale Forschungs– und Gedenkstätten der klassischen deutschen Literatur in Weimar and Centre National de la Recherche Scientifique in Paris (Berlin and Paris: Akademie-Verlag and Editions du CNRS, 1970–), 26:69. See also Heinrich Heine, *Historisch-kritische Gesamtausgabe der Werke*, ed. Manfred Windfuhr et al. (Hamburg: Hoffmann und Campe, 1973–), 13/1:382.

[4] Heine, *Historisch-kritische Gesamtausgabe*, ed. Windfuhr, 9:1031–33.

[5] Cazden, *A Social History of the German Book Trade*, 302, 309.

first collected edition of Heine to appear.[6] His publisher Julius Campe was enraged and attempted to combat the edition with a price war but was unable to do so.[7] This edition had gone into five printings by 1860 and by 1864 had sold eighteen thousand sets in the United States.[8] It might be mentioned in passing that no work of Heine's sold that many copies in Germany during his lifetime, except probably the *Book of Songs* (*Buch der Lieder*) by the time it had reached its thirteenth edition at the end of his life; the circumstance suggests what Heine's success in Germany might have been if it had not been for the censorship. When in 1859 the winner of a Turner Society essay contest was awarded a set of Heine, it was probably the Philadelphia edition.[9] In 1861 a seventh volume was added, containing a longish biography by Godfrid Becker. Like virtually all commentators before modern times, Becker deplored Heine's polemics against Platen and Börne but otherwise gave a generally positive account, comparing Heine at considerable length to Aristophanes.[10] Becker was also an early propagator of what I shall call the victim topos. This is a device to explain Heine's almost universally assumed unreliability in moral, aesthetic, and, in some cases, political matters by the determinants of the oppressive time in which he lived. He was, writes Becker, "an intellectually large, temperamentally deep nature, receptive for everything beautiful, good and true, and he might really have become what he claimed to be with so much pomp," but he was damaged by a sick society that thrust him into phantasy.[11]

---

[6] A pirated edition had been begun in Amsterdam a year earlier, but the Philadelphia edition was completed sooner. See Cazden, *A Social History of the German Book Trade*, 334, n. 55; see also Walter Wadepuhl, "Zur amerikanischen Gesamtausgabe von Heines Werken," in Wadepuhl, *Heine Studien* (Weimar: Arion, 1956), 174–80.

[7] Julius Campe to Heine, 14 April, 10 June 1855, *Heinrich Heine Säkularausgabe* 27:301, 330–31.

[8] Cazden, *A Social History of the German Book Trade*, 312. The edition was also exported to Europe, where, despite Campe's protests, it sold fifteen hundred sets.

[9] Carl Wittke, *Refugees of Revolution: The German Forty-Eighters in America* (Philadelphia: University of Pennsylvania Press, 1952), 155.

[10] Heine, *Sämtliche Werke* (Philadelphia: Köhler, 1865), 7:lxxiv, cxiii, cxiii–cxxx. John Weik had gone out of business by this time and the edition had passed into other hands.

[11] Heine, *Sämtliche Werke* (Philadelphia), 7:clxiv–clxv.

When, toward the end of the century, there was a dispute, partly within the German-American community, concerning the erection in New York of the Lorelei Fountain, the Heine monument originally financed by the Empress Elisabeth and intended for Düsseldorf, the piano manufacturer Steinway intervened with a vigorous article, asserting that Heine was "incomparably the most popular of all German poets, not excepting Goethe or any other; ranking, by universal recognition, with the very first men of genius of all the world's ages" and that "considerations of aristocratic, political, and race animosity and sullenness, harbored against Heine because of the license of his pen and because of his Jewish birth, were exclusively accountable for the adverse decision."[12]

Of course, if he had been so universally acknowledged, the dispute would not have arisen, and in fact there was substantial negative opinion about Heine among German-Americans, as there was in the homeland. An article that appeared in a German-American encyclopedia in 1871, in addition to being very inaccurate, deplores all of Heine's works after the 1830 revolution, accuses him of frivolity and of "raging invectives against Christianity" in his waning days.[13] In 1899, then falsely believed to be the centenary of Heine's birth, a conservative pillar of the German-American community, H. A. Rattermann, made a speech in the German Literary Club of Cincinnati in which he praised Heine's lyrical poetry — indeed the evening concluded with "Lieder" performances — but refused to discuss his life in France, accusing him of false wit, crudeness, subjectivity, superficiality, nihilism, and lack of principle or patriotism.[14]

---

[12] William Steinway, "The Heine-Fountain Controversy," *Forum* 20 (Sept. 1895–Feb. 1896): 740.

[13] *Deutsch-amerikanisches Conversations-Lexicon*, ed. Alexander J. Schem (New York: Gerhard, 1871), 5:239–40. The article may have been lifted from a German encyclopedia; it refers to Strodtmann's but not to Weik's American edition and also to an otherwise obscure Italian critical work. It is odd, however, that the Brockhaus contained an article five years earlier that, while not much friendlier, is much more accurate in regard to facts: *Allgemeine deutsche Real-Encyklopädie für die gebildeten Stände: Conversations-Lexikon* (Leipzig: Brockhaus, 1866), 7:765–66.

[14] H. A. Rattermann, "Heinrich Heine als Dichter," *Gesammelte ausgewählte Werke* (Cincinnati: Selbstverlag des Verfassers, 1906–12), 9:399–428. Rattermann, who named his son "Friedrich Schiller," was an "anti-slavery democrat," that is, an opponent of Lincoln

In the Freedom Stall Where the Boors Live Equally 45

The most positive views of Heine are found, not surprisingly, on what today we would call the Left. In 1872 there appeared in Boston an imitation of Heine's most radical major work, *Germany: A Winter's Tale* (*Deutschland: Ein Wintermärchen*), subsequently published in several formats and smuggled into Europe, that depicts Heine as returning to life after the founding of the Reich and discovering to his amazement that Germany is not a republic with a president but a monarchy with a kaiser; he rages against the Prussians and the dissoluteness of the upper classes, calls for the guillotine, and predicts the uprising of the common people. The poem used to be ascribed to the German-American radical Karl Heinzen, who published it, but it is now known to be the work of a German radical, Otto Hörth.[15] Another passionate admirer of Heine was the anarchist and radical freethinker Robert Reitzel. In his essay of 1895 he evaluates Heine as a religious as well as a political revolutionary who was the victim of his own sincerity. "He was imprudent or honest enough to present himself whole with all his inconsistencies, with all his foolishnesses and paradoxical ideas." If Reitzel held anything against Heine, it was his baptism, which Reitzel defends on the grounds of insincerity but regards nevertheless as "dishonoring of himself and an example harmful to public morals." Reitzel, who included the Jewish religion in his antireligious attitude, insisted that Heine was no friend of the Jews.[16]

---

and the Civil War and a supporter of Douglas, an opponent of religious freethinking and of women teaching school, indeed of American women in general, whom he regarded as a major source of corruption in the nation. See Sister Mary Edmund Spanheimer, *Heinrich Armin Rattermann: German-American Author, Poet, and Historian 1832–1923* (Washington, DC: Catholic University of America, 1937), 21, 34–35, 40, 50.

[15] *Ein neues Wintermärchen; Besuch im neuen deutschen Reich der Gottesfurcht und der frommen Sitte* (Boston: Expedition des "Pionier," 1872). The Yale Library also has a miniature, sold for five cents, with the imprint "Herausgegeben vom Verein zur Verbreitung radikaler Prinzipien." The work is ascribed to Heinzen by Carl Wittke, *Against the Current: The Life of Karl Heinzen (1809–80)* (Chicago: University of Chicago Press, 1945), 279, n. 11, among other sources, but see Gerhard Friesen, "Heine II," *Heinrich Heine: Dimensionen seines Wirkens: Ein internationales Heine-Symposium*, ed. Raymond Immerwahr and Hanna Spencer (Bonn: Bouvier, 1979), 96–113.

[16] Robert Reitzel, "Stunden der Andacht mit Heinrich Heine," *Des armen Teufels gesammelte Schriften* (Detroit: Reitzel Klub, 1913), 2:203–4, 227–28, 226–27. For Reitzel's argument that the contempt in which the Jews are held is their own fault because of their clannishness and holding to religious forms in which no modern man believes, see 231. Reitzel's Heine essay is dated 23 May 1895 by Adolf Eduard Zucker, *Robert Reitzel* (Philadelphia: America

As a figure on the boundary between the first and the second constituencies we might consider the Harvard professor Kuno Francke, around the turn of the century probably the most prestigious mediator of German literary culture in the U.S. In his *Social Forces in German Literature*, published in English in 1896, Francke develops an often-admiring but ambiguous view of Heine. Francke sees him as a true patriot and defends his doctrine of sensualist emancipation as "only a new form of that ideal of free humanity toward which all German culture from Luther to Goethe" strives. He praises the essay on religion and philosophy in Germany, compares Heine to Whitman, and ascribes to him "republican sympathies." But Francke sees much of this virtue as more assertion than achievement. Heine "never placed his genius in the service of those ideals," and his career was "poisoned by a fundamental falsehood," his baptism; in addition, Francke like many other critics evaluates Heine's poetry by Goethean standards and finds it wanting. He also has a version of the victim topos. "Is it too much to say that of all the writers of his time Heine is the saddest example of the intellectual degeneration wrought by the political principles of the age of the Restoration?"[17] However, in his edition of the *German Classics*, the most ambitious effort of its time to make major texts of the German canon available in English translation, he accorded considerable space to Heine; forty-seven poems and six prose pieces are preceded by a longish, although evaluatively qualified, biographical essay by William Guild Howard.[18] But after World War I, when Francke's prestige and raison d'être had been grievously battered both by anti-German sentiment and German-American resentment of his moderation, he was wholly positive toward Heine in a book in German on cosmopolitanism, locating him in the development of the German idea

---

Germanica Press, 1917), 60. Zucker, incidentally, is much concerned to distinguish Reitzel from Heine: "There is never the filth with which Heine in very poor taste interlarded his most beautiful works. Moreover, we find that Reitzel takes his lifework seriously, and unlike Heine, does not feel moved to mock his works by ironical conclusions. As a character Reitzel stands far above Heine" (54–55).

[17] Kuno Francke, *Social Forces in German Literature: A Study in the History of Civilization* (New York: Holt, 1896), 519, 521, 522, 525, 523, 526–27.

[18] *The German Classics*, ed. Kuno Francke (New York: The German Publication Society, 1914), 6:1–212.

of humanity, and, incidentally, taking his Jewishness to be a quite natural determinant of his enlightened views.[19]

The substantial amount of discourse on Heine in nineteenth-century America is embedded in the general interest in German literature and culture that governed American intellectual life for much of the century and up to World War I. Most of this discussion, however, is more quantitatively broad than deep, and some of it is fairly repetitious. A great deal of it is found in general essay-writing in histories of German literature, some designed for school use. It has been said that these histories were "small and unscholarly volumes.... They sacrificed thoroughness and comprehensiveness to pragmatism and leisurely appreciation" and "largely resemble lectures."[20] Evaluations were often dependent, though at a distance, upon contemporary German opinion. Thus they are mostly negative at the outset about Heine, since his reputation was at a low ebb at the time of his death and for about two decades afterward; it improved in the United States as it did in Germany later in the century. Partly this change resulted from improved information; one watershed was the appearance of Strodtmann's biography in 1867; a number of other German works were republished also in the U.S. One very remarkable event was the appearance in 1892 of an English translation of *The Family Life of Heinrich Heine* (*Heinrich Heines Familienleben*), edited by Heine's nephew Ludwig von Embden, in which it appears that Heine loved his mother, was kind to his sister, and affectionate to his wife. This news seems to have been received with astonishment and was constantly pointed out as a characteristic mitigating his sins.[21] American opinion was also influenced by the

---

[19] Kuno Francke, *Weltbürgertum in der deutschen Literatur von Herder bis Nietzsche* (Berlin: Weidmann, 1928), 81–82. On Francke's position, see my essay, "Heine as *Weltbürger*? A Skeptical Inquiry," *Modern Language Notes* 101 (1986): 612–19; also in Sammons, *Imagination and History: Selected Papers on Nineteenth-Century German Literature* (New York, Bern, Frankfurt am Main, and Paris: Peter Lang, 1988), 100–101.

[20] Richard Spuler, *"Germanistik" in America: The Reception of German Classicism, 1870–1905* (Stuttgart: Heinz, 1982), 77.

[21] The point was made even earlier by James K. Hosmer, *A Short History of German Literature*, 2nd ed. (St. Louis: G. I. Jones, 1879), 539. See for example John Firman Coar, *Studies in German Literature of the Nineteenth Century* (New York: Macmillan, 1903), 168; H. B. Sachs, *Heine in America* (New York: Appleton, 1916), 12; and Charles Godfrey Leland in his introduction to his translation of Embden's book, cited by Sachs, 28.

British; in fact, at times it is difficult to separate the strands of American and British Heine reception.[22] Especially important were George Eliot's famous essay "German Wit" of 1856, actually a review of Weik's Philadelphia edition,[23] and an equally famous one by Matthew Arnold in 1862.[24] Both of these were republished in the United States; especially Arnold's figured prominently in the discussion, although some commentators disputed the high rank in European literature that he assigns to Heine.[25] Also affecting the level of understanding was William Sharp's level-headed, sometimes sardonic biography, published simultaneously in London, New York, and Toronto in 1888.[26]

Much of the American discussion, however, was also limited in significant ways. It is noticeably marked by the puritanical streak that long survived in American intellectual discourse. Virtually all commentators, unsurprisingly, took offense at Heine's polemics against Platen and Börne, but many also found him a frivolous scoffer in matters of religion and morals and unsound in politics. Consequently we find several variants of the victim topos. James K. Hosmer, for example, concludes his account in for him typically autobiographical, anecdotal form with a vignette of the Venus de Milo in the Louvre, visited in 1870. "May we not see in the statue a type of Heine's genius, — so shorn of strength, so stained and broken, yet, in the ruin of beauty and power so unparalleled?"[27] Similarly, John Firman Coar ends his section with the remark, "One cannot read the *Memoirs* of Heine or his

---

[22] Note, for example, that Sol Liptzin's study, *The English Legend of Heinrich Heine* (New York: Bloch, 1954), tends to conflate the American with the English reception as it goes along.

[23] [George Eliot], "German Wit: Heinrich Heine," *Westminster and Quarterly Review* n.s. 9 (1856): 1–33.

[24] Matthew Arnold, "Heinrich Heine," *Cornhill Magazine* 8 (1862): 233–49.

[25] On this evolution and the influence of Eliot and Arnold, see Henry A. Pochmann, *German Culture in America: Philosophical and Literary Influences 1600–1900* (Madison: University of Wisconsin Press, 1957), 334.

[26] William Sharp, *Life of Heinrich Heine* (London: Walter Scott; New York: Thomas Whittaker; Toronto: W. J. Gage, 1888).

[27] Hosmer, *A Short History of German Literature*, 545.

last poems and not feel the great sadness of a poet conscious of his failure."[28] Mention might be made here also of J. G. Robertson, who, though British, was the author of a history of German literature that was published also in the United States and, in the absence of a better one, was for decades the standard work. Robertson spoke of Heine's "satire and cynicism, which only expressed itself in petty personalities for want of worthier objects. Heine suffered by living in an age when there were no great causes to fight for,"[29] a judgment that most modern Heine scholars would find incomprehensible.

Related to this gesture of rescuing Heine, so to speak, with the left hand, is what I will call the splitting topos. Very common in Heine reception in Germany as well, it simply divides Heine's corpus and often also his personality into a segment that can be appreciated and one that is ignored or disdained. Characteristic of this view is the tendency to see him as an unresolvably contradictory or incongruent phenomenon; rarely is any effort made to seek coherence in him, largely because he is assumed from the outset to have lacked integrity. In general this is a matter of restricting appreciation to the *Book of Songs* and the *Travel Pictures*, with occasional mention of *The Romantic School* and the essay on religion and philosophy. Thus William Hurlbut, who regarded Friedrich Wilhelm III as a "really excellent king" and was disgusted by the Young Germans, in 1849 found the first two *Travel Pictures* the most important work of Heine's and praised the *Book of Songs*, while suggesting that volumes three and four of the *Travel Pictures* are "to be read ... by as few persons as possible" and referring to *The Romantic School* as "an entertaining abomination," consigning *Atta Troll* and *A Winter's Tale* to oblivion, and detecting in the "lamentable" *New*

---

[28] Coar, *Studies in German Literature*, 192.

[29] John G. Robertson, *A History of German Literature* (New York: Putnam's; Edinburgh and London: Blackwood, 1902), 510. Robertson's history has been revised and republished several times; it should long since have been retired, but no one has undertaken the task on modern principles. Its most recent version is the sixth edition, ed. Dorothy Reich et al. (London: House & Maxwell, 1970); the segment concerning Heine has undergone some augmentation but is very similar to the original.

Poems (*Neue Gedichte*) an "evil spirit."[30] Frederick H. Hedge also praises the *Travel Pictures* and *Book of Songs* but denies that Heine was a great poet and rejects Arnold's view, observing that a "mocker" cannot have "contributed most to the liberation of humanity."[31] A Chautauqua lecture course published in 1904 proposes to "elucidate what is best in Heine"; that turns out to be the *Book of Songs*, while *Atta Troll* and *A Winter's Tale* "cannot be regarded as German classics."[32]

However, not all commentators split him in the same way. Coar, whose book is "an attempt to trace the elements of democratic thought in some characteristic forms of this literature," insists that Heine was a democrat, while rejecting *Atta Troll* and *A Winter's Tale* as versified polemic, and concluding that "Heine, the man, was a democrat; Heine, the poet, was anything but a democrat."[33] Examples of splitting Heine could be multiplied almost endlessly.[34] There were, to be sure, less ambiguously negative judgments. In 1856 Heine was described as "not a man to command approval or love.... He was possessed, like many other men of genius, with a gigantic selfishness.... No one can say that

---

[30] [William Hurlbut], [review of *Travel Pictures, De l'Allemagne, Book of Songs, Atta Troll, The Salon I–IV*, and *New Poems*], *North American Review* 69 (July–October 1849): 217, 223, 240–41, 232, 238, 239–40, 246. The essay makes a very odd impression with its alteration of fascination and horror. Despite its severe criticisms, it shows an increased knowledge of Heine. It has been called "the first fundamental closure of American Heine criticism" and estimated "in its comprehensive layout, its thoroughness exhibited over long stretches" as "despite its religious limitations, the greatest achievement of American Heine criticism up to that point" by Gerhard Weiss, "Die Aufnahme Heinrich Heines in Grossbritannien und den Vereinigten Staaten von Amerika (1828–1856): Eine Studie zur Rezeption des Menschen und Prosakünstlers" (Ph.D. diss., Mainz, 1955), 196.

[31] Frederick Henry Hedge, *Hours with German Classics* (Boston: Roberts Brothers, 1887), 513, 518, 503. In his bulky anthology *Prose Writers of Germany* (New York: Francis; London: Sampson Low, 1855), Hedge did not include a single Heine text.

[32] Richard Hochdoerfer, *Introductory Studies in German Literature* (Chautauqua: Chautauqua Press, 1904), 189, 200, 199. Hochdoerfer was professor of German at Wittenberg College.

[33] Coar, *Studies in German Literature*, vii, 161, 185, 192.

[34] See the comment on this by Martin Henry Haertel, *German Literature in American Magazines 1846 to 1880* (Madison: University of Wisconsin, 1908), 87.

In the Freedom Stall Where the Boors Live Equally 51

he did not deserve his fate."[35] And although Heine was depicted in a Chautauqua lecture course published in 1887 as "quite the most interesting and most striking literary figure that has risen among Germans since Goethe and Schiller," his last years of suffering were a retribution for his "indulgence in ribald reviling regardless of truth"; at the end his features were rigidified in a sardonic grin; he was a "thinking skeleton" with a "half-crazed brain," a shallow, lascivious character, "a blight rather than a blessing."[36]

On the other hand, there were his defenders. A Countess de Bury, evidently the Scottish wife of the critic Henri Blaze de Bury, wrote a most vivacious and penetrating review of the French version of *Lutetia*, praising Heine's prophetic powers, his understanding of the July Monarchy, his estimation of Adolphe Thiers, and his unique sense of the potential of a military dictatorship.[37] However, most of the positive treatments tend to appear somewhat later. One A. Parker in 1880 argued that Heine's "service in the war of liberation of humanity" was "truly a great service to posterity."[38] At least one commentator found occasion to point out in 1896 that Heine was an inspiration to socialists. "That Heine is esteemed by Socialists as the poet of revolt against established social institutions, is unknown to most. His fierce protests against injustice in Church and State are not found in the dainty blue and gold gift-editions of his *Book of Songs*; they live rather in the red tablets of the hearts of the struggling masses." The curious essay concludes with the remark that a Chicago anarchist recited Heine's poem "The Weavers" ("Die schlesischen Weber") on the night before

---

[35] [George Ripley], "The Last Years of Heinrich Heine," *Putnam's Monthly Magazine* 8 (July 1856–January 1857): 526. The article is a longish review of Alfred Meissner's memoir of Heine. For an evaluation, see Weiss, "Die Aufnahme Heinrich Heines," 307–9.

[36] William Cleaver Wilkinson, *Classic German Course in English* (New York: Chautauqua Press, 1887), 297, 298–99, 318.

[37] [Review of *Lutèce*], *North American Review* 83 (July–October 1856): 287–316. The author is identified and the essay commented upon by Weiss, "Die Aufnahme Heinrich Heines," 301–6. See also Heine, *Historisch-kritische Gesamtausgabe*, ed. Windfuhr, 13/2:1879–82. I am grateful to Dr. Volkmar Hansen of the Heinrich-Heine-Institut, Düsseldorf, for making information on this point available to me.

[38] In *Lippincott's Magazine*, as paraphrased by Sachs, *Heine in America*, 50.

he was hanged.[39] It was 1913, however, before two Vassar professors stressed Heine's modernity: "Thus he is truly the first poet of modern life with its rude and hard antagonisms."[40] Beginning in 1886 and for decades afterwards Heine texts were repeatedly edited for American students learning German. Most commonly employed was *The Harz Journey* (*Die Harzreise*), though other selections from the *Travel Pictures*, usually *Ideas: The Book of Le Grand* (*Ideen: Das Buch Le Grand*), and some poems were sometimes offered. The *Harz Journey* text was often expurgated of its more offensive passages.[41]

Things become a little more interesting when we look at Heine's reception among writers. Longfellow, though he is often cited as one of the earliest American commentators on Heine, is not one of the more impressive and appears to be dependent on received German opinion; in 1842 he attacked Heine for blasphemy and atheism, lack of taste and refinement, and absence of sincerity and spirituality, and concludes that he is "not sufficiently in earnest to be a great poet."[42] Sachs has rightly said of this article that it "affords an excellent illustration of a man of talent and genius failing to understand the significance of Heine in the literature of Europe," and he points out that Longfellow was privately influenced by Heine and that he cited

---

[39] Marion Mills Miller, "Heinrich Heine," *The Bachelor of Arts* 2 (1895–96): 789–90. This convoluted essay manages to put Heine in a neo-Romantic light and associate him with Gautier's theory of art, make injudicious remarks about the cosmopolitanism, i.e., incapacity for patriotism, of the Jews, and call attention to Heine's constituency on the Left. The Chicago anarchist was George Engel, hanged in 1887 for his participation in the Haymarket Riot. I have not been able to find confirmation of this story, but another of the anarchists, Michael Schwab, who was condemned but later pardoned, quoted the poem in his autobiographical sketch. See Philip S. Foner, ed., *The Autobiographies of the Haymarket Martyrs* (New York: Humanities Press, 1969), 111–12.

[40] Lilian L. Stroebe and Marian P. Whitney, *Geschichte der Deutschen Literatur* (New York: Holt, 1913), 196.

[41] John Hargrove Tatum, *The Reception of German Literature in U.S. German Texts, 1864–1918* (New York, Bern, Frankfurt am Main, and Paris: Peter Lang, 1988), 89–92. Some forty-five text editions are listed on 245–370.

[42] Henry W. Longfellow, "German Writers: Heinrich Heine," *Graham's Magazine* 20 (1842): 134–37.

The Romantic School as an authority.[43] Mark Twain, who was clearly an admirer of Heine, ventured a translation of the "Lorelei" poem, having also undertaken a hilarious demolition of another, botched translation.[44] Not surprisingly, Heine was greatly admired by Walt Whitman, who "especially emphasized Heine's contemporaneity, his freedom and fearlessness in applying ideas to life," and his insistence "on the necessity for embodying and actually living the theories of the nineteenth century."[45] James Russell Lowell, Longfellow's successor as professor of modern languages at Harvard, tried his hand at translating Heine and alluded to Atta Troll in a poem of his own; he clearly admired Heine, though he was something of a splitter, referring to the sort of impropriety "which, if it makes Germans laugh, as we should be sorry to believe, makes other people hold their noses."[46] But the champion admirer among American writers was certainly William Dean Howells, who learned German in order to read Heine and became so much of a disciple stylistically that Lowell warned him to "sweat the Heine out of your bones." Heine, wrote Howells, "dominated me longer than any one author that I have known"; "my literary liberation began with almost the earliest word from him"; "he undid my hands, which I had taken so much pains to tie behind my back." Howells meant by this that Heine taught him that literature could be joined directly to life.[47] He had some misgivings about Heine's more questionable side, but he was not a splitter: Heine "was not a very good Jew, but he asserted nobly the dignity of Judaism; he

---

[43] Sachs, *Heine in America*, 14–18. The most judicious analysis of Longfellow's Heine commentary will be found in Weiss, "Die Aufnahme Heinrich Heines," 112–13, 133–42, 169–72.

[44] Mark Twain, *A Tramp Abroad*, Volume 1, Chapter 16, "An Ancient Legend of the Rhine," *Author's National Edition* (New York and London: Harper, [1920]), 3:119–29.

[45] Pochmann, *German Culture in America*, 466–67. See also Sachs, *Heine in America*, 71–72.

[46] James Russell Lowell, "The Dancing Bear," in *The Complete Works* (Boston and New York: no pub. [Fireside Edition], 1910), *Poems* 4:184–85; "Lessing," *Writings* (Boston and New York: Houghton, Mifflin, 1896), 2:170.

[47] William Dean Howells, *My Literary Passions* (New York and London: Harper and Bros., 1895), 125–30. For examples of poems of Howells quite evidently influenced by or, one should say, imitating Heine, see Sachs, *Heine in America*, 172–81.

was a doubtful Christian, but he felt to the heart the beautifulness of Christ; he was a poor pattern of Protestantism, yet he was as far from being a Catholic as from being a pagan or a Puritan." Moreover, Howells is the only American I have encountered to speculate in a surprisingly modern way on Heine's effect upon reader consciousness. "What Heine does for the reader, who is also a writer, is to help him find his own true nature, to teach him that form which is the farthest from formality; to reveal to him the secret of being himself."[48]

Perhaps the oddest case of Heine reception among American writers is that of Ezra Pound, who published translations and adaptations of seven poems along with an ironic epistle in 1909. Pound did not know German well, though ignorance of a foreign language normally did not discourage him. How the anti-Semite and subsequent fascist collaborator came to be an admirer of a Jewish and politically radical poet is one of the incongruous puzzles of Heine reception. Pound himself indicates that he was attracted by Heine's opposition to "Philistia's pomp and Art's pomposities."[49] Peter Demetz has seen Pound's struggle with German literature as a symptom of allegiance to a kind of Goethean "world literature."[50] But I think that it is just a symptom of Pound's scavenging in the literary tradition, and, in the case of Heine, a consequence of splitting, since it is hard to imagine that Pound would have continued to admire Heine if he had been able to see him whole.

Pound's adaptations bring us to the topic of translation, the obvious link between the second constituency of readers competent in German and the third of those with little or no German. Translations of the poetry are legion. "Few, if any, German poets have exceeded Heinrich Heine's record of currency in English translation"; in the fifteen years after World War II he was "by far the most translated German poet of the past century."[51] According to Pochmann's count, Heine ranked eighth in frequency among German poets translated from 1830 to

---

[48] [William Dean Howells], "Editor's Easy Chair," *Harper's Monthly Magazine* 107 (1903): 483.

[49] Ezra Pound, *Personae* (New York: New Directions, 1926), 46.

[50] Peter Demetz, "Ezra Pound's German Studies," *Germanic Review* 31 (1956): 279–92.

[51] W. LaMarr Kopp, *German Literature in the United States 1945–1960* (Chapel Hill: University of North Carolina Press, 1967), 67.

1864, and third, behind Goethe and Uhland, from 1865 to 1899, the highest frequency falling in the years 1865 to 1879.[52] The challenge of translating Heine's verse has continued to inspire efforts until the present day, and has not even been noticeably blunted by the appearance of Hal Draper's translation of Heine's complete poetical works.[53] I consider this the definitive translation, though I should probably declare an interest, as I became a kind of silent partner in the enterprise prior to publication. Draper also made a collection, poem by poem, of every known English version; he turned this material over to me, and I transferred it to a translation center at the University of Texas, where it will be available for comparative and theoretical studies.[54]

The Englishing of Heine's prose proceeded more slowly. The first item to appear in the United States was a fragment of the *Travel Pictures* taken over from the *Athenaeum* in London in 1828.[55] The first full work, and for nearly two decades the only one, to appear in American translation was the preliminary German version of the book that was to be called *The Romantic School*. It appeared in Boston in 1836 with the title *Letters Auxiliary to the History of Modern Polite Literature in Germany* in a translation by a New Hampshire banker named George Wallis Haven.[56] The early appearance of this work may account for its prestige in the nineteenth century, for it had considerable influence and "really became a text book on German literature."[57] Whether this was altogether advantageous to the American reception of German Romanticism is another question; in any case, Gerhard

---

[52] Pochmann, *German Culture in America*, 329–35.

[53] Hal Draper, trans., *The Complete Poems of Heinrich Heine: A Modern English Version* (Boston: Suhrkamp/Insel, 1982).

[54] A first result of the study of these materials is André Lefevere, "Why the Real Heine Can't Stand up in/to Translation: Rewriting as the Way to Literary Influence," *New Comparison*, no. 1 (Summer, 1986): 83–92. Oddly, Lefevere makes no acknowledgment of Draper's collection.

[55] Scott Holland Goodnight, "German Literature in American Magazines Prior to 1846" (Ph.D. diss., University of Wisconsin, 1907), 162.

[56] On Haven and the reception of this work, see Heine, *Historisch-kritische Gesamtausgabe*, ed. Windfuhr, 8/2:1106–9.

[57] Sachs, *Heine in America*, 75.

Weiss thinks this work came to be displaced by Wolfgang Menzel's history of German literature.[58] However, Weiss also points out that Heine, along with August Wilhelm Schlegel and Coleridge, helped to model in America a mode of criticism adequate to Romantic literature.[59]

The chief translator of Heine's prose was to be Charles Godfrey Leland. A kind of literary jack-of-all-trades, Leland's main claim to fame was a long series of low-comic ballads written under the name of "Hans Breitmann" in a German-English jargon. He began with *Pictures of Travel*, which came out in 1855 with the Philadelphia pirate of Heine's collected works in German. This work went into five editions by 1866 and nine by 1882; it had sold ten thousand copies by the time Leland began to bring out the complete prose works in 1891.[60] Heine got wind of the success of this translation and was greatly pleased.[61] Leland then attempted verse translations and brought out a version of the *Book of Songs* in New York in 1864. In the course of time he conceived the project of translating all of Heine's prose works. He began to publish the edition in London in 1891 and by 1905 had, with the aid of others, produced a twelve-volume edition of Heine in English, which was then published also in New York. In the following year he brought out with the New York firm of Croscup and Sterling a twenty-volume edition; though initially published for subscribers only, it became the standard English Heine and is, in fact, still in print. Although other translations of Heine's prose have been and continue to be sporadically undertaken, even today they are sometimes adaptations of Leland rather than fresh versions.[62]

---

[58] Weiss, "Die Aufnahme Heinrich Heines," 94–95.

[59] Weiss, "Die Aufnahme Heinrich Heines," 111.

[60] Sachs, *Heine in America*, 81; Heine, *Historisch-kritische Gesamtausgabe*, ed. Windfuhr, 7/2:577. See also Weiss, "Die Aufnahme Heinrich Heines," 255–71. Weiss found twelve reviews bound in a printing of 1858 (260–64).

[61] Heine to Michel Lévy, 4 October 1855, *Heinrich Heine Säkularausgabe* 23:461.

[62] For example, Heinrich Heine, *Ideas: The Book Le Grand*, in *Poetry and Prose*, ed. Jost Hermand and Robert C. Holub, The German Library, vol. 32 (New York: Continuum, 1982); *History of Religion and Philosophy in Germany*, ed. Paul Lawrence Rose ([Townsville]: Department of History, James Cook University of North Queensland, 1982).

This is unfortunate, for Leland was a more facile than gifted translator. As he launched into the project, he wrote to his friends, "I am translating *all* of Heine, a very congenial and easiest of easy tasks," and "I thank God that it is extremely easy and congenial work."[63] In retrospect one wonders if the result might have been better if he had found the task more difficult. Even in his own time there was dissatisfaction with his work; many reviewers were disappointed and found it difficult to believe that the translation was the product of so experienced and prominent a literary figure.[64] He bowdlerized the text in places, causing one British reviewer to remark that "Heine is inexpurgable, and squeamish people had best have nothing to do with him."[65] Leland's habit of footnoting the text with pedantic or censorious comments also irritated some readers, among them Howells.[66] A twentieth-century reader has complained that "Leland as a commentator is frequently irritating, often absurd, and sometimes preposterous. His awkwardly ambitious attempt to supply a corrective to what he conceives to have been Heine's frequent lapses from good judgment and taste, as well as the poet's alleged defects of literary form, is the one thing that can fairly be urged against this generally competent edition."[67] Not only Leland's judgment but also his knowledge of Heine is by now wholly obsolete. It would be a great desideratum to be able to set beside Draper's complete poems a reasonably complete, modern edition of Heine's prose works in English. Such a project does not seem very likely at present, however.

As we move through the turn of the century closer to our own time, an increasing Jewish preoccupation with Heine becomes noticeable.

---

[63] Leland to E. R. Pennell, November 1890; to David MacRitchie, 8 April 1891, in Elizabeth Robins Pennell, *Charles Godfrey Leland: A Biography* (Boston and New York: Houghton, Mifflin, 1906), 2:339, 345.

[64] Sachs, *Heine in America*, 82–84.

[65] R. M'Lintock, review of the first volume of Leland's edition, *Academy* 40 (July–December, 1891): 257; M'Lintock is very critical of the quality of the translation as well.

[66] [Howells], "Editor's Easy Chair," 482. In the same place Howells complained of "a certain heaviness" in Leland's style.

[67] Michael Monahan, *Heinrich Heine: Romance and Tragedy of the Poet's Life* (New York: Nicholas L. Brown, 1924), 198.

Like other features of the American reception, this development appears to reflect a process taking place in the homeland. Initially, the German-Jewish attitude toward Heine had been quite negative. Prominent Jewish figures in German cultural life, such as Berthold Auerbach, rejected Heine as materialistic, degenerate, and unpatriotic.[68] The leading proponent of Jewish emancipation, Gabriel Riesser, even tried to challenge Heine to a duel in the aftermath of his book on Ludwig Börne.[69] In 1893 a rabbi was in the forefront of the agitation to prevent a monument to Heine from being erected in Mainz.[70] Gradually, however, the attitude of Jewish cultural spokesmen to Heine improved, a sign, perhaps, of the increasing confidence and sense of belonging among assimilated German Jews.[71] Gustav Karpeles was a lively admirer of Heine whose writings were also known in the United States. Major Jewish Heine scholars began to emerge such as Helene Herrmann and Erich Loewenthal (both of whom perished in the Holocaust). In time there was also a strain of Jewish appropriation of Heine.[72] It culminated in Max Brod's effort of 1934 to remove Heine entirely from German literary history and place him in an imaginary sequence of Jewish writers.[73]

As far as I can see, Jewish commentators are not prominent in the American discussion in the nineteenth century, although what appear to be Jewish names occasionally turn up among the translators. There is one exception, however, who may be regarded as the pioneer of Jewish Heine reception in America: Emma Lazarus, who began to

---

[68] See especially Auerbach's early essay, published around the midpoint of Heine's career, *Das Judenthum und die neueste Literatur: Kritischer Versuch* (Stuttgart: Brodhag, 1836).

[69] Jakob Venedey to Heine, 17 August 1841; Heine to Venedey, 19 August 1841, *Heinrich Heine Säkularausgabe* 25:334-35; 21:413-15.

[70] Ludwig Marcuse, *Heine: Melancholiker, Streiter in Marx, Epikureer* (Rothenburg ob der Tauber: J. P. Peter, Gebr. Holstein, 1970), 455.

[71] See Hans Otto Horch, *Auf der Suche nach der jüdischen Erzählliteratur: Die Literaturkritik der 'Allgemeinen Zeitung des Judentums' (1837-1922)* (Frankfurt am Main, Bern, and New York: Peter Lang, 1985), 104-15 and passim.

[72] See the essay on this in my *Heinrich Heine: The Elusive Poet* (New Haven and London: Yale University Press, 1969), 446-65.

[73] Max Brod, *Heinrich Heine: The Artist in Revolt* (New York: Vallentine, Mitchell, 1957), esp. 218-22.

translate Heine at the age of fourteen, during the Civil War, and was much drawn to Heine's melancholy and his dichotomy of Hellene and Jew. In an essay of 1884 she wrote, "He was a Jew, with the mind and eyes of a Greek. A beauty-loving, myth-creating soul was imprisoned in a Hebrew frame; or rather, it was twinned, like the unfortunate Siamese, with another equally powerful soul, — proud, rebellious, oriental in its love of the vague, the mysterious, the grotesque, and tragic with the two-thousand-year old Passion of the Hebrews."[74] This is a quite original version of the victim topos, for she traces Heine's contradictions and dualities to this dichotomous heritage. "He was a changeling, the victim of one of Nature's most cruel tricks, and his legacy to the world bears on every page the mark of the grotesque caprice which had begotten him."[75] Lazarus herself seems to have been victimized somewhat by what has been called Heine's "Marrano pose," for she asserts, "We must go back to the Hebrew poets of Palestine and Spain to find a parallel in literature for the magnificent imagery and voluptuous orientalism of the 'Intermezzo.' ... His was a seed sprung from the golden branch that flourished in Hebrew-Spain between the years 1000 and 1600."[76] However, Lazarus does not wish to appropriate Heine for Judaism. "It would convey a false impression to insist unduly upon the Hebrew element in Heine's genius, or to deduce therefrom the notion that he was religiously at one with his people"; his was a "sympathy of race, not of mind," and "the deluded Jew who takes up his work to chuckle over his witty sarcasms against Christianity will be grievously disappointed suddenly to receive a stinging blow full in the face from the same merciless hand."[77]

In 1866 she published, at the age of seventeen, fifteen Heine translations in a volume of poems and in 1881 a volume of Heine's

---

[74] Emma Lazarus, "The Poet Heine," *The Century Illustrated Monthly Magazine* 29, n.s. 7 (November 1884–April 1885): 210–11.

[75] Lazarus, "The Poet Heine," 211.

[76] Lazarus, "The Poet Heine," 212, 215. Her father was probably of Sephardic background; see Dan Vogel, *Emma Lazarus* (Boston: Twayne, 1980), 13. See also Philipp F. Veit, "Heine: The Marrano Pose," *Monatshefte* 66 (1974): 145–56. This work is one of the most illuminating essays on Heine's self-understanding; it has been almost totally ignored.

[77] Lazarus, "The Poet Heine," 216.

Poems and Ballads, incidentally the first book of Heine translations to be republished after World War II.[78] Her own poetry exhibits many echoes of Heine. Sachs remarks perceptively, "Very curious is the link between that bitter, mocking, cynical spirit and the refined, gentle spirit of Emma Lazarus."[79] This contrast is best illustrated by her effort to continue the project Heine began with his poem "Donna Clara," a poem in the *Book of Songs*, which was written at the time of his intensive Jewish studies in 1823 and images an elegant Sephardic gentleman masking his identity in order to seduce and then humiliate an anti-Semitic noblewoman.[80] Heine wrote at the time that the poem was the first of a trilogy; in the second part the hero was to be scorned by his own child and in the third this child, having become a Dominican, was to have his brothers tortured to death.[81] Heine never wrote these two poems, but Emma Lazarus did, under the titles "Don Pedrillo" and "Fra Pedro," in unrhymed trochaic tetrameter, Heine's most supple meter but one that in English, I am afraid, calls up irrepressible echoes of *Hiawatha*.[82] Emma Lazarus followed Heine's description literally; nevertheless, there is something incongruous about the succession, for Heine's poem is marked by a spirit of vengeance and defensive malice; Lazarus's poems by helpless submission to persecution without a note of protest or rebellion.[83] Here lies one of the problems of Jewish and particularly American Jewish appropriation of Heine. His Jewish persona was militant, aggressive, rudely polemical toward Christian religion and gentile structures of oppression. Assertions that the Jewish

---

[78] Emma Lazarus, *Poems and Translations*, printed privately in 1866, then in the following year in New York by Hurd and Houghton; Heine, *Poems and Ballads* (New York: Worthington, 1881; republished with illustrations by Fritz Kredel, New York: Hartsdale, 1947). See Aaron Kramer, "The Link Between Heine and Emma Lazarus," *Publication of the American Jewish Historical Society* 45 (1955/56): 248–57, and Kopp, *German Literature in the United States*, 69–70.

[79] Sachs, *Heine in America*, 117.

[80] Heine, *Historisch-kritische Gesamtausgabe*, ed. Windfuhr, 1/1:312–19.

[81] Heine to Moses Moser, 6 November 1823, *Heinrich Heine Säkularausgabe* 20:122.

[82] *The Poems of Emma Lazarus* (Boston and New York: Houghton Mifflin, 1888), 2:213–22.

[83] Vogel, *Emma Lazarus*, 119, disagrees, finding the force of the poems in irony. The contrast with Heine's direct assault upon the sensibilities of the reader remains, however.

Reform was an effort to establish "a little Protestant Christianity as a Jewish company, and they make a *tallis* out of the wool of the Lamb of God, a vest out of the feathers of the Holy Ghost, and underpants out of Christian love, and they will go bankrupt and their successors will be called: God, Christ & Co.," or, about Felix Mendelssohn, "If I had the good fortune of being a grandson of Moses Mendelssohn, I would certainly not use my talent to set the pissing of the Lamb to music"[84] were the last thing the Jews, seeking integration and tolerance, wanted to hear, either in Heine's own time or later, and thus this tone tends to be edited out of Jewish reception.

Another indication of the tendency to appropriate Heine is an article in *The Jewish Encyclopedia* in 1904, which is admittedly confined to "considering Heine in his relations to Judaism." Here it is asserted that "His wit was essentially Jewish"; "the next eighteen years of his life [in Paris] were devoted in the main to a series of propagandist efforts which were Jewish in method if not in aim"; he was a mediator between France and Germany as the Spanish Jews had been between Christians and Moors; he had many Jewish acquaintances, and his brief stint as a student in Berlin with the Society for Culture and Science of the Jews "was deep enough to stamp his work with a Jewish note throughout his life"[85] — all highly debatable propositions. A somewhat different tone appears in Lewis Browne's biography, *That Man Heine*, of 1927. Browne, who had been a rabbi at the Free Synagogue in Newark, had left the rabbinate to devote himself full-time to writing. His biography was conceived out of a lively contempt for literary criticism and scholarship, and shows it;[86] it is vivacious but not very precise or accurate. Virtually alone among Heine biographers, Browne finds him enduringly influenced by his Hebrew School experience, which steeped him in Biblical lore and made his soul "definitely that of

---

[84] Heine to Immanuel Wohlwill, 1 April 1823; to Ferdinand Lassalle, 11 February 1846, *Heinrich Heine Säkularausgabe*, 20:72; 22:194.

[85] [Joseph Jacobs], "Heine, Heinrich," *The Jewish Encyclopedia* 6 (New York and London: Funk and Wagnalls, 1904): 327–30.

[86] So Browne tells us in *The Final Stanza: A Hitherto Unpublished Chapter of "That Man Heine"* (San Francisco: The Book Club of California, 1929), iii–iv.

a Jew."[87] Browne develops a version of the victim topos in explaining the Platen polemic. "Christian Germany was largely to blame for the chapter, the Christian Germany that had fretted and harried and badgered the Jewish Heine until he had gone half-mad with hate." Browne's superintending thesis is that Heine was never able to belong to a community, even after his "return" to Judaism at the end of his life.[88] Browne's interpretation of Heine should probably be seen in the light of his reading of the modern Jewish situation, which was that the Jews should be excluded, by force if necessary, from their traditional commercial and bureaucratic occupations and enabled to take up the same variety of trades and vocations as gentiles. He thought Stalin a particularly positive force in this endeavor but also invested hope in the settlements in Palestine.[89]

As in Germany, there were significant contributions to Heine scholarship from Jewish sources. An important one was Rabbi Israel Tabak's study of Heine's Jewish knowledge, a valuable beginning to an understanding of that question, for gentile German scholars found Judaic matters exotic and were often very uninformed about them.[90] If Tabak makes too much of Heine's Biblical allusions — the stock in trade of any German-language writer — and adduces Talmudic parallels in unconvincing numbers, these are correctable faults and less important than his showing that Heine was often ignorant of or inaccurate about commonplace Jewish matters. Mention might also be made here of the Kohut-Rutra Collection that has made the study of Heine and his context so convenient at Yale. Rabbi George Alexander Kohut, who

---

[87] Lewis Browne with Elsa Weihl, *That Man Heine* (New York: Macmillan, 1927), 13. Oddly, this notion is revived in the most recent Jewish-oriented publication, containing translations of the *Rabbi*, the essay on Shylock, and the *Hebrew Melodies*, where support is claimed from an admittedly idealized painting of a *cheder* by Moritz Oppenheim made three-quarters of a century later. *Jewish Stories and Hebrew Melodies by Heinrich Heine*, ed. Elizabeth Petuchowski (Masterworks of Modern Jewish Writing Series, New York: Markus Wiener, 1987), 5–6.

[88] Browne, *That Man Heine*, 189, 368.

[89] Lewis Browne, *How Odd of God* (New York: Macmillan, 1934), 228–37.

[90] Israel Tabak, *Judaic Lore in Heine: The Heritage of a Poet* (Baltimore: Johns Hopkins University Press, 1948). Today German scholars once again seem to be out of touch with common Jewish matters of the sort that an American simply picks up from the environment.

founded Yale's Judaica collection with the materials collected by his father, the Conservative rabbi Alexander Kohut, gave his collection of Heine books and manuscripts to Yale in the late 1920s, supplemented with a collection he purchased from the Munich dramatist Arthur Ernst Rutra, consisting largely of Heine's French editions as well as works of his contemporaries, especially Ludwig Börne and the Young Germans. These items, in many cases quite rare, have been of inestimable value to my own studies for many years.[91]

In 1937 there appeared what probably became the most influential book on Heine in America in modern times: Louis Untermeyer's biography, published together with a volume of poem translations.[92] Untermeyer had been translating Heine's poems for a long time, at least since 1916. He had come to be known as the "American Heine,"[93] and by 1937 he had produced a larger fraction of Heine's total poetic corpus than any other translator; this continued to be the case for forty-five years until the appearance of Draper's volume. It has been said recently that Untermeyer "tries to make Heine a little less cynical";[94] my own opinion, after having made a considerable number of comparisons, is that Draper's versions are regularly more vivacious as well as more faithful. The biography has a number of virtues; it is well informed for its time, properly skeptical about anecdotal traditions, and judicious in its evaluations; and it brings a poet's sensitivity to the texts. However, there is something of a tendency to appropriate Heine for Untermeyer's own standpoint of wholly secular Jewishness. Concerning Heine's Jewish activities and studies in Berlin Untermeyer remarks, not imperceptively, "It was wholeness that Heine wanted at twenty-five. He could bear the 'dark inheritance,' but not maladjustment; it was the

---

[91] On the Kohut-Rutra Collection, see Carl F. Schreiber, "The Kohut Collection of Heineana," *Yale University Library Gazette* 6, no. 3 (1932): 49–53; and Hermann J. Weigand, "Heine Manuscripts at Yale: Their Contribution Concerning Him as Man and Artist," *Studies in Philology* 34 (1937): 65–90.

[92] Louis Untermeyer, *Heinrich Heine: Paradox and Poet. The Life*; Heinrich Heine, *Paradox and Poet: The Poems* (New York: Harcourt, Brace and Company, 1937).

[93] Kopp, *German Literature in the United States*, 70.

[94] Lefevere, "Why the Real Heine Can't Stand Up," 86.

sense of division which gripped him with secret terror."[95] The difficulty is, I think, that Untermeyer ascribes to Heine more of an undivided Jewish identity than he was actually able to achieve. He is said to be a "Jewish Jew," in Thorstein Veblen's phrase, "a disturber of the intellectual peace"; he endeavored to unite nationalism and universalism, like Isaiah; he was not a Nazarene but an "emotional, quick-tempered, transplanted Oriental: the true Semite, never so sensitive as when he covers his heart with a cynical shrug or a coarse witticism"; he possessed a "particularly Jewish wit"; in his late "Hebrew Melodies" ("Hebräische Melodien") "Background, diction and emotion are characteristically Jewish in the voluptuous use and celebration of the senses, in the hot colors and sharp flavors.... No Hebrew poet has ever been more unreasonably confident, more hand-in-hand with God."[96] In this last judgment Untermeyer's interpretive perspicacity seems to have broken down altogether. The biography ends with a long poem that Heine is imagined to have composed at the hour of his death and that ends with the *Sch'ma Yisroel*, a most improbable conceit.[97]

This Jewish appropriation of Heine was never without its implicit or explicit resistance. During World War II Sol Liptzin endeavored to balance Heine's character as "a product of his Jewish heredity and his German environment" and to distinguish his shifting attitude toward Jewish religion from his continuous sense of Jewish fellowship.[98] After the Holocaust had intervened, an article in *Commentary* attacked efforts to claim Heine for Judaism on the grounds that he had been an "inauthentic Jew," pursuing the illusion of a transcendence of Judaism in cosmopolitan humanism. His "return" to Judaism was not a choice for authenticity but a choice not to be inauthentic any longer. "You cannot choose not to be a Jew, you can only choose to be an authentic

---

[95] Untermeyer, *The Life*, 93.

[96] Untermeyer, *The Life*, 292, 293, 294, 303, 337–38.

[97] Untermeyer, *The Life*, 379–84.

[98] Solomon Liptzin, *Germany's Stepchildren* (Philadelphia: Jewish Publication Society of America, 1944), 68, 72.

or inauthentic Jew."⁹⁹ Like all arguments of this kind, this one runs the risk of accepting and reifying the categories of the oppressor.

Among the publications objected to in this article was one edited by Hugo Bieber that had originally been called *Confessio Judaica* when it was published in Germany in 1925 and then was republished in New York under the title *Jüdisches Manifest* (Jewish Manifesto).[100] This is simply a chronological compendium of Heine's writings and other utterances on Judaism. It is interesting to observe, however, that when Bieber was asked by the Jewish Publication Society of America to compile a biographical anthology in English, he did not retain this format but produced an entirely new book covering the whole of Heine's life. Overall it is balanced and perceptive. Bieber is critical of Heine's judgment as well as admiring of his struggle "for justice and freedom"; he devotes considerable space to Heine's Jewish interests and experience, but judiciously, observing, for example, that "he only gradually and with great difficulty attained to an independent judgment of Jewish history, in which, however, the traces of anti-Jewish influences never wholly disappeared"; and that "what allied him to Judaism without, however, uniting him with it, was his dislike for Christianity."[101] Bieber had earlier written an article in which he was quite critical of Jewish appropriations of Heine, and it may have been this insight that caused him to alter his biographical strategy.[102]

In my opinion, that era of Jewish interest represents the last chapter of significant Heine reception in America. For one thing, the Heine discussion came to be even more internationalized than it had been

---

[99] Martin Greenberg, "Heinrich Heine: Flight and Return. The Fallacy of Being Only a Human Being," *Commentary* 7 (Jan.–June 1949): 225–31.

[100] Hugo Bieber, *Heinrich Heine: Confessio Judaica* (Berlin: Welt-Verlag, 1925); *Jüdisches Manifest* (New York: Mary S. Rosenberg, 1946). The new edition is augmented with materials Bieber found when editing Heine's conversations: *Heinrich Heine: Gespräche, Briefe, Tagebücher, Berichte seiner Zeitgenossen* (Berlin: Welt-Verlag, 1926). This publication had the misfortune of appearing at the same time as H. H. Houben, *Gespräche mit Heine* (Frankfurt am Main: Rütten & Loening, 1926), and never achieved the same visibility.

[101] Hugo Bieber, *Heinrich Heine: A Biographical Anthology*, English translations made or selected by Moses Hadas (Philadelphia: Jewish Publication Society of America, 1956), 11, 30, 26. This is a posthumous publication, completed by Hadas after Bieber's death.

[102] Hugo Bieber, "Recent Literature on Heine's Attitude Toward Judaism," *Historica Judaica* 10 (1948): 175–83.

before with the presence on the American scene of works imported from abroad, not only Max Brod's biography, mentioned earlier, but also one of the several incarnations of Ludwig Marcuse's, which appeared in translation in 1933.[103] There were also the popular biographies written in French by Antonina Vallentin and François Fejtö, originally appearing in 1934 and 1946 respectively and then republished most recently in 1970.[104] Heine scholarship, which has increased its momentum decade by decade, is naturally international and in any case comes more and more to be restricted to academic consumption. While such things are difficult to measure, I believe that today there is no significant general reception of Heine in the United States outside the academic community. A contemporary enthusiast who has rediscovered him was moved to say, "Heine's very spirit is roaming among us," but I think this is an optical illusion caused by the mass of scholarly publication.[105] People generally associate nothing with his name except perhaps a memory of a musical setting. What little does appear in the public domain is often amateurish and trivial.[106] Even within the academy I have found that nonspecialists know little about him, although, as I found out in the reviews of my biography, this ignorance does not always inhibit them from publishing their opinions. Most current American Heine scholarship, with the perhaps eccentric example of my own and that of one or two others, is totally

---

[103] Ludwig Marcuse, *Heine: A Life Between Love and Hate* (New York: Farrar & Rinehart, 1933).

[104] Antonina Vallentin [?pseud. for Julien Luchaire], *Poet in Exile: The Life of Heinrich Heine* (New York: Viking, 1934); François Fejtö, *Heine: A Biography* (London: Wingate, 1946), both republished Port Washington, NY, and London: Kennikat Press, 1970.

[105] Heinz R. Kuehn, "Rediscovering Heinrich Heine," *Sewanee Review* 97 (1989): 124. See also the hopes expressed by Robert C. Holub, "Heine and the New World," *Colloquia Germanica* 22 (1989): 101–15. However, this lecture, delivered in China, is not very deeply informed.

[106] Examples are Kuehn's essay, cited in the previous note; Philip Kossoff, *Valiant Heart: A Biography of Heinrich Heine* (New York and London: Cornwall Books, 1983), for which the verdict "worthless" would not be excessive; or Henry Regensteiner, "Heine in Retrospect," *Midstream* 33, no. 11 (November 1987): 43–46. Of doubtful utility is Alfred Kazin's essay "One of us?" *New York Review of Books* 28, no. 17 (5 November 1981): 24–25. It was unwisely employed as a foreword to Heine, *Poetry and Prose*, ed. Hermand and Holub, vii–xiii.

derivative of German models and exhibits no particularly American note. There are no Heine texts edited for American students currently in print; my own effort to produce such a textbook was, I believe, the last, and the fiasco attending its publication appears in retrospect as a sign that the time for such things was past.[107] In general this situation is a symptom of the total lack in our culture of interest in the German literary tradition of the past. That Heine was an exception to that tradition and in some ways a belligerent dissident from it can have no effect as long as the entire context with which he contended remains unapprehended. This may change in the future, but there are no signs that it will happen soon.

A malevolent observer might look upon this outcome as a fair recompense for Heine's contemptuous lack of interest in America, "that Freedom Stable where / All the boors live equally."[108] Nevertheless, he was gratified by what he heard of his American reputation, and he might have continued to be by much if not all of it for something like a century after his death.

---

[107] *Heine–Selections* (Englewood Cliffs: Prentice Hall, 1970). Prentice Hall vigorously solicited this text but, when it had been edited to everyone's satisfaction, sat on it for some three years. I believe the purpose was to make me angry enough to withdraw it. Soon after publication it was remaindered. It was republished by Preston in New York in 1976 on the strength of colleagues' recommendations. But they must have been supplied out of pure collegiality, for none of the colleagues ever used the book, leaving me in a somewhat embarrassed situation with the publisher.

[108] Lines from the poem "Jetzt wohin?" ("Now, Where To") from *Romanzero*, Heinrich Heine, *Sämtliche Schriften*, ed. Klaus Briegleb et al. (Munich: Hanser, 1968–1976), 6/1:101; translated by Draper, *The Complete Poems*, 633.

The Fame of Theodor Storm in America in the Late Nineteenth and Early Twentieth Centuries

Clifford Albrecht Bernd

The *NATIONAL UNION CATALOGUE* offers an interesting point of departure for any study of the American reception of German literature, for in this work we can find extensive listings of German literary texts published in the United States. I have spent many hours counting and perusing texts of German literature read in the schools and colleges of the United States during the period in which German was the most widely studied modern language, namely during the fifty-odd years between the Civil War and America's entry into World War I. That time span constituted the era in American education when the study of German language and literature enjoyed a vogue never known before and never experienced subsequently.[1] It was a time when enrollments in German in high schools were almost three times higher

---

[1] The urge to write this essay was piqued, in part, by Inga E. Mullen's book *German Realism in the United States: The American Reception of Meyer, Storm, Raabe, Keller and Fontane* (New York: Peter Lang, 1988). Professor Mullen claims throughout her book that the above-named writers were hardly known to American readers prior to the second half of the twentieth century. In the statement that follows herewith a counterargument is presented that with regard to Storm such a claim is unfounded. This writer was not only known but even exceedingly well-known to millions of readers in America of yesteryear, from the time of the Civil War onwards.

than those in French and fourteen times higher than in Spanish.[2] It was a time when German private schools — Catholic, Protestant, and nondenominational — mushroomed in the central Atlantic and midwestern states, from Connecticut to Missouri and from Maryland to Minnesota, something hardly known in earlier American history (except in Pennsylvania) and certainly not known in the post–World War I period.[3] It was a time, moreover, when German in our colleges and universities had acquired, in the words of a former head of Columbia's German Department, an "indispensable position among the branches of study,"[4] and it was a time when a United States Commissioner of Education could report that "the German language has actually become the second language of our Republic, and a knowledge of German is now considered essential to a finished education."[5]

Since it was almost axiomatic in those days that the study of German in the United States had, as Victor Lange has recently reminded us, as "its ultimate target and its self-evident justification ... not merely the acquisition of a practical skill but the prospect of exploring the impressive realization of the 'genius' of that language in its ... literary documents,"[6] there can be no reason for surprise when we note, via the *National Union Catalogue*, that precisely during that period when the study of German in the United States flourished most profusely, editions of German literary texts were published in America in far greater abundance than ever before or ever since. The period from the Civil War until the United States declared war on Germany in World War I constituted, hence, not only the heyday of German language

---

[2] Edwin H. Zeydel, "The Teaching of German in the United States from Colonial Times to the Present," *German Quarterly* 37 (1964): 356.

[3] Ibid., 353–54.

[4] Louis Viereck, *German Instruction in American Schools* (New York: Arno Press, 1978), 591.

[5] Quoted by Zeydel, 345.

[6] Victor Lange, "Thoughts in Season," in *German Studies in the United States: Assessment and Outlook*, ed. W. F. W. Lohnes and V. Nollendorfs (Madison: University of Wisconsin Press, 1976), 5. See also V. Lange, "The History of German Studies in America: Ends and Means," in *Teaching German in America: Prolegomena to a History*, ed. D. P. Benseler, W. F. W. Lohnes, and V. Nollendorfs (Madison: University of Wisconsin Press, 1988), 6.

instruction in America, but also the heyday of the publication of German literary texts in the United States.[7]

Which were the works of German literature that were printed most frequently and therefore presumably most widely read during that enviable period in the history of the reception of German literature in North America? Two titles in the *National Union Catalogue* stand out particularly conspicuously; Schiller's *Wilhelm Tell* and Storm's *Immensee*.

*   *   *

That Schiller should have been read so widely in the United States at the time can cause no real surprise. He became, after all, following the Schiller centenary celebrations of 1859 the most beloved writer in Germany itself. Things were no different in America. Goethe's works, especially *Hermann und Dorothea*, were certainly given their share of attention, but in the final analysis Schiller's plays inspired the greatest admiration and affection,[8] and not least of all because Schiller was considered — especially after 1848 — a champion of freedom, in contrast to Goethe, whom many looked upon with a certain disdain because, as it was said, he had compromised himself by becoming "the hireling of princes."[9]

If we need not be too surprised about the popularity of Schiller, we do need to be astonished, however, about *Wilhelm Tell*'s taking a commanding lead over all of Schiller's other plays,[10] for that was not

---

[7] John Hargrove Tatum, *The Reception of German Literature in U.S. German Texts 1864–1918* (New York: Peter Lang, 1988), 224–382, lists in chronological order the titles of the works published in each of those fifty-four years (excluding, however, translations in English).

[8] Henry A. Pochmann, *German Culture in America: Philosophical and Literary Influences, 1600–1900* (Madison: University of Wisconsin Press, 1957), 332.

[9] Carl Wittke, *Refugees of Revolution: The German Forty-Eighters in America* (Philadelphia: University of Pennsylvania Press, 1952), 311.

[10] The history of German literature that was most widely read in the United States after the middle of the nineteenth century, by Edward Evans of the University of Michigan, stated unequivocally that *Tell* constituted the "high point" in the whole of Schiller's artistic oeuvre. E. P. Evans, *Abriß der deutschen Literaturgeschichte* (New York: Leypoldt & Holt, 1869),

the case in America prior to the mid-nineteenth century, when *Maria Stuart* and *Die Jungfrau von Orleans* were held in higher esteem.[11] After World War I *Tell* also did not receive as much acclaim.[12] To what may we attribute the unusual fascination with *Tell* in the half century following the Civil War?

I think the answer is intimately tied to the reason for the extraordinary flowering of German studies in our schools and colleges during those years, namely the growth of German immigration to gigantic proportions as a result of the German revolutions of 1848. Albert Faust, a former chairperson at Cornell, estimated that some nine hundred thousand German immigrants came to the United States as a direct consequence of the 1848 revolutions.[13] Louis Viereck tells us that between two and one-half to three million German immigrants must have landed in the United States in the half century following 1848.[14] The overwhelming majority of these immigrants gathered and remained in a multitude of "Little Germanies" in many American cities, and these immigrants were firmly united, we know, in their resolve to keep their mother tongue alive for their children and children's children.[15] That was the main reason for the almost incredible flowering of German studies in America during the historical period to which we are referring.

The yeast for this mass German immigration was, as history books tell us, the so-called Forty-Eighters, those political refugees whose lives had been left with a permanent scar as a result of the abortive German upheavals of 1848. These Forty-Eighters, the most homogeneous and largest group amongst the estimated five and a half million German

---

189.

[11] Zeydel, 336, 337, 341.

[12] The listings in the *National Union Catalogue* offer telling information about the popularity of *Wilhelm Tell* in America both before and after World War I.

[13] Albert Bernhardt Faust, *The German Element in the United States* (New York: Houghton Mifflin, 1909), 1: 585.

[14] Viereck, 557.

[15] Ibid. Also: *The Forty-Eighters*, ed. A. E. Zucker (New York: Columbia University Press, 1950), 77.

immigrants in the whole of the nineteenth century,[16] influenced with their ideas and their ideals the earlier German immigrants whom they met in German communities in the United States soon after their arrival and with whom they then quickly intermarried. In turn, these Forty-Eighters established the institutions to which the subsequent waves of German immigrants up to World War I attached themselves.

In short, the Forty-Eighters influenced not only the huge volume of German immigration to the States in the nineteenth century but also the growth of German institutions in America. Most especially the sudden increase in the teaching of German must be attributed to the impact the Forty-Eighters made.[17] I do not wish to minimize the contributions of distinguished non–Forty-Eighters like Henry Wadsworth Longfellow, George Ticknor, Bayard Taylor, and other such sages at American universities in the fostering of German studies at the time, but their labors alone would never have produced the gigantic upswing in the study of German that took place if it had not been for the Forty-Eighters. Carl Schurz, that notable Forty-Eighter who became "the uncontested leader of German-Americans"[18] and who never flagged in reminding his fellow German-Americans that their children should learn German,[19] had a far broader appeal than any of the eminent nonnative professors of German.

But if we now accept the theory that the Forty-Eighters gave the main impetus to the spectacular growth of German studies at the time, it seems thoroughly understandable why Schiller's *Tell* should have become such an extraordinarily important text in German instruction. For in that play the Forty-Eighters, as well as all the other German-Americans who came under the influence of the Forty-Eighters, could

---

[16] *Germans to America: 300 Years of Immigration, 1683 to 1983*, ed. Günter Moltmann (Stuttgart: Institute for Foreign Cultural Relations, 1982), 9. See also the statistics in Peter Marschalck, *Deutsche Überseewanderung im 19. Jahrhundert: Ein Beitrag zur soziologischen Theorie der Bevölkerung* (Stuttgart: Ernst Klett, 1973), 35ff., 48ff.

[17] Wittke, 300ff.

[18] Hans L. Trefousse, *Carl Schurz: A Biography* (Knoxville: University of Tennessee Press, 1982), 253.

[19] See, for instance, Schurz's speech "The German Mothertongue," *Speeches, Correspondence, and Political Papers of Carl Schurz*, ed. F. Bancroft (New York: G. P. Putnam's Sons, 1913), 5: 334–38.

rediscover the political ideals they had championed.[20] *Wilhelm Tell* was, after all, a drama par excellence of political revolution, a drama about the quest for freedom from monarchical despotism, and also a drama about the pursuit of a national unity — precisely what the 1848 insurrections, according to Schurz, were all about.[21] Could the political refugees of 1848 have wanted a more ideal work of literature which they could use to teach German (and the ideals of German culture) to their children and children's children?

*   *   *

The case for Storm's *Immensee* amongst these refugees must have been hardly less compelling, as the huge number of printings of that novella in the United States reveals. Perhaps, however, it was not so much the particular story of *Immensee* as it was the biography of Storm that appealed to the Forty-Eighters, for in Storm they could find the writer with whom they could best identify. He, too, was one of them, and what a Forty-Eighter he was! He hailed from that part of the German-speaking world on which the eyes of all Forty-Eighters had been most keenly riveted and about which the members of the German National Assembly meeting in Frankfurt talked most of all, namely Schleswig-Holstein.[22] Friedrich Engels said that the 1848 revolutionary movement in Germany first really came to life when the rebellions in Schleswig-Holstein erupted.[23] In none of the German rebellions of 1848 did more of the causes that the Forty-Eighters so ardently espoused come together than in those that broke out in Schleswig-Holstein. And in no other place did more Germans from every part of the German-speaking world volunteer, risk, and sacrifice their lives in order that the petty kingdoms and dukedoms of the time might receive a more just government. Not only did the Schleswig-Holsteiners want

---

[20] Wittke, 311.

[21] "The so-called 'Forty-eighters' were striving principally for the realization of two great ideals: national unity and representative government." *Speeches, Correspondence and Political Papers of Carl Schurz* 5:469.

[22] Alexander Scharff, *Schleswig-Holsteinische Geschichte* (Würzburg: Ploetz, 1982), 64.

[23] Karl Marx and Friedrich Engels, *Werke* (Berlin: Dietz, 1959), 5:393.

to be free from a monarchical government in which they possessed no democratic representation, but they also wanted liberation from an oppressive foreign yoke, from an autocratic Danish rule that was thoroughly alien to their German life-style. In no other parts of Germany did the twin goals of the Forty-Eighters, the quest for democratic liberty as well as the pursuit of a national unity free from foreign domination, coincide so seamlessly as in Schleswig-Holstein. In no other parts of Germany was the defeat of these rebellions felt with as much anguish as in Schleswig-Holstein, and in no other parts of Germany was, as a result of the failure of these rebellions, as large a percentage of Germans then forced into exile. The ruthlessness with which the victorious royal Danish government proceeded to expel anyone who had been politically active for the cause of democracy in Schleswig-Holstein was unmatched anywhere else in German-speaking lands. Approximately a quarter of a million Schleswig-Holsteiners left for America, swelling the ranks of the Forty-Eighters there and keeping, as history books tell us, the ideals of the revolutions alive longer in America than in purged Schleswig-Holstein itself.[24] Even the majority of the intellectual leadership of this rebellion left for America.[25]

The writer to whom these Forty-Eighters could relate most was Storm. He had been an eyewitness to all the depressing events in the insurrections around him. He had been unusually outspoken in the demand for sedition from monarchical rule, for democratic government, for freedom for Germans from foreign domination, and for a national unity of all Germans in a republican form. He had been conspicuously active for the cause of the rebellion not only as a poet but also as a sardonic journalist and in the leadership he exerted on behalf of the revolutions.[26] Few others had publicly denounced the oppressive political conditions of 1848 as vehemently as he did, and certainly no other German writer at the time had suffered the anguishing life in political exile that he was forced to experience for twelve long years.

---

[24] Otto Brandt, *Geschichte Schleswig-Holsteins*, 7th ed. (Kiel: Walter Mühlau, 1976), 290.

[25] Zucker, *The Forty-Eighters*, 68–69.

[26] Frithjof Löding, *Theodor Storm und Klaus Groth in ihrem Verhältnis zur schleswig-holsteinischen Frage: Dichtung während einer politischen Krise* (Neumünster: Karl Wachholtz, 1958), 60ff.

Could the Forty-Eighters have found a more ideal contemporary writer to cherish than Storm?

To the political refugees of 1848 from Germany he was very much the counterpart of what the exiled Thomas Mann represented for the refugees from Hitler's Germany a century later. There could be no mistake about why the refugees of 1848 revered Storm so highly, and if there are any doubts about this, one only needs to read the introductions to the many editions of Storm's works that were published in the States when German instruction flourished as a result of the impetus of the Forty-Eighters. These introductions seek again and again to prejudice young readers of succeeding generations in favor of Storm by calling attention to his prominence as both a supporter of as well as a victim of the 1848 revolutions.[27] Just as with Thomas Mann, however, it was perhaps not so much one single work, like Mann's *Buddenbrooks* or Storm's *Immensee*, that won the affection of the political refugees from Germany following the 1848 revolutions or following Hitler's rise to power, but rather it was the salient and salutary roles each of these two writers played in denouncing the evil political conditions of their respective times in Germany that made their works popular among their fellow political refugees.

But if the emigrés of 1848 did prefer *Immensee* (and not any other novella by Storm) to introduce their American children and children's children to the literature of their ancestral fatherland, this was not without reason. *Immensee* was, after all, the one particular work of Storm written precisely at the very crest of the revolutionary euphoria in German lands and, moreover, a work in which the author had succeeded in presenting a moving lesson on how a man is condemned to stand by helplessly while his happiness erodes as a result of the destructive actions of time. Such a poetic message, composed at the time of the turmoil the Forty-Eighters themselves had experienced,

---

[27] Typical are the following sentences taken from Robert N. Corwin's introduction to an edition of Storm's *Auf der Universität* (New York: Henry Holt, 1910), vi: "From the time of his admission to the bar, Storm's career is closely associated with the fate of his native state. Schleswig-Holstein, whose inhabitants were in large part German, had long chafed under Danish rule. The struggle for independence, begun in the revolution of 1848, ended disastrously in 1852. With the tightening of the Danish bonds, Storm's license to continue the practice of his profession was made dependent upon his anti-Danish sympathies. He was therefore forced into exile."

could hardly have failed to appeal to their collective emotions. What attracted these refugees living subsequently in the United States no less to *Immensee* must also have been the welcome consolation they surely received when they could quickly savor how the passing of time offered its compensations, foremost among these the bitter-sweet pleasure of reflection, of pausing in later life to meditate on what had been as well as what might have been. The wistful resignation associated with looking back at a time irretrievably past stood out, on the first and last pages of *Immensee*, as an unusually conspicuous hallmark of this novella, and more obviously so than in perhaps any of Storm's other tales. This was a story almost made to order for a Forty-Eighter who had escaped to America but who could not forget.

Thus *Immensee*, like *Wilhelm Tell*, secured a firmly established and prominent place in the canon of German literature taught in American schools and colleges when German instruction in the United States thrived as a result of the influence of the Forty-Eighters. Indeed, Storm's novella came to be so securely anchored that it was not until the middle of the twentieth century that it could be entirely dislodged from its enviable position. In 1927 one of the most prominent American Germanists, B. Q. Morgan of Stanford University, could still say, "*Immensee* has been, and will doubtless continue to be, more widely read by American High School and College students than any other single work in the German language."[28] Even as late as 1949 George Schulz-Behrend of the University of Texas could comment, "It is probably safe to say that no other modern foreign language text has found [in the United States] wider use than *Immensee* ... [and] the demand for it is still strong."[29]

*   *   *

Yet, despite the tremendous vogue that *Immensee* enjoyed in the curriculum of American schools and colleges, it would be misleading if we were to assume that Storm was famous in the United States in the

---

[28] Theodor Storm, *Immensee*, ed. B. Q. Morgan and E. O. Wooley (Boston: D. C. Heath, 1949), iii.

[29] George Schulz-Behrend, "Forever *Immensee*," *German Quarterly* 22 (1949): 159.

nineteenth century (and later) solely because millions of young Americans read that one particular work. Storm's fame also spread with the American publications of other novellas. Five editions of *In St. Jürgen* (with thousands of copies) appeared on the American book market between 1901 and 1917. Four editions of *Geschichten aus der Tonne* were published in Boston between 1894 and 1914. *Auf der Universität*, *Pole Poppenspäler*, *Psyche*, *Im Sonnenschein*, *Ein grünes Blatt*, and *Carsten Curator* also became familiar texts in the heyday of German instruction in the United States. In 1908 a Boston publisher offered, for the first time in America, a school and college edition of *Der Schimmelreiter*. It sought to win many new young American friends for Storm by claiming that this novella (rather than *Immensee*) was "probably the best of Theodor Storm's stories from an aesthetic and technical point of view."[30] The argument "sold," and *Der Schimmelreiter* has remained "an enduring college classic" ever since.[31] Another novella that has succeeded in making Storm known to a continuous stream of college students is *Aquis submersus*. In 1909 Calvin Thomas of Columbia University, "one of the greatest authorities in America on German literature,"[32] used his considerable gifts of pedagogical persuasion to draw attention to it, "The art of Storm," Thomas said, "culminated in *Aquis submersus*."[33] The cult of this novella was then nourished further, indeed immeasurably, when less than six months later George Madison Priest of Princeton also called it Storm's "best work."[34] Such statements from such exceedingly prominent members of the German teaching profession must have helped to place this novella high on college reading lists. This must have been the case particularly at Princeton, where George Priest and a

---

[30] *Der Schimmelreiter: Novelle von Theodor Storm*, ed. J. Macgillivray and E. J. Williamson (Boston: Ginn, 1908), v.

[31] David Brett-Evans, "Theodor Storm: An Enduring 'College Classic,'" in *Deutung und Bedeutung: Studies in German and Comparative Literature Presented to Karl-Werner Maurer*, ed. B. Schludermann et al. (The Hague: Mouton, 1973), 185–86.

[32] *New York Times*, 5 November 1919, 15.

[33] Calvin Thomas, *A History of German Literature* (New York: Appleton, 1909), 377.

[34] George Madison Priest, *A Brief History of German Literature* (New York: Charles Scribner's Sons, 1909), 305.

devoted pupil of Calvin Thomas, Harvey Waterman Hewett-Thayer, held for several decades the two senior positions in German. Their high opinion of *Aquis submersus* doubtless encouraged two young German-American members of Princeton's teaching staff to introduce more students to this novella by publishing (in 1942) a college edition with the prefatory statement: "*Aquis submersus* ... is frequently acknowledged to be Storm's greatest work."[35]

*   *   *

Truly, the Forty-Eighters, with their immense esteem for their fellow political refugee Storm and with the powerful influence they exerted on succeeding generations of American schoolmasters and college professors, accomplished an extraordinary feat. The phenomenal run of Storm texts edited and annotated for high school and college reading made Storm an established feature of instruction in countless classrooms of America's secondary schools and colleges. As a result, he gained entrance into the mainstream of American culture, where his fame then spread in ever-widening ripples, with many translations published all across the country, from New York and Philadelphia on the eastern seaboard to as far west as Portland, Oregon, on the Pacific coast.[36]

---

[35] *Deutsche Novellen*, ed. A. van Eerden and B. Ulmer (Boston: Houghton Mifflin, 1942), 213.

[36] According to the *National Union Catalogue*, eight translations of *Immensee* were published in New York, Philadelphia, Chicago, Cleveland, and Portland between 1863 and 1912. A translation of *Der Schimmelreiter* appeared in the anthology *The German Classics* (New York: German Publication Society, 1914). A second translation quickly followed in a competing anthology *The Harvard Classics* (New York: Collier, 1917). Selections of Storm's poetry in translation were included in numerous collections of German verse published in the United States from 1865 onward. See Bayard Quincy Morgan, *A Critical Bibliography of German Literature in English Translation 1481–1927* (New York and London: Scarecrow Press, 1965).

Lifting the Cultural Blockade: The American Discovery of a New German Literature after World War I — Ten Years of Critical Commentary in the *Nation* and the *New Republic*

WULF KOEPKE

THE FAVORABLE IMAGE OF Germany, the Germans, German culture, and its beneficial influence on the United States was so powerful that it took an all-out effort in 1917 to prepare the nation for war with the brutal "Huns." If this was not yet a total war, it was certainly a total propaganda war, and the consequences are well known. Many place-names and family names were changed out of fear or patriotism or both; German-speaking groups were afraid to use the language in public; schools and colleges stopped teaching German which had been the unquestioned first foreign language (24 percent of all high school and college/university students);[1] many states imposed a ban on the teaching of German; even German music was banned, and operas had to be sung in English. Still, underneath the anti-German mood the old connections remained. The ban on German music had lost its force by 1920, and German operas could be sung in German again. The "cultural blockade" against German art, literature, science, and philosophy began disappearing with the physical blockade.

---

[1] See the essay by Clifford Bernd in this volume.

There were lasting effects, however. Even after the U.S. Supreme Court struck down as unconstitutional the state laws banning the teaching of German in 1923, few students learned German, and the teaching of foreign languages in general was significantly reduced. While the old positive image of Germany persisted, the new image of the aggressive and dangerous Germans remained as well, resulting in the ambiguous American view of the Germans still prevalent today.

Oswald Garrison Villard, the *Nation*'s chief editor, voiced in 1919 the American suspicion of "the militarization of the intellect, which is Germany's crime,"[2] and the formula of the "two Germanies" was already current in 1919,[3] meaning the Germany of the Prussian military vs. the Germany of culture. Books were published entitled *The Causes of Germany's Moral Downfall*[4] as well as *The Moral Recovery of Germany*.[5] From now on, the political behavior of the German people became a moral question, which it has remained.

Moral, economic, and political issues got intertwined in a more complex manner when the conditions of the peace treaty at Versailles became known. The *New Republic* became outspoken in its verdict that this treaty would never work and that the chance to build a democratic society in Germany rested on the possibility for an economic recovery. Later, the *Nation* as well as the *New Republic* were concerned with Germany's ability to pay war reparations and with the living standard of the Germans. Events in Germany were followed attentively. The assassination of Walther Rathenau was mourned, the swing to center–right-wing governments after 1923 was viewed with concern, the election of Hindenburg to the presidency caused some alarm. Hitler's putsch in Munich in 1923 did not escape notice, and the questionable Bavarian system of justice was exposed — which brought

---

[2] *Nation*, 10 May 1919, 755.

[3] *Nation*, 24 May 1919, 828.

[4] See Robert James Hutcheon, *New Republic*, 25 June 1919, 260.

[5] *New Republic*, 9 July 1919, 297.

Lion Feuchtwanger to write the novel *Erfolg*[6] — causing Hitler to write a letter to the editor of the *Nation*.[7]

On the other hand, good will and charity never ceased. An article in the *Nation* on 30 August 1919, "The Tale of College Teachers of German" (289f.), focused on the plight of Germanists who were fired for lack of enrollment or some pretext, and it printed a letter by Ernst Feise, who was later to become prominent in German studies. Still a German citizen at the time, he was dismissed from his position and also denied a visa to return to Germany. With the rising inflation in Germany and Austria, universities and their faculties began to suffer. An emergency committee headed by Franz Boas went into action, and agencies like the Rockefeller Foundation responded generously. Werner Sombart reported on the deplorable standards of living in Germany,[8] Albert Einstein described the plight of German scholars,[9] and repeated calls for help for German authors were printed, for instance by H. L. Mencken.[10]

Also, the opportunistic avoiding of the word *German* — until very recently, Germans were usually disguised as *Central Europeans* — was soon ridiculed. A reviewer of a new translation of Gottfried Keller's Seldwyla novellas made fun of the attempts of the translator to characterize Keller as purely Swiss and not German.[11] Herbert C. Herring attacked the prejudice against the German language.[12]

---

[6] For some of the background, see *Jahrmarkt der Gerechtigkeit*, ed. Wolfgang Müller-Funk (Tübingen: Stauffenburg, 1987), in which several studies analyze different aspects of the system.

[7] 2 September 1925, 256. The letter from Uffing dated 28 June 1925 takes issue with an article by Louis Fischer on "Class Justice in Germany" that had relied on Emil Gumbel. Hitler says he spent thirteen months in prison, not six, and had no privileges.

[8] *New Republic*, 24 May 1922, 362–65.

[9] *New Republic*, 18 October 1922, 197.

[10] *New Republic*, 31 January 1923, 254.

[11] *Nation*, 24 January 1920.

[12] "We Never Say German," *New Republic*, 17 January 1923, 200–1.

The memoirs of the kaiser, the crown prince, Ludendorff, Hindenburg, and others were carefully reviewed, generally with disapproval.[13] During the earlier twenties, most history books on the world war — and there were many — presented the Allied point of view. Although the *New Republic* was much more preoccupied with the Soviet Union than Germany, it still carried firsthand accounts of German events, which were even more frequent in the *Nation*. The *Nation* also published articles by Theodor Wolff, Kurt Tucholsky (as Ignaz Wrobel), Hans Goslar, and Arthur Eloesser. The November 7 issue in 1928 was under the heading "Ten Years of a New Germany."

The open-minded attitude and the growing interest in this "new Germany" are clearly in evidence in the book review sections. What is remarkable is that, at the time of the virtual interdiction of the German language, a large number of books were reviewed that had not yet been translated into English: novels, biographies, history books, memoirs, and scholarly books from diverse disciplines. Obviously, there were still reviewers and readers fluent in German, which would not be the case in later years.[14]

In contrast to the general mood in the country, which doubted whether the United States should get involved in world politics, especially in the messy affairs of Europe, the vigorous young book industry was keen on importing and exporting books and was on the lookout for new authors and new countries. The liberal periodical press reflected these concerns, defending New York as a bastion of cosmopolitanism in a country dominated by isolationist attitudes. Books were at first imported via England, but the American publishers were not always satisfied with the British choices and translations, so they began to explore the European continent on their own. Especially Alfred and Blanche Knopf and W. B. Huebsch — the latter first for his own company, then for Viking — were active in Europe. Three geographical areas were at first of primary interest: France, Russia, and Scandinavia.

---

[13] *New Republic*, 21 January 1920, 240f., Walter Lippmann on Ludendorff; 139f., Alfred Hoernle on the kaiser's "Apology"; 19 July 1922, 230f., on the crown prince, and others.

[14] This is true even for the *New Republic*. A few examples: 1 October 1919, Wilhelm Stekel, *Der nervöse Magen*, 26 November 1919, *Heines Sämtliche Werke* (Insel Verlag); 18 January 1922, Gerhart Hauptmann, *Anna*; 7 May 1924, books on history (two in German); and the above-mentioned memoirs.

The German-speaking countries were not considered prime targets. The Germanists had taught much German literature, but predominantly the period of Goethe and Romanticism,[15] and the names familiar to Americans after Heine would be Richard Wagner, Friedrich Nietzsche, Sigmund Freud, and Albert Einstein. With the virtual elimination of German instruction, the knowledge of classical German literature faded away, leaving vague memories of Goethe and Heine,[16] and the book industry, unencumbered by previous knowledge, took a fresh look at the present.

The *New Republic* reveals the nature of this void and how it was filled. It reviewed a translation of poems by Rainer Maria Rilke, labeling him "A Mystic."[17] It then reviewed Jacob Wassermann's *Christian Wahnschaffe*, translated as *The World's Illusion*, characterizing it as "essentially a Continental book," a "visionary book," "romantic," "a sort of half Slavic, Franciscan romance," definitely not realistic, and not a novel of the conventional kind.[18] Molnar's *Liliom* was a hit on Broadway,[19] but Georg Kaiser's expressionist play *From Morn to Midnight* in 1922 was not.[20] Gerhart Hauptmann was well known. His idyll *Anna* was reviewed in German[21] and his *Hannele* got a decent review by Stark Young in 1924[22] in spite of a mediocre production. But the new discoveries were mainly in fiction. Wasser-

---

[15] See John Hargrove Tatum, *The Reception of German Literature in U.S. German Texts, 1864–1918*, Studies in Modern German Literature, no. 2 (New York, Bern, Frankfurt am Main: Peter Lang, 1988); Richard Spuler, *"Germanistik" in America: The Reception of German Classicism, 1870–1905* (Stuttgart: Akademischer Verlag Hans-Dieter Heinz, 1982).

[16] Reviews of books by and on Goethe and Heine in the *Nation*, for example, 29 June 1921; 26 June 1922; 19 March 1924; 15 October 1924; 10 December 1924; 6 October 1926 — most of it on Goethe. No other German authors of the past were noteworthy for the *Nation*.

[17] *New Republic*, 24 May 1919, 127.

[18] *New Republic*, 23 March 1921, 113.

[19] *New Republic*, 6 July 1921, 299.

[20] *New Republic*, 12 July 1922, 189f.

[21] *New Republic*, 18 January 1922, 226f.

[22] *New Republic*, 27 February 1924, 21.

mann's next novel, *The Goose Man*, was duly noted,[23] and so was *Gold*.[24] A review of Schnitzler plays[25] praises the playwright, describing his works as texts one ought to know, and criticizes the translation. Then there are unexpected reviews of authors and works hardly known in the United States. The purpose of the review of Clara Viebig's *Daughters of Hecuba*, which describes the fate of German women during the war, is mainly political. "We can ask nothing more of American women whose hearts are still filled with hate than to read the book."[26]

But the *New Republic* also noted, at least now and then, the coming events of German literature. Stark Young commented on a mediocre production of Ernst Toller's *Man and the Masses* (*Masse Mensch*), upholding the stature of the play,[27] and Robert Morss Lovett noted the significance of *Buddenbrooks*[28] when the translation appeared. The *New Republic* did not review the subsequent *Death in Venice* or other publications by Thomas Mann, but a review of Georg Hermann's *Jettchen Gebert* (=*Hetty Geybert!*) said that it was "like Buddenbrooks."[29] The preoccupation with the war and recent history would explain that Bernhard Kellermann's *The Ninth of November* was reviewed.[30]

Thus the slow shift is noticeable from a preoccupation with the "German mind" and the war and German militaristic mentality to a reception of German literature as fiction or drama. Also, the fact remains that Scandinavian novels received special attention, and that the overriding literary events were the appearance of James Joyce's *Ulysses* and Marcel Proust's *A la recherche du temps perdu* gradually translated into English.

---

[23] *New Republic*, 27 September 1922, 24; and 29 November 1922, 18–20.

[24] *New Republic*, 4 June 1924, 51f.

[25] *New Republic*, 8 August 1923, 53.

[26] *New Republic*, 18 October 1922, 202.

[27] *New Republic*, 30 April 1924, 262.

[28] *New Republic*, 9 April 1924, 7f.

[29] *New Republic*, 10 September 1924, 53.

[30] Robert Morss Lovett, *New Republic*, 11 March 1925, 76f.

That the *Nation* offers a substantially different picture, although its evaluations are quite similar, is primarily due to the influence of one man, Ludwig Lewisohn. He had been a German professor at the University of Wisconsin and Ohio State University and was unusual in that he wrote a book on contemporary German literature.[31] He was born in Germany but had come to the United States as a small child. His nostalgic loyalty to his native land was so strong that he offended the university communities during the war and had to resign. Later, in the mid-twenties, Lewisohn lived in Europe and traveled to Palestine. He saw the dangerous isolation of the Jews in Germany and Austria; he rediscovered his Jewishness and became an active Zionist.[32] Still, he always remained a mediator between German and American culture. He translated plays by Gerhart Hauptmann, novels by Wassermann and Werfel, poetry, especially by Rilke, and he chose Thomas Mann as his great hero, whom he never tired of praising, especially after the appearance of *The Magic Mountain* in English translation in 1929.[33]

The translations of *Der Zauberberg*, Feuchtwanger's *Jud Süß* (*Power*) and Erich Maria Remarque's *Im Westen nichts Neues* (*All Quiet on the Western Front*) were the crowning events of the reintroduction of German literature to America, establishing the Germans as masters of the "philosophical" novel, the historical novel, and the antiwar novel — but they did not come unprepared. In the *Nation* Lewisohn wrote a laudatory obituary of the poet Richard Dehmel;[34] in the 15 May 1920 issue he surveyed "The German Theatre of Today," mentioning Wedekind, Georg Kaiser, Sternheim, and antiwar plays. In the issue of 3 July 1920 he reviewed a new translation of *Der Tod des Tizian* by Hofmannsthal, stressing the considerable literary stature of the author.

---

[31] *The Spirit of Modern German Literature* (New York: W. B. Huebsch, 1917).

[32] Lewisohn has described his life's story in *Up Stream: An American Chronicle* (New York: Boni and Liveright, 1922); and *Mid-Channel: An American Chronicle* (New York: Harper & Bros., 1929); Joseph Wood Krutch describes the years at the *Nation* in *More Lives Than One* (New York: W. Sloane Assoc., 1962), in which he gives a sympathetic and humorous picture of Lewisohn.

[33] See my article "Thomas Mann und Ludwig Lewisohn: Ein Beitrag zum Thema 'Thomas Mann und Amerika' aufgrund unveröffentlichter Briefe Thomas Manns," *Colloquia Germanica* (1978): 123–48.

[34] *Nation*, 6 March 1920, 294–96.

In the 1 December 1920 issue he published his own translation of five poems by Rilke; in the 8 December 1920 issue H. L. Mencken reviewed Lewisohn's translation of Wassermann's *Christian Wahnschaffe*. Mencken agreed that "it was worth doing into English," but he, too, pointed out that this was not a novel of the expected kind. "Thus the chronicle, to an American, cannot carry much conviction despite its fine passion and its vivid details." The book was too epic, not plot-oriented, too "fantastic."

In the 13 April 1921 issue "The Progress of Poetry" in Germany was reviewed by Lewisohn. He gave an overview from Mörike to Liliencron, Rilke, and George and on to the "expressionists," to Däubler, Benn, and Trakl, praising Werfel, whom he considered the new "genius." Lewisohn's primary function was, however, that of a drama critic. He, too, praised Molnar's *Liliom*[35] and was critical of Kaiser's *From Morn to Midnight*, declaring that "Kaiser ... is not a great writer."[36] In his view, the production of *Rose Bernd* by Gerhart Hauptmann on Broadway, with Ethel Barrymore playing the titular main role, was a failure,[37] but the play was great, and the failure was due to the ignorance of the performers and producers as to who Hauptmann was.

The 1 March 1922 issue carried Lewisohn's article "Republican Germany and the Arts," which gave him an opportunity to extol Thomas Mann. Arthur Eloesser (who was Lewisohn's cousin) wrote about Gerhart Hauptmann on the occasion of the dramatist's sixtieth birthday.[38] Lewisohn criticized the translation of Hauptmann's *Phantom*, 10 January 1923, but called the story itself "of the utmost significance." Lewisohn used every opportunity to criticize American ignorance of German literature. In the 14 March 1923 issue he offered a choice of his translations of German poetry: Nietzsche, Hofmannsthal, George, Hesse, and Werfel. In the 26 September 1923 issue he published his translation of Thomas Mann's "Hungry Souls" ("Die

---

[35] *Nation*, 11 May 1921, 695.

[36] *Nation*, 14 June 1922.

[37] *Nation*, 11 October 1922.

[38] *Nation*, 15 November 1922, 520f.

Hungernden"), a key text by Thomas Mann in his estimate.[39] The novel *Buddenbrooks* was for him, naturally, "a very great book";[40] finally, he wrote a long article for Thomas Mann's fiftieth birthday in 1925,[41] mostly a glowing review of the yet untranslated *Der Zauberberg* and of Arthur Eloesser's biography of Thomas Mann.

Not that Lewisohn or the *Nation* were uncritical about Germany and German culture. In 1922 Arthur Eloesser saw German theater in a state of crisis; the age after Hauptmann was still awaiting the transformation through "a great democratic organization."[42] In 1925, when he came to Berlin, Lewisohn diagnosed not only the isolation of Jews, but also a lack of vitality after the end of expressionism. His report on 13 May 1925 concludes, "And life, on the entire Continent today, is sterile." He saw forces at work "re-medievalizing Europe." Lewisohn very astutely saw the political danger signals, but his partisanship for expressionistic forms of style prevented him from doing justice to the incipient *Neue Sachlichkeit* (New Objectivity) — he obviously overlooked the latest trends.

The *Nation* did not have to rely on Ludwig Lewisohn alone for reports and reviews on things German, and after he left, others carried on, notably his successor Joseph Wood Krutch, who was not a Germanophile but knowledgeable in German literature. A list of German books reviewed or recommended in the *Nation* between 1920 and 1926 is instructive, especially compared to the *New Republic*, and sometimes surprising: *Der Pastor von Poggsee* by Gustav Frenssen;[43] *Paracelsus* by Erwin Guido Kolbenheyer;[44] *The Goose Man* by Wassermann (this last review stating "that Wassermann's name may be mentioned without too much apology with the names of the greater

---

[39] *Nation* 26 September 1923, 318f.

[40] *Nation*, 16 April 1924, 443.

[41] "Thomas Mann at Fifty," *Nation*, 9 December 1925, 667.

[42] *Nation*, 7 June 1922, 700f.

[43] *Nation*, 5 July 1922, 22.

[44] Roy Temple House, *Nation*, 1 November 1922, 476.

Russians");[45] recent histories of German literature by Kurt Martens, Klabund, Franz Blei, and Kasimir Edschmid;[46] a biography of Sudermann;[47] *Gold* by Wassermann;[48] *The Ninth of November* by Bernhard Kellermann;[49] *Der gute Weg* by Otto Flake;[50] *Faber* by Wassermann; *Die Insel der großen Mutter* by Hauptmann; and *Fräulein Else* by Schnitzler.[51] Emil Ludwig began his conquest of the American market with *Genie und Charakter*;[52] his rapidly appearing biographies were much criticized but always taken seriously. After Thomas Mann's *Buddenbrooks*, his novella *Herr und Hund* was published, then *Death in Venice*,[53] and soon afterwards *Royal Highness*.[54] Oswald Spengler's *Der Untergang des Abendlandes* (*The Decline of the West*) found a much friendlier reading than one might have expected;[55] Lewisohn introduced a new poet of genius, Ernst Waldinger;[56] and Krutch reviewed Werfel's play *Juarez and Maximilian*.[57] The interest in German music continued during this period, and also the German films, *Siegfried* and *Metropolis* for instance, stood out as superior to films made in Hollywood.[58]

[45] J. W. Krutch, *Nation*, December 1922, 624.

[46] W. O. Zinnecker, *Nation*, 19 September 1923, 300f.

[47] Roy Temple House, *Nation*, 13 August 1924, 170.

[48] J. W. Krutch, *Nation*, 27 August 1924, 218f.

[49] Dorothy Brewster, *Nation*, 26 August 1925, 237.

[50] *Nation*, 2 September 1925, 261.

[51] J. W. Krutch, *Nation*, 18 November 1925, 579f.

[52] Roy Temple House, *Nation*, 4 March 1925, 245.

[53] J. W. Krutch, *Nation*, 25 March 1925, 330f.

[54] J. W. Krutch, *Nation*, 21 April 1926, 454f.

[55] Allen Tate, *Nation*, 12 May 1926, 532–34.

[56] Ludwig Lewisohn, *Nation*, 13 October 1926, 363f.

[57] J. W. Krutch, *Nation*, 27 October 1926, 435.

[58] J. W. Krutch, *Nation*, 16 September 1925, 311; 23 March 1927, 323f.; on *Metropolis*, also *New Republic*, 30 March 1927, 170f.

There was as much preoccupation with recent history, current events, and the struggle for democracy in Germany in the pages of the *Nation* as in the *New Republic*. It was obvious, however, that the *Nation* arrived earlier, by 1924 at the latest, at the point where German books were viewed like others, without special apology or negative bias. This may have been in keeping with the changing mood of the country, but in the case of the *Nation* it was also the result of an editorial orientation: to give the new Germany a chance to rebuild and to succeed. The *Nation* was against the crushing reparations, etc., and it wanted an active policy of the U.S. in Europe not discernable in the *New Republic*, which also reflected a changing attitude toward Germany. While the *Nation* had more firsthand accounts of living conditions and the mood of the country, the *New Republic* remained more systematic in its analysis of the political situation and its call for fairness toward the Germans.

The *New Republic* gave Lion Feuchtwanger's *Power* a short review, calling it a "good solid novel of the old-fashioned kind," considering it very "German" and criticizing that Jud Süß's last transformation was not convincing. "Mistiness," said the reviewer, was as much a German trait as "thoroughness."[59] The *Nation* was a little more positive, saying, "Feuchtwanger is a poet," and, "It was a racy and kaleidoscopic picture."[60] When the *New Republic* reviewed *The Devil* by Alfred Neumann, another book on its way to best-seller status, the review already included the statement, "With two such books as Feuchtwanger's 'Power' and Neumann's 'The Devil' to their credit, it might be said that the Germans have evolved a new type of historical novel."[61] Similarly, in his review of Feuchtwanger's *The Ugly Duchess* Clifton Fadiman in the *Nation* spoke of Feuchtwanger's "enthusiastic admirers," while he himself remained critical — Feuchtwanger was no "great novelist," but he had a "happy genius for reiteration," and "he has applied a modern economic realism to the writing of historical

---

[59] T. S. M., *New Republic*, 9 February 1927, 338.

[60] Lisle Bell, *Nation*, 2 February 1927, 122f.

[61] T. S. Matthews, *New Republic*, 15 August 1928, 337f.

fiction."[62] The parallel statement in the *New Republic* is "Herr Feuchtwanger has done his job so well that he defeats himself."[63] But then Clifton Fadiman, reviewing *The Devil* in the *Nation* called it "as brilliant a piece as 'Power,'" and spoke of "the third living German novelist of international importance."[64]

In contrast to this reluctant acceptance of Feuchtwanger and of the historical novel's "new type," the reception of *The Magic Mountain* was enthusiastic, although it was not a novel of the conventional kind, and some people thought it "possesses all the worst faults of the discursive epic, but its author lacks the genius to make the grade."[65] Ludwig Lewisohn, on the other hand, wrote in his autobiography *Mid-Channel*, "I read Thomas Mann's *Der Zauberberg*, assuredly the completest and most enduring work of our age, perfect in form, incredibly searching in thought and rich in creative energy."[66] In the *Nation*, after Lewisohn's article "Thomas Mann at Fifty," a reviewer, "D. I.," gave a survey entitled "New Books in Germany" that included Emil Ludwig's biographies, Alfred Döblin's *Wallenstein* and *Berge, Meere und Giganten*, Stefan Zweig's books, and Alfred Neumann's *Der Teufel* (*The Devil*), and said, "Since 'Der Zauberberg' by Thomas Mann, no German book has appeared which obviously towers above all of its contemporaries."[67] Joseph Wood Krutch called his survey of the American book market in spring 1927, "Spring Novels and the Magic Mountain." *The Magic Mountain*, he stated, "stands out above all the others."[68] Robert Morss Lovett in the *New Republic* recognized the "great

---

[62] *Nation*, 1 February 1928, 126f.

[63] *New Republic*, 28 March 1928, 200.

[64] *Nation*, 19 September 1928, 273f.

[65] *The Living Age*, 15 August 1927; see my article "Die Exilschriftsteller und der amerikanische Buchmarkt," in *Deutsche Exilliteratur seit 1933* ed. John M. Spalek and Joseph Strelka, (Bern, Munich: Francke, 1976), vol. 1, *Kalifornien*, 115 (note 55), also 101f.

[66] Lewisohn, *Mid-Channel*, 141.

[67] *Nation*, 11 May 1927, 531f.

[68] *Nation*, 8 June, 1927, 637–39.

qualities of a masterpiece," calling it "The Epic of Decay" and "an allegory of a sick world."[69]

The floodgates of the historical novel had opened, as well as those for contemporary German novels. In 1928 the *Nation* discussed books by Klaus Mann, René Schickele (*Maria Capponi*), Bruno Frank, Alfred Neumann, Emil Ludwig, Jacob Wassermann, Arthur Schnitzler, Hermann Sudermann (*Der tolle Professor*), Arnold Zweig (*Der Streit um den Sergeanten Grischa*), Fritz Reck-Mallesczewen, Fritz von Unruh, Max Brod (*Tycho Brahe*), Oskar Maria Graf, Felix Salten, Waldemar Bonsels, and Ricarda Huch (*Garibaldi*). Ernst Toller's contribution to the 7 November 1928 "German" issue, on the theater, mentioned Brecht, Bronnen, and Zuckmayer.

Also in 1929, the *Nation* devoted its space to quite an array of "imports" from the German-speaking countries, whether translated or not. There were reviews of Ricarda Huch, Sudermann, Heinrich Mann's *Diana* ("a stern artist and a completely disenchanted social thinker" who does "not resemble his brother"),[70] Franz Werfel's *Class Reunion* ("in the German manner"),[71] Alfred Neumann, Thomas Mann's essays, Hermann Hesse's *Steppenwolf* (rather negative!), and even Albert Ehrenstein's adaptation of a Chinese novel, *Robbers and Soldiers*. Lewisohn advertised Harry Slochower's biography of Richard Dehmel, and Stefan Zweig made his entry with "Adepts in Self-Portraiture."[72]

But the real event was Erich Maria Remarque's *All Quiet on the Western Front*. Krutch called it "not only impressive in itself but still more so when taken in conjunction with the others,"[73] meaning Dos Passos and Henri Barbusse. This theme of the war stories, already introduced in the previous year with Arnold Zweig, was then continued with reviews of books by Rudolf G. Binding, Georg von der Vring,

---

[69] *New Republic*, 6 July 1927, 180f.

[70] E. M. Benson, *Nation*, 10 July 1929, 45.

[71] J. W. Krutch, *Nation*, 31 July 1929, 121f.

[72] Angus Burrell, *Nation*, 10 April 1929, 431.

[73] *Nation*, 10 July 1929, 43.

Joachim Ringelnatz[74] and a favorable review of Ludwig Renn's *Krieg*.[75] War or antiwar stories had always raised attention, Kellermann's book mentioned before, for example, and many others, documentary or fictional.[76]

The *New Republic* confirms this picture. In 1928 and 1929 it reviewed books by Emil Ludwig, Thomas Mann (praising the novella *Unordnung und frühes Leid* [*Disorder and Early Sorrow*]), Alfred Neumann, Bruno Frank, Arthur Schnitzler, Frank Thieß, Hans Heinz Ewers, René Fülöp-Miller, Hermann Sudermann, Heinrich Mann (*Mother Mary* "will not increase the reputation of the family"),[77] René Schickele; and then the war novels. *Sergeant Grischa* was "one of the best novels of the war that has yet appeared."[78] *All Quiet on the Western Front* was an impressive work; the reviewer stated, "I have said nothing in criticism of this book, and there is little I will say."[79] *War* by Ludwig Renn, however, failed to convince the writer of the short review, who stated that "Herr Renn has not, as his predecessor has done, pierced through our minds and shaken our hearts."[80] The predecessor, of course, was Remarque.

The *New Republic* had also arrived at the conclusion of G. H. Danton in his article "Germany Ten Years After," that "what is best in

---

[74] James B. Wharton, *Nation*, 17 July 1929, 69f.

[75] James B. Wharton, *Nation*, 14 August 1929, 173.

[76] "An Honest German," review of *Mein Kampf gegen das militaristische und nationalistische Deutschland*, by Friedrich Wilhelm Foerster, *Nation*, 13 April 1921, 557f.; review of *The German Revolution*, by Heinrich Ströbel *Nation*, 9 April 1924, 403f. The *New Republic* (11 February 1920, 320) made a case out of the fact that *A German Deserter's War Experiences*, used for British and French propaganda, had been forbidden in the United States; it mentioned the stand against the war by Fritz von Unruh, in Clara Viebig's novel cited above, and in Stefan Zweig's biography of Romain Rolland (reviewed by Robert Morss Lovett, 19 October 1921, 22f.) where Zweig defended Rolland's pacifist stance. Again, it is significant that apart from memoirs by Ludendorff, Hindenburg, the kaiser, the crown prince, etc., German "apologists" did not find space in these journals.

[77] T. S. Matthews, *New Republic*, 13 February, 1929, 357.

[78] Ibid., 355f.

[79] T. S. Matthews, *New Republic*, 19 June 1929, 130.

[80] *New Republic*, 14 August 1929, 349.

Germany is German 'kultur'";[81] and T. S. Matthews summed it up a year later, "In a literary way, at least, Germany has come back into the society of nations."[82] And he mentioned that "such names as Mann, Feuchtwanger, Zweig, Neumann, Thieß, von Unruh, Frank and Schickele" were proof of that and should be familiar to American readers. Thus although the individual reviews were often critical and liked to fault the books for their "Germanness," the stature of German literature as a whole had grown considerably in a very few years. The boom of German novels, both on contemporary and on historical topics, was to continue; after Feuchtwanger, Neumann, and Remarque, then Zweig, Hans Fallada (*Kleiner Mann, was nun?*, 1932; translated as *Little Man — What Now?*, 1933), Vicki Baum (*Menschen im Hotel*, 1929; translated as *Grand Hotel*, 1930), and Franz Werfel (*Die vierzig Tage des Musa Dagh*, 1933; translated as *The Forty Days of Musa Dagh*, 1934) all had their successes. Thus the German exiles after 1933 could count on a favorable bias — with the qualifications that the depression also affected the book market, and that there was a resurgence of American patriotism in the thirties.

Indeed, the cultural blockade was over. The new German literature, especially after 1925, attracted publishers and readers. Prose fiction was much more successful than stage plays. There were good reasons for this: Broadway proved incapable of adapting plays in the new German style, expressionist or postexpressionist. Fiction was not under the strictures of institutional censorship, and before 1945 the production of novels was not yet a great financial risk. The German and Austrian novels combined interesting subject matter with a probing psychological approach, often Freudian. That was liberating for an American audience trying to shake off the yoke of confining Puritanism. At the same time, there was also a less savory side. World War I propaganda had left the idea that there was a "dark side" in the German psyche. This idea was confirmed by movies like *Das Kabinett des Dr. Caligari* and later by Fritz Lang's film about the murder of a child, *M*. The novels also were examining such dark sides; the literature of the twenties was full of crimes and trials, and it had a predilection for

---

[81] *New Republic*, 18 April 1928, 275f.

[82] "Made in Germany," 24 April, 1929, 285.

abnormal states of the psyche. Thus the illicit curiosity about the dark sides of humanity was satisfied, while readers were always able to say, "Those people are not like us Americans; they are the 'others.'"

There is astonishing little commentary on the political and ideological spectrum of German literature. Authors like Kolbenheyer and Frenssen were treated like Thomas Mann, Feuchtwanger, Remarque, Renn, and Toller. The specifically German message got lost on its way across the Atlantic. Also, book reviewers did not ask what such books said about the health of German democracy, while a few pages earlier in the same issue that same question may have been debated. The gap between politics and culture that the German authors wanted to close was quite visible in their American reception. As some of the above quotations indicate, the respect for German culture may have, once more, colored the image of Germany. For example, while antiwar fiction was readily received, the equally vigorous prowar fiction in Germany remained unknown and unnoticed.

The exploration of new areas of psychology, social life, and history in the German novels had a decidedly liberating effect in America, a country ruled by isolationism, moral censorship, prohibition, and a defensive attitude toward the world. The New York book market, expression of the cosmopolitan island within the country, was juggling its liberal convictions and its moral and financial pressures. It was easier to publish daring literature when it was "foreign." German literature had a slightly scandalous character; the novels were not made to order, were told in a "strange" manner, and contained much reflection. Intellectuality and thoroughness became the expected trademark. Psychological interest was also one of the expected ingredients, probing into the subconscious depths of the psyche. The interest in Freudian analysis was unabated during this decade, and C. G. Jung was making his entry into America as well.

The consolidation of the American book market on the basis of middle-brow taste coincided with this influx of German imports. The German novels, like Scandinavian and Russian novels before them, occupied the fringes rather than the center of the market. This trait they shared with the new French novels as well, which ranged from solid tales like *Les Thibaults* to Proust's novel cycle and to unsettling experiments like André Gide's *The Counterfeiters* (*Les Faux-Monnayeurs*), which reached the American market at the same time as *The Magic Mountain*. What the American public accepted from Germany was the antiwar novel, the historical novel, the biography with a psychological dimension, and the "philosophical" novel reflecting on the present. Germany remained a somewhat unsettling country, fascinating, if not outright demonic. The previous "romantic" image had turned into a modern and definitely threatening image. This was combined, in spite of contradictions, with a respect for the "philosophical" nature of the Germans, their thorough knowledge and expertise, and their earnest desire to do good. Humor was definitely not part of this concept of things German. Some variations were allowed for Austrian works; they were granted the light touch, and a measure of elegance.

It is easy to see how such clichés could survive and be reinforced by political events or propaganda. It is also evident that the German literature after 1925 did not contradict the idea of "two Germanies" — a beneficial one and a destructive one. The reception of these books had a specific social function in the United States, but it also reinforced the image of Germany. Negative reviews of works by German exiles during World War II would routinely fault their "Germanness" and their Teutonic clumsiness.

The academic discipline of Germanistics — struggling for its very survival — had almost no part in this new appraisal of recent German literature. Until well after World War II it kept concentrating on the past rather than the ugly present. There was one point where the interests of the academics, the New York liberals, and the public at large coincided: Thomas Mann's work, specifically *The Magic Mountain*. *The Magic Mountain* was to have a key function in bringing these groups together, in legitimizing Germany and German culture, and in opening academic studies for contemporary literature. Thomas Mann not only provided the ultimate proof for the validity of the new German culture, but he also legitimized the novel as more than distraction and entertainment, and he made depth psychology respectable. His American prestige went well beyond the usual idea of the reception of literature.

The sketch presented here is, of course, incomplete. Much more source material would be needed to document the different facets of the reentry of German literature into the United States. The outline is clear, however; the German-American encounter of the 1920s was very significant, and it should not be overlooked in a general history of literary reception.

Gerhart Hauptmann in the United States

WARREN R. MAURER

IT WOULD SEEM USEFUL, for reasons of contrast and perspective, to begin a discussion of Gerhart Hauptmann's reputation in the United States with a brief review of his place in German literary history. Hauptmann's work — some fifty plays, twenty-five novels and shorter prose works, half a dozen verse epics, and numerous poems, also an abundance of fragments, essays, speeches, and diaries — has been popularized in films and television productions and internationalized through translations into more than thirty languages. Just a few random statistics make it clear that he is one of Germany's most widely published and performed authors. *The Weavers* (*Die Weber*, 1892) appeared in no fewer than 253 editions between 1892 and 1942; *The Sunken Bell* (*Die versunkene Glocke*, 1896) in 160 editions between 1896 and 1930, and *The Beaver Coat* (*Der Biberpelz*, 1893) in 108 editions between 1893 and 1942. Not only were these plays read, but they were also performed — and continue to be performed. A random theater season — 1958–59 — saw, for example, forty-two productions of fifteen different dramas for a total of 823 performances.[1]

Nor was Hauptmann's impressive oeuvre ever denied commensurate critical attention. A glance at recent bibliographies confirms that scholarly interest continues, albeit with somewhat less vigor (as compared with that in the work of competing figures like Brecht or

---

[1] See Roy C. Cowen, *Hauptmann: Kommentar zum dramatischen Werk* (Munich: Winkler, 1980), 68, 78. For a general introduction to Hauptmann (1862–1946) and his work, see Warren R. Maurer, *Gerhart Hauptmann* (Boston: Twayne, 1982).

Kafka) than it enjoyed during the first half of our century. During that period almost every critic concerned with German literature seems to have felt compelled to comment on him, with the result that in 1952 Hermann Weigand concluded that "more has been written about Hauptmann than about any other author except Goethe; that to a wide and devoted following he came over many decades to be regarded as the incarnation of the poetic spirit. His appeal was broad, deep and lasting."[2]

Part of this appeal was, to be sure, a function of extraliterary qualities. Embodying much of the impressive humanity and disingenuous charisma of his caricature in the Mynheer Peeperkorn figure of Thomas Mann's *Magic Mountain* (1924) — but also endowed with the born actor's talent for self-promotion — he seemed, to the many who knew him, "regal," "majestic," or even a "prototype of man."[3]

Honors and material rewards were neither niggardly nor slow in coming. The recipient of many awards, including the 1912 Nobel Prize for Literature, honorary doctorates (the first, in 1905, from Oxford), and the highest distinctions an appreciative nation could bestow, Hauptmann enjoyed the rare privilege of seeing his work studied in the public schools and of having his birthdays celebrated as national events throughout Germany. His renown brought him into contact with numerous foreign luminaries, and his work served as an inspiration not only for fellow countrymen (including Bertolt Brecht) but also for such authors as Eugene O'Neill, James Joyce, and Anton Chekhov. Especially in Russia, where the first collected edition of his works appeared between 1902 and 1905, and where for a time he was that country's most popular dramatist, his influence was enormous.[4]

The veneration of the German nation for Hauptmann was fully reciprocated by him, and his more mystical than rational identification with it also contributed to some dubious chapters in his life. For a man

---

[2] Hermann J. Weigand, "Gerhart Hauptmann's Range as Dramatist," *Monatshefte* 44 (1952): 317.

[3] See Eberhard Hilscher, *Gerhart Hauptmann* (Berlin: Verlag der Nation, 1969), 5, and Hans Daiber, *Gerhart Hauptmann: Oder der letzte Klassiker* (Vienna, Munich, Zurich: Molden, 1971), 7.

[4] For secondary literature relating to Hauptmann's influence abroad see Sigfrid Hoefert, *Gerhart Hauptmann* (Stuttgart: Metzler, 1974), 112–14.

who was identified in a newspaper poll as early as 1906 as second in popular recognition only to Kaiser Wilhelm[5] and who was early compared with (and increasingly saw himself as something of a reincarnation of) Goethe, the temptation to view himself as the spiritual figurehead of his nation proved irresistible — to the eventual detriment of his reputation at home and abroad. To be sure, he had seemingly begun his career on a note of rebellion (largely artistic in *Before Sunrise* [*Vor Sonnenaufgang*]; more political in *The Weavers*), but he had also taken refuge in the notion that an artist worthy of the name is ipso facto apolitical. By the time of World War I, however, he is alleged to have declared his readiness to give up literature to devote himself to politics and, in a paroxysm of nationalistic fervor, wrote a number of propagandistic poems such as one commemorating his third son's induction into the army entitled: "Come, Let Us Go to Die" ("Komm, wir wollen sterben gehn").[6] And by 1921 he had become so strongly identified with the political life of the Weimar Republic that he felt obliged to deny widespread rumors that he was a presidential candidate. Nevertheless, Thomas Mann (and others) continued to see in him an unofficial "King of the Republic," and Reichspräsident Friedrich Ebert declared on the occasion of the author's sixtieth birthday in 1922, "By honoring Gerhart Hauptmann the German nation honors itself."[7]

Unfortunately for his subsequent reputation at home and abroad, Hauptmann failed to separate himself forcefully from the German state when it was taken over by the Nazis. Whether we ascribe the lapse to a congruence of personal weltanschauung with that professed by the new regime, accept his alleged confession of cowardice, or blame an excessive political flexibility, which at the end of World War II found him ingratiating himself with East German communists, the fact remains that he stayed in Germany and, outwardly at least, arranged his comfortable life so as to coexist with the new rulers with a minimum

---

[5] See Peter Sprengel, *Gerhart Hauptmann: Epoche — Werk — Wirkung* (Munich: C. H. Beck, 1984), 226. For an overview of Hauptmann's political proclivities see 221–35.

[6] In the *Centenar* ed. of *Gerhart Hauptmann: Sämtliche Werke*, 11 vols., ed. Hans-Egon Hass and Martin Machatzke (Frankfurt am Main: Propyläen, 1966–74), 11:663–64. Henceforth cited as *Werke*.

[7] "Mit einer Ehrung Gerhart Hauptmann's ehrt das deutsche Volk sich selbst." Quoted by Sprengel, 226. See also *Werke* 11:964.

of friction.[8] There were, to be sure, mitigating circumstances. In contrast to such famous emigrés as Heinrich and Thomas Mann, Alfred Döblin, Franz Werfel, or Bertolt Brecht, a decision to go into exile was not forced upon him by Nazi anti-Semitism or anti-Bolshevism. The fact that he was already seventy-one years old in 1933, that he felt — rightly or wrongly — that emigration would stifle his artistry, and that he wished to be buried in his native soil may be mentioned in his defense.[9]

Had Hauptmann joined the ranks of fellow German artists and intellectuals in America he might have been spared some of the bitterness of his last years. Perhaps the low point came on the night of 14 February 1945 when he witnessed one of the most destructive conflagrations of the war. In a statement which was later to become a staple of GDR propaganda he wrote, "I have personally experienced the demise of Dresden under the Sodom and Gomorrah hells of English and American airplanes. Splendid rivers flowed out from Dresden through the world, and England and America drank thirstily from them. Have they forgotten this?"[10]

Although never free of ambiguity, Hauptmann's image of America was not always so dark. Growing up during a period of massive German emigration to the United States, he recalls that, as a teenage agricultural trainee on the estate of an uncle, one stood as a matter of course "with one foot in America."[11] And although his knowledge of American literature was casual, it was probably no more so than that of other Europeans without facility in English. In his autobiography *Das*

---

[8] See Wolfgang Leppmann, *Gerhart Hauptmann: Leben, Werk und Zeit* (Bern, Munich, Vienna: Scherz, 1986), 8, 353, 359–60, 364–65; and Ferenc Kormendi, "A Walk with Gerhart Hauptmann," *Reporter*, 2 November 1967, 50. On Hauptmann's relationship to the Third Reich see also Hilscher, 412–27 and Sprengel, 230–35.

[9] Maurer, 3–4.

[10] "Ich habe den Untergang Dresdens unter den Sodom- und Gomorra-Höllen der englischen und amerikanischen Flugzeuge persönlich erlebt.... Von Dresden aus ... sind herrliche Ströme durch die Welt geflossen, und England und Amerika haben durstig davon getrunken. Haben sie das vergessen?" Gerhart Hauptmann, "Die Untat von Dresden," *Aufbau* 6 (1950): 109. See also Siegfried H. Muller, "Gerhart Hauptmann's Relation to American Literature and his Concept of America," *Monatshefte* 44 (1952): 338.

[11] "... mit einem Fuß in Amerika." *Werke* 7:619.

Abenteuer meiner Jugend (1937, The Adventure of My Youth) he claims to have learned to read from a translation of James Fenimore Cooper's *Leatherstocking Tales* and says that he identified so strongly with the fictional chieftain Chingachgook that for a time he was nicknamed after him. Cooper's forest descriptions proved useful background for his early drama *Germanen und Römer* (Germanic Tribes and Romans), and the boy-hero Phaon of his novel *Die Insel der großen Mutter* (1924, *The Island of the Great Mother*) also begins his education by reading Cooper.[12] In addition to Cooper, Hauptmann was also familiar with Walt Whitman, Emerson, Longfellow, Mark Twain, and Poe (whose essay "Eureka" he especially admired) and, among contemporary authors, he later expressed admiration for Sinclair Lewis, Theodore Dreiser, and Eugene O'Neill; some of O'Neill's dramas he had even seen performed in Berlin.[13]

In addition to such purely literary contact Hauptmann also became more personally involved with America on several occasions. Under the oppressive atmosphere of Prussian militarism, and together with his brother Carl and some student friends, he had in 1882–83 discovered Étienne Cabet's novel *Voyage en Icarie* and learned of the attempt by Cabet and his followers to establish model socialist-utopian settlements in Texas and Illinois some thirty-five years earlier. Attempting a similar experiment, the group founded a Pacific Society (Gesellschaft Pazifik) and named Carl and Gerhart ministers respectively of science and culture for the American venture. The designated president, Alfred Ploetz, was actually dispatched on a reconnaissance trip to the United States in 1884. He soon found, however, that Cabet's settlements had fallen into a sad state of decline and that American conditions in general were not conducive to utopian plans. Abortive though it was, this episode brought Hauptmann an undeserved reputation as a socialist agitator.[14]

---

[12] *Werke* 5:347, 708; 7:822; and Muller, 333.

[13] See Muller, 333; and Frederick W. J. Heuser, *Gerhart Hauptmann: Zu seinem Leben und Schaffen* (Tübingen: Max Niemeyer, 1961), 69.

[14] See also Muller, 334–35; Hilscher, 38–39, and Leppmann, 72–73 for further details of this abortive venture.

Hauptmann was able to explore the United States firsthand (albeit only the eastern seaboard) on two occasions; in 1894 at a time of great personal problems and again in 1932 at the height of his renown. The turbulent premiere of *Before Sunrise* on 20 October 1889, and the subsequent successes and sensationalism aroused in Europe by *Das Friedensfest* (1890, *The Coming of Peace*), *Einsame Menschen* (1891, *Lonely Lives*), *The Beaver Coat*, and even *The Weavers* passed by the American cultural establishment with barely a ripple. To be sure, *Before Sunrise* had been staged three evenings in succession by the German-language Thalia Theatre in New York, beginning on 11 January 1892, and elicited these comments by an anonymous reviewer:

> A study in Socialism, by Gerhart Hauptmann, one of the German followers of Ibsen, was brought forward at the Thalia Theatre last night under the title of "Vor Sonnenaufgang." Briefly recapitulated, the story of the play has to deal with the inevitably irrepressible conflict between capital and labor. A young journalist is sent into the mining regions to investigate the relations between employers and employed. While thus concerned he is thrown into contact with the charming daughter of one of the hated monopolists. He is an ardent lover and he captivates the girl. But he is likewise a young man with a theory. His investigations show that the father of his bride-expectant is a drunkard and her mother is an infidel. This determines him, and he relentlessly breaks off the match, and the young woman kills herself with a convenient household utensil — a carving knife. And capital continues triumphant, while labor languishes.[15]

The flippant tone of these remarks fails to camouflage the reviewer's superficial understanding of what he has seen. The "mother" referred to quite inaccurately as an "infidel" (hypocrite is more like it) is actually the heroine's stepmother; the suicide is accomplished with a hunting knife, not the ludicrous "kitchen utensil," and the entire play is, of

---

[15] *New York Times*, 12 January 1892, 4. Also quoted by Walter A. Reichart, "Die früheste Hauptmann-Kritik in Amerika," in *Marginalien zur poetischen Welt: Festschrift für Robert Mühler*, ed. Alois Eder et al. (Berlin: Duncker & Humblot, 1971), 271–72.

course, much more than a simplistic socialist tract. As Theodor Fontane pointed out the day after the German premiere, "the tone with works such as this, which have much of the ballad about them, is almost everything."[16] Even naturalistic art benefits from virtuosity (for example, in the arbor love scene), and the play remains a memorable compendium of the ideas and moods of the people, places, and events it reflects.

Attention to Hauptmann and his works waned in America during the next two years. The *Review of Reviews* reported some relevant French commentary from the *Nouvelle Revue* of June 1893, in which the author was presented as "Germany's great coming dramatist," whose *Weavers* "became widely known all over Europe, for the German government forbade its production on the boards of a state theatre, as its performance might have led to public disturbances."[17] The French critic was then quoted to the effect that "Hauptmann's great merit is one rare in Germany, namely, that of having the power to create living personalities who speak in a natural manner according to their character and their conditions.... We shall be curious to see if in France people will appreciate, as he deserves, the writer whom the Germans do not hesitate to proclaim their only modern poet."[18]

It is typical for the state of cultural transmission of the time that this first substantial report on Hauptmann should arrive via a French intermediary; more typical yet is the similar role played by England. In a "London Letter" printed in the *New York Times*, Arthur Waugh reports, "Rumors — very faint as yet — have reached London of the coming of a new Continental dramatist, who is, it is suggested, to step upon the pedestal from which the exertions of Mr. Clement Scott are supposed to have thrust Ibsen.... His literary temperament is spoken of as one of extreme gloom, unrelieved by any shaft of humor."[19]

---

[16] "Der Ton ist, bei Arbeiten wie diese, die viel von der Ballade haben, nahezu Alles." Theodor Fontane, "Gerhart Hauptmann, 'Vor Sonnenaufgang,'" in *Gerhart Hauptmann*, ed. Hans Joachim Schrimpf (Darmstadt: Wissenschaftliche Buchgesellschaft, 1976), 13.

[17] Quoted by Reichart, "Hauptmann-Kritik," 273.

[18] Ibid., 273.

[19] *New York Times*, 6 January 1894, 9.

When Hauptmann arrived in New York four weeks later, on 4 February 1894, he was not only virtually unknown in this country, but he was also burdened by a number of handicaps; as a dramatist he was at the mercy of a theater tradition that could not compare with that of his homeland; as a Naturalist he was part of a movement that would remain largely alien to Americans for some twenty more years, and as a Silesian German he drew his characters, situations, language, and inspiration from a milieu that was almost incomprehensible to American audiences. To be sure, German drama had been steadily performed in New York, Philadelphia, Boston, Chicago, Milwaukee, and St. Louis since William Dunlap's 1798 adaptation and staging of August von Kotzebue's *Menschenhaß und Reue* as *The Stranger*. Unfortunately this choice of author remained typical for the general level of sentimental, farcical, melodramatic fare that was to dominate the American stage for years to come. Even the immigrants of 1848, many of whom arrived with their artistic sensibilities still intact, were soon homogenized by the "melting pot" to the point where they too patronized the vapid, Americanized, happy-end versions of French plays by the likes of Rostand and Sardou and later preferred Hermann Sudermann over Hauptmann by a wide margin. By the mid-nineties the profit motive and star system had become so dominant in New York that even Heinrich Conried had to prostitute his fine Irving Place Theatre with performances of trivia in order to finance an occasional culturally significant German play.[20]

Another problem was that Naturalism, Hauptmann's most congenial mode, was antithetical to the optimistic, didactic, and puritanical temper. When Ibsen's *A Doll House* was staged in 1883 it was given a happy ending in the form of a sermon about a woman's place in the home, and in 1937 Arthur Hobson Quinn still claimed that "it must be recognized that great as the power of Ibsen and Strindberg may be,

---

[20] For the status of the American theater in 1894 see Peter Bauland, *The Hooded Eagle: Modern German Drama on the New York Stage* (Syracuse: Syracuse University Press, 1968), esp. vii, 1, 4, 23–24, 43; and Edith Cappel, "The Reception of Gerhart Hauptmann in the United States" (Ph.D. diss., Columbia University, 1953), 10–21. This unpublished dissertation provides the most detailed record of Hauptmann's reception available to date.

they present those facts of life which men must forget if life is to be noble or even endurable."[21]

An equally daunting problem was that of translation. As Lilian Furst has noted, "a translation is no guide to a Naturalist play.... Precisely because of the German achievement in the field of dramatic language, characteristic speech-patterns, dialectical coloring, verbal gestures, silences, etc., the problems of translation apply to German Naturalism more than to any other movement and largely account for its unwarranted neglect outside Germany."[22]

It would have been hard to concoct a better demonstration of German-American culture shock than that produced by the first English language performance of a Hauptmann play in America: the Charles Henry Meltzer translation of *Hanneles Himmelfahrt* (1893, *The Assumption of Hannele*) performed in the Fifth Avenue Theatre on 1 May 1894. Through a coincidence that would have further alienated puritan sensibilities had the details been known, Hauptmann found himself in the United States at the time. After eight years of marriage to Marie Thienemann, whose financial resources had made his literary calling possible in the first place, he had, during the German premiere of *Hannele* in 1893, become passionately attached to the young actress Margarethe Marschalk, whom he eventually married. Rejecting his proffered solution of a ménage à trois, and in a desperate maneuver to shock some sense into her wayward spouse, Marie fled with their three sons to the household of Alfred Ploetz, who had settled in Meriden, Connecticut. The ploy worked. After considerable tragicomic commotion, during which he even considered suicide, Hauptmann followed in hot pursuit. Meanwhile, two emigrant impresarios, Carl and Theodor Rosenfeld, who had produced *Before Sunrise* in Berlin in 1889 and had also been responsible for the New York production, decided to enhance publicity for their impending staging of *Hannele* (set for April 23) with the rumor that its famous author had come to America expressly to oversee their production. Not yet satisfied with this, they tried to generate additional revenue with the revelation that the title role of their sensational play would be performed by a fifteen-year-old actress

---

[21] Quoted by Bauland, 4.

[22] Lilian R. Furst and Peter N. Skrine, *Naturalism* (London: Methuen, 1971), 64.

named Alice Pierce — a move which provoked more outrage than they had bargained for. Almost immediately Commodore Elbridge T. Gerry, president of the Society for the Prevention of Cruelty to Children and champion of legislation to regulate the appearance of minors on the stage, mobilized his considerable political influence to prevent the performance. In a letter to Mayor Thomas F. Gilroy, which was also released to the press, Gerry demanded that Pierce be prohibited from appearing in *Hannele*. His long diatribe attacked the play wildly but centered on two arguments: the alleged godless nature of the work, and the danger to the moral and mental health of a participating minor. As especially blasphemous he considered the appearance on the stage of a person identified as "The Stranger" but who plainly represented none other than the Saviour himself.

As soon as the letter became public, Theodor Rosenfeld rushed to the mayor's office and tried to persuade Mayor Gilroy that the drama was actually morally edifying and should be performed as planned. Taking the same approach that Hauptmann himself had used with a reporter upon his arrival a few days earlier, Rosenfeld claimed that "The Stranger" represented no real person at all but was only a figment of Hannele's feverish imagination. (To the literal-minded the flaw in the argument was that the alleged apparition was played by a quite palpable actor.) He also argued that Miss Pierce was older than fifteen (by three months), that she provided the sole support for her widowed mother, and that it would be cruel to deprive the family of much needed income. Pleading ignorance of the details of the dispute, Gilroy summoned the principals to a public hearing on April 24, at 11:00 A.M. in City Hall. Present in addition to the mayor were Commodore Gerry, the Rosenfelds with their attorneys Maurice and Samuel Untermeyer, Alice Pierce with her mother, Hauptmann, and the actress Maud Banks, who had a role in the play and was known for her efforts on behalf of female emancipation.

Given the social, religious, and political orientations of the disputants, the outcome was all but inevitable. Gerry repeated the arguments of his widely publicized letter and refused a compromise of softening some of the more "objectionable" lines of the play; Maud Banks praised its high ethical tone and movingly recited the lines of the scene where Hannele talks to her dead mother, and Hauptmann sat in mute, uncomprehending silence. When Samuel Untermeyer dared suggest that Commodore Gerry had no right to appoint himself censor of others' work, the latter played his trump card against his foreign-born detractors, loudly proclaiming, "I am not a censor. I am an American citizen, born and raised in this country. Every American citizen has a right to raise his voice against sacrilegious blasphemy."[23] Theodor Rosenfeld, who had been naturalized a few weeks earlier, thereupon elbowed his lawyer aside, pounded his fist on the table, and shouted, "I am an American citizen, Mr. Mayor, and I will have my rights!"[24] By now Mayor Gilroy had heard enough. Declaring himself both an enemy of censorship and an admirer of the theater, he nevertheless concluded, "The decent sense of the community, I believe, will be shocked and outraged by the appearance on the American stage of a character representing Jesus, whose name has been mentioned so frequently here, and I am compelled to disapprove of it. I refuse to grant the application."[25]

The application, of course, related only to Miss Pierce's appearance on stage, and while Gerry and his allies may have hoped that the decision would scuttle the entire production, they failed to reckon with the persistence of the Rosenfelds. The brothers hired the twenty-five-year-old wife of James O'Neill (Eugene's celebrated actor father) to play the adolescent Hannele and set a new opening date for the first of May. If they were still hoping, however, that the pattern established in Germany with *Before Sunrise* and *The Weavers* would repeat itself in New York, they were disappointed. This production, too, had now had its well publicized scandal, but success failed to follow. *Hannele* was performed only twice under their auspices; once on the evening of April 30 as a dress rehearsal for invited critics, men of letters, political dignitaries, clergymen, and others whom they hoped to win over, and again on May 1 for the general public. Although the reviews were not unfavorable regarding the acting and staging, the play itself was almost

---

[23] Quoted by Frederick W. J. Heuser, "Gerhart Hauptmann's Trip to America in 1894," *Germanic Review* 13 (1938): 19.

[24] Ibid., 19.

[25] Ibid., 20.

110   The Fortunes of German Writers in America

universally condemned. The only glowing notice came from Meltzer (the translator!) who claimed in the *New York Herald*, that

> when the curtain descended upon the last scene ... a revulsion of feeling set in that was anything but complimentary to Messrs. Gerry and Gilroy.... So pure, so sweet, so elevating was the effect ... on all, that one could not but wonder what it was that caused our self-appointed censors to take so strabismic a view of so harmless, so lovable a composition.... Only the Passion Play of Oberammergau and Wagner's *Parsifal* make an impression such as is produced by Gerhart Hauptmann's play.... More serious and satisfying work than was accomplished by all concerned in this difficult task I have rarely witnessed on the New York stage.[26]

Other critics were less enthusiastic. Although there was some debate regarding the degree of religious affront to audiences, it was generally agreed that despite its brevity the play was boring. Thus the *New York Times* opined, "From whatever point of view the piece is regarded, it is not worth one tithe of the fuss that has been made about it in the public press.... It could never flourish, not because of any offense which it might offer to religious sentiment but because it is sickly, morbid, hysterical, unintelligible, and utterly and irremediably tedious and dull."[27] And while the *Tribune* critic grudgingly granted the drama "some poetical phrases ... some impressive passages," he also complained that much of it was

> no more interesting or dramatic, except possibly to medical students of hysteria, than the delirious ravings of the patients in a clinic.... An atmosphere of the strenuous but sentimental piety of the Salvation Army pervaded a considerable part of the play.... [It] is not likely to succeed for any considerable length of time, and it ought not to succeed. It may attract audiences of restless sensation-seekers for a few weeks, but it is not a work of genuine

---

[26] *New York Herald*, 1 May 1894, 6.

[27] *New York Times*, 2 May 1894, 5.

merit and it affronts both the verities and sanctities which are still cherished by the people whose influence in this community is for the good.[28]

When Alfred Ploetz reported on Gerhart Hauptmann in America to his readers in Germany two months later, he tried to soften the disappointment over *Hannele*'s failure. His claim that most reviews had been favorable contradicts the available evidence, and his professed belief that the hostility directed at the play was the result of puritanical and chauvinistic attitudes shared by only a small minority of Americans at that time is open to question.[29]

Be that as it may, *Hannele* did draw attention to recent trends in European drama, and the more sophisticated reviewers began to realize that an important new writer had appeared. Sporadic commentary in the *Critic*, for example, gradually became more positive. The difficulty of an adequate translation of *Hannele* was pointed out, as was also the subtle psychology which was apt to be overlooked by an audience unaccustomed to exposure to such matters in the American theater. Indeed, a year later William Guthrie even insisted that "'Hannele,' the little stranger from overseas, who was so inhospitably treated by our New York volunteer censors of the stage, is one of the masterpieces that defy criticism."[30]

By 1910, when the actress Minnie Fiske made a final effort to establish an English translation of *Hannele* on Broadway, the accusations of blasphemy and immorality had largely given way to carping over questions of form and style — whether it was a play at all or "only" a poem. This production closed after sixteen performances.[31]

The year 1894 brought a second, milder, Hauptmann sensation: the first American performances of *The Weavers*. Here, as in Europe, the drama was exploited as agitprop; it was staged as a thinly disguised, socialistically oriented attack on capitalism. First performed on the

---

[28] *New York Tribune*, 2 May 1894, 6.

[29] See Alfred Ploetz, "Gerhart Hauptmann in Amerika," *Neue deutsche Rundschau* 5 (1894): 723-28.

[30] Quoted by Cappel, 49.

[31] See Bauland, 15.

evening of 9 October 1894 by amateurs in the Thalia Theatre under the sponsorship of a labor group calling itself "Free Stage of New York" (Freie Bühne von New York), it featured the well-known anarchist-terrorist John Most in the role of Old Baumert. Not only was the cast woefully inadequate to the task of bringing Hauptmann's subtle masterpiece to life, but the producer clumsily tried to sharpen the political attack. "Not that he omitted passages," as Blankenagel has summarized his meddling, "but rather that he arbitrarily made additions which Hauptmann never would have written. There were more vulgarisms, tirades, and a long bombastic speech by Jäger in which he attacked the manufacturer Dreissiger. As a result, the fourth act became a botched farce."[32] When, a few weeks later, Most tried to produce the play in Newark, New Jersey, the *New Yorker Volkszeitung* of October 29 declared on its front page, "*The Weavers* Dangerous to the State. Performance of Hauptmann's Play Prohibited by the Newark Police, Due to the Presence of Strikers."[33] Again, as in the case of *Hannele*, a meeting of the politically powerful had been called — this time including the mayor of Newark, his police commissioner, and the district attorney — in which the mayor declared that, except for the fact that the play was "crass, tasteless, and therefore not ennobling," he had nothing against it, but with the district attorney reminding his honor that "we are the guardians of morality."[34] This time, however, it was the arguments of the police commissioner which carried the day. Pointing out that there were a thousand local workers who had been unemployed for nine weeks and whose families were starving, he thought it dangerous to allow an agitator like Most to stir them up further. Should he dare to speak, he would be arrested. Permission to perform the play was denied.[35]

Strangely, when *The Weavers* was performed twelve times in Chicago a short time later — again as a vehicle for protest — there were

---

[32] J. C. Blankenagel, "Early Reception of Hauptmann's 'Die Weber' in the United States," *Modern Language Notes* 68 (1953): 337.

[33] "Die Weber staatsgefährlich. Aufführung des Hauptmannschen Stückes von der Newarker Polizei verboten, weil dort Striker [sic] sind." Quoted ibid., 337.

[34] Quoted ibid., 338.

[35] Ibid., 338.

no censorship problems. And when in April 1896 Heinrich Conried tried a short German-language run of the play in his Irving Place Theatre (alternating it with Hauptmann's *Kollege Crampton* [*Colleague Crampton*]), it was well received by its audiences, if not by the critics. Indeed the *New York Times* concluded, "Hauptmann is not a great dramatist in any sense."[36]

Fortunately, another drama, *Die versunkene Glocke* (*The Sunken Bell*), proved more compatible with American tastes and did much to further Hauptmann's reputation among audiences and critics. Staged more than twice as often as any of his other plays, it was sufficiently nebulous to permit a wide range of speculation regarding its meaning, and the vestiges of Naturalism still remaining in the original virtually disappeared in translation. First produced in German by Conried at his Irving Place Theatre and on tour in 1897 and 1898, the English translation, again by Meltzer, attracted considerable attention in productions in Baltimore, Boston, Chicago, Milwaukee, Philadelphia, Pittsburgh, St. Louis, and Washington. It was lauded by critics and scholars for its power and significance as serious drama, for a perceived kinship with Goethe and *Faust*, and for its "charm," that is, for the beauty of its poetry and its ineffable fairy-tale atmosphere. From an standpoint, Conried's production, featuring a distinguished German cast headed by Agnes Sorma, appears to have been the most successful presentation of any of Hauptmann's works in America.[37] From the popular perspective, however, credit is due to a more unlikely source — the E. H. Sothern–Julia Marlow repertory company, which introduced the author to Broadway and to the afore-mentioned cities during the 1889–90 and 1906–7 seasons. Although much attention was focused on the star (Marlowe) and spectacular stage effects (rising steam, colored lighting, a green rubber mask for the Nickelmann character, and the like) the play itself was frequently the object of critical abuse, even though the overall reception was positive. Thus Henry Austin Clapp, the dean of Boston reviewers, directed his censure mainly against the inadequacies of American audiences, concluding that "the mental

---

[36] Quoted by Walter A. Reichart, "Gerhart Hauptmann's Dramas on the American Stage," *Maske und Kothurn* 8 (1962): 225.

[37] See Reichart, "Hauptmann's Dramas on the American Stage," 226.

level of dramatic work [in America] is generally so low that a change of this sort has an ineffably tonic and soul-stirring value."[38] And Weisert, in his detailed discussion of the reception of the play in America, perhaps best summarizes its importance in the words, "The fact remains that during the first decade of this century plays like *The Sunken Bell* could be put on in America with some hope of artistic and financial profit. Hauptmann's play did its share to bring about that situation."[39]

With the exception, however, of a few efforts by the Irving Place Theatre to provide German language productions of Hauptmann dramas — notably *Colleague Crampton* in 1896; *Fuhrmann Henschel* (1899, *Drayman Henschel*) with Adolph Sonnenthal in the title role in 1899, and *The Beaver Coat* in 1909 and 1912 — the popularity of the author's work on the American stage had reached its highpoint with the Sothern tour of *The Sunken Bell* and began to fade quickly thereafter.[40] After 1910 serious, professional American theater (as opposed to the little-theater movement and amateur theatricals) again declined rapidly, with the result that only two or three further efforts to perform Hauptmann require mention here.

Foremost among these was Emanuel Reicher's production of Mary Morrison's translation of *The Weavers*, which opened at the Garden Theater in New York on 14 December 1915 and enjoyed a run of eighty-seven performances. Only then, some twenty-five years after its heyday in Germany, were American audiences and critics becoming receptive to Naturalist drama, and critical acclaim for the work was enthusiastic and virtually unanimous. *Theatre Magazine* called it "one of the most stirring realistic dramas dealing with modern social conditions;" the *New York Times* now saw in it "one of modern Germany's great plays," and Heywood Broun hardly exaggerated the general tenor of its critical reception with the headline of his *New York Tribune* review, "Art at its Best in 'The Weavers.'"[41]

---

[38] Quoted by John Weisert, "Critical Reception of Gerhart Hauptmann's 'The Sunken Bell' on the American Stage," *Monatshefte* 43 (1951): 223.

[39] Ibid., 234.

[40] See Cappel, 200.

[41] Quoted by Bauland, 21; *New York Tribune*, 15 December 1915, 11.

A final attempt to stage Hauptmann on Broadway was less successful. In 1922, while the author's sixtieth birthday was being widely celebrated in his homeland, Arthur Hopkins produced a badly translated (Lewisohn) version of *Rose Bernd* at the Longacre Theater. With the celebrated American actress Ethel Barrymore in the title role, the play ran from September 26 to December 9 to mixed reviews for the star and lack of appreciation (or even ridicule) for the work itself. Robert Benchley — to cite just the best-remembered of the reviewers — compared the dialogue and situations to "a reading from *Snow White and Rose Red*."[42]

Since 1922 individual performances in English (of *Hannele* in 1924 and 1947 and *The Beaver Coat* in 1956) have come and gone with hardly a trace, and the only opportunities to see live performances of Hauptmann have been rare college and university performances — notably the excellent German production of *The Beaver Coat* in 1967 by the West German Tourneetheater under the direction of Wilhelm Michael Mund.[43]

Fortunately, Hauptmann's renown in America was not limited to his achievements as a dramatist. In the United States the reasons for this were the awarding of the Nobel Prize to the fifty-year-old author in 1912, his emergence as a novelist, and the increasing availability of his works in translation. The Nobel Prize made him difficult to ignore and, while there were the usual reservations as to the worthiness of the laureate, the influential *New York Times* repeated the by now familiar comparison that "in the opinion of many critics [Hauptmann was] the most distinguished dramatist since Goethe," printed A. H. Hohlfeld's judgment that he was the "world's greatest living writer," and congratulated its readers for having overcome the narrow-mindedness that had rejected *Hannele* as blasphemous in 1894.[44] The latter conclusion, of course, may have been overblown and premature. When the novels *Der Narr in Christo Emanuel Quint* (1910, *The Fool in Christ Emanuel Quint*) and *Atlantis* (1912) appeared in translation soon after their

---

[42] Quoted by Cappel, 323.

[43] See Klaus W. Jonas, "Gerhart Hauptmann in Amerika und England," in Schrimpf, 427.

[44] *New York Times*, 6 October 1912, 14; and 15 December 1912, Book Review Section, 1. See also Cappel, 170, 201, 210.

publication in Germany, the old religious and chauvinistic atavism continued to surface. And although *Quint* was cited as "proof of earnest artistic endeavor in the service of a great ethical purpose" and as "the best work of [Hauptmann's] gradual decadence" and received generally favorable reviews, it was also attacked as "a satire on Christianity — nothing short of sacrilegious."[45] *Atlantis*, an admittedly self-indulgent novel based on the author's trip to the United States in 1894, found little favor. As in Europe, much was made of the uncanny way in which it had anticipated the sinking of the *Titanic*, but the unflattering light in which the author portrayed the darker side of "Americanism" — its puritanism, cultural backwardness, and capitalistic excess — was hardly conducive to a warm welcome.[46]

Hauptmann's growing recognition in America is also reflected by the history of translations of his works in this country. Excerpts from William Archer's translation of *Hannele* had appeared as early as 1894 in *Werner's Readings and Recitations*, and individual scenes were also published in *A Library of the World's Best Literature* in 1896 and in the *Ridpath Library of Universal Literature* in 1898.[47] By 1900 complete translations of *Lonely Lives*, *The Sunken Bell*, and *The Weavers* were also readily available, but the most ambitious and successful project was the translation and publication of *The Dramatic Work of Gerhart Hauptmann*. This nine-volume edition, which appeared in New York between 1913 and 1929, represents the effort of a number of translators under the editorship of Ludwig Lewisohn and contains thirty dramatic works, including all of Hauptmann's best-known plays from *Before Sunrise* to *Veland*. Even after World War II the author has continued to challenge translators, and between 1945 and 1978 there have been new (sometimes multiple) translations of *Flagman Thiel* (*Bahnwärter Thiel*) *The Heretic of Soana* (*Der Ketzer von Soana*), *Before*

---

[45] Quoted by Cappel, 170, 175.

[46] Ibid., 185–88.

[47] *Werner's Readings and Recitations* (New York: Edgar S. Werner, 1894); *A Library of the World's Best Literature* (New York: T. A. Hill, 1896); *Ridpath Library of Universal Literature* (New York: Globe, 1898).

Sunrise, Hannele, The Weavers, The Beaver Coat, Drayman Henschel, and *Rose Bernd.*[48]

The pinnacle of Hauptmann's renown, at home as in America, had, of course, been achieved much earlier — in 1932, to be precise. The year-long celebration of his seventieth birthday, which by a kind quirk of fate coincided with the centennial of the death of Goethe (with whom he identified ever more strongly), brought a harvest of acclaim: the Goethe Prize of Frankfurt; a theater named after him in Breslau; a celebration and speech by Thomas Mann in Munich; similar celebrations in Prague, Vienna, Dresden, Hamburg, and Leipzig, to give just a sampling. By now perhaps the best-loved personality in Germany, his fame had reached such proportions that it even spilled across the Atlantic and provided the occasion for a second trip to the United States.[49]

Principal organizer, impresario, press agent, interpreter, general factotum, and eventual historian of the visit was Columbia University professor and long-time Hauptmann friend and admirer Frederick W. J. Heuser. Never before, according to Heuser, had a German national been so celebrated in America, and never had the press preoccupied itself to such an extent for three whole weeks with a mere author.[50] From his triumphal motorcade arrival in New York's City Hall, where he was warmly received by the popular Mayor James A. ("Jimmy") Walker on February 26, to his tumultuous farewell on March 16, the daily stream of honors bestowed upon him was avidly reported by the

---

[48] See, for example, *Flagman Thiel*, trans. Adele S. Seltzer, in *Great German Short Novels and Stories*, edited with an introduction by Victor Lange (New York: Modern Library, 1952), 332–62; *The Heretic of Soana*, trans. Bayard Q. Morgan with an introduction by Harold von Hofe (New York: Frederick Ungar, 1958); *Gerhart Hauptmann's Before Daybreak*, trans. Peter Bauland (Chapel Hill: University of North Carolina Press, 1978); *The Weavers, Rose Bernd, Drayman Henschel, The Beaver Coat, Hannele: Five Plays by Gerhart Hauptmann*, trans. Theodore H. Lustig (New York: Bantam Books, 1961); *Three Plays: The Weavers, Hannele, The Beaver Coat*, trans. Horst Frenz and Miles Waggoner with an introduction by Horst Frenz (New York: Frederick Ungar, 1980).

[49] Maurer, 118. For a detailed, day-by-day account of Hauptmann's 1932 trip, see Heuser, *Gerhart Hauptmann*, 67–91.

[50] Heuser, 91.

New York Times and other leading newspapers.[51] And although the ostensible reason for the trip was his centennial Goethe address, Hauptmann also enjoyed the benefits of a highly privileged tourist. The main celebration occurred at Columbia University on February 29, where he was awarded an honorary doctorate. The following day, before a sellout crowd, he delivered his Goethe address, which was also broadcast by radio to the entire United States, Canada, and Germany. Repetitions of the speech took him to Harvard, Johns Hopkins, and George Washington universities. Other highlights included visits to Harlem and to a house in New York once occupied by Poe; a three-day stay in Craigie House in Cambridge where Longfellow had lived; a meeting with President Hoover and a reception in his honor by the political elite of Washington, as well as introductions to such notables as Theodore Dreiser, Sinclair Lewis, Helen Keller, Lillian Gish, and Eugene O'Neill — whose *Mourning Becomes Electra* he had an opportunity to see and admire. Finally, at a Lotus Club dinner in his honor, Ethel Barrymore provided what was probably the most moving testimonial. Having rushed to New York by train from an engagement in Ohio just to meet the author, she stammered this tribute:

> It is a very difficult place to speak after Dr. Hauptmann. I am not a speaker, but I wish just to tell you that it is the greatest moment of my life tonight to be sitting at the table with Dr. Hauptmann. It makes me feel as if I were sitting with Beethoven, with Goethe, and Hauptmann.
>
> I feel that so much, I have nothing else that I can say. It is true ... that my favorite role is Rose Bernd of Hauptmann of all that I have ever played — and I have played many, many roles. Thank you! I can't say any more.[52]

Yet in spite of such effusions — in this case by the doyenne of American actresses — it is a telling commentary that no commercial theater was

---

[51] Cappel, 406, counts seventeen *New York Times* reports on Hauptmann's activities between 2 February and 17 March.

[52] Quoted by Reichart, "Hauptmann's Dramas on the American Stage," 232.

moved by Hauptmann's presence to risk a production of one of his plays during (or immediately after) his visit.

The fact that it was Heuser, a Columbia University professor, who assumed responsibility for the visit, points to another aspect of the author's fame in America which needs at least to be mentioned, the role of schools, colleges, and universities. As early as 1900 a school edition of *The Sunken Bell* (with an introduction and notes by Thomas Stockham Baker) was published in New York by Henry Holt and Company. Here, as in later editions of various works by Hauptmann, the practice of combining language instruction with an introduction to significant literary works certainly assured some familiarity with the author to numerous students struggling to learn German over the years.

At a more advanced level, American scholars have contributed a substantial proportion of the research devoted to Hauptmann. Thus Walter A. Reichart's "Fifty Years of Hauptmann Study in America (1894–1944): A Bibliography" lists 614 items, with very little slackening during the war years.[53] Beginning with an essay simply entitled "Gerhart Hauptmann" by William Guthrie in the *Sewanee Review* in 1895 and soon followed by substantial contributions from Harvard professors Kuno Francke and John A. Walz, the author continued to attract the attention of such notable American Germanists as Heuser (Columbia), Siegfried H. Muller (Adelphi), Fred B. Wahr (Michigan), Hermann Weigand (Yale), Klaus W. Jonas (Pittsburgh), and Reichart (Michigan) himself. For these individuals the study of Hauptmann has been an obvious labor of love. Not only were they often personally acquainted with him (Heuser, Muller, Reichart, and Wahr), but the significant American Hauptmann collections at Harvard, Columbia, Adelphi, Pittsburgh, and especially Michigan are the result of their intense efforts.[54]

When we summarize Hauptmann's relationship to the United States, several things ought still to be mentioned. As in Germany, his flamboyance and daring originality provoked an initial notoriety which, as often as not, distracted from a deeper appreciation of his works.

---

[53] Walter A. Reichart, "Fifty Years of Hauptmann Study in America (1894–1944): A Bibliography, *Monatshefte* 37 (1945): 3–5.

[54] See Jonas, 428–39.

Furthermore, the two most memorable episodes, the *Hannele* scandal of 1894 and the trip to America in 1932, give a somewhat skewed image of his reception. While *Hannele* nicely illustrates the difficulty of injecting an exotic, foreign playwright into a woefully unprepared theater tradition and audience, the final result of the episode was much heat and little light. Likewise, it should not be overlooked that the 1932 trip was largely an exercise in celebrity. Without Professor Heuser's efforts it is doubtful whether the trip would have been undertaken and, if it had, whether it would have attracted the attention it did. On the other hand, Heuser, who like some of his colleagues may be suspected of "Hauptmann idolatry," did much to promote the author among that segment of the population — especially college and university students — best prepared to appreciate him. In Germany today Gerhart Hauptmann has achieved the status of a modern classic; in the United States he has been largely relegated to the obscurity of the academy.

Kafka in America: His Growing Reputation during the Forties

JÜRGEN BORN

W. H. AUDEN, WHO IN 1947 characterized our age as the "age of anxiety" in an often quoted-title, wrote as early as 1941, "Had one to name the artist who comes nearest to bearing the same kind of relation to our age that Dante, Shakespeare and Goethe bore to theirs, Kafka is the first one would think of."[1] Six years later, however, Edmund Wilson, well-known American writer and critic, the author of *To the Finland Station* (1940) and *The Wound and the Bow* (1941), took issue with what he called the "Kafka adulation" of his time. "To compare Kafka with Joyce and Proust and even with Dante ... is obviously quite absurd." Wilson concludes his essay, "A Dissenting Opinion on Kafka," "I do not see how one can possibly take him for either a great artist or a moral guide."[2]

These quotations mark two extreme positions in the Kafka criticism of the forties, a decade that offers an amazingly wide and varied range of evaluations and interpretations of this author's work. I shall return to this decade after some general considerations regarding the reception of foreign authors in the United States.

---

[1] W. H. Auden, "The Wandering Jew," *New Republic*, 10 February 1941, 185f.

[2] Edmund Wilson, "A Dissenting Opinion on Kafka," *New Yorker*, 26 July 1947, 58–64; adverse criticism of Kafka in the United States prior to Wilson's essay was limited to Edwin Berry Burgum, "Kafka and the Bankruptcy of Faith," *Accent* 3 (Spring 1943): 153–67; and Harry Slochower, "The Limitations of Franz Kafka," *American Scholar* 15, no. 3 (Summer 1946): 291–97.

The fame of a writer abroad, be it in the United States or in any other country, is established to a certain extent by those who helped to introduce him to the country concerned. Who was it that stood up for or voiced an opinion against this writer, who recommended, and who rejected his books?

Ultimately, of course, it is the author's own works that establish his reputation, and the fame of a writer depends largely on the translator's skill, on his or her ability to find linguistic equivalents that carry the meaning the author intended to convey. With reference to Kafka, some readers might find a title like "The Sentence" more evocative than "The Judgment"; to others a title such as "The Verdict" might be more appealing (and more appropriate, after having read the story). Each of the three titles has, of course, a different implication, suggesting a different interpretation. Marthe Robert, distinguished French critic and essayist, in an article published in 1961, pointed out convincingly how French Kafka translators of different periods have chosen the language of their particular time. She demonstrated how they translated Kafka's novels and tales in the vein of surrealism and, subsequently, in the idiom of existentialism.[3]

As to Kafka's present reputation in America, he has, of course, become accepted as a modern classic. He is read in college German classes in the original and in translation in college English classes by a considerably larger group of students. The novels *The Trial* or *The Castle* are included in courses on the twentieth-century European novel, his stories "The Metamorphosis" and "The Judgment" have become as well known as Edgar Allan Poe's "The Pit and the Pendulum" or Melville's "Benito Cereno." Orson Welles's arbitrary and individualistic production of *The Trial* with Anthony Perkins as Joseph K. (1963) was successfully shown in the United States as well as in Europe; Maximilian Schell's sensitive film version of *Das Schloß* was presented in Europe as well as in the United States. An unfortunate supplicant who is passed from office to office in order to settle his case, say with the Internal Revenue Service, may call his experience "kafkaesque" and can expect to be understood by educated people.

---

[3] Marthe Robert, "Kafka en France," *Mercure de France* (1961), no. 342, 241–53.

Kafka in America

In my deliberations I should like to return, however, to an earlier stage of the Kafka discussion in the United States, to the 1940s.[4] It was during this decade that Kafka was first introduced to literary circles in New York, Boston, Chicago, and San Francisco. To talk about "The Metamorphosis" at that time was, to quote a line from "The Waste Land," "so elegant / so intelligent." It should be mentioned that the *Southern Review*, with contributions by Philip Rahv, John Kelly, and Austin Warren, was among the first and most active voices in the discussion of Kafka in America. It was in the very beginning of this decade that Klaus Mann introduced the American reading public to Kafka's novel *Amerika* and that his father wrote an introduction to *The Castle*.[5] It was at the end of this decade that Heinz Politzer published his fundamental essay "Problematik und Probleme der Kafka-Forschung";[6] in his seminal critique he demanded an end to the fashion of "translating" Kafka in the vein of a current jargon — be it that of existentialism, that of the "Theology of Crisis" or the jargon of psychoanalysis.[7]

In the course of the 1940s Kafka experienced a most lively and, as is evident from my few quotations from W. H. Auden and Edmund Wilson, controversial debate. Among those who participated, two groups can be distinguished; first we have highly esteemed native critics quite familiar with the tradition of literary criticism in the United States, for instance, Austin Warren and Edmund Wilson; and second we have European refugees like Johannes Urzidil, Hannah Arendt,

---

[4] Peter U. Beicken has given an excellent account of the American Kafka reception in Hartmut Binder's *Kafka-Handbuch* (Stuttgart: Alfred Kröner, 1979), 2:776–86; Beicken, in turn, makes reference to Ann Thornton Benson's dissertation "The American Criticism of Kafka, 1930–1948" (University of Tennessee, 1958).

[5] Franz Kafka, *Amerika*, translated by Edwin Muir with a preface by Klaus Mann and an afterword by Max Brod (Norfolk, Conn.: A New Directions Book, 1941); and Franz Kafka, *The Castle*, translated by Edwin and Willa Muir with an introduction by Thomas Mann (New York: Alfred A. Knopf, 1941).

[6] Heinz Politzer, "Problematik und Probleme der Kafka-Forschung," *Monatshefte* 42, no. 6 (1950): 273–80.

[7] Politzer's warning anticipates many a point in Friedrich Beißner's very influential contribution *Der Erzähler Franz Kafka* (Stuttgart: W. Kohlhammer, 1952); Beißner refers to Heinz Politzer's article, thus fully recognizing the importance of his colleague's statements.

Heinz Politzer, and others, who were eminently familiar with Kafka's social background, with the particular political and ethnic tensions in Prague, and more specifically, with the antagonism between the German-speaking minority and the Czech-speaking majority, familiar too with German, Austrian, and Czech anti-Semitism. Consequently, the critics of the first group, those born, raised, and educated in America, were inclined to look more closely at the *text* of Kafka's novels and tales in the fashion of the criticism of the time, the still flourishing New Criticism. The critics of the second group, those of European origin and orientation, particularly Urzidil and Politzer — though literary critics of extraordinary sensitivity — could not help bringing to bear their own experience of having lived in Prague. Indeed, their personal acquaintance with Kafka and with his environment was hailed — though sometimes overestimated — by American Kafka enthusiasts. Thus Urzidil on 7 June 1948 wrote to the Austrian painter Hans Fronius in Vienna, "Hier haben sich die amerikanischen 'Kafkianer' auf uns gestürzt, weil wir ihn persönlich kannten, und wir konnten uns des Ansturms begierig Einzelheiten sammelnder Literaten kaum erwehren.... [D]ie Fülle der Haarspalterei, mit der jetzt jeder jüdische und nichtjüdische Intellektuelle sich selbst durch Kafka-Analysen legitimieren zu sollen glaubt, übersteigt das Maß des Erträglichen."[8] Hannah Arendt, although she never lived in Bohemia, was familiar from her studies of social history with the structure of society in the Austro-Hungarian Empire. She was intimately familiar with the mechanisms of the bureaucratic apparatus, the self-perpetuation of an institution functioning efficiently to the point of senselessness, even counter-productivity.

Of the introductory essays written in 1940 by Klaus and Thomas Mann, Klaus Mann's contribution shows a far more sympathetic understanding of Kafka: of the man and his work. Thomas Mann's introduction to *The Castle* is an undistinguished, perfunctory piece of writing done at the request of his New York publisher, Alfred A.

---

[8] Johannes Urzidil, "Brief an Hans Fronius," *Der Turm* (Vienna) 2, nos. 9–10 (1946/47): 356.

Knopf.[9] Indeed, the publisher had to urge his author and to remind him of his promise to write this introduction; finally, he did so, but, it seems, with little enthusiasm. For the most part he closely follows Brod's preface to the German edition of the novel and finally arrives at a characterization of Kafka as a "religious humorist." Mann entitled his introductory essay "Homage"; had he instead called it "Trying to Like Kafka," it would have been more consistent with his real attitude.

Klaus Mann's introduction to *Amerika* reflects an understanding of both the Prague writer and the American reader whom he is eager to introduce to Kafka's novel. "May we speak of 'fame,' " he asks, "in the peculiar case of an author who neither sought nor gained popularity and never was a 'success' in the ordinary sense of the word?" Yet the actual effect of Kafka's work has been "more intense and lasting than that of many a literary sensation of the day: his subterranean influence has proven penetrating and mysteriously strong." Quoting from Rilke, Klaus Mann continues, "What we call fame is nothing but the sum of all mistakes circulating about one individual."[10] Klaus Mann regrets that even Kafka, "for all his aristocratic reserves, was not spared awkward misinterpretations," and that he had erroneously been identified with the surrealists as well as with "a certain decadent Viennese school."

Of the essays introducing Kafka's *Amerika* and *The Castle* at the beginning of the forties, the various reviews of the first novel (during the last quarter of 1940) and of the second novel (in the spring of 1941) show that Klaus Mann's introduction to *Amerika* received by far more attention and sympathy than his father's introduction to *The Castle*. The *New Yorker* of 19 October 1940 calls Klaus Mann's preface "a first-rate introduction to Kafka's work." Philip Rahv, in the *Nation* of 26 October 1940, quotes from Klaus Mann's preface the observation that Kafka makes no attempt to give a realistic account of America, that he is, in fact, quite inaccurate "in every detail, yet the picture as a whole

---

[9] See Jürgen Born, "Thomas Mann's Homage to Franz Kafka," *Oxford German Studies* 7, no. 3 (1972): 109–18.

[10] For Klaus Mann's preface to Ksafka's *Amerika* see note 5. The German original of Klaus Mann's quotation from Rilke reads, "Denn Ruhm ist schließlich nur der Inbegriff aller Mißverständnisse, die sich um einen neuen Namen sammeln." See R. M. Rilke, *Auguste Rodin*, first published in 1903 by Bard & Marquard, Berlin.

has poetical truth." Babette Deutsch, in the *New York Herald Tribune Books* of 8 December 1940, paraphrases Klaus Mann's comment on Kafka's psychological predicament, his "father complex that dominated and all but destroyed him." The reviewer of the *Canadian Forum* of December 1940 calls the introduction to *Amerika* "a brilliant preface to Kafka's book"; in the course of his article he warns that readers "who overlook Klaus Mann's mild rebuttal" of Kafka's assumed ambition of writing *Amerika* in the vein of Dickens and who "try to read it as a Dickens novel, will meet with irritating disappointment."

Compared to Klaus Mann's introduction to *Amerika*, his father's introduction to Kafka's last novel found little response among the reviewers — although Thomas Mann was by far the better-known author and *The Castle* is artistically more advanced and generally considered the more significant novel of the two. Angel Flores, who in the autumn of 1941 reviewed *The Castle* for *Books Abroad*, complains that most of Kafka's critics see in this author's work "only themselves as Thomas Mann does when he compares Kafka with Tonio Kröger."[11]

Among the American critics who made Kafka's novels and tales the subject of intensive analysis, Austin Warren assumed a leading position. This widely recognized critic and scholar in the field of literary theory published his article "Kosmos Kafka" in the autumn issue of the *Southern Review* 1941.[12] He characterizes the "world" of Franz Kafka. This concept of a "world" is found among others in Walter Benjamin's famous essay written in 1934 and in Erich Heller's stimulating contribution published in 1948.[13] Still, what Warren specifically means by a novelist's world or kosmos is more complex. In *Theory of Literature*, which he published together with René Wellek in 1948, Warren calls it "this pattern or structure or organism, which includes

---

[11] Angel Flores's review appeared in *Books Abroad* 15, no. 4 (October 1941): 480.

[12] Austin Warren, "Kosmos Kafka," *Southern Review* 7, no. 2 (Autumn 1941): 350–65.

[13] Walter Benjamin, "Franz Kafka / Eine Würdigung," *Jüdische Rundschau* (Berlin) 39 (1934), no. 102–103 (21 December 1934), 8 and no. 104 (28 December 1934), 6; Erich Heller, "The World of Franz Kafka," *Cambridge Journal* 2 (1948): 11ff.

plot, characters, setting, world-view, 'tone.'"[14] Warren claims convincingly that Kafka's novels "evoke a world as self-coherent and characteristic as that of Dickens, of Dostoevski, of Proust, of Poe, of Hawthorne. Like Hawthorne's and Poe's, Kafka's is a limited, a lyric, world. Kafka is a metaphysical poet in symbolist narrative." Warren goes on to give evidence of the self-coherent structure of Kafka's world by presenting pertinent examples from the novels and tales. He shows that Kafka's fictional texts have much in common and thus constitute a poetic world of their own, unmistakably *his* world. Warren's analysis is an excellent example of a type of literary criticism, New Criticism, that is almost exclusively based on the text of an author's work. It does not depend on an intimate knowledge of the author's social background, the structure of the society he lived in, etc. It is, rather, based on the close reading of a text, admittedly by a person endowed with remarkable literary sensitivity. Having given Kafka's texts a close reading, Warren seems dissatisfied, understandably so, by Brod's interpretative guidance, particularly his observation that *The Trial* and *The Castle* should be "creative expression to the mysteries of Justice and Grace"; "that they are metaphysical novels," Warren adds, "we should surely have made out."

Hannah Arendt, primarily concerned with the dissolving structure of society in the twentieth century, emphasizes in her article "Franz Kafka: A Revaluation"[15] the importance of the bureaucratic hierarchy apparent in the world of Kafka's novels, particularly in *The Trial* and in *The Castle*; Kafka knew, she writes, that man caught in the bureaucratic machinery is already condemned. She holds that the public of the twenties did not take Kafka seriously because it did not understand the truth of his novels. Those readers were "fascinated by paradoxes as such," and they were no longer willing "to listen to reasons." To the public of the twenties "bureaucracy did not seem an evil great enough to explain the horror and terror" expressed in *The Trial*. Arendt maintains that people were "more frightened" by the novel than by "the

---

[14] René Wellek and Austin Warren, *Theory of Literature*, 3rd ed. (New York: Harcourt, Brace & World, 1956), 214.

[15] Hannah Arendt, "Franz Kafka: A Revaluation (On the occasion of the twentieth anniversary of his death)," *Partisan Review* 11, no. 4 (Fall 1944): 412–22.

real thing." So they were looking for "other, seemingly deeper" interpretations. They found them "following the fashion of the day, in a mysterious depiction of religious reality, the expression of a terrible theology."

Arendt emigrated to the United States in 1941, and a reflection of her own experience as a refugee from the Third Reich sounds through to us when we read in her 1944 article that Kafka's world "actually has come to pass.... [T]hose who have the doubtful advantage of having lived under the most terrible regime history has so far produced, know that the terror of Kafka is adequate to the true nature of the thing called bureaucracy.... We know that Kafka's construction was not a mere nightmare." Understandably, Hannah Arendt challenges her readers to fight determinism and to gain faith in true "liberty and faith of man." She insists that Kafka's "so-called prophecies" were but a "sober analysis" of "underlying structures which today have come into the open." Of the critics who dealt with Kafka's work during the 1940s, Arendt, because of her own experience, drew the closest parallel between Kafka's fictional work and the political reality of the 1930s and 1940s in central Europe.

Edmund Wilson's "A Dissenting Opinion on Kafka," published in 1947, is the most outspoken rejection of the Prague writer in American criticism. He starts with a metaphor, or, more exactly, a comparison.

> Franz Kafka is looming on the literary world like the meteorological phenomenon called the Brocken specter: a human shadow thrown on the mist in such a way that it seems monstrous and remote when it may really be quite close at hand, and with a rainbow halo around it. Since the publication in English of *The Trial* in 1937 ... Kafka's reputation and influence have been growing till his figure has been projected on the consciousness of our literary reviews on a scale which gives the illusion that he is a writer of towering stature.[16]

Edmund Wilson's "dissenting opinion" must be understood more in terms of his opposition to the Kafka boom, the Kafka vogue, the "cult"

---

[16] Wilson, "A Dissenting Opinion," 58.

of the "Kafkians" than in opposition to Kafka's writings themselves. Otherwise he would not have called some of his short stories "absolutely first rate, comparable to Gogol's and Poe's." Moreover, he would not have considered including Kafka, along with Virginia Woolf, in the sequence of authors he planned to deal with in *The Wound and the Bow*.[17] Leon Edel demonstrates in his comments that Wilson, in the notes for his book, originally included both Virginia Woolf and Kafka among the authors to be discussed. Wilson finally decided against it, though Kafka was, as Edel puts it, "the most wounded" among the authors Wilson treated.[18]

The Kafka discussion of the 1940s, above and beyond its contribution to our understanding of his writings, impressively reflects the philosophical and ideological conflict among intellectuals in the United States. It is essentially a conflict between a Marxist materialist or, more generally, a sociopolitical view on the one side, and a metaphysically oriented or religious view on the other. The latter opinion gained in strength after the general disappointment with the solutions offered by Marxism and psychoanalysis; as far as Marxism is concerned, the Moscow treason trials and the Hitler-Stalin pact added to the disappointment. The diametrically opposed positions in this controversy become quite apparent; thus Klaus Mann as early as 1940 recognized Kafka's "passionate concern with the problem of our spiritual existence" and expressed his amazement that "there were even attempts at analyzing from a Marxist angle certain enigmatic passages" in Kafka's books.[19] Arendt obviously does not agree with what she called the "seemingly deeper interpretations" of Kafka's narratives which people found, "following the fashion of the day, in a mysterious depiction of religious reality."[20] Edmund Wilson, with obvious irony, speaks of "the more metaphysical Kafkians."[21] Johannes Urzidil, in a contribu-

---

[17] Edmund Wilson, *The Wound and the Bow: Seven Studies in Literature* (Cambridge, Mass.: Houghton Mifflin Co., 1941).

[18] Edmund Wilson, *The Forties: From Notebooks and Diaries of the Period*, edited with an introduction by Leon Edel (New York: Farrar, Straus and Giroux, 1983), 6.

[19] Klaus Mann, preface to Kafka's *Amerika*, ix.

[20] Hannah Arendt, "Franz Kafka: A Revaluation," 414.

[21] Edmund Wilson, "A Dissenting Opinion on Kafka," 61.

tion to *The Kafka Problem* (1946), emphasizes that it is "the realm of the soul and the spirit exclusively that matters" to Kafka. Hence his "stories are not stories, his novels are not novels; they are purely spiritual architectures."[22] And in his review of Pavel Eisner's book *Franz Kafka and Prague* (1951) Urzidil warns that in "the case of a writer whose metaphysical thinking and style are unprecedented in modern literature, one should use caution in ascribing too unmitigated an influence to the merely materialistic forces of the milieu."[23]

Given the intensity of the Kafka-discussion in America during the 1940s, it is not surprising that after World War II Kafka was reintroduced to Germany and Austria via America. This fact is generally accepted nowadays by scholars. That the interest in Kafka's deeply disturbing narratives and aphorisms was kept alive during the turmoil that ravaged the European continent in the forties we owe greatly to the literary as well as to the philosophical sensitivity of writers and critics participating in the Kafka discussion in the United States.

---

[22] Johannes Urzidil, "The Oak and the Rock," in *The Kafka Problem*, ed. Angel Flores (New York: New Directions, 1946), 276.

[23] Johannes Urzidil, review of *Franz Kafka and Prague* by Pavel Eisner, *Germanic Review* 26, no. 2 (1951): 163–65.

Hoover's Mann: Gleanings from the FBI's Secret File on Thomas Mann

HANS RUDOLF VAGET

THE STORY OF GERMAN exile literature in the United States has a secret and unpleasant chapter ominously entitled "Confidential Matter." Few of the writers, artists, and scientists who, in the aftermath of 1933, fled from Germany to this country would have suspected that they were the target of elaborate clandestine surveillance conducted by the United States Federal Bureau of Investigation and rigorously enforced by its powerful boss John Edgar Hoover. Even fewer would have imagined, as refugees and exiles from fascism, mind you, the reason for which they attracted the attention of a federal agency charged with investigating subversion, organized crime, and similarly serious violations of federal law. What brought them to the attention of the FBI was the very reason for which they had left their own country: their opposition to fascism. The point is that their antifascism, viewed from certain ideological positions in the America of the 1930s, was deemed "premature." Indeed, better than any other, the slogan *premature antifascism* sums up the troubled, contradictory spirit of an era that W. H. Auden so aptly labeled "a low dishonest decade."[1]

Premature antifascism is a striking and bizarre, but also a revealing, coinage. Its origins are obscure. It seems, though, that the term was first applied as a collective label to the approximately five thousand

---

[1] W. H. Auden, "September 1, 1939," in *The Collected Poetry of W. H. Auden* (New York: Random House, 1945), 57.

American volunteers of the Abraham Lincoln Brigade who fought against fascism in the Spanish Civil War of 1936–1939.[2] The crucial word here is, of course, the term *premature*. It implies that there are two types of antifascism, one timely, the other untimely; one acceptable, the other unacceptable. The difference, it would seem, was purely one of timing. After Pearl Harbor and America's entry into the war in December 1941, antifascism suddenly no longer had the dubious ideological implications that it was thought to possess before Pearl Harbor.

How, and in what sense, could antifascism be considered a dubious proposition? To begin with, open antifascism articulated a hostility toward certain countries with which the United States, before 1941, was not at war. And hostility towards the new fascist regimes in Europe conjured up the danger of being drawn once again, as in 1917, into a war that would serve no discernable American interest. Active antifascism — whether propagated by the supporters of the Republican cause in Spain or by the refugees from Nazi Germany — was generally feared to subvert the deep-seated desire of most Americans to remain isolated from the troubles brewing in Europe. It ran counter to the slogan *America first*, which implied that the defense of American interests was to be placed ahead of the defense of any other country.

There was, however, yet another, more insidious, connotation to the slogan of *premature antifascism*. It was thought to undermine the one virtue and potential use attributed to fascism: its function as a bulwark against communism. To the collective mind of the FBI, communism appeared to be a much greater threat to Western civilization than fascism. German antifascists in this country were thus confronted by a somewhat schizophrenic situation of which they were mostly unaware: publicly they were welcomed, cheered, and, in some cases, celebrated, but secretly they were considered, at least in some important quarters, as potentially subversive. The logic of this type of thinking is strikingly simple; if fascism is the enemy of communism, then antifascists are likely to be communists. Armed with this conviction, the FBI gathered piles upon piles of information at great expense in order to show that

---

[2] See John Gerassi, *The Premature Antifascists: North American Volunteers in the Spanish Civil War 1936–1939. An Oral History* (New York: Praeger, 1986), 159f.

this or that individual preaching antifascism was actually a communist or a communist sympathizer.

I do not know how many German exile writers had an FBI file. No comprehensive study of this subterranean chapter of exile literature has as yet been undertaken. If the evidence concerning American writers is any indication, it is safe to assume that nearly all exiles were kept under surveillance. Natalie Robins, who recently reported on her probe into the "defiling" of American writers by the FBI, came up with a list of 134 names, including virtually all of the better-known writers active in the 1930s, 1940s, and 1950s.[3]

As for German authors, we know about the FBI file on Brecht, of course, from James K. Lyon's pioneering study *Bertolt Brecht in America*.[4] We can now add the name of Thomas Mann, on whom the FBI kept a watchful eye, here and in Europe, from 1937 to 1952, that is, from the year just prior to his immigration until the end of his exile in America. My efforts to obtain copies of the Mann file under the 1966 Freedom of Information and Privacy Acts yielded, over several years, a total of 153 pages.[5] This figure strikes one as arbitrary. On the one hand, it is too high — because the papers released include a good deal of useless material in the form of duplicates of publicly printed matter. On the other hand, it is too low — much too low — considering how much material was withheld. Based on internal evidence, especially a memorandum of 1947,[6] we have to assume that "evidence" was

---

[3] Natalie Robins, "Hoover and American Lit: The Defiling of Writers," *Nation*, 10 October 1987, 367–72.

[4] James K. Lyon, *Bertolt Brecht in America* (Princeton: Princeton University Press, 1980), 70f., passim.

[5] For a more complete analysis of the file than I can present here, see my "Vorzeitiger Antifaschismus und andere unamerikanische Umtriebe. Aus den geheimen Akten des FBI über Thomas Mann," in *Horizonte: Festschrift für Herbert Lehnert zum 65. Geburtstag*, ed. Hannelore Mundt, Egon Schwarz, and William J. Lillyman (Tübingen: Max Niemeyer, 1990), 173–204.

[6] Memorandum for Mr. Nichols, dated 29 October 1947: "In the case of Thomas Mann it should be noted that there are approximately 800 references in our files to this individual." In view of the fact that FBI activity relating to Thomas Mann was most intense in the years 1949–1951, we must conclude that the total number of entries in the Thomas Mann file considerably exceeds 800. Copy of this document from the FBI file on Thomas Mann is in the author's possession.

collected far in excess of 1,000 pages. Requests for additional material have been routinely denied; FBI policy protects the identity of confidential sources, the privacy of living persons, and the internal practices and procedures of the agency. In addition, Executive Order No. 123456 in the Interest of National Defense or Foreign Policy, issued in 1982 by President Reagan, further restricts scholarly access to the FBI files. Had I begun my project not in 1984 but five years earlier, I might have obtained a substantially larger file. It is hardly surprising that these additional restrictions were imposed during the Reagan years. As president of the Screen Actors Guild, Ronald Reagan had been actively involved in the communist witch-hunt in Hollywood and reported regularly to the FBI under the code name "T-10."[7]

When Mann first encountered the term *premature antifascism*, in 1943, he found it amusing and cheerfully counted himself as one of its exponents.[8] He would probably have been less cheerful had he known about the FBI's spying on him. Although the FBI file on Thomas Mann does not seem to contain the label *premature antifascist*, there can be no doubt that the Bureau considered him such a person. For indeed, Thomas Mann fit the profile. Not only was he an articulate and tireless crusader for an unambiguous anti-Nazi policy, he also openly supported the antifascist cause in the Spanish Civil War.[9]

Does the FBI file reveal anything new and worth knowing about Thomas Mann's American years? I think it does. Above all, the FBI evidence compels us to revise the rosy picture that has been painted by some scholars[10] of the good fortune of Thomas Mann in this country.

---

[7] See Herbert Mitgang, *Dangerous Dossiers: Exposing the Secret War Against America's Greatest Authors* (New York: Donald J. Fine, 1988), 31ff.; the book also has a brief chapter on Thomas Mann, 79–84.

[8] Letter to Agnes E. Meyer, 21 July 1943 (unpublished). The correspondence of Thomas Mann and Agnes E. Meyer is now in the Thomas Mann Collection of the Beinecke Rare Book and Manuscript Library of Yale University.

[9] See Mann's article "I Stand with the Spanish People," *Order of the Day: Political Essays and Speeches of Two Decades*, trans. H. T. Lowe-Porter (New York: Alfred A. Knopf, 1942), 83–87. [Henceforth: *Order of the Day*].

[10] See for example Erich A. Frey, "Thomas Mann," in *Deutsche Exilliteratur seit 1933*, ed. John Spalek and Joseph Strelka (Bern and Munich: Francke, 1976), vol. 1, *Kalifornien*, 473–526.

To most Americans, especially in the centers of liberal sentiment on the East and West coasts, he was a courageous, effective, and altogether admirable figure — one of the most illustrious figureheads, along with Albert Einstein and Arturo Toscanini, of the antifascist cause. To a very small number of persons, however, he was an untrustworthy friend and ally whose chauvinism and antidemocratic position during the World War I disqualified him as a spokesman for democracy in World War II. And then there was J. Edgar Hoover and his FBI, spearheading what one suspects were the sentiments of the silent majority. To them Thomas Mann — his great fame as a writer notwithstanding — was a question mark.

Mann wished to see Germany defeated as fervently as any American patriot. But most of the time he was at odds with official American policy and with public opinion. Consider the basic leitmotivs of his political writings and of his extensive speechmaking during the first years of his American exile. Before Pearl Harbor, he considered it his most urgent task to alert a concerned but cautious American public to the threat posed by his native country by painting Nazi Germany as a threat to all of Western civilization and Hitler as the enemy of mankind.[11] A classic case of *premature antifascism*, indeed! Once the United States had been drawn into the war, Mann was certain that Hitler's days were numbered. He then shifted his emphasis somewhat, insisting that Nazism be eradicated completely and that Germany be punished and rendered powerless. He argued for the unconditional surrender of Nazi Germany long before this was declared the official war-aim of the Allies at Casablanca in January of 1943. What he feared most, at the time, was a deal between the Western powers and the fascist regimes in Europe for the purpose of an ultimate crusade against the Soviet Union to wipe communism off the face of the earth.

Mann branded anticommunism one of the "greatest follies of our epoch."[12] He first made this untimely comment in October of 1943

---

[11] See "This War," in Thomas Mann, *Order of the Day*, 186–227 and "The Enemy of Mankind," *Gesammelte Werke* (Frankfurt am Main: S. Fischer Verlag, 1974), 13:645–55 (a 1938 address that has survived only in its English version).

[12] Thomas Mann, "The War and the Future," in *Thomas Mann's Addresses at the Library of Congress 1942–1949* (Washington, D.C.: Library of Congress, 1963), 23–43. This famous statement occurred in the following context: "I do not visualize as ideal for humanity, a

in his second address, "The War and the Future," at the Library of Congress, where a generous sinecure had been arranged for him by Agnes E. Meyer and Archibald MacLeish.[13] Later, after the war, criticism of American anticommunism became one of Mann's dominant themes. In a sense, his stance against anticommunism confirmed the charge implicit in the label of *premature antifascism* all along — the charge of sympathizing with the true ideological enemy, namely communism.

Mann himself was first publicly identified as a "communist dupe" in April of 1949, when *Life* magazine, in a notorious article, launched a vicious attack on some of the most prominent figures in the liberal camp. The occasion was the second Cultural and Scientific Conference for World Peace, which took place in March of 1949 at the Waldorf Astoria in New York. The conference was hosted by the National Council of Arts, Sciences, and Professions headed by Albert Einstein and Thomas Mann; neither one was actually in attendance.[14] *Life* covered the event in a three-page article brimming with scorn and indignation.[15] As if to warn its readers and help them identify the enemy, *Life* added a two-page-spread displaying the heads, in mug-shot fashion, of the fifty most dangerous fellow travelers and dupes — among them Thomas Mann.[16] The list contained also Albert Einstein, of course, and the likes of Charlie Chaplin, Langston Hughes, Norman

---

socialism in which the idea of equality completely outweighs that of freedom. So I hardly can be regarded as a champion of communism. Nevertheless, I cannot help feeling that the panic fear of the Western world of the term communism, this fear by which the fascists have so long maintained themselves, is somewhat superstitious and childish and one of the greatest follies of our epoch. Communism is today the bogeyman of the bourgeoisie...." (39).

[13] See Kurt S. Maier, "A Fellowship in German Literature: Thomas Mann, Agnes E. Meyer, and Archibald MacLeish," *Quarterly Journal of the Library of Congress* 36 (1980): 385–400; H. R. Vaget, "Die Fürstin: Ein Beitrag zur Biographie des späten Thomas Mann," in *Internationales Thomas-Mann-Kolloquium 1986 in Lübeck*, Thomas-Mann-Studien, no. 7 (Bern: Francke, 1987), 113–38.

[14] See Cedric Belfrage, *The American Inquisition 1945–1960* (Indianapolis and New York: Bobbs-Merrill, 1973), 92–99; Kenneth O'Reilly, *Hoover and the Un-Americans: The FBI, HUAC, and the Red Menace* (Philadelphia: Temple University Press, 1983).

[15] "Red Visitors Cause Rumpus," *Life*, 4 April 1949, 39–41.

[16] "Dupes and Fellow Travelers Dress Up Communist Fronts," ibid., 42–43.

Mailer, Arthur Miller, Lillian Hellman, Dorothy Parker, Aaron Copland, and Leonard Bernstein.

As far as Thomas Mann is concerned, J. Edgar Hoover had determined long before that he had a "communistic background" and "communistic inclinations," as can be seen now from an interoffice memorandum dated 5 May 1942.[17] With that memo Hoover interceded in the matter of the visa application of the Polish writer Joseph Mischel for the sole reason, it appears, that Mischel was sponsored by Thomas Mann, who almost routinely lent his name to such applications. From FBI documents released in connection with this particular case, one can draw essentially three conclusions:

1. The director of the FBI took a personal interest in Mann's activities in this country; it even appears that Hoover had a fixation about Thomas Mann. We can only speculate about the reasons. Undoubtedly, the great visibility of Mann's political activities and the weight of his name marked him in the eyes of the FBI.

2. Hoover concluded, to his own satisfaction, that Mann had "communistic inclinations." He based that conclusion on a five-and-one-half-page summary, produced by one of his assistants, of all the evidence on Thomas Mann gathered by the FBI from 1937 to 1941.[18]

3. Finally — and this will come as no surprise, though it might make you want to laugh or cry — none of the FBI's "evidence" against Thomas Mann was gained from any of his writings. Reading literature was not the FBI's forte. Invariably, the FBI considered as incriminating the participation in, or sponsorship of, certain political demonstrations, such as the Save Czechoslovakia rally held in Madison Square Garden on 9 September 1938, or the Stop Hitler Parade of 24 March 1939. The FBI also carefully noted references favorable to Mann in the *Daily Worker*, the newspaper of the American Communist party, or in the *Deutsches Volks-Echo*, the German daily of the Social Democrats in New York. Only in one instance is there even the semblance of a substantive charge, when one of the FBI agents reported that Mann's 1938 lecture, "The Coming Victory of Democracy," was "extremely Communist in

---

[17] See the facsimile of the memorandum in my "Vorzeitiger Antifaschismus und andere unamerikanische Umtriebe," 198f. (See footnote 5 for complete citation.)

[18] Ibid., 182ff., 197.

its presentation of the case for Democracy."[19] In all likelihood what bothered this particular agent was Mann's plea, referred to earlier, for a reconciliation of democracy and socialism.

Subsequent developments suggest that the *Life* article of April 1949 was intended to prepare the ground for a number of follow-up actions. It appears to have been the opening salvo in a campaign that was to continue for over two years. Ultimately, however, all efforts to intimidate and silence Thomas Mann were in vain. He was too famous and too well-connected even for the FBI. Unbelievable as this may seem to us today, Mann himself was unaware of the rather extensive surveillance by Hoover and his "Special Agents in Charge"; his diary records not even the slightest suspicion. Nor did he suspect any foul play by a government agency when it seemed to him that some sort of concerted campaign against him was going on.

Thomas Mann experienced a real scare only when he found his name on a list of forty persons identified by the House Committee on Un-American Activities as being "affiliated" with one or several "communist front organizations." The story was on the front page of the *Los Angeles Times* on 15 April 1951,[20] and we can well imagine how it affected Mann's breakfast that morning in his home in Pacific Palisades. Publication of such lists was usually the first step in a process that could lead to a summons before the dreaded committee. And this, in turn, might well lead to travel restrictions, blacklisting, public humiliation, and, worst of all, a complete upsetting of what, in Mann's case, had always been a very precariously balanced existence. The accusation by HUAC referred once again to Mann's cosponsorship of the World Peace Conference in 1949, on which *Life* had published that insidious article, and to his signing, in 1950, of the so-called Stockholm Appeal for a worldwide ban of nuclear weapons. Mann made himself "unavailable for comment" to all *Los Angeles Times* reporters and had his daughter Erika refer them to a carefully worded, previously published statement, which read in part, "Without questioning the sincerity of anyone's desire for peace but considering the prevailing mood and

---

[19] Ibid., 181.

[20] "Judy Holliday, Jose Ferrer Linked to Red Front Units. Top Oscar Winners, Other Notables Named by Congress Committee," *Los Angeles Times*, 5 April 1951, 1, 20.

atmosphere, I am convinced that any peace movement generally believed to be Communist inspired or controlled is bound to hurt rather than help the cause of peace in this country."[21]

Mann had good reason to feel concerned. The case of his fellow exiles Bert Brecht and Hanns Eisler, who were both called before HUAC, indicated clearly enough that the committee's accusation, however unsubstantiated, was no empty threat. What is more, Mann himself had already experienced the humiliating effects of the FBI witch-hunt the previous year. He had been scheduled to deliver the sixth of his annual addresses at the Library of Congress in April 1950. But this lecture was never held, because a few weeks before the scheduled date Mann was pressured to cancel on the urgent pleading of Luther Evans, the Librarian of Congress, and of Agnes E. Meyer, his Washington friend and benefactor. Evans had been shown a "dossier" with supposedly incriminating evidence drawn particularly from Mann's trip to East Germany in August 1949 to receive the Goethe Prize of the city of Weimar.[22] It is not difficult to guess the provenance of such a dossier. Evans, in order to protect the Library, which itself had increasingly become the target of FBI and HUAC probes, saw no choice but to ask Thomas Mann to withdraw.[23] Mann agreed reluctantly, though not without some lingering bitterness. Thus ended Thomas Mann's distinguished association with the national library of his host country.

Nothing, however, embittered and depressed him more than the obsessive campaign waged against him by one Eugene Tillinger, who, from 1949 to 1951, wrote four denunciatory articles about Mann, which were published in FBI-front journals. In the end, however, they failed to trigger action by HUAC; all they produced was one official reprimand of Thomas Mann in the House of Representatives.

---

[21] Ibid., 20.

[22] See my "Vorzeitiger Antifaschismus und andere unamerikanische Umtriebe," 189. See also Mann's account of his trip, "Germany Today: A Famous Exile's Impression of a Ruined, Vanquished Land and an Unchanging People," *New York Times Magazine*, 25 September 1949, 14, 26, 28–30, 32–34.

[23] See my article, "Die Fürstin," 137. (More complete citation in note 13.)

Tillinger is somewhat of a mystery man. From a brief *New York Times* obituary we know that he died in 1966 at age fifty-eight[24] and that he was a journalist working for various American news organizations in the 1940s and 1950s. For the earlier part of his biography we have to turn to the Manfred-George-Archiv in Marbach. It turns out that young Tillinger worked from 1928 to 1933 for the Ullstein tabloid *Tempo* in Berlin, where he was a protégé of Manfred George, formerly an editor at *Tempo* and from 1939 to 1965 editor of the German-language daily *Aufbau*. He went to Vienna in 1933 and from there, probably in 1938, fled via France to the United States — a familiar pattern among exile writers in this period. It is unclear why he became fixated on Thomas Mann.[25] It may have something to do with the two curt letters Tillinger received from Thomas Mann in 1945 and 1946 when Tillinger served as secretary of Rex Stout's Society for the Prevention of World War III.[26]

However this may be, in December of 1949 Tillinger launched his first attack under the title "The Moral Eclipse of Thomas Mann." Following the lead of *Life* magazine, Tillinger harped again on the World Peace Conference in New York. The most recent provocation he pointed his finger at was Mann's brief but triumphant trip to East Germany. "From his magic mountain in Hollywood," wrote Tillinger sarcastically, "Mann journeyed as an American citizen to the land of Goethe, raising in the wake that double standard of morality cultivated by the Nazis and Communists."[27] Tillinger portrays Mann as "America's Fellow-Traveler No. 1" with a long history as a political turncoat. The obvious aim of the article is to discredit Mann's criticism of American anticommunism and to characterize it as the logical consequence of Mann's profound and lifelong amorality in political matters.

---

[24] *New York Times*, 15 October 1966, 29.

[25] In his letter to the *Freeman* (see note 34) Thomas Mann suggested that Tillinger was motivated by a desire to distract from his own flirtation with communism in the past. I have found no evidence to support this charge.

[26] See *Die Briefe Thomas Manns: Regesten und Register*, ed. Hans Bürgin and Hans-Otto Mayer (Frankfurt am Main: S. Fischer Verlag, 1982), vol. 3 (1944–1950), 45/489, 46/53.

[27] Eugene Tillinger, "The Moral Eclipse of Thomas Mann," *Plain Talk* 4 (December 1949): 53–58.

FBI documents show that Tillinger sent his article, which appeared in *Plain Talk*, to "My dear Mr. Hoover."[28] It seems he wanted to make certain that the "Boss" knew of his good work, for he eagerly offered more of his services. Tillinger's next attack was occasioned by Mann's joining the American Peace Crusade which protested the war in Korea and demanded the admission into the United Nations of the People's Republic of China. Urged by Agnes E. Meyer, Mann soon distanced himself from the Peace Crusade when he learned that one of its leaders, Paul Robeson, was a prominent communist courted by Stalin. Tillinger argued that Mann's denials and disclaimers meant nothing, coming as they did from a writer without political morality. To make this point, Tillinger cited Mann's denial that he *had* signed the Stockholm Peace Appeal (which Mann had in fact signed), and then reproduced Mann's signature as it had been printed in *Les Lettres Françaises*, the weekly of the French Communist Party. Hence, no doubt, the awfully clever title of Tillinger's article, "Thomas Mann's Left Hand."[29] It appeared in the *Freeman*, the same FBI sponsored publication as in the earlier case, but now renamed.[30]

Tillinger's third article was entitled "Thomas Mann and the Commissar" and repeated some familiar arguments.[31] It was triggered by Mann's open letter to his colleague, the poet Johannes R. Becher, who was now minister for cultural affairs in the German Democratic Republic.[32] When Tillinger's fourth and final attack appeared — a lengthy, tedious piece in *American Mercury*, entitled "The Case Against Thomas Mann"[33] — Mann was out of the county on his fourth

---

[28] See the reproduction in my "Vorzeitiger Antifaschismus und andere unamerikanische Umtriebe," 201.

[29] Eugene Tillinger, "Thomas Mann's Left Hand," *Freeman* 1, no. 13 (26 March 1951): 397–98.

[30] See the editorial note in the first issue of the *Freeman*, 2 October 1950, "*The Freeman* is dedicated to the cause of freedom. It is the outspoken voice protesting against the Trojan horse of Communism and socialism within our walls."

[31] Eugene Tillinger, "Thomas Mann and the Commissar," *New Leader* 34 (18 June 1951): 6–8.

[32] "Johannes R. Becher zum Gruß," *Gesammelte Werke* 13:870–71.

[33] *American Mercury* 75 (1951): 51–61.

postwar trip to Europe. By that time his mood had improved and he was able to shrug off the whole affair. Initially, though, he was so furious that he considered a libel suit against Tillinger. Fortunately, he gave up this idea on the advice of a lawyer who wisely argued that such a suit would only shorten Mann's life. He thus contented himself with a sharp reply to the *Freeman*, which he asked his daughter Erika, an expert polemicist, to compose.[34]

It is perfectly understandable, it seems to me, that Mann should feel gloomy and disappointed in the face of the widespread anticommunist hysteria that characterized the McCarthy era. What alarmed him were so many indications that he was the target of increasingly irritating harassment. It seemed that with the denunciation in *Life* in April of 1949 open season had been declared on him. He noticed that whenever he was attacked, *Time* magazine was eager to report on it and to reinforce the FBI cliché of Thomas Mann as the typical "communist dupe."[35] *Time* and *Life* were published, of course, by Henry R. Luce; we are probably safe to assume that both magazines were fed from the same secret source of confidential information. When Mann read another such article in the summer of 1951,[36] in which the "evidence" against him was summarized, he thought that *Time* magazine actually encouraged the idea of calling him before the HUAC.[37] But even then he did not suspect that this was all instigated by a government agency and directed by a man who, on the shakiest of grounds, had determined once and for all, a long time before that Thomas Mann had communist inclinations and thus represented a threat to American democracy.

Mann's worst fears did not come true. The only official action against him came from the floor of the House and had no practical consequences. Representative Donald L. Jackson, in whose California district Mann lived, commented on his illustrious fellow citizen in the House of Representatives on 18 June 1951. Jackson read or had placed

---

[34] "Thomas Mann's Affiliations: Dr. Mann Objects," *Freeman* 1, no. 21 (21 May 1951): 536.

[35] *Time*, 12 February 1951, 21.

[36] "Ideologies: The Company He Keeps," *Time*, 25 June 1951, 27.

[37] Thomas Mann's diary (unpublished), 23 June 1951. Copies of Mann's diaries are at the Thomas Mann Archiv, Zurich.

the complete text of Tillinger's diatribe, "Thomas Mann and the Commissar," into the *Congressional Record*. Expressing serious doubts about Mann's "loyalty," he concluded his remarks with an unsubtle warning, "Mr. Mann should remember that guests who complain about the fare at the table of their host are seldom invited to another meal."[38]

And indeed, Thomas Mann felt no longer comfortable, or welcome, in the land of FDR, which of course, the United States no longer was. For a time he would console himself with an observation by his English friend, Harold Nicolson, who had advised him to distinguish between weather and climate in America, "Though at present the weather is undeniably bad, the climate continues to be fine."[39] At the height of the campaign against him, in 1951, Mann began to have doubts about even the climate in America. It was in such a mood of disappointment and gloom that he wrote to Agnes E. Meyer on 30 August 1950, "[I]t saddens me to see that this land of pioneers and of liberty is supporting all over the world the old, the used-up, the corrupt; in a constantly changing world, America plays the policeman of the status quo."[40]

And yet it would be misleading to conclude that Thomas Mann was a victim of the anticommunist hysteria of the McCarthy era. Compared with most of his fellow exiles, he was relatively safe. His fame and his Washington connections made him virtually untouchable. Nor is it justified to say that it was the harassment of the years 1949 to 1951 that drove him into a second exile to Switzerland. It does appear, however, that the events of 1951 confirmed and strengthened his longstanding desire to spend the final years of his life in Europe; they probably hastened the decision to do so.

When he did decide not to return to America, in the summer of 1952, Mann wrote to Agnes E. Meyer, "Help me dispel the impression

---

[38] 18 June 1951, *Congressional Record*, 82nd Congress, 1st Session, 97, pt. 5:6687f.

[39] Thomas Mann, "One Does Not Lead the World by Terror," *St. Louis Post Dispatch*, 15 August 1948; reprinted in: Thomas Mann, *Tagebücher 1946–1948*, ed. Inge Jens (Frankfurt am Main: S. Fischer Verlag, 1989), 930–31.

[40] Letter to Agnes B. Meyer, 30 August 1950; *Briefe 1948–1955 und Nachlese*, ed. Erika Mann (Frankfurt am Main: S. Fischer Verlag, 1965), 165. [My translation]

that I am turning my back on America."[41] In a sense, however, this is precisely what happened. During the last three years of his American exile Mann felt increasingly misunderstood, slandered, and, at least in one case, humiliated. Like thousands of other Americans he saw his constitutionally guaranteed freedom of speech and freedom of association more and more restricted. Although he felt no overt bitterness toward the country that had offered him refuge in 1938 and citizenship in 1944, and that had been decisive in defeating Nazi Germany, there is no denying the fact that he left America a disappointed man.

---

[41] Letter to Agnes E. Meyer, 7 November 1952 (unpublished). For permission to use and to quote from unpublished material I am grateful to Professor Golo Mann.

The Reception of Arthur Schnitzler in the United States

Donald G. Daviau

Arthur Schnitzler's reception in the United States has had a long and eventful history beginning in 1897 with a German production of *Liebelei* at the Irving Place Theater in New York and continuing steadily to the present day. Among Austrian writers known in the United States he occupies a prominent position. All but four of his works have been translated into English, a substantial number of them more than once, and his plays have been performed in German and English as well as in Russian and French. While critics have generally deemed the quality of the translations to be good, the adaptations of his works for theater, film, and television are probably inferior to those of anyone else. Yet his reputation has managed to transcend the misuse — if not mutilation — of his original texts, and from about 1911 on, critics in the United States have accepted him as a world class author.

The reception of Schnitzler is significant for several reasons. 1) Since he is considered today as one of Austria's greatest writers, and by some possibly the premier Austrian author of the twentieth century, the way in which his works have been received in the United States provides a valuable look at differing cultural and literary tastes, 2) studying the translations and adaptations of his works contributes to an understanding of how original texts are handled by publishers and directors for presentation to American audiences. 3) The reactions of scholarly critics as well as of newspaper and periodical reviewers over the years reveal the changing critical fashions of academia and of the general media by the way they have responded to Schnitzler's world and works. 4) The continued reception of Schnitzler is proof of the universality of the characters and situations in his writings. He emphasized character over plot and created human beings and constellations of characters and interpersonal relationships that continue to attract and speak to readers and viewers everywhere. As Robert A. Kann has expressed so aptly, "The comprehensiveness of Schnitzler's work does not rest on the fact that his characters represent all classes of Austrian society but that, taken as a whole, they represent all human problems regardless of the social setting in which they are cast."[1]

In order to trace more than ninety years of reception in a short presentation — considering that the reception of Schnitzler in Sweden and Russia has been given book-length studies[2] — I have to quantify much of the material and proceed by time periods: 1) from the beginning in 1897 to 1931; 2) from 1932 to 1961; 3) from 1962 to the present. Within each section I will enumerate the works available in English translation, the number of performances and films, and give an assessment of the critical response, both academic and popular. In this way it will be possible to document the shifting pattern of the reception, its breadth, and its basis. In terms of reception theory I am following the methodological approach of Felix Vodicka[3] and Gotthart Wunberg,[4] who stress the important role of critics in helping to gain acceptance for foreign literary works.

---

[1] Robert A. Kann, "Arthur Schnitzler: Reflection of the Evolution of his Image," *Wisconsin Studies in Contemporary Literature* 8, no. 4 (1967): 552.

[2] Margot Elfving Vogel, *Schnitzler in Schweden: Zur Rezeption seiner Werke* (Stockholm: Almqvist and Wiksell International, 1979). Elisabeth Heresch, *Schnitzler und Russland* (Vienna: Braumüller, 1982).

[3] Felix Vodicka, *Die Struktur der literarischen Entwicklung* (Munich: Fink, 1976).

[4] Gotthart Wunberg, "Modell einer Rezeptionsanalyse kritischer Texte," in *Literatur und Leser*, ed. Gunter Grimm (Stuttgart: Reclam, 1975), 119–33.

1897-1931

The first part of this study has been greatly aided by the work of Beatrice Schrumpf, who in an M.A. thesis at Columbia University written for Otto P. Schinnerer, a study that was praised by Schnitzler himself, traced the reception up to 1931, the year of Schnitzler's death.[5] Following *Liebelei* in 1897 the Irving Place Theater presented five more German productions — *Freiwild* (1899), *Das Vermächtnis* (1900), *Die letzten Masken, Der grüne Kakadu, Literatur* (1907), and *Das weite Land* (1915) — before it closed its doors in 1918. The first production of a Schnitzler play in English was also of *Liebelei*, translated as *Flirtation*, performed at the Progressive Stage Society in New York in 1905. Up to 1931 there were seventeen additional productions of Schnitzler's plays, including five of the *Affairs of Anatol*, three more of *Liebelei*, now translated as *Reckoning* (1907) or *Playing with Love* (1916 and 1929), three of *The Green Cockatoo*, and single performances of *The Fairytale, Literature, The Gallant Cassian, The Call of Life, Round Dance*, and the pantomime version of *The Bridal Veil*.

Three plays have commanded the greatest attention on stage and in film: *Anatol*,[6] *Liebelei*,[7] and, after 1950, *Reigen*.[8] American directors have remained fascinated by the characters Schnitzler created despite their inability to portray them convincingly. To these plays can now be added *Das weite Land*, which received new life through Tom Stoppard's

---

[5] Beatrice M. Schrumpf, "The Perception of Arthur Schnitzler in the United States" (M.A. thesis, Columbia University, 1931).

[6] See Sarah Luverne Walton, "*Anatol* on the New York Stage," *Modern Austrian Literature* 2, no. 2 (Summer 1969): 30–44.

[7] Stephanie Hammer, "Fear and Attraction: *Anatol* and *Liebelei* Productions in the United States," *Modern Austrian Literature* 19, nos. 3/4 (December 1986): 62–74. See also Leroy R. Shaw, "Modern Austrian Dramatists on the New York Stage," in *Österreich und die angelsächsische Welt*, ed. Otto Hietsch (Vienna: Braumüller, 1968), 2:547–63.

[8] See Gerd K. Schneider, "The Reception of Arthur Schnitzler's *Reigen* in the Old Country and the New World: A Study in Cultural Differences," *Modern Austrian Literature* 19, nos. 3/4 (December 1986): 75–90; and Sarah Luverne Walton, *Arthur Schnitzler on the New York Stage* (Ann Arbor: University Microfilms, 1971).

adaptation, *Undiscovered Country*.⁹ Curiously and lamentably, none of the productions to the present day has, according to the critics, seemed to do justice to the plays; they have at times been "adapted" almost beyond recognition. Some adaptations, particularly the musical and film versions, have used little more than Schnitzler's main characters and a bare semblance of the basic plot line. Some of the re-creations possess their own artistic unity and integrity, but most often they fail to render the meaning and spirit of the original. As a result, the stage and film versions have not contributed all that they might have to enhancing Schnitzler's reputation. Indeed, Schnitzler's stature as a dramatist has been built despite, not because of, the U.S. productions. Directors here have experienced particular difficulties with *Anatol*; as Stephanie Hammer has noted, "A truly definitive theatrical interpretation has never been established. Instead (especially in the case of the major revivals) problematic production follows problematic production, each one differing radically from the last, each one in its own way disturbing and unsatisfying to some of the critics, regardless of whether the director and actors handle the play as comedy of manners, farce, or existential or psychological drama."[10]

The first version of *Anatol* and one of the greatest was the 1911 New York production at the Little Theater, starring John Barrymore. This play has been adapted and performed more than any other, with over a dozen productions up to "The Loves of Anatol" at the Circle in the Square Theater in New York in 1985. Particularly notable was the 1931 version starring Joseph Schildkraut. In 1921 *The Affairs of Anatol* also became the first film version of a Schnitzler play, a major production by Cecil B. De Mille, starring Wallace Reed, Elliott Dexter, and Gloria Swanson. Only the basic idea was taken over into this version, and it bears little resemblance to the original play. Another film production in English in 1931, *Daybreak* (*Spiel im Morgengrauen*) starring Ramon Novarro, while more faithful to the original, was not successful.

---

[9] Kurt Bergel, "The Recent Reception of Arthur Schnitzler's *Das weite Land* on Two American Stages," *Modern Austrian Literature* 19, nos. 3/4 (December 1986): 91–96.

[10] Hammer, "Productions," 66.

Liebelei, entitled variously *Flirtation*, *The Reckoning*, *Playing with Love*, *The Love Game*, *Light-o'-Love*, and *The Lovers and the Losers*, was produced nine times in English adaptations between 1905 and 1987, the most recent version being Tom Stoppard's *Dalliance* (1989). Although critics have often regarded *Liebelei* as Schnitzler's finest drama, the reception by theater audiences, even in the case of good performances, has been lukewarm at best. This lack of success contrasts not only with the enthusiasm for the play in Europe, but also with the popularity of Max Ophüls's 1932 French film, which still won rave reviews at the New York Film Festival in 1974. Despite its universality the play's identification with Vienna at the turn of the century has tended to reduce its appeal as time goes on. Nevertheless, attempts continue to be made to produce it commercially — witness Stoppard — attesting to its intrinsic appeal.

The production history of *Reigen* in the U.S. has paralleled, to some degree, that in Germany and Austria, where the play was banned from the stage from 1922 to 1982. Translated as *Hands Around* in a private, limited printing for subscribers in 1920, the play created the same stir in the United States that it had in Berlin, where a lawsuit became necessary in 1920 to acquit the work of a charge of pornography.[11] In New York John Hess Sumner, head of the New York Society for the Suppression of Vice, brought suit against Max Gottschalk for selling *Hands Around*. On 27 November 1929 Judge Brodsky dismissed the complaint, finding "not a single line, not a single word, that might be regarded as obscene, lewd, lascivious, filthy, indecent or disgusting within the meanings of the statute."[12] However, shortly thereafter the decision was reversed at another trial, and the reversal was upheld by the Court of Appeals.[13] The French film *La Ronde* by Max Ophüls was also banned in New York in 1950. Not until 1955 could the play be produced at the Circle in the Square in Greenwich Village in a new translation by Eric Bentley. Since then it has been performed repeatedly.

---

[11] Wolfgang Heine, ed., *Der Kampf um den Reigen* (Berlin: Rowohlt, 1922).

[12] *Publishers' Weekly*, 14 December 1929, 2758.

[13] Schrumpf, "Perception of Schnitzler," 15.

Early on Schnitzler received little attention; his name was frequently misspelled in the commentaries and reviews. Granville Barker's translation of *Anatol* in 1911 brought the first real attention, which then continued to grow, ascending to a high point in 1917, declining in 1918 and 1919, and then rising again steadily to a peak in 1932. In addition to numerous reviews of his works, interviews with the author and articles with pictures were published.[14] Interest was widespread throughout the United States, judging by the quantity and distribution of the reviews. One major difference with Europe was the absence of any special attention to Schnitzler in 1912 and 1922, the years of his fiftieth and sixtieth birthdays. Another significant contrast involved the absence of anti-Semitism in all of the American commentaries. But the fact that he was Jewish also did not gain him any particular advantage with New York audiences, as Shaw has noted.[15] *Anatol*, the most frequently performed and published work, served as the main measure of Schnitzler, spreading the standard European image of him as a decadent aesthete with a limited artistic range.

Ashley Dukes, who produced the translations for the Modern Library edition of Schnitzler's works in English, played an important role in spreading Schnitzler's reputation but also perpetuated the cliché about Schnitzler as a limited, frivolous writer.

> Schnitzler ... is content to take as his theme only a few scenes from life, and even in those few scenes he recurs continually to a single passage.... His dramatic method is the intellectualization, the refinement of the Viennese waltz. The most famous of his plays is *Liebelei*.... But, in reality, they are all *Liebelei*.... The moralist will find 'flirtation' a euphemism, but Schnitzler has nothing to do with moralists or morality. His subject is always

---

[14] The most comprehensive bibliographies are: Richard H. Allen, *An Annotated Arthur Schnitzler Bibliography* (Chapel Hill: University of North Carolina Press, 1966); and Jeffrey B. Berlin, *An Annotated Arthur Schnitzler Bibliography 1965–1977* (Munich: Fink, 1978). Allen's dissertation "Arthur Schnitzler's Works and their Reception: An Annotated Bibliography (University of Michigan, 1964) contains a useful section entitled "The Critical Reception of Schnitzler's Works" (21–97) that is not contained in the printed version. Another important article is that of Herbert Seidler, "Die Forschung zu Arthur Schnitzler seit 1945," *Zeitschrift für deutsche Philologie* 95, no. 4 (December 1976): 567–94.

[15] Shaw, "Austrian Dramatists," 550–51.

The Reception of Arthur Schnitzler in the United States 151

the same — the lover and the mistress or two.... His power lies chiefly in the creation of an atmosphere ... it is indescribably charming and completely aimless.[16]

In general, however, periodical reviewers viewed Schnitzler in a positive vein as representing his age rather than in negative terms of artistic limitations. Academic critics, on the other hand, followed the German criticism and tended to perpetuate the image of a Schnitzler limited in thematic range.

Up to 1926 Schnitzler's reputation was based mainly on his early plays, for the latest play performed up to 1931 was *The Call of Life* (*Der Ruf des Lebens*), which had first appeared in German in 1906, and the last drama published in English translation was *Professor Bernhardi* (1912). In the meantime American audiences have seen *Undiscovered Country* and *Professor Bernhardi* but have still not had the opportunity to view performances of the substantial body of major dramas written after 1912. Nor in fact have these dramas ever been available; for, surprisingly, there has been no interest in even translating the later plays until very recently. A volume containing the last four plays, which had never been translated previously, is currently in preparation.[17] The European view that the later plays showed a falling off of ability and contained more or less repetitions of the early themes carried over to the scholarly opinion in the United States.

In the period to 1931 there was usually one production of a Schnitzler play each year (except for 1919), and the time between the appearance of the original and the translation grew shorter and shorter. *Professor Bernhardi*, published in German in 1912, was translated into English in 1913. The reviews often mentioned that the productions were inadequate, but charitably the critics did not hold the performances against the plays or the author. As late as 1929 the critic Edwin Green called *The Green Cockatoo* perhaps the most extraordinary one-act

---

[16] Ashley Dukes, *Reigen, The Affairs of Anatol, and Other Plays* (New York: The Modern Library, 1933), vii–viii.

[17] The volume, to be published by Ariadne Press, contains *The Sisters or Casanova in Spa*, *Seduction Comedy*, and *The Way to the Pond*.

play in our time. Evidently he was unaware that this particular work had been written in 1899.

As in Europe, Schnitzler's reputation in the United States was built on his one-act plays, which in addition to being performed were also anthologized in such standard works as the Modern Drama Series[18] and the Modern Library of the World's Best Books.[19] His reputation as a master of the one-act form has remained consistent to the present day. Discussions of him also appeared in books and articles devoted to modern drama. Percival Pollard, in *Masks and Minstrels of New Germany* (1911), headed one chapter "Vienna's Essence: Arthur Schnitzler." Pollard struck a theme that has also persisted: Schnitzler as a representative of Vienna, presenting its charm and grace but also its license. "His eroticism is far more insidious than the brutalities of Wedekind. His pictures of the patrician fastidiousness in amatory etiquette which characterizes peculiarly the last and staunchest stronghold of aristocracy in the modern world, Vienna, are so enchanting that they lure us toward licentiousness."[20] In 1912 Archibald Henderson wrote an overview of Schnitzler's dramatic works up to that point, stating that "the three plays, *The Fairytale*, *The Legacy*, and *Light-o'-Love* justify Schnitzler's title of world-dramatist and align him with the serious social dramatists of our age, headed by Ibsen, Björnson, Hauptmann, Sudermann, Shaw, and Brieux."[21]

An early translator and enthusiast, B. Q. Morgan, praised *Liebelei* but also stressed the view that Schnitzler's forte actually lay in the one-act dramas. "One of Schnitzler's earliest works *Liebelei* remains his high-water mark in the drama, and in view of the distinct limitations of his art, it may be doubted that he will ever rise above it, or even reach it again."[22] Other important articles appeared in James Huneker, *Ivory*

---

[18] *The Lonely Way, Intermezzo, Countess Mizzie: Three Plays by Arthur Schnitzler*, ed. Edwin Björkman (New York, 1915; and Boston: Little, Brown Co., 1922).

[19] *Anatol, Living Hours, The Green Cockatoo*, ed. Ashley Dukes (New York: Boni and Liveright, 1917).

[20] Percival Pollard, *Masks and Minstrels of New Germany* (Boston: W. Luce, 1911), 277.

[21] Archibald Henderson, "Arthur Schnitzler," in *European Dramatists* (Cincinnati: Stewart and Kidd, 1918), 399–429.

[22] Bayard Q. Morgan, "Arthur Schnitzler," *Drama*, no. 7 (August 1912): 13.

Apes and Peacocks (1915),[23] and Ludwig Lewisohn, *The Modern Drama* (1915).[24] Of particular significance was an interview with George Viereck, entitled "The World of Arthur Schnitzler," in *Glimpses of the Great* (1930).[25] Also noteworthy with regard to the growth of Schnitzler's reputation was his inclusion for the first time in the *Encyclopaedia Britannica* in 1926.

The year 1926 also served as a pivotal point in the reception, for it was then that the emphasis shifted from the dramas to the prose works, primarily because Simon & Schuster, which in 1925 had become Schnitzler's chief U.S. publisher, brought out only prose, except for one republication of *Professor Bernhardi*. All of the later prose works were published in translation within a short time after the German version. The growth of interest in Schnitzler is also evidenced by the increase in the number and geographical diversity of the reviews. The *Affairs of Anatol* in 1911 had received eleven reviews, almost all in New York publications, while *Therese* in 1928 was accorded seventy-seven reviews in newspapers and journals all over the country.

The earliest prose translations, six short stories, appeared in *Viennese Idylls* in 1913.[26] This and all of the subsequent translations were well received, if not for the stories themselves, then at least for Schnitzler's craftsmanship, which reviewers almost universally praised. The outstanding event in terms of the reception of the prose works was the publication in 1926 of *Fräulein Else*, the first work issued by Simon & Schuster. The book had to be reprinted twice in rapid succession and by 1931 had reached its tenth printing. *Beatrice, None but the Brave, Daybreak, Therese, Rhapsody*, and *Flight into Darkness* were all accorded favorable reception, but none approached the success of *Fräulein Else*.

The prose tale, *Casanova's Homecoming*, one of Schnitzler's favorite works, first printed in English privately in 1921 for subscribers and then for general sale in 1922, created the same censorship controversy as *Hands Around*. The vigilant John Sumner again brought suit, and the

---

[23] (New York: Scribner's, 1915; also 1926), 210–17.

[24] (New York: B. W. Huebsch, 1915), 154–63.

[25] (New York: Macaulay Co., 1930), 395–409.

[26] Trans. Frederick Eisemann (Boston: J. W. Luce, 1913).

book was banned until Simon & Schuster successfully defended it in court in 1930. Authors such as H. L. Mencken and Theodore Dreiser, who testified on Schnitzler's behalf, and the newspaper reports, which were all favorable toward publishing the book, stressed Schnitzler's reputation as a writer, leaving little question that by 1930 he was regarded as a classic author of undisputed stature. By that time his standing in America was more positive than in Austria and Germany, where his fame had declined in the later years because of the changing tastes and fashions and the rise in anti-Semitism that accompanied the growth of national socialism. The contemporary critic Hans Weigel described the situation in Vienna in the late 1920s as follows: "Arthur Schnitzler lebte, arbeitete, war halb berühmt und halb vergessen" (Arthur Schnitzler lived, worked, was half famous and half forgotten).[27] Weigel later regretted that he, along with other critics of the time, failed to recognize Schnitzler's greatness adequately.

In summing up Schnitzler's reputation in the U.S. in 1931, we can agree with the assessment of Beatrice Schrumpf, who, on the basis of her comprehensive examination of the translations, the secondary literature, and the reviews, described him as "one of the greatest authors living today, well-known and well-liked in the United States if one is to judge by the number of plays produced here and by the number of his plays and stories translated and published here."[28]

1932-1961

While the reception of Schnitzler up to 1931 took place mainly in the popular rather than in the academic sphere, the reverse has been the case since then. In the generation from 1932 to 1962 his reputation in academic circles continued to grow primarily on the basis of the diligent efforts of two American scholars: Otto P. Schinnerer at Columbia University and Sol Liptzin at New York University. Schinnerer had written the afterword to the protested edition of *Casanova's Homecoming* and had helped to clear the book of allegations of pornography. In

---

[27] Hans Weigel, *Arthur Schnitzler in Memoriam* (Graz, Vienna, Cologne: Styria, 1979), 152.

[28] Schrumpf, "Perception of Schnitzler," 1.

subsequent years he produced a series of important interpretative and bibliographical articles that helped to blaze the trail for other scholars to follow.[29] It was always expected that he would produce the definitive book on Schnitzler at that time, but he died without ever doing so.

The first book on Schnitzler in English came instead from Sol Liptzin, who equaled Schinnerer in his enthusiasm and admiration for Schnitzler, views that he still possesses. His book thoughtfully appraised Schnitzler in positive terms, and through the advantage Liptzin enjoyed of consulting with Schnitzler, it contributed above all to a detailed understanding of the genesis of some of the major works. Although written in 1932, it has been the only overview of Schnitzler by an American scholar. Liptzin also included a chapter on Schnitzler in his second book, entitled *Germany's Stepchildren*, in 1935. Thus, while Schnitzler's books were banned and burned in Germany in 1933 and prohibited in Austria after the anschluss in March 1938, his reputation was maintained and kept alive in the United States along with and in some cases by the exiled writers. An important event in this connection was the rescue of the *Nachlaß*. The Schnitzler family feared that the extensive and valuable literary estate would be confiscated and destroyed in Vienna. A young student, Eric Blackall, who was studying in Vienna in the mid-1930s, agreed to ship out the *Nachlaß* with his possessions and was thus able to preserve it for future scholars.

The cultivation of Schnitzler's literary status was enhanced in colleges and universities by the choice of his works for inclusion in textbooks. His works were recognized as ideal textbook selections, for they provided significant literature that could be read at a relatively early stage of language learning with a minimum of editorial intrusion. One example, and perhaps one of the most successful textbooks of all time, was Lawrence M. Price's edition of *Der blinde Geronimo und sein Bruder*, which was first published in 1928 and remained in print until the 1970s.[30] Another widely used text was Schinnerer's edition of *Der*

---

[29] See Allen, Annotated Bibliography, 113–15.

[30] (Boston: Heath, 1928).

grüne Kakadu, *Literatur*, and *Die letzten Masken*,[31] three of the plays which had proved to be among the most popular with audiences up to 1931 and have remained staples of the Schnitzler repertoire to the present. Allen Porterfield's *Arthur Schnitzler: Stories and Plays*, which appeared in 1930, also became a prominent text.[32] There is no information available about Schnitzler's inclusion in general texts during this period such as Horst Jarka has compiled for the postwar era,[33] but it is entirely possible that most students of German between 1932 and 1962 encountered Schnitzler at some point in the course of their language and literature study.

As for the works themselves, there were many fewer publications during this period from 1932 to 1962 than previously. All of the translations that appeared during these thirty years were published in England and were mainly reissues of the earlier editions. Simon & Schuster failed to continue publishing or republishing Schnitzler's works, an indication either of diminishing interest or sales.

With regard to stage performances, the same decline occurred. *The Gallant Cassian* was performed in New York in English in 1934 and *Professor Bernhardi* in 1936. One scene from *Anatol*, "Abschiedssouper," was performed in 1938 together with Thornton Wilder's *The Happy Journey* by the McDonald Club Players in the Guild Hall of the Little Church Around the Corner. Orson Welles attempted a production of *Anatol* in 1938 on his radio program, "The Mercury Theater of the Air," and *Anatol* was again performed in 1946 at the Equity Library Theater.[34] Reviewers praised the atmosphere of old Vienna, but the free translation which rendered "leichtsinniger Melancholiker" as "Austrian philosopher" raised the ire of the *New Yorker Staatszeitung und Herald*.[35] There were four additional performances of *Anatol* in 1952, 1956, 1958, and 1959. The 1958 performance stands out

---

[31] (New York: Appleton Century Crofts, 1928).

[32] (New York: Holt, 1930).

[33] Horst Jarka, "Austrian Literature in Editions for American Undergraduate Students," *Modern Austrian Literature* 8, nos. 3/4 (December 1975): 151–67.

[34] Walton, *Arthur Schnitzler on the New York Stage*, 26.

[35] Ibid., 38.

because it was the only one to present all seven scenes. In 1961 television station KNXT in Hollywood showed three scenes of *Anatol*. This less than successful local affair is notable only because it manifested the attempt to upgrade the theatrical medium on television. The two musical versions of *Anatol* in 1959 in New York and one by Tom Jones in 1961 in Boston are better forgotten, for Schnitzler's play served only as a "suggestion" for the main character of these musical extravaganzas.

The many exiles flocking to the United States in the late 1930s included the Viennese writer and theater director Ernst Lothar, who together with the journalist and author Raoul Auernheimer established an Österreichische Bühne in New York in 1941 to present plays in German. Both men were great admirers of Schnitzler, and Auernheimer can be considered a Schnitzler epigone, so closely did he imitate Schnitzler's form and technique. *Liebelei* was one of the plays selected for performance before the short-lived venture ended. Lothar also had an opportunity to present an understanding of Schnitzler to his students at Colorado College, where he taught drama courses for four years along with directing plays.

Lothar returned to Vienna in 1946 in American uniform, charged with restoring theater life in Austria. He then returned to the post he had left in 1938 as director of the Theater in der Josefstadt. In that capacity during the early 1950s he mounted a cycle of Schnitzler's works that he feels began a Schnitzler renaissance.[36] He also made excellent dramatic adaptations of *Leutnant Gustl* and *Fräulein Else* that further contributed to Schnitzler's revival in Austria and Germany.

The situation in the U.S. developed differently. Throughout the years from 1932 to 1961 Schnitzler's reputation was maintained more than enhanced, an achievement in itself considering the circumstances of the late 1930s, World War II, and the aftermath. From a high point in 1932, when there were thirteen articles in English as well as Liptzin's book, research dwindled to a minimum during the twenty-seven years from 1933 to 1960, which according to Allen saw a total of twenty-eight articles on Schnitzler written in English in the U.S. for an average of approximately one article a year. No books and few dissertations

---

[36] Ernst Lothar, *Das Wunder des Überlebens* (Vienna, Hamburg: Zsolnay, 1961), 379.

appeared. Six textbooks included Schnitzler selections. Not until 1961 did the real growth begin to occur.

1962-Present

The momentum given to Schnitzler's reputation in Europe by Ernst Lothar in the 1950s finally carried over to the United States in 1961, given impetus by the occasion of the hundredth anniversary of the author's birth. To commemorate this event, Schnitzler's publisher, S. Fischer, began to produce a new edition of his collected works, bringing out a two-volume set of *Die dramatischen Werke* in 1962, two volumes of *Die erzählenden Schriften* in 1965, and a volume of *Aphorismen und philosophische Betrachtungen* in 1967. The anniversary year also served Robert O. Weiss, then at the University of Kentucky, as the appropriate time to found the International Arthur Schnitzler Research Association with the announced goal of stimulating research on Schnitzler and the age in which he lived. Weiss had obtained a microfilm of the materials in the *Nachlaß*, now deposited in Cambridge University, and made this copy available to scholars. The association held annual meetings, produced the *Journal of the International Arthur Schnitzler Research Association*, which in 1967 was renamed *Modern Austrian Literature*, and in 1967 funded the publication of Allen's *An Annotated Arthur Schnitzler Bibliography* to help scholarship.

These events clearly stimulated the volume of research. From a low of no articles at all in English in 1960, there were six in 1961, eight in 1962, and fourteen in 1963. The number of essays in books, dissertations, and selections in textbooks continued to expand from this point on, justifying Jeffrey B. Berlin's entitling the introduction to his bibliography "The Meaning of the 'Schnitzler-Renaissance.'"[37] Berlin's view was corroborated by other scholars. Elisabeth Lebensaft began her article "Schnitzler aus tschechischer Sicht" with the assertion that the Schnitzler renaissance, which had taken place during the 1960s in German and Anglo-American countries, now had spread to France,

---

[37] Berlin, 1.

Italy, Japan, and Russia.[38] Elisabeth Heresch, in *Schnitzler und Russland*, questioned whether a renaissance of Schnitzler's dramas in Russia could not parallel that occurring in the prose works since 1961.[39] In her excellent study *Schnitzler in Schweden* (1978) Margot Vogel showed a parallel growth of Swedish interest in Schnitzler during the same time. In her study *Emanzipation bei Arthur Schnitzler*, Barbara Gutt also stressed the idea of a Schnitzler renaissance during the 1960s, accompanied by a revisionist process in the attitude toward his work.[40]

A revision of Schnitzler's reputation had become necessary, for although serious studies had been published in the earlier years, the predominant general view of Schnitzler continued to be based on the three works *Anatol*, *Liebelei*, and *Reigen*. The new research, which had the advantage of access to the *Nachlaß*, to the letters of Schnitzler, and to his unpublished diaries, which is one of the most important documents that he left as his legacy not only of himself but also of his age, enabled scholars to take the measure of the whole man and his thought rather than concentrating only on the early works. The author's son, Heinrich Schnitzler, who taught in the Theater Arts Department at the University of California, Los Angeles for ten years, played an important role in stimulating research by freely granting permission to publish correspondences, to read the diaries, and by giving helpful advice and suggestions. He also contributed importantly through the correspondences he edited together with Therese Nickl and through his generous support of the Austrian scholar Reinhard Urbach, who produced some of the most meaningful Schnitzler research based on familiarity with all of the available unpublished material. His book *Arthur Schnitzler* was published in English by Frederick Ungar in 1973, and his many contributions, although published in German, were used by American scholars.

Frederick J. Beharriell in his seminal article, "Arthur Schnitzler's Range of Theme," had documented in 1951 that Schnitzler's interests and concerns extended well beyond the two themes of love and death,

---

[38] Elisabeth Lebensaft, "Schnitzler aus tschechischer Sicht," *Modern Austrian Literature* 16, no. 1 (March 1983): 17.

[39] Heresch, *Schnitzler und Russland*, 142.

[40] Barbara Gutt, *Emanzipation bei Arthur Schnitzler* (Berlin: Volker Spiess, 1978), 8.

a myth established at the beginning of his career that resists eradication. Despite all the evidence the stereotype of Schnitzler as an aesthete and decadent, as the creator of Anatol types, has still not been completely eliminated among scholars and certainly not in the popular media. A television series from England in 1978, hosted by Alistair Cooke, was entitled "Vienna 1900: Games of Love and Death." The paperback book (Penguin, 1979) carried the same title, continuing the cliché of a frivolous Schnitzler limited to two themes. The television productions offered poor adaptations of four of Schnitzler's prose works and detracted from, rather than added to, Schnitzler's reputation.

Whereas the reception up to 1931 had been pronouncedly more popular than scholarly, the situation was reversed in the period after 1961. Very few new translations of Schnitzler's works in English have been published; only reprints of earlier ones have appeared. Directors continued to feature *Anatol*, *Liebelei*, and *Reigen*. *Anatol* was performed at the Hartford Stage in 1984 and at the Circle in the Square in New York in 1985. *Liebelei*, under the title "Flirtations," appeared at the Nassau Repertory Theater in 1981. Although the production received favorable reviews, it achieved only a local success.[41] This limitation holds true generally for productions outside of New York. No record exists for performances at colleges and universities. A brilliant professional performance of *Professor Bernhardi* in English in Los Angeles in 1985 received no reviews and therefore does not exist except for the fortunate 250 members of the audience privileged to see it.

Schnitzler's *La Ronde* continued to be performed but without American directors ever finding a satisfactory tone. The production of the Ragtime Theater opened on 7 September 1978 and closed on 24 September.[42] The production of the Equity Library Theater in New York in 1979 premiered on 1 February and closed on 18 February. A musical version in 1980 at the Playhouse in the Mall in Paramus, New Jersey, received moderately positive reviews, while a production at the Ohio Theater in New York, which set the action in New York in the 1920s, resulted in a travesty of the original work not appreciated by the critics. By contrast, Tom Stoppard's *Undiscovered Country* was per-

---

[41] Hammer, 68.

[42] Schneider, 85.

formed in 1979 at the National Theatre in London, in 1982 at the Arena Stage in Washington, D.C., and in 1985 at the Mark Taper Forum in Los Angeles to very good reviews.[43] The later play shows a more mature, probing Schnitzler than the earlier works and provides an indication of how the awareness of the later plays would contribute to changing the image of Schnitzler from that based exclusively on the early works.

New translations include Schnitzler's autobiography of his early years, *My Youth in Vienna* (1970); *The Mind in Words* and *Some Day Peace Will Return*, both published by Ungar in 1972; and *The Little Comedy and Other Stories* published by Ungar in 1977, an attempt to make available works that had not been translated earlier such as *Sterben* and also to bring new, current translations. Frederick Ungar, one of the main supporters of Austrian literature in the United States, wrote the introduction himself. These attractive, worthwhile volumes failed to achieve financial success, according to Ungar. Another notable volume, Schnitzler's *Plays and Stories* (1982), was edited by Egon Schwarz.[44] The book contains the standard works *Flirtations*, *La Ronde*, *Countess Mitzi*, *Casanova's Homecoming*, and *Lieutenant Gustl* in earlier translations revised for this republication. In 1978 the Ashley Duke volume of the Modern Library was reprinted without altering his misconceived introduction, thus perpetuating his false view of Schnitzler. Also in 1978 AMS Press reprinted the 1913 volume *Viennese Novelettes*, which was followed in 1989 by a dozen reprinted works: *Beatrice* (1926), *Casanova's Homecoming* (1930), *Daybreak* (1927), *Dr. Graesler* (1930), *Flight into Darkness* (1931), *Fräulein Else* (1925), *Little Novels* (1929), *None but the Brave* (1926), *Professor Bernhardi* (1928), *Rhapsody* (1927), and *Therese* (1928). *Books in Print* for 1989–90 lists twenty-one titles for Schnitzler currently available in English, six of them British publications.

Other translations have appeared in the Peter Lang series. In 1986 Paul F. Dvorak produced a volume entitled *Illusion and Reality: Plays*

---

[43] Bergel, 94.

[44] (New York: Continuum, 1982).

and Stories of Arthur Schnitzler[45] featuring some of the earliest dramatic sketches such as *The Highstrung Woman* and *New Year's Eve*, along with other early prose works. These are not significant beyond expanding the number of titles in English, and the introduction unfortunately contributes to perpetuating the myth of Schnitzler as a narrow writer. "Traditionally Schnitzler's work is associated with the thematic formulae of fascination with love and death and with the interplay of reality and illusion that express the psychological, impressionistic concerns of the day. Arthur Schnitzler's work can in fact be cast in this narrow mold."[46] In the same series C. J. Weinberger also contributed an excellent translation of *Frau Berta Garlan* (1988).

The Schnitzler renaissance beginning in 1962 has taken place primarily in academic circles with numerous publications that take into account the major correspondences and the diaries. The new generation of Austrian and German critics take Schnitzler seriously as the most important diagnostician of his time, a writer whose themes include social analysis and politics as well as philosophy and psychology. In the process every aspect and phase of Schnitzler's life and career from the earliest scientific reviews and poetry to the works published posthumously have been examined, creating in the aggregate a more accurate portrayal.

Throughout the period from 1962 to the present, Schnitzler has become a staple of the canon of Austrian literature, and reaches students at all levels from lower-division textbooks to graduate seminars. In the 1960s and 1970s Schnitzler selections could be found in fourteen textbooks, according to Jarka. He has been the subject of over twenty dissertations in the last twenty years, a number of which have then been published as books. In addition, Schnitzler figures prominently in the numerous courses devoted to the Austrian turn of the century that became popular during the 1980s.[47] Both scholars and the general

---

[45] (New York: Peter Lang, 1986).

[46] Ibid., xiii.

[47] Jorun B. Johns, "Survey of Courses on Austrian Literature and Culture in the United States," *Österreich in amerikanischer Sicht* (New York: Austrian Institute, 1989), 3:13–21.

public have encountered Schnitzler prominently featured in the numerous books devoted to the fin de siècle.[48]

While American theater audiences continue to view productions presenting the image of a light-hearted, carefree Schnitzler, the standard concept of him at the turn of the century, recent scholars have penetrated the façade and broken with the imitative practices of literary historians to present a more accurate understanding of the serious and important nature of Schnitzler's work. The standard composite image today views Schnitzler as a serious moralist and as a masterful psychologist and psychoanalyst, who served as a commentator of the human spirit or of the *comédie humaine* in the broader sense, a writer who tried to describe his society, particularly the upper middle class in its social-historical context. As an author influenced by Nietzsche, Schnitzler questioned all values and preferred to allow his works to end in ambiguity rather than to make choices, for as the impressionist he was, he realized that every choice could be rendered false in the next moment by a change of circumstances. Schnitzler was particularly concerned about the role that social institutions play in the life of human beings and did not believe in the possibility of changing individuals but only in altering society by changing the organizations. He made little attempt to solve problems but concentrated on showing the fragility of existence and the possibilities in life. Schnitzler's work shows that no matter how human beings act, the actions are usually wrong. He also knew that it was not possible to make generalizations about life since everything depends on a single circumstance, which often occurs as a result of chance. Above all, Schnitzler devoted himself in his writings to striving scrupulously for what he considered to be the truth, and for that reason he usually only wrote what he had observed and experienced. The same honesty prevails in his diaries. He is, at times, viewed as a realist and even as a naturalist.

The shift from emphasis on the early works to the later works has reinforced the view of Schnitzler as a critic of, rather than as an exponent of, the impressionistic life-style. Schnitzler viewed life in Machian terms of constant flux and investigated it in terms of relative

---

[48] See "Bibliography," in *Major Figures of Turn-of-the-Century Austrian Literature*, ed. Donald G. Daviau (Riverside: Ariadne Press, 1990), lxii–lxv.

values. He believed strongly in the role of chance in life, undermining determinism. He also believed in free will. Although he was skeptical toward all organized religions, he was no atheist. In a similar way, he mistrusted politicians and did not belong to any political party. But he did not ignore politics. Rather, he fought against corruption, defended ethical values, and confronted political ideas in his works and in his philosophical writings. For example, in the thoughtful essay *Some Day Peace Will Return*, the pacifist Schnitzler argues strongly against war, while at the same time resignedly accepting that human beings by their nature would always be prone to engage in it.

It seems to be in the nature of reception of foreign authors that they never become truly assimilated but remain other or "foreign" in their new environment. Although Schnitzler is regarded as a world-class author because his writings are built on universal values that remain as valid today as in their own time, the history of his reception provides evidence that he is regarded more for being a representative of a specific age and country rather than out of any feeling of spiritual kinship with his universal themes. In colleges and universities he is taught in the context of German programs as a representative of his literary era. Students study Schnitzler to learn about Austria at the turn of the century, and while parallels and contrasts with the U.S. may be drawn, the relevance of Schnitzler's thought to America hardly seems to play a role. Often the courses are taught in German, which reinforces the difference. Even the courses in English translation emphasize Schnitzler as a historical representative of the Austrian literature and culture of a specific period. The same situation prevails among the broader public either reading the works in translation or seeing them as stage or film productions. Like other foreign authors Schnitzler remains a representative of a different time, society, and world. Attempts to perform Schnitzler in an American setting have met with little success. General articles about Schnitzler by popular commentators almost invariably mention him as a representative of his own society. Works like *Freiwild*, which involves the institution of dueling, faded quickly from the repertoire because it bears no relevance to American life.

At the beginning of the 1990s the reception of Schnitzler seems poised for further growth, even if at a slower pace than in the previous thirty years. The diaries will continue to appear at the rate of one or two volumes a year, Jeffrey Berlin will publish an update of his Schnitzler bibliography, which at present extends only to 1977, and *Modern Austrian Literature* will publish a special Schnitzler issue in December 1991 on the sixtieth anniversary of Schnitzler's death. As mentioned, the works themselves have been given new life, with twenty-one titles currently in print in English translation, and the volume of the previously untranslated late dramas is scheduled to appear in 1991. Schnitzler is an acknowledged author in the German and Austrian literary canon as well as world literature. From all standpoints his reception in the U.S., which must be ranked among the more extensive and more lasting among Austrian writers, seems destined to continue.

From Austria to America via London: Tom Stoppard's Adaptations of Nestroy and Schnitzler

GUY STERN

FEW CONTEMPORARY ENGLISH OR American playwrights are currently — and understandably — attracting as much scholarly attention as Tom Stoppard. His unusual provenance — he was born in Czechoslovakia, raised in Singapore, India, and Great Britain[1] — the all-pervasive dazzle and the frequent profundity of his dramas have made him, even at midcareer, into an international curiosity. As one of his more recent English investigators puts it, "The shelves are already beginning to groan with exegeses of the work.... Because Stoppard is cerebral, scholarly, allusive and elusive, he tends to attract the professional heavies; and the Americans and the Germans have moved in with a vengeance...."[2]

If the extent and, to my mind, the high quality of Stoppard scholarship comes therefore not unexpected, one aspect of it nonetheless surprises, at least initially. Whereas the translations and/or adaptations of playwrights are usually relegated to the appendices of monographs or the asides of articles, Stoppard's are often treated on a par with his

---

[1] For a succinct biography of Stoppard till 1979 see Felicia Hardison Londre, *Tom Stoppard* (New York: Frederick Ungar, 1981), Chap. 4; for an update till 1984 see Chronology in Harold Bloom, ed. *Tom Stoppard: Modern Critical Views* (New York, New Haven, Philadelphia: Chelsea House, 1986), 175–79.

[2] Michael Billington, *Stoppard the Playwright* (London and New York: Methuen, 1987), 10.

original plays. Given the conscious intertextuality of virtually all of Stoppard's texts, J. G. Schippers argues, "It would seem clear that Stoppard's interlingual rewritings of Schnitzler and Nestroy, rather than being regarded as peripheral to his 'own,' his 'original,' his 'real' work (as such writings rightly are with many if not most writers), should in effect be accorded a place somewhere near the heart of his oeuvre...."[3] And so it has. In addition, through the vehicle of his adaptations, specifically of three Austrian dramas, still performed in the United Kingdom, Canada and the U.S., he has revived interest in them in America, very much so in the spirit of the inquiry pursued by this conference. It will be argued in this paper that his adaptations, while often diverging from the originals, have not violated the sources but rather have reinvigorated them.

Through close comparisons between Stoppard's German-language sources and his adaptations, past scholarship has been able to advance some valid general conclusions; these are buttressed, in many instances, by comparisons between the first rough translations by intermediaries — Stoppard's knowledge of German is negligible — and his highly accomplished final versions. There appears to be wide consensus on the following brief remarks concerning Schnitzler's *Das weite Land* and *Liebelei* and Nestroy's *Einen Jux will er sich machen*.[4] Schnitzler's *Das weite Land*, it will be recalled, concerns the mores of a decaying society. An upper-middle-class industrialist, himself engaged in several adulterous affairs, kills his wife's lover in a duel, more out of a sense of humbled pride than moral outrage. In *Liebelei* the working-class mistress of a Viennese reserve officer learns only after the lethal outcome of a duel that a married aristocratic woman was the *grande passion* of her lover and she but a diversion. The end of the play implies her impending suicide. Nestroy's *Jux* recounts the adventures of two truant shopkeeper's assistants in Vienna, which interlink with their

---

[3] J. G. Schippers, "Schnitzler's Stoppard or Humpty Dumpty im Wiener Wald," in *Linguistics and the Study of Literature*, ed. Theo D'Haen, DQR Studies in Literature, no. 1 (Amsterdam: Rodopi, 1986), 249–50.

[4] Johann (Nepomuk) Nestroy, *Einen Jux will er sich machen*, in *Komödien*, ed. Franz H. Mautner (Frankfurt am Main: Insel, 1970), 2:435–519; Arthur Schnitzler, *Die dramatischen Werke*, 2 vols. (Frankfurt am Main: Fischer, 1972); *Liebelei*, in *Die dramatischen Werke* 1:215–64; *Das weite Land*, in *Die dramatischen Werke* 2:217–320.

employer's quest to prepare for his wedding and his attempt to thwart his ward's elopement with her apparently unsuitable lover. Here then are Stoppard's major changes previously recognized in secondary literature:

1. Stoppard has depoliticized the immediate situations in Schnitzler[5] and foregoes "the precisely-rooted social comedy of the original [Nestroy]."[6]

2. By his additions and deletions Stoppard has infused Nestroy's originals with "an organized demonstration of the 'mystery' of life and the inadequacy (if not iniquity) of all 'clockwork' systems which seek to impose" an ending. Stoppard thus shows that the protagonists have through their adventures in Vienna "a foundation for a better future — a liberating encounter with the 'mystery' of life."[7]

3. What Tim Brassell observed about Stoppard's Nestroy adaptation also applies to his reworking of Schnitzler. "It shows how a more or less ready-made structure of plot and characters enables him [Stoppard] to turn his almost undistracted attention to injecting his raw materials with the greatest possible ... invention."[8] Or, as Stoppard himself puts it, "I welcome adaptations for the good reason that I don't have continual ideas for new plays...."[9] "For someone like me who enjoys writing dialogue but has a terrible time writing plays, adaptation is joy time."[10]

---

[5] Schippers, 266.

[6] Billington, *Stoppard*, 149.

[7] Richard Corballis, *Stoppard: The Mystery and the Clockwork* (Oxford: Amber Lane Press, 1984), 180, 183.

[8] Tim Brassell, *Tom Stoppard: An Assessment* (London and Basingstoke: MacMillan Press, 1985), 256. Gore-Langton refers to Stoppard's adaptations as "passive eclecticism [which] is the theatre's benefit." Robert Gore-Langton, "See-Sickness at the National," *Plays and Players* 373 (Oct. 1984): 17; (Interview with Stoppard).

[9] Quoted in Malcolm Page, *File on Stoppard* (London and New York: Methuen, 1986), 83.

[10] Commenting elsewhere on his adaptations Stoppard adds, "My inventions for *Undiscovered Country* were guilty secrets, almost admissions of failure, bits of non-Schnitzler trying not to look un-Schnitzler put in because I couldn't make things bounce properly. But with *On the Razzle* I abandoned quite early on the onus of conveying Nestroy intact into English." See his "Across Nestroy with Map and Compass: Programme Note to National

4. Stoppard's adaptations transform the original texts through literary allusions, puns, verbal pyrotechnics, anachronisms and "foreign language games."[11]

5. Perhaps most important, Stoppard partially deconstructs his sources. "Stoppard's plays have dramatized such an interpenetration of text and text, re-contextualizing the works of others (Shakespeare, Ford, Strindberg, Beckett, T. S. Eliot, Wilde, Albee, Genet ...) into some of the most original drama on the modern stage.... Stoppard's adaptations of other playwrights [i.e. Schnitzler and Nestroy] may also be considered a form of intertextuality."[12]

Stoppard himself has commented on his inspired deconstructions in his Introduction to *"Dalliance" and "Undiscovered Country."* In adapting *Liebelei*, he admitted to having added something of a feminist manifesto. "Christine's [final] denunciation of Theodore turns Schnitzler's view of Christine on its head." And "the cuts [in *Das weite Land*]," Stoppard explains, "were made during rehearsals, partly for pace and partly in compliance with the director, Peter Wood...."[13] As to Nestroy, he admits "the prime concern [is] to make the tale as comic an entertainment as possible."[14]

While in general agreement with both Stoppard and Stoppard scholars, I miss in their explanations one of the pervasive purposes underlying the adaptor's changes and at least one of the means he employed in bringing those purposes about. These constitute one of the quintessential elements held in common by the English playwright and his Austrian predecessors. I refer, of course, to their profuse theatricalism — often achieved by theatricality. By that I mean the constant and deceptive role playing of the characters and the perceptible and

---

Theatre Production," reprinted in Page, 81. Compare also Gore-Langton interview, 17.

[11] Schippers, 262.

[12] Kenneth Meyer, "'It Is Written': Tom Stoppard and the Drama of the Intertext," *Comparative Drama* 22, no. 2 (1989): 105ff., 119.

[13] Tom Stoppard, *"Dalliance" and "Undiscovered Country,"* adapted from Arthur Schnitzler with an introduction by Stoppard (London and Boston: Faber & Faber, 1986), x, ix.

[14] Tom Stoppard, *On the Razzle*, adapted from *Einen Jux will er sich machen* by Nestroy with an introduction by Tom Stoppard. (London: Faber & Faber, 1982), 7.

imperceptible shifting between reality and illusion; these often become visible through the masking, unmasking, and recostuming of characters and through the bold juxtaposing of two levels of reality, of the action on stage and the action of a play within a play.[15] Since these theater techniques are, as is well known, endemic to many dramas of Nestroy and Schnitzler, it is not too much of a simplification to say that a good many changes that Stoppard imposes on the originals are infusions of more Nestroy on Nestroy and more Schnitzler on Schnitzler.

Perhaps that is what Stoppard meant to imply when hoping that *Undiscovered Country* would be "largely faithful to Schnitzler's play in word and, I trust, more so in spirit ..." even though he had succumbed to the temptation of adding "a flick here and there."[16] Stoppard's "flicking" of Schnitzler's play towards two of Schnitzler's main themes, Eros and Thanatos, begins with the title. While Stoppard's predecessors have rendered *Das weite Land*, literally as *Distant Country* or *Vast Domain*, — probably borrowed from Theodor Fontane's *Effi Briest*[17] — Stoppard resolutely lifts his appellation from a drama, in fact from the most famous soliloquy in world literature, Hamlet's "To be or not to be." He also thereby shifts emphasis — from Schnitzler's "vast country" of the soul to Hamlet's unknowable country of the dead, "from whose bourn no traveller returns."[18] Stoppard announces with that title change that he will maximize Schnitzler's game of sex, love, and death and minimize psychological explorations. Or as J. P. Stern puts it, "What he [Stoppard] portrays here, as he did in *Rosencrantz and Guildenstern Are Dead*, is his own understanding that the most interesting issue is not the enigmatic unpredictability of people's souls but the profound attraction of death."[19] Having thus, via his title, first

---

[15] Albert Bermel, *Farce: A History from Aristophanes to Woody Allen* (New York: Simon and Schuster, 1982). Bermel's definition (see p. 62 and p. 335) will prove useful. "Somewhere between realism and fantasy is theatricalism, which reminds the spectators that they're present at a performance. This is self-conscious art.... There may be a play within a play...." "Theatricalism is a kind of assertiveness, saying 'This is theater and nothing else.'"

[16] Stoppard, *"Dalliance" and "Undiscovered Country,"* ix–x.

[17] Corballis, 175.

[18] *Hamlet*, act 3, sc. 1.

[19] J. P. Stern, "Anyone for Tennis, Anyone for Death?" *Encounter* 53 (Oct. 1979): 27.

intoned a note of death, he begins the play with a note of sexual innuendo, speculations about a philandering husband's whereabouts are not voiced by his wife, as in Schnitzler, but by their chambermaid.[20]

Stoppard uses a variety of devices to tilt Schnitzler's play towards the theatrical. When Friedrich, the drama's posturing protagonist, deceitfully addresses his friends from the balcony of his house and displays false friendship to a man he will soon capriciously kill in a duel, Stoppard turns Schnitzler's neutral form of address "meine Herrschaften" ("ladies and gentlemen") into "friends, Romans, and countrymen."[21] The allusion to Mark Anthony's manipulative speech heightens the moment's atmosphere of hypocrisy — and of playacting. Stoppard achieves a similar effect when he has a society woman implausibly sharpen a famous Marxian saying into a travestying epigram "Friedrich takes from each according to his needs...."[22]

But Stoppard expands Schnitzler's text most consistently towards theatricalism where the original already introduces actors or playwrights as dramatis personae or alludes to the theater. In Schnitzler's drama Anna Meinhold-Aigner (called Mrs. von Aigner in Stoppard's adaptation), the mother of the slain duelist, is a renowned tragedienne. Schnitzler, vague as to the causes for her tragic outlook on life, merely implies that her roles may have colored her views. Stoppard goes one step beyond: the stage world consistently destroys her outlook on the real world. Even before her entrance, Dr. Mauer, the most "reliable" character, says of her, "Perhaps after all those years in the theatre, real life took her by surprise."[23] Elsewhere, after one of her misanthropic remarks, Genia, one of the main characters, speculates that von Aigner's roles may have induced her bitterness "so that life and melodrama sometimes seem a little difficult to separate."[24] Stoppard has followed here his own proclivity for interplaying appearance and reality — as illustrated by his own play *The Real Thing*, where the play within the

---

[20] Stoppard, *"Dalliance" and "Undiscovered Country,"* 61.

[21] Stoppard, *"Dalliance" and "Undiscovered Country,"* 124.

[22] Stoppard, *"Dalliance" and "Undiscovered Country,"* 63.

[23] Stoppard, *"Dalliance" and "Undiscovered Country,"* 68.

[24] Stoppard, *"Dalliance" and "Undiscovered Country,"* 91.

play opens the drama and dumbfounds the audience, or as in the dual stage-reality of *The Real Inspector Hound*.[25] But in so doing he has also come close to Schnitzler's technique of playing off *Schein* against *Sein* — appearances versus reality — which course through the Austrian playwright's *Der grüne Kakadu* (*The Green Cockatoo*), where the anticipatory playacting of the French Revolution becomes stark reality — if for all the wrong reasons. Or, to draw on a parallel in his prose fiction: in Schnitzler's short story "Das Tagebuch der Redegonda" ("Redegonda's Diary")[26] two imaginary worlds — that of the author and that of his protagonist — dovetail so closely with the "factual" world that fiction and reality become inseparable. Also by changing the words "tragedy" to "melodrama" for *Das weite Land* Stoppard has synchronized the unidentified roles of Frau von Aigner more closely with Schnitzler's designation of this play as a "tragicomedy."

Given Stoppard's ambivalence about "the mythical figure of the dedicated writer"[27] and his obvious delight, in *Travesties* and *Artist Descending a Staircase,* in the Dadaists' iconoclastic destruction of poetic egos, it is not surprising that he continues to caricature serious or pompous artists. In *Undiscovered Country* a famous pianist, his mourners erroneously hypothesize at his funeral, may have committed suicide as "an artistic tantrum,"[28] and the rather commonplace wife of Rhon, a self-inflated writer of tragedies, is sarcastically apostrophized as "his muse."[29] And Rhon's indignation at a philistine becomes even more pretentious when it is wasted on someone who, as Stoppard would have it, remembers about a play only "lots of Frenchmen in wigs

---

[25] Tom Stoppard, *Travesties* (New York: Grove Press, 1975); Tom Stoppard, *The Real Inspector Hound* (London: Faber and Faber, 1983).

[26] Arthur Schnitzler, *Der grüne Kakadu*, in his *Die dramatischen Werke* 1:465–98; Arthur Schnitzler, "Das Tagebuch der Redegonda," in his *Die erzählenden Schriften* (Frankfurt am Main: Fischer, 1961), 1:985–91.

[27] Ronald Hayman, *Tom Stoppard*, 3rd ed. (London: Heinemann, 1979), 142.

[28] Stoppard, *"Dalliance" and "Undiscovered Country,"* 63.

[29] Stoppard, *"Dalliance" and "Undiscovered Country,"* 114.

and I think it rhymed. Yes ... people in wigs rhyming.... The girl had consumption."[30]

In looking back on Stoppard's "collaboration" with Schnitzler roughly seventy years after the appearance of the original, one can see, as one of the critics put it, "why Stoppard enjoyed working this particular play.... [Among other things] it keeps a very Stoppardian balance between the artificial and the real."[31] By adding to this pervasive aspect of *Das weite Land*, emphasizing the theatricalism already in the original, he grafted Schnitzlerisms upon Schnitzler.

Occasionally Stoppard, with the same intention, adds allusions to the theater and incongruous, alienating remarks to Schnitzler's text. For example, Friedrich, the protagonist of the drama, admonishes his tennis partner "to take up some local [Austrian] pastime — light opera or psychoanalysis."[32] Such allusions and incongruities, even outright anachronisms, abound in Stoppard's *Dalliance*, his adaptation of Schnitzler's *Liebelei*. Modern advertising slogans such as "Accept no substitutes"[33] intertwine with Viennese bon mots. Unlike Schnitzler's original male characters, who think of dalliances as "adventures," Stoppard's profligates liken them to grand operas, operas, and operettas.[34] Or he grafts parodies of dramas ancient and modern on the original. Shakespeare (i.e., *Hamlet*, act 1, sc. 2) is invoked, when one of the women speaks of her job as a seamstress. "'Seams, madam?'" her lover quips, "'I know not seams.'"[35] Similarly, the same character, Theodore, does a takeoff on a film title when he anachronistically, but presciently, asks, after his doomed friend ceases playing the piano, "Has someone shot the piano player?"[36]

---

[30] Stoppard, *"Dalliance" and "Undiscovered Country,"* 110.

[31] Billington, 136.

[32] Arthur Schnitzler, *Das weite Land*, in *Die dramatischen Werke*, 2:83.

[33] Stoppard, *"Dalliance" and "Undiscovered Country,"* 15.

[34] Stoppard, *"Dalliance" and "Undiscovered Country,"* 7, 9.

[35] Stoppard, *"Dalliance" and "Undiscovered Country,"* 18.

[36] Stoppard, *"Dalliance" and "Undiscovered Country,"* 21.

But Stoppard's most dynamic, daring, and innovative theatricalisms stand out in the opening and closing stage directions of act 1 and throughout the final act, which is radically and purposefully cast adrift from its original setting. Stoppard's adaptation opens with Fritz, who at the play's denouement is the loser in a deadly duel, practicing target shooting with a pistol — and repeatedly missing. At the end of act 1 Fritz, having by now been challenged by the husband of his mistress "picks up one of the targets.... He moves the target behind the candles for a better look. The target catches fire. He stands holding the candelabra in one hand, and the blazing target in the other, the only light now in the room."[37] Stoppard's embroidery makes for a most theatrical curtain.

He reserves his most incisive change, however, for act 3. In Schnitzler's original it is set, as the previous act, in the modest apartment of the heroine and her father. Taking his cue from the fact that the father is a member of the pit orchestra of the Josefstadt theater and the heroine a copyist of scores, also (as Stoppard has it) for the same orchestra, Stoppard shifts the setting to the forestage and backstage of that theater. In previous scenes he had painstakingly laid the groundwork for this resetting. Unlike the two pairs of lovers in Schnitzler's *Liebelei*, who sing a patriotic ditty during their impromptu dinner party, Stoppard wrote for the lovers a saccharine aria, "The False Hussar," obviously an inversion of the superannuated German hit-song "Der treue Hussar" ("The Faithful Hussar") and, in Stoppard's fiction, a song from an operetta playing that season at the Josefstadt theater. Also, he adds further plausibility to the shift by converting Mizi, the heroine's confidante, from an unemployed seamstress to the theater's wardrobe mistress, thereby giving that character some additional "brilliantly funny" moments on stage, particularly as she wrestles with the tight tunic of an overweight tenor.[38]

The purpose of these changes is obvious. Stoppard contrasts the unsubstantial and artificial world of theater, almost indistinguishable from the effete world inhabited by his male characters, with the

---

[37] Stoppard, *"Dalliance" and "Undiscovered Country,"* 29.

[38] Irving Wardle, "Comedy of Queasy Compromise: *Dalliance*," *The Times* (London), 28 May 1986, 18.

substantive life and sincerity of his heroine. Sensing the incongruous congruity between stage action and the pretentious high society she has come to know through her lover and his friend, she rebels and finds herself as a person. There is no thought of suicide in Stoppard's adaptation.

As so often in his dramatic oeuvre, Stoppard provides deeper meaning through his mastery of theatricalism. As one of his explicators puts it, "through stage directions and the dramatic subtext, Stoppard continually provides information that is significant, if extra-literary."[39] By observing how he shifts from Schnitzler's setting to his own for the contrastive purpose explained above, we learn a great deal about his conscious striving for effect. His stage directions opening act 3 read in part:

> The transition between Act Two and Act Three should be made without an intermission. The effect should be that the scenery of Act Two should now be seen to be cleared from the stage of the Josefstadt by the opera stagehands. The stagehands get the stage into a 'rehearsal-state.'... The transition is being supervised by a STAGE MANAGER.[40]

In short, the worlds of illusion and reality blend through the interlocking of the settings.

As one of his interpreters implies, Stoppard's plays must not only be read but — even primarily — witnessed.[41] Perhaps that theory, to which my article also subscribes, accounts for the fact that not scholars, but at least two theater critics, have come to appreciate Stoppard's theatricalism and its purpose in his adaptation of Schnitzler's *Liebelei*.[42]

---

[39] Stephen Hu, *Tom Stoppard's Stagecraft* (New York: Peter Lang, 1989), 7.

[40] Stoppard, *"Dalliance" and "Undiscovered Country."* See stage directions in the transition into act 3.

[41] Hu, 6–8.

[42] One further reviewer of the London production of the play recognized the additional theatricality of Stoppard's version but deplored it as a falsification of Schnitzler. "The pathos of theatricality and the tragic ambiguity of public performance are vital parts of Stoppard's own art, but they have nothing to do with *Liebelei*.... Mr. Stoppard, ... you must not call it Schnitzler." John Peter, review of "Dalliance," *Sunday Times* (London), 1 June 1986, 49.

"Stoppard," noted a reviewer after the American premiere in New Haven, "has placed us in a half-world where the emotions created by a playwright mingle ambiguously with what we're made to think of as the real thing."[43] And still more pointedly, the theater critic of *Punch*, after the world premiere in London, traced Stoppard's transformations to their origins. "But by moving the final scene ... to the backstage area ... during rehearsals for a mindless operetta, Stoppard manages to invoke the shades of Pirandello, Pinero, *as well as those of Schnitzler himself*."[44]

When Stoppard adapted Nestroy's prototypal Austrian *Volksstück*, *Einen Jux will er sich machen*, he took even greater liberties. He himself has likened his method to "cross-country hiking with map and compass, where one takes a bearing on the next landmark and picks one's own way towards it."[45] Hence the plot stays more or less intact, the dialogue only intermittently, and the flavoring of regional dialect not at all. Instead, Stoppard suffuses the drama with his own verbal and pantomimic pyrotechnics, ranging from bilingual puns to malapropisms and from running gags to sight gags reminiscent of the Marx brothers. Confronted by the panegyrics of the grocer's assistant Weinberl to "greengrocerdom" and the sale of "zwei Groschen Gabri," "ein' g'faulten Lemonie" and "ein' Zuckerkandl" (act 1, sc. 2), Stoppard has recourse to converting Austrian grandiloquence into misquoted *King Lear*.[46] Once more, incongruous theatricity triumphs, and an Austrian *Posse*, shorn of its localisms and embellished by Shakespeare, turns into universal farce.

Again Stoppard never lets us forget that we are at a play. Very early in the drama, before most of the theatrics commence, one of the characters in Stoppard's version remarks, "One false move and we could

---

[43] Alan Wallach, "Stoppard's *Dalliance* With a Love Story," *Newsday*, 31 March 1987, sec. 2, p. 7.

[44] Sheridan Morley, review of *Dalliance*, by Tom Stoppard, *Punch*, 4 June 1986; repr. in *London Theatre Record* 6, no. 11 (1986): 570.

[45] Stoppard, Introduction to *On the Razzle*, 7.

[46] Stoppard, *On the Razzle*, 43.

178   The Fortunes of German Writers in America

have a farce on our hands."[47] And at the end of the play, the two truants, outdoing Nestroy's game of disguises and mistaken identity, do a riotous replay of their Viennese razzle by assuming various roles in a lightninglike recap session.[48] With one deft touch Stoppard reshapes Nestroy's diabolus-ex-machina ending — i.e., the apprehension of two robbers by the junketing shop-assistants — into a playlet within the play.

Stoppard further enhances the theatrical nature of the play by his stage design. He endows the grocery store with a trap door and chute through which characters enter and exit bedroom-farce-fashion. "Stoppard enjoys to the full [in *On the Razzle*] the flapping open and shut of cupboard trapdoors and bedroom windows … [sometimes] developed to splendid absurdity."[49] Or he brings a sextet on stage — pun intended by Stoppard — to play a serenade.[50] In the London and Toronto production (which I saw) the scenery emerges from behind giant music sheets substituting for Nestroy's vocal interludes. Also, Stoppard inserts allusions to drama and theater; "Scaramouche" invokes a stock character of the commedia dell' arte[51] and Don Juan recalls, of course, countless dramas and Mozart's opera.[52] Also, the Viennese police is compared to comic-opera cops, and a besotted Austrian newspaper refers to "the barbarian baroque universe of Sir Walter Scotch."[53]

Once more, Stoppard has recourse to alienation through anachronisms. The aforementioned newspaper, for example, deplores the

---

[47] Stoppard, *On the Razzle*, 22.

[48] Stoppard, *On the Razzle*, 78.

[49] Jim Hunter, *Tom Stoppard's Plays* (New York: Frederick Ungar, 1981), 53.

[50] Stoppard, *On the Razzle*, 33.

[51] Stoppard, *On the Razzle*, 24.

[52] Stoppard, *On the Razzle*, 68.

[53] Stoppard, *On the Razzle*, 62.

abandonment of "decent Aryan standards"[54] and one of the characters, pretending to a knowledge of Italian, mutters "la dolce vita."[55]

It would have been surprising if the razzle-dazzle of Stoppard's theatricalism had previously gone unnoticed. A standard history of farce analyzes several Stoppard plays (minus the adaptations) as part of a chapter entitled "Theatricalism After Pirandello."[56] But while Bermel greatly applauded this characteristic of Stoppard's playwriting, another critic faulted Stoppard's theatricality. "The question is whether full parodic theatricality, in the licenced interplay of pastiche as dialogue, can possibly find room for anything so grave as a centre of gravity."[57] The very opposite, I believe, holds true in *On the Razzle*. Stoppard himself has hinted at the reason why Nestroy's play intrigued him. One of the essentials he retained from his source, he says, is "the almost mythic tale of two country mice escaping to town for a day...."[58] To adhere to this mythic quality, to show the serious purpose beneath the mirth, Stoppard distanced his adaptation from Nestroy's setting of time and place. "[*On the Razzle*] is still set in Vienna (though about fifty years later than *Einen Jux*) but not essentially so."[59] The theatricalisms, more of Stoppard's time than of Nestroy's, in which even dialogue parodies itself and hence becomes unreal, further remove it from the original. Yet that very fact leads it back to Nestroy's intent of showing the pathos of seeking one day's adventure as compensation for the dreary workaday life to follow forever after. To one of the first-night critics that serious purpose became immediately apparent. "But he [Nestroy] gives a disturbing glimpse — as does Stoppard — of the apprentices' need to experience life, if only for a few hours, so that the

---

[54] Stoppard, *On the Razzle*, 62.

[55] Stoppard, *On the Razzle*, 47.

[56] Bermel, 336, 347–49.

[57] Andrew Kennedy, "Natural, Mannered, and Parodic Dialogue," *Yearbook of English Studies* 9 (1979): 54.

[58] Stoppard, Introduction to *On the Razzle*, 7.

[59] Stoppard, Introduction to *On the Razzle*, 7.

daily routine will be richer with memories."[60] "Farces," it has been said, "imply that life is more or less the same as in other regions [than those set on stage]."[61] By his use of theatricalism, together with other shifts, embellishments, and prunings, Stoppard has preserved Nestroy's concealed social criticism for our times.

How does Stoppard achieve his effects? Several of Stoppard's means of adding to the theatricalism of all three Austrian dramas have been discussed in full by previous studies and, en passant, throughout this article. Yet there is one Stoppardian device employed in many of his plays, including his adaptations, that has attracted only sporadic attention. Hu, with specific reference to Stoppard, points out that "personal choices in dress ... may reflect as much about a character's personality as his lines."[62] That is far too modest a claim for Stoppard's whirlwind of rapid costume changes — occasionally taking place right before an audience. In his play *After Magritte* one of the characters turns transvestite, donning his wife's clothing in order to substitute for her tailor's dummy; in *Night and Day* nudity, flaunted by the heroine's understudy while she herself remains prone in bed, dramatizes her erotic phantasies. In *Travesties*, where the title's linguistic root already suggests change of dress and disguise, the narrator, Henry Carr, changes from an old man to a young dandy right on stage by doffing his coat and shawl, while other characters disguise themselves on stage by putting on toupees and sunglasses.

Stoppard found few occasions to exercise his proclivity for disguises and costume changes in *Undiscovered Country*, his first and most restrained adaptation from the German. True, there is the barest hint of such legerdemain when he has one of Schnitzler's minor characters jocularly claim that he is the Archduke Ferdinand traveling incognito.[63] But he fully indulges his penchant in the other dramas. In *Dalliance*, during the play within the play at the Josefstadt theater, Stoppard builds the comic relief that precedes the stark ending around

---

[60] Rosemary Say, review of *On the Razzle*, by Tom Stoppard, *Sunday Telegraph*, rpt. in *London Theatre Records* 1, no. 6 (1981): 493.

[61] Bermel, 311.

[62] Hu, 7.

[63] Stoppard, *"Dalliance" and "Undiscovered Country,"* 97.

the ill-fitting tunic of the tenor. Mizi, the wardrobe mistress, has outfitted him with a snugly fitting uniform. Fulminating, he changes the lines in one of his arias to "I can't sing in this bloody thing! / It's too tight — it's far far far too tight." And he "leaves the stage in a huff" and sans tunic.[64] Stoppard's theatricality through robing and disrobing his actors and actresses runs riot — and becomes riotously funny — in *On the Razzle*. An elaborate conceit allows him to bedeck various Austrian characters in — of all things — Scottish costumes. The conceit is that opera-loving Vienna has gone madly Scotch-native after the local premiere of Verdi's *Macbeth*. A delicacy called *Sachertartan* and Scotch kilts have become *le dernier cri de la mode*. The near unisex nature of Scotch habiliment also facilitates the quick-changes of one of the characters from male to female attire.

Near the climax of the comedy Stoppard adds one more farcical element. The roles of a coachman and a chambermaid, little more than walk-ons in Nestroy's *Posse*, have been fleshed out. In Stoppard's version the coachman vacillates between utmost propriety and maniacal sexuality; the maid's suddenly aroused libido matches his. As a result, her various entrances, following each other in quick succession, reveal her in progressive stages of déshabillé. In short, Stoppard, in quest of greater theatricality, employs both verbal and visual pyrotechnics.

*   *   *

A comparison of Stoppard's adaptations with their original sources leaves room for additional ruminations. What wry feelings must have seized Stoppard when, five years after writing *Travesties*, in which the Dadaist Tristan Tzara is one of the main characters, he encountered a character by the name of Rosenstock, Tzara's real name, in Schnitzler's *Das weite Land*. It was pure coincidence, of course. When Schnitzler wrote his tragicomedy in 1910, Tzara was only fourteen years old. Was Stoppard tempted to add some Dadaistic lines to the role? Or was he satisfied to retain Schnitzler's repartee, which occurs after Rosenstock has unintentionally produced a rhyme?

---

[64] Stoppard, *"Dalliance" and "Undiscovered Country,"* 48.

FIRST HIKER: Ah, you're a poet, then?
ROSENSTOCK: Only in a crisis.[65]

Did Stoppard resist the temptation to embellish because any addition would have been gilding the rosebush?

Finally there is the matter of Stoppard's exile status and its impact on his work, since the dramatist left Czechoslovakia in infancy during the Hitler period. One scholar, remarking "that exile is a recurrent Stoppardian theme," attributes his affinity for it to the fact that "England and English were foreign to him in his childhood."[66] His origin may also account for his penchant for adapting plays from Central Europe and for his most politically motivated action to date, his leadership of a protest in behalf of Vaclav Havel.

One final and at the moment unanswerable question: Will Stoppard do further adaptations? One critic believes so and suggests that the verb to *stoppard* be added to drama criticism to describe his innovative adaptations.[67] At any rate, he will not be deterred by the fact that approval of *stopparding* has by no means been unanimous. Criticisms range from the snide quipping that *On the Razzle* is only "for the scholar and the bent pinky fingers"[68] to the more searching question about the legitimacy of such an enterprise. "[Stoppard] had added his own improvements in a manner that is artistically questionable."[69] I do not hold with this view; rather, I believe that his adaptations have introduced or reintroduced three deserving Austrian dramas to an English-speaking audience, and I predict that in his next adaptation, if he undertakes one, his flights of theatricalism will cruise once more over as yet undiscovered lands, continuing in his own way Schnitzler's

---

[65] Stoppard, *"Dalliance" and "Undiscovered Country,"* 98.

[66] Londre, 138.

[67] Michael Billington, review of *On the Razzle*, by Tom Stoppard, *Guardian*, 22 Sept. 1981; repr. in *London Theatre Record* 1, no. 6 (1981): 490.

[68] Review of *On the Razzle*, by Tom Stoppard, *Variety*, 29 January 1986, 64.

[69] Billington, *Stoppard*, 168.

famous self-definition "Wir spielen immer, wer es weiß, ist klug"[70] (We play eternally; clever he who knows it). In short, this quintessential hallmark of Viennese literature is now reaching an American public via a Czech-English writer. Or, to put it aphoristically and in the spirit of a Stoppardian pun, "He has poured old Wien into American bottles."

---

[70] Schnitzler, *Paracelsus*, in *Die dramatischen Werke* (Frankfurt am Main: Fischer, 1972), 1:498.

Franz Werfel: Waiting for His Time to Come

TERRY REISCH

TEN YEARS AFTER FRANZ Werfel died at his writing desk in California, his colleague and friend Friedrich Torberg wrote a two-page personal comment on Werfel's work entitled "God's Child and God's Singer," which he concluded with the statement, "Franz Werfel, who died prematurely ten years ago, will still have to survive for a short interval, before his time comes.... When this, his time, is here again (a third time, for it has has been here twice already), he will be recognized as one of the last in the German-speaking world who may be called 'poet.'"[1] The "second" and "third" times of which Torberg speaks, Werfel's exile in America and the anticipated renewal of interest in his work,[2] especially the former, are extremely significant and rare

---

[1] "Franz Werfel, vor zehn Jahren zur Unzeit gestorben, wird noch eine kleine Zwischenzeit überleben müssen, ehe seine Zeit kommt.... Zu seiner Zeit, wenn sie erst wieder da ist (ein drittes Mal, denn zweimal war sie es schon), wird er erkannt sein als einer der letzten im deutschen Sprachbereich, die sich noch Dichter nennen dürfen." Friedrich Torberg, "Gottes Kind und Gottes Sänger," *Welt und Wort* 11 (May 1956): 148.

[2] The "first" time which Torberg is implying is Werfel's initial popularity in German-speaking literature. As a major figure of the expressionist movement (starting with "Der Weltfreund" in 1911) and of post–World War I literature, he was a highly visible and respected poet and novelist, being voted in 1926 by the magazine *Die schöne Literatur* as the most popular German-speaking writer of the present, before even Hauptmann, S. Zweig, and Rilke. The renewal of interest in Werfel in America, which will be discussed in the conclusion, is already evident in the scholarly reception, in the increased number of studies in recent years. See Lionel B. Steiman, "Franz Werfel — His Song in America," *Modern Austrian Literature* 20, Special Reception Issue, nos. 3/4 (1987): 55–69; Carl Steiner, "Showing the Way: Franz Werfel's American Legacy," *Modern Austrian Literature*

examples of an Austrian writer achieving fame in North America, for Werfel was the most successful popularly received author in America of the period, primarily with his enormous best-seller, *The Song of Bernadette* (*Das Lied von Bernadette*).[3] This popularity, and the accompanying financial security, drew contempt and envy from some exiles struggling for existence; it led Bertolt Brecht to speak of "dem heiligen frunz von hollywood, dem geschwerfel."[4] But although his popularity and success were assured by *Song*, Werfel was neither unknown nor unsold in America before he sailed into Hoboken, New Jersey, on 13 October 1940 aboard the *Nea Hellas*. Indeed, his position as an established author in the American publishing world at the time of his exile was as strong as that of Thomas Mann.[5] Unfortunately, in the context of the postexile fame of German-language authors, Werfel's position suffered severely after his death and the publication of his last novel, *Star of the Unborn* (*Stern der Ungeborenen*). However, unlike other exile authors, Werfel has recently had the distinction of having a previously untranslated work published in America, namely, with the 1989 publication of *Cella; or, The Survivors*.[6] His fame in America has been a series of successes and failures, his decline or rise in popularity alternatingly explained by his style, his philosophizing, his themes, his sentimentality, or simply the cultural gap between Werfel's Europe and the American audience. The best way to ascertain the roots of Werfel's popularity, in the true meaning of the word, is to hark back to what the popular press thought of his works and, on the basis of Werfel's

---

20, Special Reception Issue, nos. 3/4 (1987): 71–79; Lionel B. Steiman, "Franz Werfel," in *Major Figures of Modern Austrian Literature*, ed. Donald G. Daviau (Riverside, Cal.: Ariadne Press, 1988), 423–57. See Lionel B. Steiman, "Franz Werfel," *Austrian Fiction Writers, 1875–1913*, ed. James Hardin and Donald G. Daviau, vol. 81 of *Dictionary of Literary Biography* (Detroit: Gale Research, 1989), 300–12.

[3] *The Song of Bernadette*, trans. Ludwig Lewisohn (New York: Viking Press, 1942); hereafter referred to as *Song*. Other simplifications of titles are: *The Forty Days of Musa Dagh*, trans. Geoffrey Dunlop (New York: Viking Press, 1934) = *Musa Dagh*; *Star of the Unborn*, trans. Gustave O. Arlt (New York: Viking Press, 1946) = *Star*.

[4] Though this wordplay cannot be done justice in translation, it roughly means that Brecht was speaking "of Saint Frunz of Hollywood, of the Werfeling."

[5] Joseph P. Strelka, *Exilliteratur* (Bern: Peter Lang, 1983), 161.

[6] *Cella; or, The Survivors*, trans. Joachim Neugroschel (New York: Henry Holt, 1989).

greatest exile success, *Song*, and his greatest exile failure, *Star*, extract those experiences and factors that led to his "second time" and that possibly could lead to Torberg's hopeful "third time."

Werfel's first real success with the American reading public had been his novel *The Forty Days of Musa Dagh* (*Die vierzig Tage des Musa Dagh*), which had first appeared in the Geoffrey Dunlop translation in November 1934 and became a Book-of-the-Month Club selection in 1935. Thus did Werfel become not only an unofficial hero of the American people but also an American best-seller, outselling all other books published that year.[7]

Embezzled Heaven (*Der veruntreute Himmel*)[8] appeared in the United States a few days after Werfel had arrived on the East Coast. While still aboard ship, he had written a letter to his parents, who had not heard from him since the end of August, "Now America lies ahead of us, this time a very unknown continent. I hope that I am received as a friend."[9] Although he had reason to be apprehensive — his last effort to publish a translated work in America, *Hearken Unto the Voice* (*Jeremias — Höret die Stimme*),[10] had appeared to positive reviews but less than best-seller sales — *Embezzled Heaven* had been chosen as a Book-of-the-Month Club selection, which assured the novel moderate sales figures, however lukewarm the critical reception. With the publication of *Song* in 1942, however, Werfel's name became known throughout North America and he was assured both critical and financial success.

While this acclaim was unprecedented for an exile author, indeed, any author — the total sales of *Song* surpassed those of any book in the history of American publishing up to that time — the overall volume of reception of Werfel's previous works in America was not insignificant: between 1925 and his death in 1945, he had had translated and

---

[7] *Register* (New Haven, Conn.), 20 Feb. 1938; John R. Frey, "America and Franz Werfel," *German Quarterly* 21 (March 1946): 127.

[8] *Embezzled Heaven*, trans. Moray Firth (New York: Viking Press, 1940).

[9] "Nun liegt Amerika vor uns, diesmal ein sehr unbekannter Kontinent. Ich hoffe, daß ich freundschaftlich erwartet werde." Peter Stephan Jungk, *Franz Werfel: Eine Lebensgeschichte* (Frankfurt am Main: Fischer, 1987), 285.

[10] *Hearken Unto the Voice*, trans. Moray Firth (New York: Viking Press, 1938).

published no less than eleven prose works,[11] twenty short pieces in periodicals, one collection of poems, and six dramas, four of which were produced on American stages. Each was reviewed in some measure, depending upon its popularity. Of all these works, most critics reviewing *Song* in 1942 naturally remembered Werfel for *Musa Dagh* and *Embezzled Heaven*, the two latest works, and occasionally for *Hearken Unto the Voice* and the production of *Eternal Road* (*Der Weg der Verheissung*) in 1936. *Jacobowsky and the Colonel* (*Jacobowsky und der Oberst*), although it was an original drama by Werfel, was produced on Broadway in an adaptation by S. N. Behrmann that was generally considered to be more his work than Werfel's — even by Werfel, as evidenced by many telegrams to various people connected with the play: "I implore you not to reject every thing for what I am fighting with perhaps the last heartpower I have"; "I beg you on my knees to restitute the end of scene IV"; "I am depressed to death because I feel helpless."[12]

So it remained that Werfel became famous in America and Canada for his *Song of Bernadette*, and four years later, shortly after his death, notorious for his last work, *Star of the Unborn*. For everything that *Song* had done to make Werfel a "household name," *Star* did to alienate the American reading public from the author's works. Reviewers who had been rapturously enchanted with *Song* were "nauseated" by *Star* and found its religiosity "the most spectacularly disgusting since Wagner's."[13] It is this discrepancy that makes a reception study both fascinating and necessary: Werfel's overall views had not changed in the years between *Song* and *Star*, and the same weltanschauung was the basis for both works, the one that he had propounded since he was a young author.[14] What was it in *Song* that appealed so much to the reading public and popular critics that made it "a classic comparable with a Beethoven symphony, an epic poem by Milton, and a Shake-

---

[11] Frey, 125–26.

[12] Jungk, 320.

[13] Eric Bentley, "The Bishop Orders Our Tomb," *New Republic*, 4 March 1946, 322–23.

[14] Harald von Hofe, "German Literature in Exile: Franz Werfel," *German Quarterly* 19 (Nov. 1944): 267–68.

spearean drama."[15] And what in *Star* repelled reviewers so much that one spoke of the "twisted mind" that had produced it, while another wished that Werfel's friends had done the world a favor and burned every page of the manuscript?

When one views not only the reception of the works in question but also readers' previous relationship to Werfel's work, their expectations of it, also what Werfel expected of them, and above all the adjustment of the public's expectations by the popular press, one should be able to explain the spontaneous success of *Song* and the public's shock at and rejection of *Star*.

The story of the genesis of the novel *The Song of Bernadette* and of the suspenseful excitement of Werfel's escape was retold by almost every critic and reviewer who covered the book, since Werfel had made it part of his "Personal Preface." Werfel, escaping from the advancing German forces, reached the pyrenean city of Lourdes in order to cross Spain to Portugal, the route taken by countless exiles, and one which played a great part in many exile tales. During the several weeks in Lourdes Werfel heard his own death reported by British radio. He also "became acquainted" with the story of Bernadette Soubirous, who had witnessed the apparition of "a lady in white" and who was canonized in 1933. In Werfel's own words, "One day in my great distress I made a vow, I vowed that if I escaped from this desperate situation and reached the saving shores of America, I would put off all other tasks and sing, as best I could, the song of Bernadette."[16]

The second most popular quote from the preface is Werfel's statement, "I have dared to sing the song of Bernadette, although I am not a Catholic, but a Jew." But more than 75 percent of the reviewers failed to mention the next statement, one that is more germane to Werfel's whole work than *Song*, "I drew courage for this undertaking from a far older and far more unconscious vow of mine. Even in the days when I wrote my first verses I vowed that I would evermore and everywhere in all I wrote magnify the divine mystery and the holiness

---

[15] "Catholic Editor Hails Novel by Franz Werfel as Classic," *Washington Post*, 2 Oct. 1942.

[16] *Song*, 6.

of man — careless of a period which has turned away with scorn and rage and indifference from these ultimate values of our mortal lot."[17]

This preface was to have a great effect on the public visibility of the novel. During the writing, however, both Werfel and his American editor Ben Huebsch had had doubts as to the eventual success of such a book. "But he did not believe in the possible success of the work from the very beginning: Protestant America would barely be interested in a Catholic miracle, especially for a theme that in the middle of a world war would have to seem completely irrelevant. Ben Huebsch ... shared the views of the author; he was also convinced that the story of Bernadette Soubirous would have no chance on the book market and stated that he was willing to publish the novel only because all other books by Franz Werfel had been published by Viking Press."[18] This lack of expectation on the part of Werfel is important in the context of this study, for it shows that he in no way was consciously attempting to write a "best-seller," nor did he even anticipate a positive response to his work. Therefore, although he was "writing for an American audience" as Carl Steiner mentions in his essay "Showing the Way: Franz Werfel's American Legacy,"[19] he was also writing for himself, as he states quite clearly in the preface. The preface, however, was to cause Werfel as much criticism from his fellow exiles as the religiosity of the book itself. Erich von Kahler accused him of using his highly personal vow as a "sensational lead-horse."[20] Even Werfel's sympathetic biographer points out that the vow was not quite as binding as

---

[17] *Song*, 7. The failure to recognize this basic premise in Werfel's work led not only to eventual misunderstandings in the theme of *Song* but also to misinterpretations of Werfel's purpose in writing *Star*.

[18] "Aber an einen etwaigen Erfolg des Werks glaubte er von Anfang an nicht: das protestantische Amerika würde für ein katholisches Wunder wohl kaum zu interessieren sein, für eine Thematik noch dazu, die inmitten des Weltkrieges gänzlich irrelevant erscheinen mußte. Ben Huebsch ... teilte die Bedenken seines Autors, auch er war überzeugt, die Geschichte der Bernadette Soubirous werde auf dem Buchmarkt keine Chance haben, erklärte sich nur deshalb bereit, den Roman zu publizieren, da bisher auch alle anderen Bücher Werfels bei Viking Press erschienen waren." Jungk, 290.

[19] Steiner, 78.

[20] Erich von Kahler, "Franz Werfel's Poetry," *Commentary* 5 (January–June 1948): 186–88; quoted from Foltin and Spalek, "Franz Werfel," in *Deutsche Exilliteratur seit 1933*, ed. John M. Spalek and Joseph Strelka (Bern: Francke, 1976), 655.

Franz Werfel

Werfel described it in the preface, "Even during the passage from Lisbon to New York, Werfel had written the notation in his notebook 'almost determined to [write] Bernadette' — he was not so unconditionally ready to write this work as he later wanted it to appear in his personal preface to 'Bernadette.'"[21] Although the vow has no bearing on the positive reception of the novel itself — the critics lauded Werfel for a myriad of reasons — it played a major role in creating a special aura about the work and building the public's relationship to the author, as is proven by the almost unanimous quoting of those key elements of the preface.[22]

Therefore, the first element in setting the tone for the positive reception of *Song* lay in the three-fold novelty of its genesis: Werfel's escape from certain death, his sacred vow to honor a saint in prosepoetry, and the "great mystery" that "a Jew has written it."[23]

The intrigue and suspense in this genesis alone, duly related and quoted by the popular press, lent the novel an air of mystery and excitement, before the public knew the plot or had read the novel. However, the number of mentions of the "mystery" of a saint's story written by a Jew were minor compared to the mass of quotes from the story of Bernadette itself and to the reactions of the press to the theme of a simple peasant girl being visited by the Virgin Mary. Although this was and is a typical pattern for popular literary reviews, the quoting and synopsizing of the plot in the press on *Song* took on massive propor-

---

[21] "Noch während der Schiffspassage von Lissabon nach New York hatte Werfel die Bemerkung 'Zur Bernadette fast entschlossen' in sein Notizbuch eingetragen — er war zu diesem Werk keineswegs so unbedingt bereit, wie er es in seinem persönlichen Vorwort zur 'Bernadette' später glaubenmachen wollte...." Jungk, 289.

[22] Of the over 240 reviews in the popular press between April 1942 and April 1944, nearly 85 percent quoted or synopsized the preface. (Some "reviews" were simply brief notices of publication.)

[23] Daniel A. Poling, "New Books To Read: 'The Song of Bernadette' by Franz Werfel," *Christian Herald*, 6 May 1942. Most reviewers surprised by the "mystery" of a Jew writing the story of a Catholic saint overlooked not only the above-mentioned quote in the preface (p. 7; at note 17 above in text), but also the themes in Werfel's previous works, especially *Embezzled Heaven*. Indeed, it was even stated that the themes glorified in the work were probably not Werfel's intention, for "it would be odd that a Jew ... should pose as a Defender of the Faith of Catholics." James M. Gillis, C.S.P., "What's Right With the World. Deposuit Potentes: Exaltavit Humiles," *Catholic News* (N.Y.), 27 May 1944.

tions, and most quotes were preceded with lavish qualifiers such as *extraordinary*, *unique*, *classic*, *masterful*, and *sublime*.

Within weeks of *Song*'s initial release at the end of April 1942, those reviewers who offered an opinion on the novel were singularly adoring in their criticism. Those critics whose interests lay in the spiritual aspect lauded the sincerity and goodness in the telling of the saint's life, those who viewed the novel from a literary standpoint found Werfel's historical-objective approach well-suited to allow the reader to develop his own conclusions about Bernadette.

A typical positive review in the days preceding and directly following the publication of *Song* also included a list of Werfel's more popular successes in America. As previously mentioned, Werfel's name was not unfamiliar to many, a situation which was not the case for most exile authors and their previous works in America. In the most vague reviews, he is mentioned as "an internationally prominent Jewish writer,"[24] "in the last lap of a race for recognition as one of Europe's leading novelists,"[25] who had had a "long and laudable career"[26] before he fled. Some reviewers preferred to look at Werfel's work in the context of European or German-exile literature, which was still one more way to identify Werfel to readers with some basis for their expectations. One article lists him among "the illustrious company of the greatest European writers of our time: Lion Feuchtwanger, Thomas and Heinrich Mann, Maurice Maeterlinck, Anna Seghers, Jules Romains."[27]

In particular, a great majority of book reviewers who had commented on his several previous successes used them as a basis for their remarks on *Song*. Remaining in the minds of many were *The Pure in Heart*, *Musa Dagh*, and his most recent American publication, *Embezzled Heaven*. The most frequently mentioned book in the reviews of *Song* was *Musa Dagh*, which had appeared nine years earlier, and it

---

[24] A. P., "'The Song of Bernadette,'" *Evening News* (Sault Sainte Marie, Mich.), 27 July 1942.

[25] Madonna Todd, "'The Song of Bernadette' Portrays Child Visionary As Symbol of Beauty, Light," *Houston Press*, 29 May 1942.

[26] "'The Song of Bernadette,'" *Ottawa Evening Citizen*, 23 May 1942.

[27] "'The Song of Bernadette' Fulfills A Vow," *Lubbock Evening Journal*, 31 May 1944.

was mentioned usually to introduce Werfel to the reader, as in "Franz Werfel, who first won fame for 'The Forty Days of Musa Dagh,'"[28] or "The German writer who became known to a wide American public through his novel 'The Forty Days of Musa Dagh.'"[29] Reviews such as these were more helpful to the reader who did not recognize Werfel's name, or who could not place the name with the work, to form very general expectations, more specific of course if the reader had indeed read *Musa Dagh* and could thereby identify more readily with the author's style and themes.

However, the better-informed reviewers who knew more of *Musa Dagh* than simply that it had been a best-seller used it as a comparison for the reader to judge better the aspects which the reviewer was pointing out about *Song*. Examples of the vaguest of the comparisons would be generalizations about the two works, here the ones that found *Song* better than or equal to *Musa Dagh*, such as "Werfel is a master of prose and theme, we need only remind you of his 'The Forty Days of Musa Dagh,'"[30] or "Another great treat is in store for those who enjoyed 'Musa Dagh.'"[31] Others described *Musa Dagh* as "gargantuan and massive," whereas *Song* was "lyrical,"[32] or they compared "'Musa Dagh,' a prose epic" with *Song*, a "splendid testimony to the mission of Bernadette," "marked by superb taste."[33] These types of reviews go one step beyond those which simply mention previous works by giving a general analysis and a comparison with *Musa Dagh*. Again, this was most helpful for those readers who had actually read the 1934 novel, but for the uninitiated it served to form a general horizon of expectations.

---

[28] Rosamond Milner, "Books and By-Products: Werfel's Finished 'Song of Bernadette,'" *Louisville Courier Journal*, 10 May 1942.

[29] Ted Robinson, "'The Song of Bernadette' Fulfills Refugee's Vow," *Cleveland Plain Dealer*, 17 May 1942.

[30] Christine Waela, "'The Song of Bernadette,'" *Columbus Dispatch*, 10 May 1942.

[31] M[elvin] J. V[incent], "Social Fiction: 'The Song of Bernadette,'" *Sociology and Social Research* (University of Southern California) 27 (18 Sept. 1942): 81.

[32] Robert Whitehand, "Franz Werfel Tells Story Of Miracles of Lady of Lourdes," *Daily Oklahoman*, 14 June 1942.

[33] Francis X. Connolly, Ph.D., "Book Tour," *Catholic Mirror*, July 1942, 30–31.

The reviews most obviously helpful in lending an initiated reader an understanding of the qualities of *Song* were those which compared specific aspects of it with those in *Musa Dagh*. The most frequent positive commonality between the two works was found in the characterizations of the two novels.[34] (See below for a more complete discussion of the characterizations.) Also mentioned was the "definite religious slant" that both works as well as others in the Werfelian canon exhibited.[35]

The other previous work by Werfel that was used as a basis for appreciation of *Song* was the last work published in America, *Embezzled Heaven*, which was at times mentioned in the same sentence as *Musa Dagh*, these two works being his best known and received. The same three types of comparisons that were used with *Musa Dagh* were also, but to a lesser extent, employed with *Embezzled Heaven*. The simple mention of the work was used less, reviewers preferring to comment on some aspect of it, due most likely to the more common religious themes in the two works. For example, Werfel's "sympathetic touch" in portraying the Catholic faith in *Song* is reminiscent of *Embezzled Heaven*;[36] one reviewer finds *Song* almost a continuation of the 1940 work,[37] and Werfel's interest in Catholic hagiology, which was "revealed in 'Embezzled Heaven,'" is seen to be revived in *Song*.[38]

The rumor that persisted after the publication of *Embezzled Heaven*, that Werfel had converted to the Catholic faith because he was "so conversant with Catholicism" in this work, was reiterated in some reviews of *Song* in nonsecular publications,[39] and although the rumor

---

[34] Pearl Mahaffey, "World Events and the Common Man," *Christian Evangelist* (St. Louis, Mo.), 30 July 1942.

[35] Jessie Kennedy Snell, "I've been reading," *Free Press* (Colby, Kan.), 8 July 1942.

[36] Mahaffey, "World Events and the Common Man."

[37] Maxine Hirsh Bader, "In Reviewing Werfel Novel, Rabbi Looks for New Unity," *American Jewish Outlook* (Pittsburgh, Pa.), 11 Dec. 1942.

[38] Reece Stuart, Jr., "Werfel Fulfills His Vow Beautifully Singing the Song of the Little Saint of Lourdes," *Des Moines Register*, 17 May 1942.

[39] John S. Kennedy, "A Great Spiritual Experience," *Catholic Transcript* (Hartford, Conn.), 14 May 1942; "'The Song of Bernadette' by Franz Werfel," *Catholic Tribune* (St. Joseph, Mo.), 11 July 1942.

was mentioned in passing, it was obviously an interesting piece of trivia for the potential reader of *Song*.

Other works of Werfel that were less known but nonetheless had been published in America were also used by some reviewers as a comparison for their opinions on *Song*. *Hearken Unto the Voice* was mentioned in passing as a previous Werfel work,[40] as was *Eternal Road*,[41] the very early *Barbara*,[42] (the translated title of which was *The Pure in Heart*) and his poetry, the majority of which had not yet been translated into English. One unique comparison is made between *Song* and the 1929 publication *Class Reunion* (*Der Abituriententag*). The reviewer finds "the duel between Bernadette and Sister Marie Therese (or better perhaps, between the nun and her own pride)" reminiscent of the struggle between Adler and Sebastian.[43]

Thus, in the light of Werfel's status as an "established author" and his previous American publications, predominantly *Musa Dagh* and *Embezzled Heaven*, *Song* was seen by most critics to be a work of art worthy of the author of those works. But even given all the positive allusions to his previous works, *Song*, like any other work to be criticized, also had to stand on its own in the eyes of the critics.

Once a basis for the expectations of the reader had been set, through citing the preface, synopsizing the story and/or history of Bernadette, and comparing the novel to previous works, the typical reviewer set to the task of evaluating the themes and style of *Song*.

Above all else, the popular press agreed in its for Werfel's structural integrity and stylistic elegance. The two elements that led to this applause were his objective, historical approach — the "slow-moving

---

[40] "Recent Fiction: 'The Song of Bernadette,' By Franz Werfel," *Advance*, 1 Oct. 1942; Connolly.

[41] Albert Hubbell, "Franz Werfel Keeps His Vow," *Chicago Sun*, 11 May 1942.

[42] Marianne Hauser, "Incense in the Grotto: 'The Song of Bernadette,' by Franz Werfel," *New Republic*, 29 June 1942, 900–1. "Those familiar with Werfel's earlier writings, particularly his poetry and 'Barbara,' will hardly be surprised that he should have been drawn by the story of Lourdes."

[43] John S. Kennedy, "A Great Spiritual Experience."

196   The Fortunes of German Writers in America

story of European novelists"[44] — and the "sensitive, reverent"[45] character renderings. His objectivity and use of the form of the historical novel were lauded for their lending an air of detachment to the story, allowing the reader to draw his own conclusions and not be forcibly "converted,"[46] and yet his characterizations were praised for creating a vividness, beauty and tenderness not possible in a biographical form. His precision and detail are paralleled with that of Proust, but "without the burden of the latter's structural complexity."[47] However, a very few critics found that Werfel the dramatist and philosopher had turned the novel into "an interminable discussion which went on in church and state," the result of which is that "one finds oneself skipping many pages of medical and psychiatric theorizing and religious and political arguments to join her [Bernadette]."[48]

Other minor complaints were aimed at Werfel's use of some "vulgarity and blasphemy,"[49] his "occasional misuse of terms" which showed his "unfamiliarity with Catholic usage"[50] and the quality of the translation. Katherine Woods's review in the *New York Times Book Review* found fault in phrases such as "love filled consoledness" and "cognition of mystical coherences," especially when found with colloquialisms like "had a hunch" and "put on an act."[51] These negative aspects were pointed out, however, by a small minority of reviewers, and were heavily outweighed by the hyperbolic praise about Werfel's style.

---

[44] Joe Pekar, "Werfel Writes About a Saint," *Morning World-Herald* (Omaha, Nebr.), 17 May 1942.

[45] David A. Appel, "Franz Werfel Writes Prose Symphony in 'Song of Bernadette,'" *Cleveland News*, 15 May 1942, 20.

[46] Sidney McGee, "'Miracle of Lourdes,'" *Nashville Banner*, 20 May 1942.

[47] Henry Montor, "Study in Sacred and Profane: the Novels of Franz Werfel and Lawrence Lipton," *Jewish Times*, 26 June 1942, 1-D.

[48] N. H. C., "Werfel Ponders A Miracle," *Kansas City Star*, 23 May 1942.

[49] "The Song of Bernadette," *Jesuit Mission*, July/Aug. 1942.

[50] A. C. D., "The Song of Bernadette," *Magnificat*, July 1942, 163.

[51] Katherine Woods, *New York Times Book Review*, 10 May 1942, 3.

It was especially on thematic questions that the reviewers usually split along clearly defined lines. Clifton Fadiman, reviewing the novel for *New Yorker*, stated this difference in viewpoint clearly, in writing that the book is difficult to judge because of its theme, and that the true believer will find "a factual history of enormous spiritual power," while the nonbeliever will see "a strange tale, crowded with improbabilities and perhaps impossibilities."[52] One reviewer, in presenting the various possible viewpoints on the novel, stated that "the scientist will suspect propaganda, the Protestant will suspect Catholic apology, and the Catholic will suspect a secular attack."[53] Indeed, the difference portrayed in the novel between "spiritual principles and radical nihilism, between those who regard the human being as a machine and those with a consciousness of the spiritual meaning of life"[54] were clearly reflected in the dichotomous opinions on the strengths of the theme.

On the one side, a large group of reviewers found the tale of the miracle at Lourdes to be a "most sympathetic and convincing representation of Catholic life,"[55] in which Werfel "rubs the noses of materialistic scientists into the hard facts of the miracles."[56] Especially in the later reviews, i.e., after October 1942, *Song* was almost unanimously considered a "Catholic" book, with some reviewers expressing surprise that Werfel had not yet become a member of the Catholic Church and some assuming that he already had.[57]

In a broader sense, some critics saw faith in general as the main theme of the novel, highlighting its appeal "to all human beings in the

---

[52] Clifton Fadiman, "Books: Three Novels," *New Yorker*, 16 May 1942, 72.

[53] Gerald Kennedy, "'The Song of Bernadette,' By Franz Werfel," *Christian Advocate*, 18 June 1942.

[54] Anon., "Typewriters Battle Swords. One of Nazis' First Foes Tells of Nihilism's Spread. Vroman Luncheon Guests Hear of Answer To Pledge To France; Poet Urges Confidence," *Pasadena Star News*, 30 May 1942. This was a quote of Werfel's talk of May 29 at the Hotel Vista del Arroyo.

[55] "The Song of Bernadette," *Northwest Review*, June 1942.

[56] Connolly, "Book Tour," 30–31.

[57] "The Song of Bernadette. By Franz Werfel," *Sign: A National Catholic Magazine*, June 1942, 697.

realm of faith, beyond dogma and beyond sect."[58] The review in *Time*, a magazine which would have had the widest national circulation of all the popular press, calls the book "an act of piety transcending blood and creed."[59] Most of the reviewers who find either general spirituality or the exaltedness of mankind as the main themes are simply extrapolating Werfel's ideas in the preface to *Song*, that he was writing to "magnify the divine mystery and the holiness of man." Thus descriptions of the theme as "man in his quest for spiritual comfort, in which even an agnostic can find the meaning of man's faith in eternal goodness,"[60] or that "belief in the Divine is nothing other than the substantially convinced recognition of the fact that the world is meaningful, that is to say a spiritual world"[61] are direct quotes from Werfel himself.

However, on the harsher side of the disagreement, one Jesuit reviewer bluntly called other reviews which dismissed the supernatural and emphasized the broader ideals of humanity and spirituality "pagan stupidity."[62] Such criticism was targeted against the more secular reviewers, who, in the eyes of some, had "turned this Catholic book into another affirmation of the transcendence of the spirit."[63]

A third, smaller group of critics, writing for the Jewish press, were also split on the main theme of Werfel's novel. Those who reviewed it positively found "a potential reservoir of faith in noble ideals which may sweep away the race bitterness and religious intolerance of the day and

---

[58] Alexander Kendrick, "Bernadette Saw a Lovely Lady: Franz Werfel's Story of Lourdes," *Philadelphia Inquirer*, 13 May 1942.

[59] "Modern Miracle: Song of Bernadette — Franz Werfel," *Time*, 8 June 1942, 90.

[60] Harold D. Carew, "The Lady of Lourdes," *Pasadena Star-News*, 23 May 1942, 7–8.

[61] Paul H. Hallet, "The Literary Pageant," *Register*, 31 May 1942.

[62] Alfred Barret, S. J., "Some Good Books: The Song of Bernadette. By Franz Werfel," *Messenger of the Sacred Heart*, Aug. 1942, 85.

[63] L. D. W., *Dominicana* (Somerset, Ohio), Autumn 1942. The reviewer goes on to predict the failure of the upcoming film version, "because of the necessity of choosing a heroine from the Hollywood queens whose experience of suffering has gone no further than their sixth spouse's mental cruelty."

bring about a new faith in humanity,"[64] or compared it to Sholem Asch's *The Nazarene* in that it attempted to be "a messenger of a new gospel which would bring Christian and Jew together."[65]

The inevitability of comparison of *Song* to other religious books was foreshadowed, although cynically, in Harry Hansen's review of 28 October 1942, in which he stated that one would think publishers were planning more books of a religious nature because of the popularity of Werfel's book.[66] And indeed, there were several such books with which *Song* was compared, predominantly with L. C. Douglas's *The Robe* and A. J. Cronin's *The Keys of the Kingdom*.[67] Although one reviewer chastised others for saluting works such as *Keys* with the same superlative that should be reserved for works such as *Song*,[68] all three works enjoyed high sales. The reason for the popularity of such books concerned with the "phenomenon of faith"[69] was the topic of several articles, and Werfel's quoted opinion was that the books found so large an audience because people respond to poetry.[70] Another reviewer dealing with the same three books concluded that the books' appearance on the best-seller lists at this time was "not an accident but rather an

---

[64] Maxine Hirsh Bader, "In Reviewing Werfel Novel, Rabbi Looks for New Unity," *American Jewish Outlook*, 11 Dec. 1942. In this report on Dr. Soloman Freehof's review of *Song*, Bader found it strange that eminent exiles such as Mann, Feuchtwanger, Zweig, and Werfel had not written books dealing with 1. the shock of finding one's home an alien place, 2. the pain of the outcast, and 3. the danger that lies around their new homeland.

[65] "Song of Bernadette," *Jewish News*, 10 March 1944.

[66] Harry Hansen, "Fiction Rivals War Books in Race for Public's Favor," *Chicago Sun Tribune*, 28 Oct. 1942.

[67] Werfel's publisher, Ben Huebsch, recalled in an article on the hundredth anniversary of Bernadette's vision how, when Werfel had noticed the attention *The Robe* was getting, he asked, "'What is this *Robe* that people are talking about?' And I told him the theme as I had gathered it from reviews. He wagged his head in acknowledgment; then, with twinkling eyes and the suspicion of a grin, ejaculated, 'Protestant competition!'" B. W. Huebsch, "Werfel Remembered," *Saturday Review of Literature*, 15 March 1958, 36.

[68] John S. Kennedy, "A Great Spiritual Experience."

[69] W. Bonner, "News of the Literary World: A New Trend in Literature. The Three Best Sellers Since 1941," *St. Petersburg Times*, 18 July 1943.

[70] Ibid.

indication that they fill a need," since World War I produced "no such testimonies of faith."[71]

As to the necessity of such works as *Song*, many reviewers voiced an opinion. It was called a story "for all who would fight against the evil influences the Nazi hordes have unloosed upon the world."[72] Werfel was seen as having produced "a religious masterpiece just when it was needed most,"[73] one that conveyed the idea "that not a material, but a spiritual principle is at stake in this World War."[74] Perhaps one of the most visible statements of the need in America for such a book was when Father Francis Shea used *Song* in a sermon at St. Patrick's Cathedral in New York on 9 August 1942, stating that its best-seller status was "proof that Americans hunger for faith and spiritual consolation," and calling it "a novel of faith, in which war-torn America sees a lamp of heaven, lighting the way through the shadows of the day and the blackout of night."[75] This homily was directed at the congregation so that they would become a "kneeling army" behind the fighting army of the country. Thus, the connection between the book and the war found some mention in the popular press.

Werfel himself had expressed similar ideas in his short piece for *Commonweal*, "Writing Bernadette," in which he saw the war as a spiritual rather than material battle. And as far as the central theme of *Song* was concerned, there did exist a parallel to the "radical nihilism which no longer regards the human being as the image of God but as an amoral machine in a completely meaningless world" facing "the metaphysical, the religious concept of life."[76] These were concepts that Werfel had formulated years before in his 1938 essay "Observations on

---

[71] *Perry Record* (Perry, N.Y.), 2 Sept. 1943.

[72] Frank Mayer, "Music, Art and Books: Werfel's Glowing Story of Bernadette of Lourdes," *Minneapolis Tribune*, 17 May 1942.

[73] "Priest Praises Werfel Novel," *Worcester Telegram*, 17 Oct. 1942.

[74] "Dr. M. J. Cohen Reviews Book At Y.M.H.A.," *Easton Express*, 14 Oct. 1942.

[75] "Cathedral Preacher Lauds Werfel's Book. Father Shea Finds 'The Song of Bernadette' a Lamp to Heaven," *New York Times*, 10 Aug. 1942; "Kneeling Army in U.S. Urged By Father Shea," *New York Herald Tribune*, 10 Aug. 1942, 11.

[76] Franz Werfel, "Writing Bernadette," *Commonweal*, 29 May 1942, 126.

the War of Tomorrow" ("Betrachtungen über den Krieg von morgen")[77] and it is true that much American propaganda portrayed the battle against Germany and Japan in terms of spiritual good vs. incarnate evil;[78] but whether the majority of the reading public consciously drew the analogy between Bernadette's struggle against the secular state and America's destiny to "defend victoriously eternal values — Christian values — against the Blitzkrieg of Satan,"[79] may be questioned. Adolf Klarmann went one step further in writing to Werfel that the book's success was due to "a deep metaphysical longing in America, a longing that extended beyond the events of the day...."[80] But the fact remains that the date of its publication and its genesis were inexorably linked to the darkest, most uncertain days of World War II.

Werfel's comments in 1942 on *Song*'s intended purpose were *ex post facto*. Indeed, his statement that he "has written this document of current portent with complete consciousness of purpose — a polemic of this war,"[81] was in answer to the question "What meaning do you feel the story of Bernadette has for readers today?" rather than to the question of why he wrote it[82] and belies his stated intentions in his much-quoted preface. As has been mentioned in connection with the genesis of the novel, Werfel had from the outset not expected a large general interest in the work.

A few clues, however, in the text itself, hint at these intentions, and in some ways validate his statements. In the final chapter, the pope speaks of "the fever of maniacal false doctrines ... threatening to plunge the human spirit into bloody madness. In the battle against this, which man must win, not only did Lourdes stand like a very rock, but the life

---

[77] *Paneuropa* 14 (March 1938): 65–77.

[78] For example, the short film series "Why We Fight," directed by Frank Capra.

[79] "I'm an American," radio broadcast on 16 March 1941, KECA, Los Angeles; quoted from Lore Foltin, "Franz Werfel's Image of America," in *Exile: The Writer's Experience*, ed. John M. Spalek and Robert F. Bell, (Chapel Hill: University of North Carolina Press, 1982), 305.

[80] Letter from Klarmann to Werfel, 5 Sept. 1942, quoted from Steiman, "Franz Werfel — His Song in America," 60.

[81] "Writing Bernadette," 126.

[82] Ibid.

of Bernadette Soubirous retained its prophetic activity within time."[83] After the address, as Bouhouhorts stands outside of St. Peter's in Rome, he looks skyward, "convinced that localized in that patch of sky above him all the saints of the Church dwelt close together on their thrones.... Under the heaven of Rome, where the saints were gathered to welcome their new comrade, flew a military plane."[84] The year was 1933, and surely the "maniacal false doctrines" were those of fascism and "radical nihilism." Thus, in a minor way, *Song* does actually touch upon the topical theme of the war, though not nearly as specifically as Werfel stated. On this topic, Lionel B. Steiman mentions that "one is tempted to conclude that his subsequent claims for the work's polemical significance sought advantage for it by relating it to the war effort, which in the temper of that time could legitimate almost any undertaking."[85] This must remain speculation, as no documentation exists — and to divine an author's intention even with documentation is at best a risky task — but the effects of the novel's theme being closely tied in with the war, at least in popular view if not in fact, were indeed helpful in 1942.

The atmosphere in post–Pearl Harbor America was obviously receptive to any book that dealt with the newly entered war.[86] It was also receptive to books of a religious nature.[87] The books that enjoyed the greatest sales overall, it follows, were those which dealt with both themes, such as Eddie Rickenbacker's *Seven Came Through* or Robert Scott's *God Is My Co-pilot*. These appear to be two phenomena that arose simultaneously, and, in historical retrospect, disappeared simultaneously.[88]

---

[83] *Song*, 574.

[84] *Song*, 575.

[85] Lionel B. Steiman, *Franz Werfel — The Faith of an Exile* (Waterloo, Ontario, Canada: Wilfrid Laurier University Press, 1985), 150.

[86] The best-sellers of 1942–45, predominantly in the "General" or "Nonfiction" category, were virtually all books on various aspects of the war.

[87] As witnessed by the three top best-sellers of 1942–43, A. J. Cronin's *The Keys of the Kingdom*, *Song*, and Lloyd C. Douglas's *The Robe*.

[88] A shift in the themes of best-sellers occurred in late 1944, gradually excluding any work of a religious nature.

However, quantifying the reception, we find that the popular press considered the main theme — either the Catholic aspect or the more general view of faith — as the primary attraction of *Song*, and mention of its topicality occurred in only 1 percent of the reviews, which even then referred only to "our troubled times" and gave perhaps a vague mention of the need for faith in this war. Therefore, one must conclude that any further speculation whether Werfel was attempting to address directly the underlying causes of the war would prove a moot point, as the "war-angle" was not picked up by the popular press. The reception does prove, however, that the religious theme, coupled with Werfel's artistry in form and characterization, and his previous reputation in America, were the primary factors for the popular success of *Song*.

Almost four years later, in late 1945, Werfel's novel *Star of the Unborn* was published posthumously and promoted to a highly expectant popular press.[89] The director of the Book-of-the-Month Club, Harry Scherman, was quoted as saying that, when the proofs of *Star* reached him, he had his "biggest thrill."[90] Another "teaser" mentioned that the book "has the boys excited at Viking."[91] Indeed, Viking was promoting the book heavily, calling it "one of the most important novels of our time,"[92] and "a literary monument."[93] Those who saw advance copies were describing it as "the best thing of his tragically short career."[94] Much as Werfel's vow and narrow escape in *Song*'s preface had been used to snatch the reader's attention to the book, here his death immediately after finishing *Star* was employed as an attention-grabber. The Viking full-page advertisement in the *New York Times Book Review* of 3 March 1946 states that "For the readers

---

[89] In the meantime, of course, Werfel had not been inactive. *Jakobowsky and the Colonel*, on which he had spent much time, opened in early 1943, and his collection of polemic essays, *Between Heaven and Earth*, appeared in 1944. However, in the former case, Werfel was not "in the limelight," as mentioned in the preface; and in the latter, the reception was mild and mixed, only ten thousand copies were printed.

[90] Harry Hansen, "A Poet Fights Back," *New York World-Telegram*, 26 Feb. 1946.

[91] Clip Boutell, "Authors Are Like People," *Dayton News*, 23 Dec. 1945.

[92] Lee Charles, "Alleged Anecdote," *Philadelphia Record*, 17 Jan. 1946.

[93] "Literary Monument," *Chicago Tribune*, 10 Feb. 1946.

[94] *Indianapolis Star*, 16 Feb. 1946.

who know and love his novels, there is a special significance in the publication of this story. Completed just a few days before his death, it is a cosmic comedy...."[95] One of the few positive reviews saw Werfel writing "in the light of a vision of death, similar to that which set the mood for Brahms' Fourth Symphony."[96] All reviewers expected, on the basis of the prepublication praise, a repeat of the success of *Song*.

Once the reviewers had had a chance to read the advance copies, the reviews became a mixture of caution and rhetoric, with expressions of disapproval side by side with positive statements couched in vague terms. The most common negative comment was that this novel was nothing like Werfel's previous works, and the reviewer would then proceed to describe Werfel's career and list those works that were indicative of Werfel's talent, usually *Song* and *Musa Dagh*. That Werfel "liked to think of this [*Star*] as his greatest achievement"[97] did not deter reviewers from finding the work "as unlike the real Werfel as it is unworthy of him,"[98] or being incredulous that the same author who wrote *Musa Dagh* and *Song* had such "adolescent yearnings for a space ship and a rocket gun à la Buck Rogers."[99] Although the book was found unworthy of the author of Werfel's previous works, allusions were made in the reception to other authors ranging from Jules Verne, H. G. Wells, Jonathan Swift, and Edgar Rice Burroughs to Lewis Carroll, Aldous Huxley, Bernard Shaw and C. S. Lewis, usually with the conclusion that *Star* is merely a "literary curiosity."[100] Regardless of the prepublication promotion measures taken by Viking — dissimilar to those undertaken for *Song* in that the primary advertising for the

---

[95] *New York Times Book Review*, 3 March 1946, 23.

[96] Julian Sullivan, "Burning the Midnight Oil," *Indianapolis Star*, 3 March 1946.

[97] "Books," *Wheeling News Register*, 24 Feb. 1946.

[98] W. G. Rogers, "Literary Guidepost," *Asbury Park Press* et al., 27 Feb. 1946. This negative review found the widest circulation in over thirty smaller newspapers throughout the country. It considers the book a "dull and dreary account which thoughtful friends should have destroyed."

[99] Clip Boutell, "Today's Book: A World That Will Never Be," *New York Post*, 27 Feb. 1946.

[100] Harrison Smith, "The Secret of the Universe," *Saturday Review of Literature*, 2 March 1946, 7.

1942 work came after the popular press and public had reacted favorably to it[101] — the press set the tone for the receptive horizon of expectations for *Star*, and it was a decidedly negative one.

The unconventionality vis à vis Werfel's other works was deplored not only in its presentation of theme but also in its style and structure: precisely those elements that had kept *Song* at the top of the best-seller list until *The Robe* appeared. The main theme was infrequently recognized as being similar to that of *Song*, that "man's salvation will come when he cuts himself loose from materialism and the wrong it does,"[102] and that there exists "the dangerous paradox which threatens us now that social goodwill so often tries to ignore man's soul in order to improve his condition."[103] The view that "the further man gets from God, the closer he approaches Him"[104] is seen to be simply "the same conclusion all men learn," but Werfel had to arrive at it after 650 pages.[105] The harshest review to find wide reception was that of Eric Bentley in the *New Republic*, cited above in the introduction. Bentley stated that he was "nauseated" because he did not like thinkers who "purport to comprehend things by declaring them incomprehensible." He found Werfel "not equipped to write a philosophical novel" and the theme "an edifice of cocksure puerility based on a foundation of unabashed ignorance." Many reviewers took part in this nonobjective defamation. Speaking of Werfel's concept of utopia, another reviewer who found wide circulation termed it "pseudo-scientific, pseudo-philosophical, and compounded with the pretension to some *Welt-*

---

[101] Viking added $10,000 to the $12,500 advertisement budget of *Song* in January 1943, with the pace of sales at "just under 2500 copies a week." The advertising campaign included "two full-page ads in the *New York Times* and *Herald Tribune* book sections, one full page ad in the *Saturday Review of Literature*, and leading space in the *Atlantic*, *Harper's*, *Nation*, *New Republic*, *Commonweal*, and *America*." "Among the Publishers," *Publishers' Weekly*, 4 Jan. 1943, 34.

[102] Emily Schossberger, "Werfel's Last Novel Limns World 100,000 Years Hence," *Omaha World-Herald*, 24 Feb. 1946.

[103] John Erskine, "Books: 'Star of the Unborn,'" *New York Journal American*, 3 March 1946.

[104] Kelsey Guilfoil, "Werfel's Last Book to Kindle Many Minds," *Chicago Tribune*, 24 Feb. 1946.

[105] N. L. S., "Werfel's Time Flight," *Kansas City Star*, 23 Feb. 1946.

geschichtliche [sic] *Anschauung* which nearly all German writers seem to feel they must have in order to keep their intellectual self-respect."[106]

The style and structure of the novel were also condemned; the work was termed "inchoate and aimless,"[107] with "vast stretches of prose in which the most elementary ideas began to seem, in their wordy endlessness, like passages of profound thought."[108] The reviewer raised the questions whether the novel was a first draft that the author did not live to rewrite or whether the translation had something to do with its "diffuseness."

Those few reviewers who were positive about the novel — although still qualifying their remarks by distancing *Star* from the previous works — either looked past its thematic and structural obscurities and found in it a "gargantuan humor" "for the eclectic, the broadly read, the mentally unfettered with a high sense of humor, who can take some round intellectual kidding,"[109] or a rich autobiographical source that will lead to "a new breed of Joyce-like commentators that will explain the whys and wherefores of its labyrinthine architecture."[110]

Thus, the very elements that had propelled *Song* to a lengthy stay at the top of the best-seller list and had garnered Werfel superlative praise from clergy, critics, and the common reader had also left the receptive atmosphere cold for *Star*. As can be seen in the reception of *Star*, its theme was seen overall as differing greatly from that of *Song*, although, when viewed in general terms, it was the same in both works. As Werfel had set down in his treatise *Between Heaven and Earth* (*Zwischen oben und unten*), it is the battle not between Right and Left but between Above and Below.[111] However, this message, so clearly portrayed in the struggle of the common, pious Bernadette against the force of worldly materialism, was in *Star* couched in a mosaic of formal,

---

[106] Lucien Price, "'Star of the Unborn,'" *Atlantic Monthly*, April 1946, 166.

[107] Anne Freemantle, "Books of the Week," *Commonweal*, 19 April 1946.

[108] Hamilton Basso, "Books: Werfel's Hereafter, A Brooklyn, and Another Thirkell," *New Yorker*, 2 March 1946, 83.

[109] "Werfel's Last Work Is a Brilliant Piece of Whimsy," *Houston Post*, 24 Feb. 1946.

[110] Charles Lee, "Final Werfel," *Philadelphia Record*, 28 Feb. 1946.

[111] *Between Heaven and Earth*, ix.

structural and stylistic devices, hidden from plain view by the artist's desire to create a "humoristic-cosmic-mystic-world–poem."[112] Isaac Rosenfeld, writing in the *New York Times Book Review*, summed up the problem with *Star* as compared to his previous works as follows:

> Whereas … in some of Werfel's earlier fiction, a given meaning is always dramatically embodied in an appropriate character, here the characters … are straw men and pallid freaks, designed to break under the weight of false doctrine that the author deliberately assigns to them…. It is unfortunate that the strengthening of a novelist's religious and moral convictions should weaken his sense of the variety, seriousness and many-sidedness of the ineradicable conflicts of life. I regret that I have not been able to write a more enthusiastic obituary, at least such as 'The Pure in Heart' and 'Musa Dagh' deserve. But to the degree that a novelist deals in straw men, he becomes himself a man of straw.[113]

As Werfel the artist had changed in the eyes of the American public, so had the receptive atmosphere in America also changed. Whereas *Song* had been thrust into a national mood of uncertainty about the future, an atmosphere of a need of hope, *Star* was published in a time of general euphoria, a wave of the highest sense of achievement and moral victory after the defeat of the Axis powers, and a sense of purpose in rebuilding what years of war had destroyed. The reading public no longer needed to be reassured about the future; nor did readers need or want anyone to determine their future for them, especially along the lines of what was presented in *Star*. Werfel's antivision of utopia was not that of most of America. L. Price states on the theme of utopia and Werfel's contribution that "when offering us a vision of future society, one should try to give us something we would leave our happy homes

---

[112] "Sein neuer Roman sei ein 'humoristisch-kosmisch-mystisches Weltgedicht….'" Jungk, 330.

[113] Isaac Rosenfeld, "California a Hundred Millenniums from Now," *New York Times Book Review*, 24 February 1946, 5.

for."[114] It is apparent from the reception that Werfel did not offer such a vision. And with this last work he slowly disappeared from view in America.

The gradual renewal of interest in Werfel has remained predominantly in the scholarly sector until very recently. The number of dissertations on Werfel has been steadily rising since the 1950s, and a resurgence of scholarly articles and books was begun in 1961 with Lore B. Foltin's *Franz Werfel 1890-1945*,[115] in the preface of which she stated that there was a "dearth" of studies on Werfel relative to those on his compatriots Rilke and Kafka. Since that study, particularly since the advent of exile, reception, and Austrian studies, the number of Werfel studies has increased immensely.[116] In 1987 a major work on Werfel's life appeared in Germany.[117] But as far as the popular reception of the primary works of Franz Werfel in America is concerned, progress has been slow at best. As Steiman mentioned in his article, those works still available in America today were his most successful: *Song*, *Embezzled Heaven*, *Musa Dagh*, and *Class Reunion* in Amereon Press. In addition however, *Verdi* is available through two publishers, Ayer Co. and AMS, *Jakobowsky* is available in the German edition edited by Gustave O. Arlt by Irvington Press, and *Song* has just been reissued in St. Martin's Press's Religious Miracle Series and is also obtainable in a large-type edition by Walker & Co.

Steiman's 1987 article, perhaps prophetically, found it paradoxical that the work that "may well have a more lasting interest for Americans," *Cella*, was not yet available in English translation. Happily, this has since been remedied with the 1989 publication of the work in the Joachim Neugroschel translation. Reviews of the book were unfortunately sparse, with both *Publishers' Weekly* and *Booklist* offering synopses

---

[114] Price, "'Star of the Unborn,'" 166.

[115] Lore B. Foltin, ed., *Franz Werfel 1890–1945* (Pittsburgh: University of Pittsburgh Press, 1961).

[116] To list all publications dealing with Werfel here would be at the least impractical. For a copious bibliography up to 1972, see Lore B. Foltin, *Franz Werfel*, Sammlung Metzler 115 (Stuttgart: Metzler, 1972).

[117] Peter Stephan Jungk, *Franz Werfel: Eine Lebensgeschichte* (Frankfurt am Main: Fischer, 1987). The English translation appeared in 1990 under the title *Franz Werfel: A Life in Prague, Vienna and Hollywood*, trans. Anselm Hollo (New York: Grove Weidenfeld, 1990).

of the plot and mentioning the similarities between the main characters, Hans and Gretl Bodenheim, and Franz and Alma Werfel.

The reasons for the slow-moving but promising renewal of interest in Werfel today must remain conjecture, at least in the popular sphere, until the popular response can be measured. Steiman concluded his essay with the prediction that "there remains in Werfel's writing a wonderful lyric purity that is by no means always lost in translation, as well as a superb gift of story-telling.... If Werfel's oeuvre ever attracts again the American readers it deserves, these are the qualities in it that will hold them."[118] This is indubitably true, but as has been seen in the reception of Werfel's most popular works, the main initial attraction for the American reader and critic has been more the general theme of his work which, as in the case of *Song*, was aided by the "gripping, quietly absorbing"[119] style of the artist, and in the case of *Star*, was shrouded by his artistry. To be seen as a true "poet" in the eyes of the American reader, Werfel will have to go through the popular process again, with his main themes as an impetus to a closer look at his superb artistry.

A detriment to the reception of the contemporary publication of *Cella*, or any other of Werfel's works, is that there exists no real expectational basis for the popular reader or critic. The jacket cover of the first edition of *Cella* advertises on the lower edge that Werfel is "Author of *The Song of Bernadette*," but this would have little meaning to the present-day general reading public. The only familiarity the work could have would derive from the public's conception beforehand of the genre, that is, Holocaust literature.[120] Any works reissued will have to survive on their literary and thematic merit alone, since most readers and critics will not have the aid of knowledge of Werfel's previous reception, unless they go back to the archives of 1942–43.

A hopeful trend in the general renaissance of the reception of German and Austrian writers in America is that anthologies are being compiled of essays written by experts for an audience with no previous

---

[118] Steiman, 64.

[119] Ibid.

[120] To this end, the jacket cover duly displays a swastika and a contorted photograph of a figure stooping before uniformed Nazis.

background in the field.[121] These present a basis for an escalation of interest in the field and would provide a beginning for popular critical "horizons of expectation."

The bright spot on the horizon for Werfel's popularity remains the recent publication of the English translation of Jungk's biography,[122] for it will provide a starting point for critics and audience alike. The conjecture that Friedrich Torberg made in 1956, that Werfel would have to "survive for a short interval" before his time came again, also described what would occur during this period. "In this interval, an unsure generation of literary consumers and distributors may place him contentedly in the wrong places in their brochures and let him be a stand-in for their own gaps."[123] Since his decline in popularity Franz Werfel has been placed in many ways: as an exile author, expressionist, Catholic author, Jewish apologist, mystic, utopist, etc. To predict a revival of Werfel as a best-selling author is a gamble at best. But on the basis of the roots of his previous popularity, one can only be as hopeful as Torberg that, perhaps after a renewed interest in his themes, he will be popularly seen once again as a true poet.[124]

---

[121] Such as the above-mentioned anthologies, *Major Figures of Modern Austrian Literature*; *Austrian Fiction Writers, 1875–1913*, vol. 81 of *Dictionary of Literary Biography*; and the upcoming series by Harry Zohn on Austrian culture.

[122] Translated by Anselm Hollo (New York: Grove Weidenfeld, 1990).

[123] "In dieser Zwischenzeit mag ihn eine unsichere Generation von Literaturkonsumenten und -konsumverteilern in ihren Prospekten getrost an falsche Stellen setzen und ihn die Lücken büßen lassen, die ihre eigenen sind," Torberg, 148.

[124] In the German, and Torberg's, meaning of *Dichter*.

The Novels of Erich Maria Remarque in American Reviews

Hans Wagener

IN FORMULATING THE TITLE for this paper, I admittedly encountered some difficulties. First, I wanted to make clear that I did not want to focus on the personal life of Remarque as reported in all the articles written in fairly serious American dailies and weeklies, as I was interested in neither his personal nor his social affairs; second, I did not want to address Remarque's work in American literary criticism in general, which would have included the scholarly work generated about him, for such an approach might have shifted the attention to the somewhat biographical studies appearing in recent years by Owen, Firda, and Taylor;[1] third, I wanted to omit all articles concerning the movie versions of the Remarque novels. Instead, I will focus only upon newspaper reviews, since the author's popular successes and failures are most faithfully mirrored in the views of these particular professional critics. The reviews contain judgments upon the literary quality of Remarque's work, valuations that were determined by the day and not by hindsight or the global perspective of his entire literary oeuvre. Finally, in contrast to most other German writers, Remarque lends himself particularly well to such an investigation, because all of his

---

[1] Specifically the books by C. R. Owen, *Erich Maria Remarque: A Critical Bio-Bibliography* (Amsterdam: Rodopi, 1984); Richard Arthur Firda, *Erich Maria Remarque: A Thematic Analysis of His Novels* (New York, Bern, Frankfurt am Main, Paris: Peter Lang, 1988); Harley U. Taylor, Jr., *Erich Maria Remarque: A Literary and Film Biography* (New York, Frankfurt am Main, Paris: Peter Lang, 1989).

novels appeared in English translation. Usually they appeared simultaneously with, and sometimes even before, the German editions, the one exception being his first novel, *Die Traumbude* ("The Dream Pad").[2] It is well known that with *All Quiet on the Western Front* (*Im Westen nichts Neues*; 1929) Remarque achieved a worldwide success that was matched by no other book except the Bible. Although the sales figures are not precisely known and have probably been exaggerated by the publishers and Remarque himself for advertisement purposes, it has been estimated that a total of 8,000,000 copies in twenty-eight languages have been sold.[3] By November 1929, the statistics, which were already a few months old, inform us that the American edition had sold 215,000 copies, and the British one, 300,000; whereas in Germany, by the month of June, over 1,000,000 copies had already been sold. However, regarding the American reviews, we must bear in mind that, in contrast to the British edition, which was published by Putnam's, the American one, published by Little, Brown and Co. of Boston, was expurgated, deleting several words, paragraphs, and entire scenes, totaling approximately ten pages.[4] It was not until 1979 that the complete Putnam's version was published in the United States. These expurgations were considered necessary in order to avoid public opprobrium, and conflict with the law; once the book had been chosen as the Book-of-the-Month Club selection, the publishers became concerned about the possibility of being charged with distributing indecent material through the mail. At least one anonymous reviewer expressed regret about these deletions. "One can only regret the stupid

---

[2] Erich Maria Remarque, *Die Traumbude: Ein Künstlerroman* (Dresden: Verlag der Schönheit, 1920).

[3] For the discussion about the sales figures, see Owen, 73 and 80ff. In "Interview mit sich selbst," *Die Welt*, 31 March 1966, Remarque himself claimed that the book sold 20 to 30 million copies in up to fifty languages, including neither pirated editions nor all the editions published in the USSR or its satellites, which do not recognize the International Copyright Laws.

[4] Apart from several words concerning the bodily functions, "two passages or episodes were expunged in America, one dealing with latrine matters of the German soldier on the open field and the other with sexual contact between a convalescing soldier and his visiting wife. Neither the German nor the British editions of the novel had undergone any form of censorship in its hardcover editions" (Firda, 59).

necessity which resulted in the suppressing or deleting of material which was included in the English edition."[5]

There was no major American newspaper or journal that did not take note of *All Quiet on the Western Front* in one form or the other, and all American reviews that I was able to examine were positive.[6] The American reviewers, indeed, did not have an ax to grind with an author who inherently pleaded for peace, equality, and brotherhood. As a result, the American reviews, in contrast to many German ones from the political Right, did not attack the author as a pacifist or a traitor to the German cause. The German reviews, it seems, no matter whether from the political Right, or the Left, have to be understood as products of the political quarrels of the time, whereas the American ones do not. This is the reason why the American reviews dwelt less on the implied pacifist message of the book, concentrating more on its credibility and ability to persuade on a purely human level. It seems as if the description of suffering had completely dominated all political and, to a certain extent, aesthetic considerations. The reviewers praised time and again the book's sincerity, simplicity, honesty, its lack of sentimentality, its realism and economy of style. "It is written with simplicity and candor, and reads as if it had been well translated. There is nothing mawkish about it, nothing 'literary' — it is not the artful construction of fancy, but the sincere record of a man's suffering. Unlike the experimental artist, the author has nothing new to say; but he says it so honestly and so well that it is like news to us, though it is bad news."[7] Or: "The greatness of the book is in its pathos unmixed with sentimentality, in its brooding sense of wasted youth, in the sharp realism of all detail, and in the supreme realization of what the war meant back home.... The hunger, the fear, the dirt, the wounds, the death after death of

---

[5] *Bookman*, July 1929, 552.

[6] The following evaluation is based on the several hundred reviews contained in the Erich Maria Remarque Collection of the Fayles Library at New York University (of which I was able to obtain copies through the Erich Maria Remarque-Archiv / Forschungsstelle Krieg und Literatur of the University of Osnabrück) and on those listed and quoted in the annual *Book Review Digest*.

[7] T. S. Matthews, *New Republic*, 19 June 1929, 130.

comrades — these are portrayed with a grave sincerity."[8] It is amazing that these reviewers overlooked the redolent sentimentality and pathos in the theme of lost youth, and particularly in the scenes involving the hero's furlough. Instead, the reviewers stressed the author's honesty. "No one can argue that this work was written purely to shock readers, or to sell on the strength of the sensational. Its very character refutes such suspicions. The book is able, solid work; it comes from the heart of a man who suffered, and it is free from trickery."[9] Only rarely was reference made to a possible hidden antiwar tendency of the book; this was at the most seen to be implied in the description of the horrors of war and its effect on the ordinary soldier in the trenches. "Theme, style, mood, and the unstated, unescapable moral of this book are so nearly right that its claim to greatness must not be dismissed."[10] The reviewer of the *Boston Transcript* called it "a great and powerful book, a Locarno in prose, the end of all war's glamour in one volume. The book is starkly simple, thoroughly lacking in all bugle calls, all flag waving, all false patriotism. It is just War."[11]

Also typical of the American reviews are references to world literature. Here one reviewer makes a comparison with Ibsen's tragedies: "... a narrative that has the lean savagery of an Ibsen tragedy."[12] Here follows a reference made to another great novel about World War I: "It is not too much to say that it ranks with Barbusse's 'Under Fire' in its profound and moving simplicity in dealing with the realities of the front line atrocities."[13]

The fact that patriotism was lacking, that the adverse effects of war on the soldiers of all nations involved was depicted, and that it had about it an air of conciliation welcomed among those who had been the enemy all made the international success of the book possible. Harvey Swados, in an article from 1956 entitled "Remarque's Relevance,"

---

[8] Leon Whipple, *Survey*, 11 September 1929, 574.

[9] Harry Hansen, *New York World*, 9 June 1929.

[10] C. M., *Catholic World*, November 1929, 246.

[11] K. Schriftgiesser, *Boston Transcript*, 1 June 1929, 2.

[12] F. E. Hill, *New York Herald Tribune*, 2 June 1929, Book section, 1.

[13] Coley Taylor, *World Tomorrow*, September 1929, 277.

reflected on the success of the book in 1929; he concluded that "It is, I believe, the clarity, the boldness, and the timelessness of these observations [of the common soldiers about war — H. W.] which account in large part for the book's astonishing reception upon its appearance just before the Crash that was to bring an end to the swinish postwar decade.... The true international note had been struck."[14]

It is not surprising that Remarque's next novel, *The Road Back* (*Der Weg zurück*; 1931), revolving around the problems that a number of soldiers returning home after World War I encounter while trying to adjust to their old environment, was compared to *All Quiet on the Western Front* and deemed by many to be wanting. Whereas many German reviews, just as in the case of *All Quiet on the Western Front*, exposed Remarque's failure to take a political stand in this later work, most American reviews, on the other hand, were surprisingly positive, even when they compared the book to *All Quiet on the Western Front*. Some critics judged it, indeed, better than *All Quiet on the Western Front*. "When I am asked whether the book is as good as 'All Quiet' I answer that it is better. As a literary production, I think that is incontestable. Remarque is a growing craftsman. But as a tract, it is also superior. It probes deeper."[15] The reason was apparently again that the American reviewers valued the book for its convincing rendering of the human verisimilitudes, not for its possible political implications and arguments. Thus Clifton P. Fadiman wrote in the *Nation*, "The book's verity, its indignation are inescapable. One does not read it. One cowers under it. You cannot tell from it whether Remarque is a great writer or, indeed, whether he is a writer at all. The story jets forth like thick blood from a wound.... Here is a terrible tale to be told, directly, frontally, quickly. And it is told."[16] And none less than William Faulkner stated, "It moves you, as watching a child making mud pies on the day of its mother's funeral moves you."[17] Albeit most comparisons with *All Quiet* did not cast shadows, some reviewers, nevertheless, were

---

[14] *Book Week*, 23 October 1966, 6, 12.

[15] P. H., *Christian Century*, 8 July 1931, 904.

[16] *Nation*, 27 May 1931, 584.

[17] *New Republic*, 20 May 1931, 23.

beginning to measure by aesthetic standards, rightfully pointing out the artificiality of the characters or the calculated effects of the rather simplistically constructed stories. Thus, William Faulkner continued his review, "Yet at the end there is still that sense of missing significance, the feeling that, like so much that emerges from a losing side in any contest, and particularly from Germany since 1918, it was created primarily for the Western trade, to sell among the heathen like colored glass. From beyond the sentimentality, the defeat and the talking, this fact at least has emerged: America has been conquered not by the German soldiers that died in French and Flemish trenches, but by the German soldiers that died in German books." And Frances Warfield came to a similar conclusion. "At any rate, Herr Remarque's dramatic effects, which in the first book were used superbly, in the second have a slight but unmistakable flavor of Hollywood."[18]

Remarque continued his story about former soldiers trying to adjust to the Germany of the Weimar Republic with the sentimental novel *Three Comrades* (*Drei Kameraden*; 1937), which he completed during his exile, and which could no longer be published in Germany.[19] The most striking feature of the American reviews is that *Three Comrades* was no longer being compared to *All Quiet*. It seems that either enough time had passed to judge Remarque's new books on their own merits, or that the subject matter was so radically different that a comparison did not suggest itself. Nonetheless, reviewers did point out similarities to Hemingway's *The Sun Also Rises*. "The sense of emasculation, though spiritual, is as definite; the constant drinking and talk about drinking as prevalent ...; the aged hope and the young despair.... Yet in spite of striking similarities, the tone of this new book is quieter, the wit less brittle, the living more intimately portrayed, almost homely."[20] Although no one grumbled about the excessive sentimentality of the love story — the movies of the late thirties and forties were replete with such an element — several American reviewers, however, observed the book's lack of political significance. "The political significance of

---

[18] *Forum and Century*, July 1931, ix.

[19] The first German edition appeared at the exile publishing company, Querido, in Amsterdam.

[20] B. E. Bettinger, *New Republic*, 28 April 1937, 364.

Remarque's record of Germany in 1928 does not quite attain the stature of that of his former works. Yet the frustration of that period and the inchoate character of a movement which was later destined to sweep the country [national socialism — H. W.] are clearly portrayed."[21] And Harry Levin, the reviewer of the *Nation*, alluded to Remarque's possible future difficulties as a writer in exile who might quickly lose the realities of his own country. "As a prophet, Erich Maria Remarque has lost his ardor because his millennium has already come and gone and because whatever happens afterward is to him uniformly trivial. He definitely resents having his chaos disturbed. Therefore, even after another ten years, it would be unwarranted to expect from him an incisive depiction of the country he no longer knows. In the meanwhile, 'Three Comrades' has successfully appeared in a woman's magazine, and nobody is going to burn it."[22] Although this judgment about *Three Comrades* expresses some truth, one might add that Mr. Levin himself was obviously no prophet. Bernard DeVoto in the *Saturday Review* stated, "It contrives to tell, gravely and implacably, more about Germany in the vortex than has been told in any other novel. One reads it with an intensity so quiet that not till the end is it recognizable as desperation."[23]

As is evident from the critical tone of these reviews, Remarque was desperately in need of a new theme for his novels; he found it in the plight of the refugees from Hitler Germany. In 1941 he published his first novel dealing with this topic, *Flotsam* (*Liebe deinen Nächsten*, 1941). As the Canadian Remarque scholar C. R. Owen wrote in 1988, referring to the American edition only,[24] "The reviews of the book were not as glowing as those of most of Remarque's novels, the differing merit of each chapter, as well as the tendency of sentimentality and melodrama being criticized; the sales were very disappoint-

---

[21] *Christian Science Monitor*, 8 May 1937, 16.

[22] *Nation*, 24 April 1937, 485.

[23] *Saturday Review*, 1 May 1937, 3.

[24] The first German edition also appeared at Querido in Amsterdam, 1941, but soon afterwards the Germans invaded the Netherlands. The entire edition was subsequently lost. The German edition was republished in Stockholm in 1949. See Owen, 234.

ing...."[25] Any positive aspects were usually outweighed by perceived negative ones. Thus the anonymous reviewer of *Time* wrote, "The theme of *Flotsam* is one of the most massive, intimate and terrible derangements of human living within human memory. Remarque, able as he is, is not quite equal to it; perhaps no human talent could be. Besides, *Flotsam* has some lyric flights that droop in mid-air; some touches of sentimental sententiousness; some comedy too national quite to cross a border; one or two bits almost of cheapness. But Remarque, like Hemingway, has the rare ability to produce writing which is both a genuine work of art and popular; and to embody a generation. For that reason *Flotsam* is a deeply moving story that makes painfully clear, to readers who have forgotten or never understood, the real meaning of the words *exile, emigré, refugee*."[26] After calling Remarque again "a skillful and powerful writer," B. R. Redman, the reviewer of the *Saturday Review*, cautions, "Remarque has, I think, created a fictional pattern that exhibits more artifice than art, and owes much to cinematic technique.... Repetition, approaching monotony, dulls the reader's sensitivity, diminishes the intensity of his response on successive occasions."[27] Other reviewers pointed out that before its publication in book form the novel had been made into a movie entitled *So Ends Our Night*. "Perhaps this accounts for much of the melodrama," Klaus Lamprecht wrote in the *New Republic*, continuing, "in fact, one has the feeling that Mr. Remarque might very well have written the great novel which the powerful and tragic theme suggests, had he not subjected himself to the rules of the screen."[28] And Robert Littell, in the *Yale Review*, arrives at the verdict, "It [*Flotsam*] is not up to Mr. Remarque's standard."[29]

This unsuccess notwithstanding, Remarque resumed the theme of refugees from Nazi Germany in his next novel, *Arch of Triumph*, (1945; German edition: *Arc de Triomphe*, 1946). This novel became Re-

---

[25] Owen, 234f.

[26] *Time*, 28 April 1941, 92.

[27] *Saturday Review*, 26 April 1941, 5.

[28] *New Republic*, 2 June 1941, 768.

[29] *Yale Review* 30 (Summer 1941): 10.

marque's second worldwide success; in the United States alone over 2 million copies were sold. In its combination of being a novel about murder and love, and refugees in Paris in 1939, i.e., right before the outbreak of World War II, the novel came rather close to the genre of nonserious literature. As a result, the reviews in the major newspapers were mixed, most of them tending to be negative. However, the themes, the plot, and their professional, if not to say slick, execution accounted not only for its great success on the book market but also for the disenchantment of some reviewers. "What is so disappointing about 'Arch of Triumph' is that it is slickly workmanlike, readable, quite exciting and interesting in spots with prose which often is suddenly very fine (for a short space), and that beyond that it is nothing."[30] Several critics, particularly those of Christian publications, had strong misgivings about many supposedly immoral plot elements. "A nauseating hodgepodge of blatant atheism, gross immorality and planned murder.... If you are interested in the management of French houses of prostitution; if you wish to learn how to commit murder without suffering the penalty of the law; if you desire to spend a few hours in the company of as low a set of scoundrels as we have met in the pages of one story you will read this ultra-realistic novel."[31] Other Christian publications, such as the *Christian Science Monitor*,[32] came to similar conclusions. The many surgical scenes were often singled out as too gruesome and realistic, and the love story was considered particularly weak.[33] Only the gravity of the refugee theme seems to have won over other critics who might otherwise have tended to be more negative. Thus, Charles Poore wrote in the *New York Times*, "It makes absorbing reading, though it is sometimes overcontrived; it is briskly paced though the lacquered writing lacks the simple spontaneity of 'All Quiet on the Western Front.' And through its penetrating stories of human fortitude it should stir even those of us who have been telling ourselves that the people who helped us win our common victory are not really

---

[30] A. C. Spectorsky, *Book Week*, 20 January 1946, 1.

[31] *Catholic World* 162 [1945/46]: 477.

[32] 22 January 1946, 16.

[33] Orville Prescott, *Yale Review* 35 (Spring 1946): 573.

as badly off as some would say."[34] Nevertheless, it is astounding to see that a book that for months was on the nation's best-seller list received so many critical and often devastating reviews. The same phenomenon is visible in the case of many movies today; the most financially successful ones are not always so well received by the critics. Ironically, the critics are powerless in curtailing the financial success if it is produced by professional acumen and routine. It is interesting to note that the film version of *Arch of Triumph* (1948), with Ingrid Bergman and Charles Boyer, turned out to be a financial disaster, perhaps a result of the poor casting.

In his next novel, *Spark of Life* (*Der Funke Leben*; 1952), Remarque presented the atrocities committed in German concentration camps. The German reviewers upbraided him for having tackled a topic of which he had no firsthand experience. Such a criticism was pitched at him in Germany whenever he addressed the Third Reich. The American reviews were, without exception, positive, and the book swiftly reached the American best-seller list. Some reviewers recognized the use of stereotypes in the characterization of the S.S. men but added a justification that "Neubauer the camp commandant, Weber his assistant, Steinbrenner and Breuer the sadistic S.S. guards, seem to be stereotypes, but all the evidence that came out of Belsen and Buchenwald would indicate that these are faithful stereotypes."[35] The same reviewer concluded by dismissing potential criticism that Remarque was not an eyewitness, "But no actual survivor of a concentration camp has been able to draw up such a savage or eloquent indictment as has Erich Maria Remarque in 'Spark of Life.'" Harvey Wados, in the *Nation*, called it an "utterly uncompromising and courageous book, the more so because its subject matter is such that it cannot be transferred to the screen; nor is it calculated to win a wider reading public for Mr. Remarque, since despite its idealism 'Spark of Life' is one of the most brutal books of our time."[36] The reviewer from *Newsweek* called it "harrowing": "the book principally communicates a world of filth and

---

[34] *New York Times*, 20 January 1946, 1.

[35] Quentin Reynolds, *New York Times Book Review*, 27 January 1952.

[36] *Nation*, 16 February 1952, 158.

pain, hunger, disease, torment, torture, an unbearable background of continuous agony and fear." Recognizing the underlying positive theme of the book — the resurgence of the human spirit amidst the horror of a concentration camp — the reviewer asserted that "Remarque has succeeded in making hope the sustaining quality of human life, and in so doing has created the finest imaginative work on one of the darkest passages of human history."[37] This irrepressible confidence in the will to survive and in the power of the human spirit in the face of all moral and physical degradation, personified in a Hemingwayesque protagonist struggling to win a moral victory, was particularly appealing to American reviewers and to the reading public as well. Thus, W. V. Clark wrote in the *New Republic*, "If one cannot read 'Spark of Life' with a sense of discovery, it is nonetheless well worth reading for what it surely is, a penetrating, heartening, consistently interesting dramatization of the power of the human spirit to survive in a world beset by subhuman dogmatisms. And that is a great deal, a very much needed great deal."[38]

With *A Time to Love and a Time to Die* (*Zeit zu leben und Zeit zu sterben*; 1954) Remarque had written another war novel, this time centering on World War II. The locus of action, a place beset by bombing raids, is the hometown of its hero instead of the Russian front. In addition, a love story assumes equal importance with the war action. Although a number of elements alluding to the Third Reich and its ideology had been excised in the German edition — many for the sake of greater authenticity, and not necessarily in order to spare the feelings of the Germans[39] — the German reviews again reproached Remarque for having written a book about a configuration of events he himself had not eyewitnessed. In the United States, however, the book swiftly made the best-seller list. The reviews in the major newspapers and magazines were largely positive. A number of reviewers compared

[37] *Newsweek*, 28 Jan. 1952, 47f.

[38] *New Republic*, 25 February 1952, 18.

[39] This charge was made by Franz Carl Weiskopf, "Die politischen Valenzen des Dr. Witsch oder der kastrierte Remarque," *Neue Deutsche Literatur* 3, no. 2 (1955): 99–107; also in F. C. W., *Gesammelte Werke* (Berlin, 1960), 328–40. Also: F. C. W., "Der kastrierte Remarque: Nochmals über den Roman *Zeit zu leben und Zeit zu sterben*," *Neue Deutsche Literatur* 5, no. 4 (1957): 108–26.

the book favorably to *All Quiet on the Western Front*.[40] However, whereas Paul Engle in the *Chicago Sunday Times* praised the "authentic feeling for the small details of street and food and smell, and for the individual qualities of men,"[41] or, as J. G. Harrison did in the *Christian Science Monitor*, claiming the "accurate evocation of an historical experience which is still far too early for the world to forget with safety,"[42] others, on the other hand, pointed out its artificial and superficial aspects, which the American reviewers easily recognized despite their lack of firsthand experience of the time and place of action. C. J. Rolo in the *Atlantic Monthly* qualified his praise, "Mr. Remarque's novel is a gripping story, full of vivid incident, and at times genuinely moving. But all in all, it has a slightly glib, faintly manufactured flavor."[43] The *New York Times* commented in a similar vein, "This is an agreeable book in its attitudes and it is told with well-practiced talent. But the inner realities do not measure up to the outer ones. Instead of being made more intense and complex by the violences which surround it, the love affair takes on some of the unreality of the ruined city itself, seen at night with only the moon to light it."[44] Fortunately for Remarque, his honorable intentions of waging war against the inhumanity of ideological systems was acutely perceived. "Remarque's voice somehow carries beyond the other voices speaking for our times, for he has not ceased throughout his career as a writer to use the full power of his emotion to excoriate war's inhumanity."[45] It is perplexing how the principal themes of the book — the battles of conscience, the search for the truth of the psychological and moral effects of the Third Reich upon the German people, and in consequence what, therefore, each individual's responsibility should be — were rarely recognized.

As a result of its philosophical probing, i.e., its merely alluding to political moods, most American reviewers did not know what to think

---

[40] E.g. *Miami Herald*, 30 May 1954; *Philadelphia Inquirer*, 23 May 1954.

[41] *Chicago Sunday Times*, 23 May 1954, 3.

[42] *Christian Science Monitor*, 20 May 1954, 10.

[43] *Atlantic Monthly*, July 1954, 83.

[44] R. G. Davis, *New York Times*, 23 May 1954, 42.

[45] Virgilia Peterson, *New York Herald Tribune Book Review*, 23 May 1954, 1.

The Novels of Erich Maria Remarque in American Reviews 223

about *The Black Obelisk* (*Der schwarze Obelisk*, 1956; Engl. 1957). Subtitled *The Story of a Belated Youth*, it is a heavily autobiographical story set in Remarque's home town, Osnabrück, during the escalated inflation of 1923. While some reviewers were able to view it as in the tradition of D. H. Lawrence, Malraux, Silone, Koestler, and George Orwell,[46] others saw some of the scenes in the tradition of Rabelais.[47] However, what eluded most of them was the hidden agenda: first, to write a book pondering basic questions about life and death; second, to write a political novel about the Weimar Republic and its road toward Hitler's fascism. Thus, even the positive review in the *New York Herald Tribune Book Review* by F. T. Marsh stated full of uncertainty, "Remarque has written a brilliant satirical novel, witty, often very funny, picaresque and serious at the same time, filled with sadness, as it would have to be. I have enjoyed every minute of it; but how to assess it as a fictional history of its time — I am not so sure."[48] And F. C. Hirsch, in the *Library Journal*, stated, "The author of 'All Quiet on the Western Front' is not at his best in his latest novel. The book, while not completely lacking in powerful scenes, fails to produce the same kind of historical reality which made Remarque's best works such important documents of an era."[49] Even Richard Plant, whose first sentence called the book "one of Erich Maria Remarque's best" concluded, "The Black Obelisk, by the way, a formerly unsalable item of Kroll & Bros., provides a marvelous, half-uncanny, half-comic ending. Too bad, Chapter 25 had to follow — a dry summary of later events. Up to Chapter 24 the novel is as full-bodied, delightful, and flavorsome as the wine consumed with gusto and in large quantities throughout the book."[50] He thus completely missed the book's political message contained in Chapter 25. Hence, it is obvious that the expectations raised by the previous Remarque books prevented the reviewers from seeing this novel as revealing a different kind of

---

[46] Maxwell Geismar, *New York Times*, 4 April 1957, 4.

[47] Richard Plant, *Saturday Review*, 20 April 1957, 22.

[48] *New York Herald Tribune Book Review*, 7 April 1957, 3.

[49] *Library Journal*, 15 March 1957, 752.

[50] *Saturday Review*, 20 April 1957, 22.

Remarque, one who comingles philosophical pondering and political expression.

In *Heaven Has No Favorites* (*Der Himmel kennt keine Günstlinge*; 1961) Remarque resumed his ruminations on the meaning of life and death; this time they were articulated through a love affair between a race car driver and a tuberculosis patient. Eliciting ambivalent reactions, Remarque was scolded by the German press for not having written another *Magic Mountain*, and he was simultaneously lauded by the American reviewers for his skill as a writer and reproved for his tendency towards sentimentality and philosophical platitude. This confused and mixed reaction becomes obvious in juxtaposing a review in the *New Yorker* with one in the *San Francisco Chronicle*. To begin, the *New Yorker* accused it of lacking plot. "Nothing memorable is said in the course of this quite long novel, and the plot is so skimpy that to reveal even half an inch of it would be to reveal all."[51] Next, the *San Francisco Chronicle* called it "Remarque's tightest, most suspenseful story to date, lacking the richness of most of his other works but compensating with an intense, fast-paced narrative."[52] The *Saturday Review* published one of the most devastating reviews, attacking the novel from almost every possible angle. "One looked forward to Mr. Remarque's ninth book if only because not even a reasonably good novel has yet been written grounded on automobile racing, as dramatic a sport as mankind has devised. Unhappily, 'Heaven Has No Favorites' does not alter the record except to add one more bad book to the list.... The ramblings on life, death, and the wonder of it all are distressing, the love-making ... is often charming; the automobile racing bears little relation to reality.... But it is in the matter of preoccupation with death, which is the primary concern of the book, that Remarque's failure is plainest.... However, my principal objection in this sort of novel is to the hackneyed treatment of race drivers ... and all the machine-masters of our age as brooding mystics or hysterical fatalists."[53] The *New York Herald Tribune Lively Arts*, proclaimed the

---

[51] *New Yorker*, 8 April 1961, 174.

[52] Curt Gentry, *San Francisco Chronicle*, 2 April 1961, 8.

[53] K. W. Purdy, *Saturday Review*, 15 April 1961, 19.

dialogue "studied and unnatural."[54] The *New York Times Book Review* sensed that the book "sometimes avoids the sentimental by mere millimeters."[55] One suspects that out of respect for the writer many reviewers refrained from arrant devastation, merely mentioning their criticisms in passing. In keeping with previous Remarque novels, motley reviews did not prevent the book from reaching the best-seller list.

Remarque's next novel, *The Night in Lisbon* (1964; *Die Nacht von Lissabon*, 1962, rev. 1963) climbed quickly to the number one slot on the American bestseller list. It is peculiar how the American reviews were couched in such vaguely positive terms. To illustrate, Orville Prescott, in his review in the *New York Times* pronounced it "a brilliant novel and a strange one, not completely successful, but hauntingly moving.... If neither Schwarz nor his enigmatic wife ever seems wholly comprehensible or wholly real, their symbolic roles as the victims of the cruelty and madness of war and Nazism are eloquent and moving. Mr. Remarque's proficiency in capturing emotional atmosphere and the special atmospheres of particular places and circumstances is as great as ever. His book rises to peaks of poetic feeling as if it were both a curse and a lamentation."[56] As always, comparison with Remarque's other books offered itself, and Maxwell Geismar in the *New York Times Book Review* stated that "now, at the age of 66, he has produced what may be his best novel."[57] As previously, other reviewers utilized *All Quiet on the Western Front* as a basis of comparison, finding *The Night in Lisbon* to be, notwithstanding, a good novel. "Remarque long ago mastered the art of keeping a story moving without at the same time appearing too glib or slick. His tortured characters here are convincing as well as sympathetic. No *All Quiet on the Western Front* (how could there be another?), this is first-rate Remarque, with less philosophizing than some of his others, but meaningful and pertinent."[58] Whereas

---

[54] Rose Feld, *New York Herald Tribune Lively Arts*, 16 April 1961, 36.

[55] Frederic Morton, *New York Times Book Review*, 26 March 1961.

[56] *New York Times*, 27 March 1964, 25.

[57] *New York Times Book Review*, 22 March 1964.

[58] William S. Lynch, *Saturday Review*, 25 April 1964, 38.

most reviewers discussed the love story, the theme of exile, and the way it is treated, only Ernest S. Pisko, in his review in the *Christian Science Monitor*, was able to uncover the philosophical theme of the novel: "It is a flight and a love story — the love of Josef Schwarz and his critically ailing wife Helene; but it also is the story of man's search for the higher meaning of life and for the significance of the defeat he suffers by clinging to a 'reality' that crumbles in his hands."[59] It is thus astonishing to observe that American reviewers repeatedly measured Remarque's novels by their story and smoothness of writing, and confessed their inability to grasp his intended message.

Remarque's posthumously published novel, *Shadows in Paradise* (1972; *Schatten im Paradies*, 1971), did capture a spot on the German best-seller list — perhaps as the result of an enormous advertisement campaign.[60] The American reviews conversely were almost uniformly devastating. One could surmise that this novel, about a German refugee in New York, lacks sufficient action. As P. A. Doyle, in *Best Sellers*, pointed out: "With this novel, Remarque, who died in 1970, has not helped his reputation as a significant writer.... [His] book drags heavily and seems almost interminable. Relatively little action occurs, not one character in the novel arouses particular interest, and the ... dialogue [is] for the most part repetitious, trivial, and tedious."[61] Several other reviews endeavored to isolate positive traits in the minor characters and in the depiction of the atmosphere of the New York of the forties, but they were nonetheless unable to overlook the nostalgia and sentimentality pervading the novel. For example, D. W. McCullough in the *Saturday Review* states, "Remarque's last novel ... is basically plotless, a nostalgic look — if nostalgia can be touched with bitterness — at refugee life in New York City during the early Forties. Remarque himself experienced such an episode, and the novel is best when it simply reflects the local color of the period: the seedy lobbies of Times Square hotels, the garrulous reunions over goulash at the apartment of a prosperous refugee, the funerals of friends who survived Hitler's

---

[59] *Christian Science Monitor*, 9 April 1964, 7.

[60] See Owen, 304.

[61] *Best Sellers*, 1 March 1972, 531.

Germany only to die of cancer or suicide in the States.... The real work of [this novel] is found in this gallery of burnt-out cases. The romantic tales the author sometimes surrounds them with are the thinnest sort of frames."[62] Robert Kirsch began his review in the *Los Angeles Times* with the statement "There is a certain sadness in writing about Erich Maria Remarque's last novel, SHADOWS IN PARADISE.... It is published posthumously. Remarque died over a year ago. I don't intend it cruelly but his life as a novelist ended long before that." And he concluded, "Remarque is trying; but the truth is that he has run out of material and his powers of invention were not equal to the dearth of lore provided by the wars. He, too, I think was a victim of those times."[63]

In his review of *The Night in Lisbon* Maxwell Geismar reflected upon the reception of Remarque's books in the United States, "Now the point is that after Remarque's early success with 'All Quiet on the Western Front' in 1929 — and to a lesser degree with the sequel novels, 'The Road Back' and 'Three Comrades,' in the 1930's — his reputation began to fade somewhat. In the forties, with such works as 'Arch of Triumph,' he had settled, apparently, for a kind of charming entertainment and love romance, yet I remember that even as I read that novel with a sense of disappointment, I was still beguiled by it.... 'The Black Obelisk' (1957) was a brilliantly satirical novel of German life at the outset of Hitler and his National Socialism...."[64] These comments summarize the reception of Erich Maria Remarque's works by literary critics in the United States up to 1957. In the following, I would like to summarize my own findings predicated on a "review of the reviews":

1. As the author of *All Quiet on the Western Front*, Remarque was hailed as having written the greatest war novel of all time and as someone who was able to describe in starkly realistic colors the suffering of the ordinary soldier in the war, regardless of his nationality. The boldness and timelessness of Remarque's observations were chiefly

---

[62] *Saturday Review*, 26 Feb. 1972, 78.

[63] *Los Angeles Times*, 17 Feb. 1972.

[64] *New York Times Book Review*, 22 March 1964.

responsible for the book's American (and international) success. All other novels spanning his career were, to a greater or lesser extent, measured by this yardstick.

2. In spite of its perceived aesthetic shortcomings, *The Road Back*, on account of its moving verity and indignation, still found grace in the eyes of many American reviewers; it was, furthermore, even considered by some to be equal or superior to *All Quiet on the Western Front*.

3. When *Three Comrades* was published, the critics' enthusiasm was somewhat diluted because of the work's want of political significance and its — mostly unrecognized — maudlin disposition.

4. *Flotsam* may be considered to mark the low point of Remarque's career in the United States. Although it garnered universal respect for the refugee theme, its melodramatic execution and episodic structure (possibly under the influence of Hollywood) failed to marshal universal approval.

5. The reviews of *Arch of Triumph* were not much more favorable. Nonetheless, in spite of the castigation of the novel for its formulaic slickness and the moral depravity of its characters and locales, it became Remarque's second worldwide bestseller.

6. *Spark of Life* earned respect for its actual theme, the power of the human spirit to survive in a German concentration camp, but not for its aesthetic qualities.

7. While *A Time to Love and a Time to Die* was hailed by many for its accuracy in describing the effects of war within Germany, others recognized its artificial and unrealistic aspects. Furthermore, they largely missed the battle of conscience in the mind of its protagonist.

8. Only a few reviewers possessed the mental acumen to perceive that *The Black Obelisk* was a novel of philosophical depth and quality, containing one of Remarque's clearest attacks on German nationalism

and a monition of the resurgence of national socialism; the rest of the reviewers merely noted the book's picaresque, satirical side.

9. *Heaven Has No Favorites* brought predominantly negative reviews that rebuked Remarque for his ostensibly superficial philosophizing about death, and for the novel's weak plot development.

10. *The Night in Lisbon* was seldom acknowledged for its philosophical theme of the preservation of the past through memory; it was able to succeed, however, on its other merits; for example, its convincing characterization and its ability to capture the atmosphere of emigré life.

11. *Shadows in Paradise* justifiably reaped mostly negative reviews. The American reviewers easily spotted the novel's weaknesses — lack of action and too much nostalgia — and commended it only for its minor characters and the re-creation of the New York atmosphere of the forties.

What distinguished the American critics' appreciation of Remarque's works from that of the European critics is essentially that the German critics categorized him as a one-book author — actually as a literary lightweight whose philosophizing was almost embarrassing. In the United States Remarque was not only consistently ranked alongside the great contemporary American writers, such as Ernest Hemingway, but he was also compared to the great German writers of the twentieth century. To illustrate this, I would like to quote what Ernest S. Pisko wrote in his review of *The Night in Lisbon*. "If one wishes to assign Remarque a rank among contemporary German writers one has to place him below Thomas Mann but at least equal to Heinrich Böll and certainly above such experimental and intentionally murky novelists as Uwe Johnson. Since 'All Quiet' Remarque has kept growing in human experience and literary craftsmanship and kept performing his original role as observer and chronicler of private lives buffeted by the storms of political events."[65] As such a "chronicler of a time of tribulation,"[66]

---

[65] *Christian Science Monitor*, 9 April 1964, 7.

[66] Ibid.

Remarque earned himself a much higher place in the critics' esteem than he ever could have in Germany, where during the Third Reich years his books could not be published and where his first books that came out after the World War II were met with cold reservation.

"Brecht, Motherhood, and Justice": The Reception of *The Caucasian Chalk Circle* in the United States

SIEGFRIED MEWS

"GERMAN LITERATURE, UNLIKE THAT of France, Italy, pre-revolutionary Russia, or Scandinavia, is on the whole so remote from the taste and the aesthetic conventions of the English-speaking world that its influence does not often make itself felt," British critic Martin Esslin, author of the influential study *Brecht: A Choice of Evils* (1959), maintains.[1] Indeed, whereas American literature has been widely read in the German-speaking countries since the nineteenth century and has experienced a revival of interest in (West) Germany since World War II, German literature has played but a modest role in the United States. Moreover, the fascination that the topic of "America" held for many German writers[2] — a fascination initially inspired by enthusiasm, but during the last few decades largely motivated by critical distance and satirical intent — is hardly matched by a reciprocal interest in Germany on the part of American literati. The present volume, which charts the fortunes of German writers in America, seeks to correct, by

---

[1] Martin Esslin, *Brecht: A Choice of Evils. A Critical Study of the Man, His Work and His Opinion* (London: Eyre & Sprottiswoode, 1959); 4th, rev. ed. (London: Methuen, 1984). All references are to the American paperback edition: Martin Esslin, *Brecht: The Man and His Work* (Garden City: Anchor Books, 1961), xv.

[2] See, for example, *Amerika! New Images in German Literature*, ed. Heinz D. Osterle (New York: Lang, 1989).

documenting the reception of German literature in the U. S., the notion — held by Esslin and others — that it has had no impact here.

Among the comparatively few twentieth-century authors from the German-speaking countries who have achieved recognition that goes far beyond the narrow circle of those with a vested professional interest in German literature, we must count Bertolt Brecht (1898–1956), the playwright from Augsburg. Brecht's significance may be summarized as follows:

> Bertolt Brecht's status as one of the major playwrights of the twentieth century is largely uncontested. In addition to writing a significant body of plays that are performed all over the world, Brecht also developed in a number of theoretical writings his theory of 'epic' or 'dialectic' theater that he applied to the 'model' productions of his own plays in the early 1950s. Furthermore, practically from the beginning of his literary career [in the early twenties] Brecht has been considered a poet of considerable power and originality; more recently, his prose fiction has attracted increased attention — although Brecht the prose fiction writer has not yet been fully recognized.[3]

It was hardly an exaggeration, then, when Esslin credited Brecht with being "one of the most significant writers of this century"[4] — an opinion that has been repeatedly echoed. As early as 1959 — approximately three years after the playwright's death — Esslin predicted, "[Brecht's] influence on the theatre may well prove as powerful as that of Kafka on the novel."[5] The spreading fame of Brecht, the playwright and director of the Berliner Ensemble, a troupe headed by his actress wife, Helene Weigel, was then mostly a (West) European phenomenon. Although one may argue that Esslin's prediction has essentially come true — biographer Ronald Hayman writes, "Bertolt Brecht is without

---

[3] Siegfried Mews, "Bertolt Brecht," in *German Fiction Writers, 1914–1945*, ed. James Hardin, vol. 56 of *Dictionary of Literary Biography* (Detroit: Gale Research, 1987), 42.

[4] Esslin, xv.

[5] Ibid.

question *the* most influential playwright of the twentieth century"[6] — Brecht's ascendance to quasi-canonical status in this country was not necessarily a foregone conclusion. Despite his residence in Santa Monica, California, during his exile in the United States from 1941 to 1947, he did not succeed in making a lasting impression on the literary and theatrical scene. Only after his departure from America was he eventually recognized as a major force in the theater.

In the case of Brecht, who had turned to Marxism in the late twenties and whose plays as well as dramatic theory are infused with his Marxist convictions, aesthetic conventions and literary criteria were not the only factors exerting influence on how his plays were received in the American theater. Rather, the playwright's political stance contributed significantly to his renown or — depending on the respective critic's perspective — ill repute. Esslin put the "curious paradox" of Brecht in a nutshell, "Brecht was a Communist, he was also a great poet. But while the West liked his poetry and distrusted his Communism, the Communists exploited his political convictions while they regarded his artistic aims and achievements with suspicion."[7] Esslin's pithy formulation of 1959, which he reiterated more than a quarter of a century later in the fourth (British) edition of his *Brecht* (1984), was originally coined in the cold-war climate of the fifties and early sixties; it has not entirely lost its applicability in the eighties and nineties.

At any rate, Esslin's major thesis that, in a psychologizing vein, proceeds from Brecht's biography and posits his constant struggling between rational intent on the one hand and poetic, subconscious impulses on the other ("reason versus instinct"[8] or "alternation between anarchy and discipline")[9] is not universally shared by Brecht critics. Yet Esslin's study, "appreciative of his genius but critical of his political convictions,"[10] ultimately redounds to Brecht's credit and is

---

[6] Ronald Hayman, *Brecht: A Biography* (New York: Oxford University Press, 1983), dust jacket. My italics.

[7] Esslin, xvi.

[8] Ibid., 238.

[9] Ibid., xii.

[10] Ibid., ix.

a far cry from recent attempts to discredit the playwright by implicating him in the sinister plot of poisoning innocent American minds.

In his best-seller *The Closing of the American Mind* Allan Bloom cites as a conspicuous example of the "astonishing Americanization" of German value relativism — a consequence of the Nietzschean revaluation of values — "the smiling face of Louis Armstrong as he belts out the words of his great hit 'Mack the Knife.' As most American intellectuals know, it is a translation of the song 'Mackie Messer' from *The Threepenny Opera*, a monument of Weimar Republic popular culture, written by two heroes of the artistic Left, Bertolt Brecht and Kurt Weill.... Lotte Lenya's rendition of this song has long stood with Marlene Dietrich's singing *'Ich bin von Kopf bis Fuss auf Liebe eingestellt'* in the *Blue Angel* as the symbol of a charming, neurotic, sexy, decadent longing for some hazy fulfillment not quite present to the consciousness." After all, Bloom asserts, in "that ambiguous Weimar atmosphere ... anything was possible for people who sang of the joy of the knife in cabarets."[11]

Bloom's sweeping statement acknowledges the much-debated extraordinary flourishing of the arts and the creative ferment in Weimar Germany — particularly in its capital, Berlin. Yet his stance is reminiscent of that taken, for example, by Otto Friedrich. Friedrich's book is appropriately titled *Before the Deluge*; in rhetorical overkill it is advertised as portraying the twenties in Berlin as "a time of political upheaval, economic instability, and a moral climate whose decadence and perversity was rivaled only by a declining Roman Empire."[12] However, whereas Friedrich tends to wax nostalgic and employ the allure of sinful decadence in the manner of the musical and film *Cabaret*, Bloom sternly condemns both the morally ambiguous climate of Berlin in the twenties and, by implication, his chief witnesses for Weimar decadence, Brecht and Weill. This condemnation rests on shaky foundations inasmuch as Bloom reduces a voluminous body of writing that is going to encompass thirty volumes in the new edition of Brecht's

---

[11] Allan Bloom, *The Closing of the American Mind* (New York: Touchstone Book, 1987), 151, 154.

[12] Otto Friedrich, *Before the Deluge: A Portrait of Berlin in the 1920's* (New York: Avon Books, 1973), back cover.

works[13] to a single play or, rather, a single song. Moreover, Bloom fails to notice that in "Mack the Knife" a contrast is established between the openly rapacious shark and knife-concealing Mack, whose threatening nature and deadly intent — like those of capitalist exploiters — are not obvious at all. "Mack the Knife," then, is a warning — admittedly a subtle one — against "the joy of the knife" rather than a celebration of it.

True, *The Threepenny Opera* is an immensely popular play, which in the Marc Blitzstein version and with Weill's wife, Lotte Lenya, in the role of the prostitute Jenny, opened on 10 March 1954 in the Theatre de Lys in New York City for a seven-year run with a total of 2,611 performances. But one may legitimately question whether the play represents the quintessence of Brecht's theater. In fact, Bloom's reductionist view of Brecht as the author of *The Threepenny Opera* and of the play as a symptomatic expression of — rather than an artistic manifestation running counter to — prevailing Weimar cultural and political norms harks back to an earlier phase of Brecht's reception in this country and is indicative of the continuing — and publicity-generating — controversy about the playwright more than thirty years after his death. For example, the 1956 obituary notice in *Time* magazine, which is tinged with cold-war rhetoric, reads, "Died: Bertolt ('Bert') Brecht, 58, slight, bespectacled German playwright (librettist for Kurt Weill's *Threepenny Opera*) who, according to ex-Communist Arthur Koestler, sold Marxism 'with great brilliance and intellectual dishonesty' to 'the snobs and parlor Communists' of Europe; of a heart attack; in East Berlin."[14]

Not much progress seems to have been made over the last thirty years in terms of a differentiated approach to Brecht, the dishonest salesman of Marxism in 1956, defender of Stalinism in 1966[15] and insidious poisoner of American minds in 1987. Admittedly, the

---

[13] Bertolt Brecht, *Werke: Große kommentierte Berliner und Frankfurter Ausgabe*, 30 vols., ed. Werner Hecht et al. (Frankfurt am Main: Suhrkamp, 1988–1991).

[14] *Time*, 27 Aug. 1956, 72.

[15] See Hannah Arendt, "What is Permitted to Jove," *New Yorker*, 5 Nov. 1966; repr. "Bertolt Brecht: 1898–1956," in *Men in Dark Times* (New York: Harcourt, 1968), 207–50.

denunciatory tone of the statements in *Time* magazine and *The Closing of the American Mind* may be considered extreme in the broad spectrum of opinions on Brecht and his work. While such statements are indicative of a clearly political slant, that is, the assessment of Brecht in terms of his presumed or actual ideology, individual plays were received in a more differentiated manner by American critics. Although there are some pertinent studies with useful information in the vast literature on Brecht,[16] it is virtually impossible to give an even remotely exhaustive account of the reception of Brecht's total oeuvre in this country. Hence one individual play may serve as an instructive example of the difficulties Brecht's works encountered. However, for various reasons *The Caucasian Chalk Circle* (*Chalk Circle*) rather than *The Threepenny Opera*, according to Esslin, "the only play by Brecht that has achieved real popular success,"[17] seems more germane to illustrate the vagaries of the reception process.

First of all, the status of *Chalk Circle* as a major play in the Brecht canon is uncontested. Esslin flatly states, "With its poetry, its use of narrators [the Singer], its two-pronged construction [the successively presented Grusha and Azdak 'stories'], its stylized action — the negative, wicked characters are masked — *The Caucasian Chalk Circle* is the outstanding example of the technique of the 'epic' drama. It is one of Brecht's greatest plays,"[18] and Brecht critic and translator Eric Bentley views it as "one of the finest examples of Brecht's revolutionary approach to theater, [which] has become a classic of the world repertoire and is widely produced throughout the United States."[19] Second, it may be argued that *Chalk Circle* is Brecht's most "American" play. Despite the fact that Brecht had been familiar with the Chalk Circle materials since the twenties, he wrote the drama during 1944 in Santa Monica. The play not only originated in the United States; in a sense it was written for the American stage since Brecht sought to make

---

[16] Suffice it to mention the biographical study by James K. Lyon, *Bertolt Brecht in America* (Princeton: Princeton University Press, 1980).

[17] Esslin, 285.

[18] Ibid., 279.

[19] Bertolt Brecht, *The Caucasian Chalk Circle*, rev. ed., ed. Eric Bentley (New York: Grove, 1987), cover.

concessions to the norms of Broadway in order to improve his chances of having it produced. Even if he ultimately failed, the world premiere of *Chalk Circle* took place in the United States. Third, overtly the play seemed to be about "motherhood and justice"[20] — topics not only of universal significance but also, in the case of motherhood, proverbially claimed to be genuinely American. Fourth, *Chalk Circle* is an extraordinarily rich play that provides a number of interpretive possibilities for directors, critics, audiences, and readers; these possibilities range from the purely aesthetic to the pronouncedly political.

Perhaps not surprisingly, both Esslin and Bentley, in their remarks cited above, attribute the success of *Chalk Circle* to its innovative technical features and pay comparatively little attention to the thematic thrust of the play with its inherent radical questioning of traditional concepts of motherhood and property rights. This thrust is summed up in the Singer's concluding words.

> And you who have heard the story of the chalk circle
> Bear in mind the wisdom of our fathers:
> Things should belong to those who do well by them
> Children to motherly women that they may thrive
> Wagons to good drivers that they may be well driven
> And the valley to those who water it, that it may bear fruit.[21]

After all, the emphasis on formal criteria accords with Esslin's observation, mentioned previously, about Western critics' preference for Brecht's "poetry" at the expense of his "Communism."[22] That the political message in *Chalk Circle* could, in the long run, be safely ignored by critics and audiences is ultimately attributable to Brecht's ambivalence toward the American commercial theater, an institution that was hardly the ideal vehicle for the staging of political plays. On

---

[20] See Richard Watts, Jr., "Brecht, Motherhood, and Justice," *New York Post*, 25 March 1966. The title of Watts's review provided the title of this article.

[21] Bertolt Brecht, *The Caucasian Chalk Circle*, trans. Ralph Manheim, vol. 7 of *Collected Plays*, ed. Ralph Manheim and John Willett (New York: Vintage Books, 1975), 229. Subsequent page references are to this edition.

[22] Esslin, xvi.

the one hand, he disdained Broadway; on the other, one of his chief concerns during his stay in New York City from November 1943 to March 1944 was producing his plays, foremost among them *Chalk Circle*. James K. Lyon remarks laconically about Brecht's futile endeavors to have his plays produced, "Just as the sight of Broadway failed to overwhelm him, so Brecht failed to overwhelm Broadway, though it was not for lack of trying."[23] Brecht's own words reflect his equivocal sentiments toward Broadway — "revulsion" versus the desire to adopt indigenous American traditions in order to succeed. "[*Chalk Circle*] was written in America after ten years of exile, and its structure is partly conditioned by a revulsion against the commercialized dramaturgy of Broadway. At the same time, it makes use of certain elements of that older American theater whose forte lay in burlesques and 'shows.'"[24]

Lyon has given a detailed account of Brecht's abortive attempts to have *Chalk Circle* produced — attempts that involved the Austrian-born actress Luise Rainer, her financial backer Jules J. Leventhal, and various translators. In the end, the play "never reached Broadway during Brecht's American years, and its non-performance remains one of the puzzles of his exile." At the same time, as Lyon suggests, "Perhaps it was just as well. By most standards, *Chalk Circle* was hopelessly at odds with the American theater of the day."[25] Precisely those features that Esslin praises as the quintessence of Brecht's "epic" theater, that is, the "use of narrators, ... two-pronged construction, ... stylized action"[26] would presumably have contributed to a quick folding of *Chalk Circle* had it reached Broadway before Brecht's departure from the United States in October 1947. These features, at any rate, did not meet with the enthusiastic approval of New York theater critics when *Chalk Circle* opened in that city in 1966.

In the absence of sufficient documentary evidence that would have been generated by a production of the play before Brecht left for

---

[23] Lyon, *Bertolt Brecht in America*, 121.

[24] Brecht, "Notes to *The Caucasian Chalk Circle*," vol. 7 of *Collected Plays*, 295–96.

[25] Lyon, 129.

[26] Esslin, 311.

Europe, one can only conjecture about the retrospectively assumed failure of *Chalk Circle*. There are, however, two clearly distinguishable lines of reasoning. Whereas Lyon attributes the shortcomings of *Chalk Circle* in terms of the American theater to formal criteria, biographer Klaus Völker also draws attention to the political dimension. "The play, originally conceived as a parable about conditions in the old days of bloodshed and oppression, was no more than a golden legend interspersed with wise social judgments and commentaries delivered by a singer. In spite of all its concessions the play was still too bold technically for those days and too political in its statement."[27]

Authorial intent as expressed in political statements is not necessarily a valid criterion in reception studies; in fact, literary history is replete with deliberate or accidental "creative misunderstandings," and Brecht, the tireless adaptor, must be counted among the great pilferers of world literature. Yet Brecht's entire theoretical work attests to his endeavors to employ formal-aesthetic features as a means to the end of changing the audience's consciousness with regard not only to the theater but to society as a whole. Thus these endeavors cannot be ignored in assessing the impact of Brecht's plays in general and of *Chalk Circle* in particular. Since on the textual level authorial intent does not manifest itself unambiguously — obviously, the possibilities of interpretation multiply during an actual performance — Brecht strove to limit the range of exegesis. Hence his attempts to endow the kitchen maid Grusha with the "gumption and cunning"[28] of her class rather than have her appear as a "sucker."[29] Grusha succumbs to the "terrible ... temptation to do good"[30] and at great risk to herself rescues the beheaded Governor's child, who has been deserted by his frivolous mother. The autobiographical component of the motherhood theme — Brecht intended to encourage his pregnant collaborator and mistress Ruth Berlau to accept maternal responsibilities — is, for our purposes, of less interest than the social (instead of biological) foundation of motherhood that is made

---

[27] Klaus Völker, *Brecht: A Biography*, trans. John Nowell (New York: Continuum Book, 1978), 303–4.

[28] Völker, 303.

[29] "Notes," 297.

[30] *Collected Plays*, 160.

explicit in the final, "Chalk Circle," scene of the play. The child is awarded to the socially productive Grusha rather than to his biological mother, who does not have his interests at heart. Although wily and scheming Azdak functions as the agent of justice, this awarding judge is far from a model character; his exploits tend to obscure his wisdom. As in the case of Grusha, Brecht was dissatisfied with the character of Azdak, a much-coveted role that allowed the full display of an actor's histrionic talent, and later sought to recast him in the role of "a disappointed revolutionary posing as a human wreck."[31]

It was neither the "disappointed revolutionary" Azdak nor the "sucker" Grusha that turned out to be the touchstone of Brecht's politics. Rather, it was the "Prologue," which Brecht later renamed "The Dispute about the Valley" in order to emphasize its integral character, that generated considerable debate. This controversy was fueled by persistent rumors that Brecht had added it as an ideological prop after his return to East Berlin. Set in Soviet Georgia at the end of World War II, the "Prologue" shows the peaceful resolution of a property dispute about a fertile valley that is claimed by two collective farms specializing in goat breeding and fruit growing, respectively. After a rational discussion all present decide to award the tract of land to the fruit growers' farm whose plan promises to make the valley more productive — a decision that parallels that of awarding the child to Grusha in the final scene of the play. On a formal level, the connection between the "Prologue" and the *Chalk Circle* proper is established by the Singer, who participates in and directs "a play with songs, [in which] almost everyone in the whole [fruit-growing] kolkhoz will take part" to demonstrate — on the thematic level — the interconnectedness of "old and new wisdom."[32]

But Brecht's potentially revolutionary message concerning the settlement of differences about property rights reached the American public only after considerable delay. In Bentley's 1947 translation of *Chalk Circle* that was published in 1948, several years before the

---

[31] "Notes," 298–99.

[32] *Collected Plays*, 144.

German original,[33] the "Prologue" is missing. This translation served as the text for the play's world premiere in Northfield, Minnesota, in the spring of 1948 and instituted the practice of staging the play without the "Prologue." Bentley explained in 1965 "that the appearance of [the] 'Prologue' was postponed" on Brecht's advice.[34] Brecht, who was scheduled to appear before the House Un-American Activities Committee in Washington, D.C., on 30 October 1947, one day before his departure to Europe, feared complications if the manuscript of the translation included the "Prologue" (the translation was delivered to the publisher at about the time of Brecht's appearance before the committee). Curiously, even without the "Prologue" one observant reviewer noticed in *Chalk Circle* and its companion piece, *The Good Woman of Setzuan*, upon their publication "powerfully stated arguments for [the] author's conviction that the world must be changed"[35] — arguments that later critics, who had the "Prologue" at their disposal, failed to detect. Bentley's explanation sounds plausible in view of both Brecht's notorious survival instinct and the fact that he does not seem to have insisted on the inclusion of the "Prologue" in the first production of *Chalk Circle* in the Federal Republic at the Städtische Bühnen Frankfurt am Main in April 1955.[36]

Since the world premiere of *Chalk Circle* at a small college theater did not attract much attention, the omission of the "Prologue" in both production and the first published text went unnoticed. The "Prologue" was not printed until 1959.[37] Subsequently included in the Grove Press editions of *Chalk Circle*, the "Prologue" was first presented in the Minnesota Theatre Company's 1965 production — as Bentley reports

---

[33] Bertolt Brecht, *Parables for the Theatre. Two Plays: The Good Woman of Setzuan, The Caucasian Chalk Circle*, trans. Eric Bentley and Maja Apelman (Minneapolis: University of Minnesota Press, 1948).

[34] Eric Bentley, "Introduction," in Bertolt Brecht, *The Caucasian Chalk Circle*, rev. ed., ed. Eric Bentley (New York: Grove, 1966), 10.

[35] Review of *Parables for the Theatre*, by Bertolt Brecht, *New Yorker*, 16 Oct. 1948, 135.

[36] See Hans-Joachim Bunge, "The Dispute over the Valley: An Essay on Bertolt Brecht's Play, *The Caucasian Chalk Circle*," *Tulane Drama Review* 4, no. 2 (Dec. 1959): 50–66.

[37] Bertolt Brecht, "Prologue to *The Caucasian Chalk Circle*," trans. Eric Bentley, *Tulane Drama Review* 4, no. 2 (Dec. 1959): 45–49.

with apparent relief in a quasi-apologetic 1966 essay, "An Un-American Chalk Circle?" — "without untoward incidents."[38] Bentley's apprehension about the reception of the "Prologue" was not entirely unjustified; in his essay he sought to make palatable to American readers the gist of the play in general and the "Prologue," a veritable "stumbling block for American audiences,"[39] in particular. Bentley correctly pointed out that the amicable, rational way in which the property dispute among the two collective farms is settled constitutes "a complete reversal of the values by which our civilization has been living."[40] At the same time, he is at pains to explain that the "Prologue" is hardly "an accurate picture of Stalin's Russia" and draws attention to the future tense in the line "'The home of the Soviet people *shall* also *be* the home of Reason!'"[41] Bentley's reference to the futuristic, utopian dimension of the "Prologue" is taken by Hayman to signify utter lack of realism — "The Utopian prologue to [*Chalk Circle*] is as unrealistic as *Twelfth Night*"[42] — and implicitly rejected by Esslin. Esslin adduces from the fact that only "a single scene, the prologue to *The Caucasian Chalk Circle*, is laid inside the promised land — a collective farm in Soviet Russia" that Brecht's aspirations for a better world — based on presumably scientific Marxism-Leninism — remained "merely a pious and touching hope — a hope, moreover, which was constantly belied by [his] own experience of the real world."[43]

Bentley's evenhanded approach toward the "Prologue" differs significantly from the incomprehension or hostility displayed by critics when *Chalk Circle* premiered in East Berlin (1954) and Frankfurt am Main (1955). Dismissed by some European scholars as "primitive

---

[38] Eric Bentley, "An Un-American Chalk Circle?" in Bertolt Brecht, *The Caucasian Chalk Circle*, rev. ed., 129. Subsequent references to the essay are to this edition (see n. 34 above).

[39] Ibid., 129.

[40] Ibid., 130.

[41] Ibid., 130 (my italics).

[42] Hayman, 286.

[43] Esslin, 259–60.

Soviet propaganda"[44] or entirely expendable without effecting the substance of the play,[45] the "Prologue" did not give offense when *Chalk Circle* finally reached New York City in a March 1966 production of the Lincoln Center Repertory Company. Although one critic rejected the "Prologue" as "poster-art,"[46] another reviewer thought it to be an "unnecessary ... part of [Brecht's] social editorializing," and opined that it added "exactly nothing to the dramatic forcefulness"[47] — an argument that fails to take into account the interrelationship between the "Chalk Circle" judgment and the resolution of the "Dispute about the Valley."

For the most part, New York critics remained unpersuaded by Brecht's distancing, nonemotional "epic" drama as a mode of presentation and tended not to engage in any extended discussion of those features that have been generally acknowledged as the hallmarks of Brecht's theater style. For example, these critics devoted little attention to the dominant role of the Singer in *Chalk Circle*, who, with his wide range of "narrative" functions, mediates between the stage and the audience, or to the innovative structure that presents the two chronologically parallel strands of action involving, respectively, Grusha and Azdak not in intertwining scenes but successively. Rather, the reviewers used as their standard of evaluation traditional theatrical fare replete with suspense, emotion, and even melodrama. They tended to stress their distance from, and differences with, Brecht partisans who defended his theory; thus Brecht the playwright won out over Brecht the theoretician. "[He] can paradoxically be at his best when denying his own theory." Accordingly, the play's strengths were judged to consist of "a melodramatic and even sentimental story" and the "frankly theatrical excitement of the flight of Grusha" in scene 3, "The Flight to

---

[44] See Willy Haas, *Bert Brecht*, Köpfe des 20. Jahrhunderts, no. 7, 4th ed. (Berlin: Colloquium, 1968), 86–87. See also Willy Haas, *Bert Brecht*, trans. Max Knight and Joseph Fabry (New York: Ungar, 1970).

[45] Ronald Gray, *Brecht: The Dramatist* (Cambridge: Cambridge University Press, 1976), 157.

[46] Douglas Watt, "Brecht's *Caucasian Chalk Circle* in Fine Lincoln Rep Production," *Daily News*, 25 March 1966.

[47] Watts, "Brecht, Motherhood, and Justice," *New York Post*, 15 March 1966.

the Northern Mountains."[48] Otherwise, one headline proclaimed, "Brecht Does Not Arouse"; it aptly summed up the generally perceived "deficiency of dramatic excitement"[49] that, less charitably, was characterized by one critic as a "pretentious bore" in need of songs along the lines of "Mack the Knife" "to steam up" the play.[50] Needless to say, using *The Threepenny Opera* as the sole yardstick by which to measure *Chalk Circle* does not reveal a very profound knowledge of Brecht's work.

A more differentiated, encompassing, and positive approach was taken by the drama critic of the respectable *New York Times*, Stanley Kauffmann, who devoted two fairly detailed reviews to the *Chalk Circle* production. Although Kauffmann hailed the arrival of "[o]ne of Bertolt Brecht's plays ... [in] New York (22 years after it was written)," he minimized its political aspects and emphasized its eminent theatricality. "[The play] is a diversion from [Brecht's] activist political plays into the arena of theatrical high jinks, with plentiful opportunities for pageantry, music, horseplay and sheer heart-tugging."[51] In the final analysis, Kauffmann praised Brecht — but he did so by taking issue with those elements that give the Brechtian theater its poignancy and relevance. "[*Chalk Circle*] was written by a man whose theater theories have proved weak; it derives from a political philosophy with which I disagree; and it teaches a moral point which is simple.... Yet I think it is a fine play."[52]

The first production of *Chalk Circle* in New York City, then, proved to be a mixed blessing in that it tended to reinforce the reception pattern that had been previously noted by Esslin. On the one hand, the critical attention that the play attracted initiated a change in the perception of Brecht who, in the 1960s, had "remained a cipher for TV,

---

[48] Watts, "Brecht, Motherhood, and Justice."

[49] Norman Nadel, "Brecht Does Not Arouse," *New York World-Telegram and The Sun*, 25 March 1966.

[50] John McClain, "Too Much Brecht," *Journal American*, 25 March 1966.

[51] Stanley Kauffmann, "At Last, *The Caucasian Chalk Circle*," *New York Times*, 25 March 1966.

[52] Stanley Kauffmann, review of *The Caucasian Chalk Circle*, by Bertolt Brecht, *New York Times*, 10 April 1966.

for Hollywood, and ... for Broadway."[53] On the other hand, the measure of recognition accorded Brecht in the theater capital of the United States may be considered inadequate for Brecht's aesthetic and sociocritical intents in that entertainment clearly dominated over the political message. To be sure, New York City did offer at least one experimental production of *Chalk Circle* that tended to conform more closely to Brecht's style and intent as practiced and preserved by the Berliner Ensemble and that endeavored to observe some basic requirements of the Brechtian theater such as sufficient "time for rehearsal, ... a dedication to ensemble playing, ... and a director's commitment to the play rather than to himself"[54] — requirements that ordinarily the commercial theater was unable to meet. More indicative of the general run of productions, however, was that by the New York Lion Theater Company in 1982. The reviewer makes only passing reference to "Brecht's nonnaturalistic, epic style"; otherwise *Chalk Circle* is declared to be a "mythic fable about the imbalance of justice" — apparently without contemporary relevance or political significance — in which "fairy-tale" elements predominate.[55]

Ironically, as Bentley points out, before Brecht achieved his breakthrough with *Chalk Circle* in New York City, his "name was a byword everywhere else: Off-Broadway in New York, in the community and resident theaters all around the country, above all in that 'university world' which now [in 1966] ... dominates American culture."[56] Thus the 1966 New York production of *Chalk Circle* had been preceded by numerous productions at college and regional theaters. Even if these productions were not necessarily conceived of and acknowledged as a "structured invitation to the imaginative cognition of reality,"[57] the potential for experimental stagings in a university or college setting was, perhaps, greater than in the commer-

---

[53] Eric Bentley, "The Caucasian Chalk Circle (I)," 1966; repr. *The Brecht Commentaries 1943-1980* (New York: Grove, 1981), 168.

[54] Gordon Rogoff, "No Longer Waiting for Brecht," *Saturday Review*, 30 April 1977, 36.

[55] Mel Gussow, "*Caucasian Chalk Circle*," *New York Times*, 30 May 1982.

[56] Bentley, "The Caucasian Chalk Circle (I)," 168.

[57] Lee Baxandall, "The Americanization of Bert Brecht," *Brecht Heute — Brecht Today* 1 (1971): 164.

cial theater. The English translation of *Chalk Circle* (initially without "Prologue") has been available since 1948, and the play has been staged in Bentley's version since then — and since 1975 also in Ralph Manheim's rendering[58] — fairly regularly all over the country. But Brecht's emergence from relative obscurity was greatly aided by a number of significant publications on his work as well as translations of his writings — publications that were not restricted to academic insiders and that provided the basis for a productive engagement with Brecht, the playwright and theoretician.[59] Although it might have appeared from the perspective of a New York reviewer in 1961 that Brecht was often invoked "as a primary force in the modern theatre" but seldom performed,[60] such a view does not take into account the by no means negligible number of Brecht productions outside of New York City. With justifiable pride one reviewer could point out that, in contrast to New York, Washington, D.C., had a permanent company at the Arena Stage that in 1961 opened its new home with a production of *Chalk Circle* "in the spirit of the Berliner Ensemble."[61]

In fact, "[s]ince the early seventies Brecht has emerged as one of the four dramatists in translation [along with Chekhov, Ibsen, and Molière] who are most frequently produced by American, non-profit, regional companies."[62] The general acceptance of Brecht by white, mostly affluent, middle-class audiences who support the regional theaters was most likely aided by noncontroversial productions; audience expectations inevitably exerted pressure on directors not to challenge their

---

[58] See note 21 above.

[59] Suffice it to mention Esslin (see note 1); John Willett, *The Theatre of Bertolt Brecht: A Study from Eight Aspects* (London: Methuen, 1959); *Brecht on Theatre: The Development of an Aesthetic*, ed. and trans. John Willett (New York: Hill & Wang, 1964); Bertolt Brecht, *Seven Plays*, ed. and introd. Eric Bentley (New York: Grove Press, 1961). For a recent, select list of publications by and on Brecht in English, see *Critical Essays on Bertolt Brecht*, ed. Siegfried Mews (Boston: G. K. Hall, 1989), 277–78.

[60] Alan Pryce-Jones, "The Script Is Only Part of the Story," review of *Seven Plays* by Bertolt Brecht, *New York Times Book Review*, 19 Feb. 1961, 7.

[61] Howard Taubman, review of *The Caucasian Chalk Circle*, by Bertolt Brecht, *New York Times*, 1 Nov. 1961.

[62] Carl Weber, "The Actor and Brecht, Or: The Truth Is Concrete," *Brecht Aufführung — Brecht Performance. Brecht Jahrbuch — Brecht Yearbook* no. 13 (1984): 63.

paying patrons' cherished and conventional convictions about property rights and motherhood.

A case in point is provided by the Denver Center for the Performing Arts, a spectacular building in which Molière's *The Learned Ladies* and *Chalk Circle* were put on as first productions. But what appeared noteworthy to one reviewer was the "simple and touching" performance of the actress portraying Grusha, and the problem of biologically versus socially determined motherhood was reduced to a "peasant girl [going] through an epic odyssey for a baby that isn't hers."[63] True, the establishment of Brecht as one of the foreign mainstays in the American theater went hand in hand with "persistent complaints by critics, academics, and theater people about the failure of many Brecht productions to achieve the desired artistic impact."[64] Yet apart from the fact that American actors (and directors) were not trained in the Brechtian method and hence encountered difficulties in developing an "epic" acting style, the playwright himself had aided and abetted the interpretation of *Chalk Circle* as pure entertainment. In a 1949 diary entry he surmised that, despite the paucity of "repertory plays" in Germany, *The Threepenny Opera* and *Chalk Circle* would have to be counted among them because they could be produced on almost any occasion because of the general themes they dealt with and the opportunity they provided for theaters to display their most common skills.[65]

Both the recent post-Marxist developments in Eastern Europe and the current of postmodernism in Western thought are not likely to reverse the prevailing pattern in the reception of Brecht. The dismal failure of socialist/communist systems on the one hand and the

---

[63] Jack Kroll, "Denver's Crown Jewel," *Newsweek*, 14 Jan. 1980, 94.

[64] Weber, "The Actor and Brecht," 64.

[65] "eigentliche repertoirestücke, dh stücke, die nahezu immer gegeben werden können, weil sie im thema sehr allgemein sind und den theatern gelegenheit für ihre allgemeinsten künste gewähren, gibt es bei den deutschen wenige" (9 Nov. 1949), Bertolt Brecht, *Arbeitsjournal*, ed. Werner Hecht (Frankfurt am Main: Suhrkamp, 1973), 2:911. These features explain, in part, the popularity of Brecht (318 performances) among German-language authors in general (Friedrich Dürrenmatt is in second place with 51 performances) and the appeal of *The Threepenny Opera* (86 performances), as well as *The Good Woman of Setzuan* (57 performances) in particular. See Horst Richardson, "Plays from German-speaking Countries on American University Stages, 1973–1988," *Die Unterrichtspraxis* 23, no. 1 (1990): 76–79.

correspondingly increased attraction of capitalism and the free-market economy on the other will hardly dispose audiences to view communist utopias on stage favorably; postmodern critics who see Brecht's early plays as an attempt "to force the audience into a continuous process of re-writing [the world]" dispense with *Chalk Circle* as apparently unsuitable to the project altogether.[66] As far as the presumable future reception of the play is concerned, the often-quoted title of one of the playwright's most famous poems, "Of Poor B. B.," seems to have gained new poignancy.

---

[66] See Elizabeth Wright, *Postmodern Brecht: A Re-Presentation* (London: Routledge, 1989), 75. Wright does not mention *Chalk Circle* at all.

Making It in the Big Apple: Heinrich Böll in the New York Press, 1954–1988

RALPH LEY

THE DAY BEFORE I began researching this paper on Heinrich Böll's reception by the New York press, I read on the front page of the *New York Times* that the state of Kansas had via a constitutional amendment just abolished prohibition, which means that for the first time in over a century Kansans can sit at a public bar and legally order a glass of beer.[1] The item reminded me of something Böll said about America during an interview with a reporter from the *New York Times* on the occasion of the 1973 dinner of PEN's American Center, at which he was guest of honor. Indicating that he felt right at home in a country where politicians fear the written word, Böll made the following observations about America: "You have all sceneries here. You have Watergate and you have press freedom. You have desert and you have New York, terrible provincialism and terrible up-to-dateness. Being American means the chance to be what you want."[2] What took so long to happen in Kansas is a metaphor for the provincialism Böll refers to (ironically, the Great Central Plains, which cover the state, used to be called the Great American Desert). Whether New York is all

[1] William Robbins, "Kansans Take Drink They Believe Signals an Economic Boom," *New York Times*, 2 July 1987, 1.

[2] Israel Shenker, "Böll, Here, Reflects on Liberty and Law and Order," *New York Times*, 15 May 1973, 30.

that up-to-date is open to question, but it is the financial and cultural capital of the richest nation on earth, the ultimate American symbol of the chance to be what you want, to be a success. To paraphrase the theme song of the city that never sleeps, popularized worldwide by the irrepressible voices of Liza Minnelli and Frank Sinatra: if you can make it there, then you can make it anywhere.

As a native New Yorker for whom the other or provincial America begins beyond the confines of the metropolitan area and as someone whose admiration for Böll the writer and the human being is considerable, I was intrigued by the question, to what extent did Böll make it in America's most sophisticated as well as most competitive city? To find out, I had of course to give myself a working definition of the New York press. The criteria I applied to the medium of the printed word were as follows. 1) The publication in question had to be located in the New York area. 2) It had to have some sort of national reputation or clout. 3) It had to review fiction on a fairly regular basis. 4) It had to have a level of sophistication that would appeal to the better-educated American, and/or it had to have a huge national circulation. 5) It had to appear daily, weekly, or monthly. I found fifteen publications which met all of these criteria. To my delight and surprise (although in my New York arrogance I should not admit the surprise) I discovered that apart from daily newspapers only three more publications outside New York clearly met the requirements except location. By including these non–New York journals in my retrospect I could make the overall selection fairly representative of the entire American middle-brow cultural scene.

There were eighteen publications in all. Among daily newspapers I picked two, the *New York Times*, as well as the *New York Herald-Tribune*, which until its demise in the sixties was the national newspaper of choice for staunch Republicans for whom the *New York Times* was too liberal. Among national publications devoted almost exclusively to book reviewing there were four: *New York Times Book Review*, *New York Herald-Tribune Book Review*, *New York Review of Books*, and *Saturday Review*. Seven weekly or biweekly journals of opinion on politics, economics, and culture, all of them with an influence far greater than their relatively small circulation would lead one to believe, made my list: the Jesuit-run *America*, the independent Catholic *Commonweal*, the conservative *National Review*, and running the gamut from progressive to ultraliberal, *New Republic*, *Reporter*, *Nation*, and *New Leader*. Two monthlies were judged sufficiently urbane to be included, *Atlantic Monthly*, which published a short story by Böll way back in 1957, and *Harper's Magazine*, which published three of his short stories, the last in 1981. The two mass-circulation newsweeklies included were *Newsweek* and *Time*. And in a class by itself was that most elitist of middle-brow publications, the *New Yorker*, which saw fit to publish a Böll story in 1978. The non–New York publications are *Atlantic Monthly* (Boston), *New Republic* (Washington), and *Time* (Chicago). For most of its existence, including its halcyon years, *Saturday Review* was published in New York. From a statistical standpoint Böll's reception by the so-called New York press has been a smashing success. His books have been reviewed more often than those of any other author, dead or alive, writing in the German language and published in America since the end of World War II. Thus far there has been a total of 127 reviews.[3] But then again, Böll has also had more books

---

[3] The reviews are listed below in chronological order. Abbreviations are as follows: A=*America*, At=*Atlantic Monthly*, C=*Commonweal*, H=*Harper's Magazine*, N=*Nation*, NaR=*National Review*, NL=*New Leader*, NR=*New Republic*, NYHT=*New York Herald-Tribune*, NYHTBR=*New York Herald-Tribune Book Review*, NYR=*New York Review of Books*, NYT=*New York Times*, NYTBR=*New York Times Book Review*, NY=*New Yorker*, NW=*Newsweek*, R=*Reporter*, SR=*Saturday Review*, and T=*Time*.

I. *Acquainted with the Night*, trans. Richard Graves (New York: Holt, 1954). (*Und sagte kein einziges Wort*, 1953): (1) SR – 16.IX.54, 17 – Jerome Stone; (2) T – 4.X.54, 106; (3) NYTBR – 17.X.54, 42 – Richard Plant; (4) A – 23.X.54, 104 – Doris Grumbach; (5) N – 15.I.55, 55 – Stanley Cooperman.

II. *Adam, Where Art Thou?*, trans. Mervyn Savill (New York: Criterion Books, 1955). (*Wo warst du, Adam?*, 1951): (1) NYHTBR – 13.XI.55, 5 – Denver Lindley; (2) NYTBR – 13.XI.55, 4 – R. Plant; (3) T – 21.XI.55, 124; (4) SR – 26.XI.55, 14 – Robert Pick; (5) C – 6.I.56, 360 – Edwin Kennebeck.

III. *The Train Was on Time*, trans. R. Graves (New York: Criterion Books, 1956). (*Der Zug war pünktlich*, 1949): (1) NW 14.V.56, 129; (2) NYTBR – 20.V.56, 4 – Frederic Morton; (3) T – 28.V.56, 112; (4) SR – 2.VI.56, 12 – R. Plant; (5) NYHTBR – 10.VI.56, 4 – D. Lindley; (6) NY – 16.VI.56, 113 – Anthony West; (7) C – 29.VI.56, 329 – E. Kennebeck; (8) N – 14.VII.56, 43 – Kay Boyle.

IV. *Tomorrow and Yesterday*, trans. M. Savill (New York: Criterion Books, 1957). (*Haus ohne Hüter*, 1954): (1) NYT – 18.X.57, 21 – Nash K. Burger; (2) SR – 19.X.57, 17 – R. Plant; (3) NYTBR – 20.X.57, 4 – Frances Keene; (4) T – 21.X.57, 114; (5) C – 1.XI.57,

134 – E. Kennebeck; (6) NYHTBR – 3.XI.57, 10 – Gene Baro; (7) NaR – 7.XII.57, 525 – J. L. Weil; (8) NL – 23.XII.57, 20 – Granville Hicks.

V. *Billiards at Half-past Nine* (New York: McGraw-Hill, 1962). (*Billard um halbzehn*, 1959): (1) SR – 28.VII.62, 39 – Joseph P. Bauke; (2) NYHTBR – 5.VIII.62, 6 – M. S.; (3) NYTBR – 5.VIII.62, 4 – Siegfried Mandel; (4) C – 19.X.62, 99 – William James Smith; (5) T – 4.I.63, 69.

VI. *The Clown*, trans. Leila Vennewitz (New York: McGraw-Hill, 1965). (*Ansichten eines Clowns*, 1963): (1) NYTBR – 24.I.65, 4 – Daniel Stern; (2) NYHT – 25.I.65, 23 – Maurice Dolbier; (3) NYT – 25.I.65, 35 – Thomas Lask; (4) T – 29.I.65, 98; (5) SR – 30.I.65, 27 – J. Bauke; (6) NYR – 11.II.65, 5 – D. J. Enright; (7) A – 6.II.65, 196 – Hugh McGovern; (8) NW – 8.II.65, 90; (9) C – 12.II.65, 645 – Bruce Cook; (10) R – 25.II.65, 53 – George Steiner; (11) NR – 20.III.65, 17 – Frank J. Warnke; (12) At – Apr. 65, 158 – William Barrett; (13) NaR – 6.IV.65, 287 – Guy Davenport; (14) N – 3.V.65, 484 – Stephen Koch; (15) NY – 20.XI.65, 241 – A. West.

VII. *Absent without Leave*, trans. L. Vennewitz (New York: McGraw-Hill, 1965). (*Als der Krieg ausbrach, Als der Krieg zu Ende war*, 1962; *Entfernung von der Truppe*, 1964): (1) NYT – 6.IX.65, 13 – Erik Wensberg; (2) SR – 11.IX.65, 42 – Edward Martin Potoker; (3) NYTBR – 12.IX.65, 4 – Kurt Vonnegut, Jr.; (4) A – 18.IX.65, 293 – James G. Murray; (5) T – 24.IX.65, 114; (6) H – Oct. 65, 132 – Katherine Gauss Jackson; (7) C – 12.XI.65, 193 – Judith Sklar; (8) NY – 20.XI.65, 241 – A. West; (9) A – 27.XI.65, 686 – William B. Hill, S.J.; (10) NR – 27.XI.65, 36 – Victor Lange.

VIII. *18 Stories*, trans. L. Vennewitz (New York: McGraw-Hill, 1966). (Selections from *Doktor Murkes gesammeltes Schweigen und andere Satiren*, 1958 and *Erzählungen, Hörspiele, Aufsätze*, 1961): (1) NYTBR – 16.X.66, 4 – J. P. Bauke; (2) NR – 12.XI.66, 33 – Edward Grossman; (3) SR – 10.XII.66, 50 – E. M. Potoker; (4) C – 23.XII.66, 354 – B. Cook; (5) NYR – 29.XII.66, 7 – D. J. Enright; (6) NYT – 31.XII.66, 17 – T. Lask.

IX. *Irish Journal*, trans. L. Vennewitz (New York: McGraw-Hill, 1967). (*Irisches Tagebuch*, 1957): (1) NYTBR – 13.VIII.67, 3 – Sean O'Faolain; (2) NYT – 25.VIII.67, 33 – Lawrence M. Bensky; (3) NYR – 14.IX.67, 10 – Conor Cruise O'Brien; (4) N – 2.X.67, 314 – Kevin Sullivan; (5) NY – 7.X.67, 191.

X. *End of a Mission*, trans. L. Vennewitz (New York: McGraw-Hill, 1968). (*Ende einer Dienstfahrt*, 1966): (1) T – 29.III.68, 104; (2) A – 20.IV.68, 549 – Thomas L. Vince.

XI. *Children Are Civilians Too*, trans. L. Vennewitz (New York: McGraw-Hill, 1970). (*Wanderer, kommst du nach Spa... Erzählungen*, 1950, and *Die schwarzen Schafe*, 1951): (1) NY – 28.II.70, 114; (2) T – 2.III.70, 80; (3) NYR – 26.III.70, 42 – D. J. Enright; (4) SR – 28.III.70, 38 – William J. Schwarz; (5) NYTBR – 5.IV.70, 5 – Ernst Pawel; (6) N – 22.VI.70, 760 – Richard Howard.

XII. *Adam and The Train*, trans. L. Vennewitz (New York: McGraw-Hill, 1970). (*Wo warst du, Adam?*, 1951, and *Der Zug war pünktlich*, 1949): (1) SR – 12.IX.70, 32 – LaVern J. Rippley; (2) NW – 14.IX.70, 118 – G. W.; (3) NYR – 5.XI.70, 22 – Denis Donoghue.

XIII. *Group Portrait with Lady*, trans. L. Vennewitz (New York: McGraw-Hill, 1973). (*Gruppenbild mit Dame*, 1971): (1) NYTBR – 6.V.73, 1 – Richard Locke; (2) NYT – 9.V.73, 45 – Anatole Broyard; (3) A – 12.V.73, 445 – Daniel Coogan; (4) NW – 14.V.73, 118 – W[alter] C[lemons]; (5) T – 28.V.73, 99 – Geoffrey Wolff; (6) NYR – 31.V.73, 35 – D. J. Enright; (7) NL – 11.VI.73, 16 – Pearl K. Bell; (8) At – July 73, 95 – Melvin Maddocks; (9) N – 30.VII.73, 88 – Charles Lam Markmann.

XIV. *The Lost Honor of Katharina Blum or: How Violence Develops and Where it Can Lead*, trans. L. Vennewitz (New York: McGraw-Hill, 1975). (*Die verlorene Ehre der Katharina Blum oder: Wie Gewalt entstehen und wohin sie führen kann*, 1974): (1) NR – 26.IV.75, 26 – B. Cook; (2) NYTBR – 27.IV.75, 1 – Michael Wood; (3) A – 17.V.75, 388 – D. Coogan; (4) NY – 19.V.75, 119; (5) NYT – 21.V.75, 41 – Christopher Lehmann-Haupt; (6) NaR – 1.VIII.75, 843 – Rene Kuhn Bryant; (7) A – 15.XI.75, 332 – W. B. Hill.

XV. *The Bread of Those Early Years*, trans. L. Vennewitz (New York: McGraw-Hill, 1976). (*Das Brot der frühen Jahre*, 1955): (1) NYTBR – 23.I.77, 7 – E. Pawel; (2) N – 29.II.77, 213 – Saul Maloff; (3) A – 12.III.77, 222 – D. Coogan.

XVI. *Missing Persons and Other Essays*, trans. L. Vennewitz (New York: McGraw-Hill, 1977). (Twenty-nine essays and reviews written between 1952 and 1976): (1) NYTBR – 6.XI.77, 14 – A. Broyard; (2) A – 25.II.78, 151 – D. Coogan.

XVII. *And Never Said a Word*, trans. L. Vennewitz (New York: McGraw-Hill, 1978). (*Und sagte kein einziges Wort*, 1953): (1) NY – 7.VIII.78, 81; (2) NYTBR – 27.V.79, 23 – Kay Walters.

XVIII. *The Safety Net*, trans. L. Vennewitz (New York: Knopf, 1982). (*Fürsorgliche Belagerung*, 1979): (1) SR – Jan. 82, 57 – Anthony Burgess; (2) NYTBR – 31.I.82, 3 – Richard Gilman; (3) NYT – 5.II.82, C–27 – John Leonard; (4) T – 8.II.82, 74 – R. Z. Sheppard; (5) NW – 22.II.82, 73 – Jim Miller; (6) NR – 3.III.82, 31 – Robert Alter; (7) NYR – 18.III.82, 46 – D. J. Enright; (8) NL – 22.III.82, 20 – Lothar Kahn; (9) NY – 14.VI.82, 129 – John Updike; (10) C – 16.VII.82, 409 – David H. Richter.

XIX. *What's to Become of the Boy? or: Something to Do with Books*, trans. L. Vennewitz (New York: Knopf, 1984). (*Was soll aus dem Jungen bloß werden? Oder: Irgendwas mit Büchern*, 1981): (1) NYT 6.X.84, 13 – A. Broyard; (2) NYTBR 7.X.84, 3. – Gordon A. Craig; (3) NW 15.X.84, 100 – David Lehman; (4) At – Nov. 84, 148 – Phoebe-Lou Adams; (5) NY – 12.XI.84, 195; (6) SR – Nov./Dec. 84, 81 – Andrea Barnet.

XX. *A Soldier's Legacy*, trans. L. Vennewitz (New York: Knopf, 1985). (*Das Vermächtnis*, 1982): (1) NW – 10.VI.85, 81 – Peter S. Prescott; (2) NYTBR – 23.VI.85, 9 – Joel Agee; (3) At – July 85, 100 – P.-L. Adams; (4) NaR – 4.X.85, 46 – D. Keith Mano; (5) NR – 21.X.85, 40 – William Boyd.

XXI. *The Stories of Heinrich Böll*, trans. L. Vennewitz (New York: Knopf, 1986). (Comprises two novellas from *Absent without Leave*, 1965; thirteen stories from *18 Stories*, 1966; twenty-four of the twenty-six stories in *Children Are Civilians Too*, 1970; *Adam and The Train*, 1970; two stories originally published in *Encounter* in 1969 and 1971; two stories originally published in *Harper's* in 1979 and 1981; *A Soldier's Legacy*, 1985; plus translated into English and sold in America than any other German-writing author since 1945, twenty-three to be exact, including retranslations. In terms of quality it is no secret that the reception has been mixed,[4] and what I would like to do in the limited scope of this paper is to share with you some of the points of criticism which struck me as particularly positive or negative or controversial or unusual in my perusal of these reviews.

seventeen newly translated stories): (1) NYTBR – 23.II.86, 42 – D. J. Enright; (2) NR – 7.IV.86, 28 – Sven Birkerts; (3) NY – 7.IV.86, 103.

XXII. *The Casualty*, trans L. Vennewitz (New York: Farrar, Straus, Giroux, 1987). (*Die Verwundung und andere frühe Erzählungen*, 1983): (1) NYTBR – 23.VIII.87, 29 – Russell A. Berman.

XXIII. *Women in a River Landscape: A Novel in Dialogues and Soliloquies*, trans. David McLintock (New York: Knopf, 1988). (*Frauen vor Flußlandschaft: Roman in Dialogen und Selbstgesprächen*, 1985): (1) NYTBR – 24.VII.88, 13 – Vivian Gornick.

---

[4] Aspects of Böll's reception in America have been treated by the following: Keith Stewart, "The American Reviews of Heinrich Böll: A Note on the Problems of the Compassionate Novelist," *University of Dayton Review* 11, no. 2 (Winter 1974): 5–10; Rainer Nägele, "Aspects of the Reception of Heinrich Böll," *New German Critique*, no. 7 (Winter 1976): 45–68, esp. 66f.; Ray Lewis White, *Heinrich Böll in America 1954–1970* (Hildesheim and New York: Georg Olms Verlag, 1979), esp. 4–9; Walter Ziltener, *Heinrich Böll und Günter Grass in den USA: Tendenzen der Rezeption* (Bern and Frankfurt am Main: Peter Lang, 1982) — with reference to Böll this study deals primarily with the reception of *Die verlorene Ehre der Katharina Blum*; Mark W. Rectanus, "*The Lost Honor of Katharina Blum*: The Reception of a German Best-Seller in the USA," *German Quarterly* 59, no. 2 (Spring 1986): 252–69; Thomas Schaller, *Die Rezeption von Heinrich Böll und Günter Grass in den USA: Böll und Grass im Spiegel der Unterrichtspraxis an höheren amerikanischen Bildungsinstitutionen* (Frankfurt am Main, Bern, New York, Paris: Peter Lang, 1988). Useful background information on the American reception of postwar German authors in general is provided by Manfred Durzak, "Die Rezeption der deutschen Literatur nach 1945 in den USA," in *Die deutsche Literatur der Gegenwart: Aspekte und Tendenzen*, ed. M. Durzak (Stuttgart: Philipp Reclam jun., 1971), 437–47; Volkmar Sander, "Die 'New York Times Book Review': Zur Rezeption deutscher Literatur in den USA," *Basis* 4 (1973): 86–97; Peter Demetz, "Die Literatur der Bundesrepublik in den Vereinigten Staaten: Kritische Notizen," in *Perspectives and Personalities: Studies in Modern German Literature Honoring Claude Hill*, ed. R. Ley, M. Wagner, J. M. Ratych, and K. Hughes (Heidelberg: Carl Winter Universitätsverlag, 1978), 110–17; Leslie A. Willson, "Das Wiederaufleben deutscher Literatur in den Vereinigten Staaten," *Inter Nationes Tätigkeitsbericht* (1982), Appendix 8, 1–6; and Volker Wehdeking, "Von Vergangenheit lange verstellt: Zur verspäteten Ankunft westdeutscher Gegenwart beim amerikanischen Leser. Die deutsche Literatur seit 1945 im Urteil des Auslandes," *Deutsche Vierteljahrsschrift für Literaturwissenschaft und Geistesgeschichte* 60 (1986): 496–517.

Böll's debut in the New York press was anything but spectacular. On 16 September 1954 Jerome Stone of the *Saturday Review* wrote a very unflattering critique of *Acquainted with the Night* (*Und sagte kein einziges Wort*), the first of Böll's novels to be translated into English. He began by borrowing a nasty observation about the German national character made by Winston Churchill during World War II to the effect that the Germans are either at your feet or at your throat. "If circumstances will not allow them to feel superior they react by insisting on feeling terribly inferior." This trait, Stone continued, is reflected in a sense of paralyzing futility and demoralization that pervades Böll's novel, otherwise undistinguished except for an occasional effective symbol of the spiritual ugliness of urban Germany. Dissatisfaction with the "happy" ending of the novel was expressed by the anonymous reviewer of *Time*, who found it both contrived and dismal. He resorted to another reputed national trait to account for the lack of real relief when Fred Bogner returns to his cramped apartment. "Like his hero," he concluded, "author Böll is apparently determined to go on suffering, even though the need for it may have passed." Equally snide — after all, the war had ended less than a decade earlier — was the concluding comment of Stanley Cooperman in the *Nation*. After opining that the somber prose, together with the dominant moods of submission and hopelessness, runs counter to the note of mild affirmation at the end, the reviewer wondered why Böll made no attempt to answer the question, "How was it possible for these appealing, sensitive folk to become the 'good citizens' of a murderous regime?" Some of this negativism was offset, however, by a very positive, very prophetic, and very perspicacious review precisely where it would do the most good. Böll was extremely fortunate in that a New York Germanist, Richard Plant, was assigned to review his novel for the *New York Times Book Review*. Plant called the form of the novel, the use of two first-person-singular narratives, a dangerous experiment that Böll carried out with the brilliance and insight of an Arthur Schnitzler. The seemingly disparate interior monologues, he wrote, combine to tell a unified story; Böll is able to distill from the "tristesse" of the inhabitants of his half-lit and undernourished town "a particular sweetness, an immediacy which is the secret seal of the born writer." The review concludes with the speculation that the advent of Böll marks the start of a literary renewal in Germany. Doris Grumbach in *America* likewise singled out Böll's ability to work wonders with atmosphere. She found Böll's language "extraordinarily effective and affecting" in its tremendous simplicity. Missing from all the reviews was any reference to Böll's sociocritical bent, his extreme uneasiness about the nascent *Wirtschaftswunder*, and his anger at the collusion of the Church with the forces of materialism, and there was no comprehension of the primary factor in Bogner's malaise, his unrequited sense of hunger for justice.

Time had at least labeled the first of Böll's novels to appear in America a "good" book; Grumbach had nothing but praise for the prose, persons, and plot of what she called a "first-rate novel"; Plant had compared Böll favorably with Dostoyevsky, Hemingway, Maupassant, and Schnitzler. The reviews were encouraging enough to induce Böll's American publisher to rush a second novel to the States, *Adam, Where Art Thou?* (*Wo warst du, Adam?*). A mildly favorable review by Denver Lindley in the *Herald-Tribune Book Review* ("not a great novel," "solid qualities," "brilliant reporting," "terse and lucid style") was followed by Plant's highly positive piece in the *New York Times Book Review*, in which once again Böll's reputation was enhanced by name-dropping. His work was mentioned in the same breath as two of the most famous American war novels, Norman Mailer's *The Naked and the Dead*, and James Jones's *From Here to Eternity*, as well as Erich Maria Remarque's *All Quiet on the Western Front*. The review in *Time* was again mixed. Here, too, Böll was described as the German Mailer but lacking Mailer's staying power. And here for the first time two criticisms were made which would become a hallmark of anti-Böll reviews but which would never be expressed as acidly as they were by the anonymous critic of *Time*. In Böll's hands, he wrote, irony is such a blunt instrument that "almost every character is killed by it even before the bullets get him." And when the self-pity that underlies the novel "shows through the chinks in his dead-pan mask [Böll] seems bent not only on living the war again but also on losing it again." In a more positive review Robert Pick of the *Saturday Review* expressed admiration for Böll's distinctive style, which "has a persuasiveness all its own and a kind of sturdy beauty." "There can be little doubt but that one day Mr. Böll will write an extraordinary novel," he concluded. In effect the final reviewer, Edwin Kennebeck of *Commonweal*, said this extraordinary novel had already been written. His critique of *Adam* was fairly positive, but he felt that the book lacked depth: a vision of senselessness is still a vision of nothing. Kennebeck then contrasted this novel with the later-written *Acquainted with the Night*, which he called an "unusual compassionate story ... firmly unified by an implicit religious point of view." Kennebeck thus became the first reviewer of the New York press to appreciate the religious dimensions of a Böllian work. Having written not too long ago in an epitaph for Böll that *Acquainted with the Night* is probably the finest Christian novel of postwar Germany,[5] I was naturally pleased to read Kennebeck's assertion that "this later work tells of a kind of dumb mortal *patience* that could renew the face of the earth."

Adam received four favorable reviews and one mixed review at the hands of the New York press. It was thus no surprise that when Böll's third book came to America less than a year later, it garnered eight reviews. The more hard-boiled critics came down rather heavily on *The Train Was on Time* (*Der Zug war pünktlich*). The problem was both the credibility of the protagonist and of the climax, the encounter between Andreas and the Polish prostitute. A charge of Wagnerian romanticism, of something typically Teutonic but counter to Anglo-Saxon tastes, was leveled against Böll. "Once his hero has run into a prostitute who looks like a Fragonard princess and plays Bach superbly," commented the *Newsweek* reviewer, "the reader will probably feel the pull of the stage management. But then the reader is not German." Frederic Morton in the *New York Times Book Review* was equally unkind, saying that Andreas never convinces, "he is simply the vehicle for a black omen" and the chaste night he spends with Olina is a "protracted cliché." *Time* saw Böll as a prisoner of the notorious German talent for feeling guilty. Kay Boyle in the *Nation* found Böll disappointingly frail and bloodless (in both senses of the word) in comparison with the German war novelists Theodor Plievier and Willi Heinrich, and the exquisitely delicate, practically feminine prose very incongruous. Among Böll's four defenders, three were quick to emphasize that his works were being published in the reverse order of their appearance in Germany; hence

---

[5] Ralph Ley, "Heinrich Böll: A Tribute," in *Dictionary of Literary Biography Yearbook 1985*, ed. Jean W. Ross (Detroit: Gale Research, 1986), 260.

The Train, even though inferior to the other two works — wrote two of the three reviewers — did not represent a chronological diminution of quality. All four reviewers, in marked contrast to the initial four, had nothing but praise for the Olina episode — a clear indication of what would become typical in the American reception of Böll: judgments colored by individual temperament and personal taste, one man's meat becoming another man's poison. Thus Denver Lindley of the *Herald-Tribune Book Review*, who evinced a view of the fine line separating sentiment and sentimentality pronouncedly different from that of Frederic Morton of the *New York Times Book Review*, could conclude his review with the contention that the encounter with Olina in a brothel "triumphs over the squalor of its setting and the skepticism of the reader to become a scene charged with insight and compassion."

In 1957 the novel *Tomorrow and Yesterday (Haus ohne Hüter)* was translated into English, the fourth book by Böll to be offered to the American public within the brief span of three years. Every review was positive except the one by J. L. Weil in the *National Review*. He attacked the novel on highly moralistic grounds, chiding the author for saddling the two young protagonists Martin and Heinrich with mothers who forgot "how to remember and pray, how to hate and love" and then expecting the boys to start fresh and ask what is immoral, to face tomorrow without a yesterday — an allusion to the title in English. Nash K. Burger of the *New York Times* indicated that Böll was a major factor in the literary renaissance finally getting under way in West Germany, pointing out that his three previous books had received "considerable critical acclaim and that the new one should do as well." The anonymous reviewer of *Time* stated flat-out that he was "the best of Germany's post-war novelists." He and Frances Keane of the *New York Times Book Review* singled out Böll's treatment of the young for special commendation. The latter said that Böll, the compassionate champion of dissidents, who has interpreted for non-German readers what it was like to be a draftee in Hitler's Reich, had now acted as interpreter for the children. Heinrich, one of the most believable youngsters in contemporary fiction, moves the reader by his "cynicism and desperate matter-of-factness." Yet "Böll never weakens the character by allowing a shade of sentimentality or pity to intrude." One of the best aspects of Böll's eminently successful story — so the *New York*

Times reviewer — is "the gropings of the two boys to understand that most nonunderstandable of adult relationships, the relationship of men and women." Granville Hicks in the *New Leader* said that Böll achieved an extraordinary freedom through a technical mastery that permitted his conviction that no event can be the same for two beholders to become reality; Böll "can identify himself with either of the boys, so different in what they have experienced, so alike in their bewilderment." Reservations concerning the novel were twofold — and they would be expressed about subsequent works by Böll: too long a cast of characters, an overuse of leitmotivs, and a repetitiveness of phrase and imagery. But these criticisms were more than offset by what Kennebeck of *Commonweal* called Böll's "extraordinary depth of feeling." The first of our critics to penetrate to the spiritual core of *Acquainted with the Night*, Kennebeck harked back to the earliest of Böll's novels to appear in America in extolling "the many strong and eloquent passages" in *Tomorrow and Yesterday* "celebrating human love and human pleasure." "But most haunting of all," he concluded, "are the gentle moments celebrating compassion, which passes, rarely and suddenly, from one person to another in a look or touch or word, clearing away clouds of fear and hatred."

When *Billiards at Half-past Nine* (*Billard um halbzehn*) was anonymously translated into English in 1962, there had been a five-year hiatus since the appearance in America of *Tomorrow and Yesterday*. Initially only three publications ran a review of *Billiards*, a clear indication that the momentum gained by having four works appear to generally positive reviews within three years had been lost. It was almost as if Böll had been forgotten. The *Saturday Review* called upon a New York Germanist to refresh the memory of its readers. Joseph Bauke wrote a respectable critique, pointing out that Böll was not the most sophisticated of writers but at least he was a good storyteller, a disciple not of Mann or of Kafka but of Hemingway. But few critics would have credited him with the ambition to write a novel about three whole generations of a family who experience the fate of 20th century Germany. "The result is not a sequel to *Buddenbrooks*, to be sure, but it is an excellent book and certainly the author's best." In an unenthusiastic review Siegfried Mandel of the *New York Times Book Review* found Böll old-fashioned, putting narrative ahead of experimentation, and his novel "too sprawling in its aim, constructed of too many patches of memory, too repetitive in theme and symbolism." And in an extremely short piece the anonymous critic of the *Herald-Tribune Book Review* called the novel impressive and fascinating but said little of substance beyond a reference to the author's "brilliant technical dexterity." It took another two and a half months for a fourth review to appear. Under the rubric "Six Novels out of the Summer Doldrums," which suggested that these were novels which publishers were not quite sure they wanted to bring out, W. J. Smith of *Commonweal* lumped together with Böll's novel (which some academicians today regard as his greatest formal success) five works of fiction totally forgotten a few months after publication. Perhaps it was a good thing the review of *Billiards* was so buried: Smith raised an extremely unflattering objection. Böll, he wrote, was automatically confronted "with the problem of sympathetically presenting a group of people who are terribly righteous, however right they may be," and he failed to handle this difficulty convincingly. After another two and a half months a fifth review appeared, again a collective one, but this time Böll was placed in the more dignified company of Günter Grass and Uwe Johnson. This extremely long review in *Time* was up to this point unique in Böll reception, for it dealt intelligently and in some depth with the political situation in West Germany. *Time* hailed all three writers for their ability and inclination to come to grips with the most overwhelming experience in Germany's history. They were persistently probing beneath a surface prosperity to the uneasy past "with a power and subtlety needed for so dark and difficult a subject." A particular and urgent accomplishment was the parallel they exposed between a new smugness and materialism in West Germany and the spirit that prevailed among self-seeking Germans under Hitler, technically innocent but morally guilty. *Billiards* was depicted as Böll's crowning achievement in a line of thoughtful novels "more notable for civilized intentions than sustained artistic power." What made *Billiards* memorable was "a whopping internal monologue of more than 50 pages, interspersed Faulkner style through the novel," the record of a woman's fifty-year struggle with Germany's most dreaded enemy — "not the Nazis who personify the known power of evil, but respectability, which would rather look the other way than cause a fuss." *Time* concluded its review, very possibly the most important in the history of Böll reception in America, with the statement that all three writers argue angrily and eloquently "that the destruction of individual character (and of nations) begins with the tiniest indifference, the smallest act of cowardice, the most microscopic compromise."

As if to make up for its sin of omission, the New York press devoted three times as many reviews to *The Clown* (*Ansichten eines Clowns*) when it appeared in 1965 as it had to *Billiards*. The fifteen critiques of the novel set a record never to be broken in subsequent Böll reception. Four were negative, one was mixed, one noncommittal, and nine favorable, some of them extremely so. Of the eight reviews that drew some sort of comparison between Böll and Grass, two, including that by William Barrett, one of the leaders of the New York intelligentsia and the foremost propagator of existentialism in America, rated them evenly, four reviews gave the nod to Grass, and two voted for Böll. Fortunately for Böll one of these two reviews appeared in the recently established and already very prestigious *New York Review of Books*. Böll, D. J. Enright wrote, is one of those rare authors who have something to say. "Unlike Uwe Johnson in *Speculations about Jacob*, Böll doesn't erect reading-difficulty into a law ... unlike Günter Grass, Böll doesn't obscure his real meaning with a barrage of private emblems." Of the negative reviews Guy Davenport's in the *National Review* was the wittiest and therefore the unkindest. The novel, he wrote, fails as satire because Böll explains his subject to death with Teutonic humor. "The Greeks made epigrams that stung like wasps; the French treat satire as if it were light, fragile, and memorable as a soufflé.... But the Germans — their humor is for Germans, and that's that." Hugh McGovern's review in *America* was the most myopic: the novel is dismissed purely and simply as a pathetically childish, spitefully biased, and woefully misinformed attack on the Catholic Church. Other negative observations by various critics: the protagonist is a professional self-pitier; the author's gripes are not integrated into the structure of the novel; as Böll's best effort to date, the novel reveals the limitations of his artistry as a conventional realist. Among the most enthusiastic boosters of *The Clown* was Daniel Stern in the *New York Times Book Review*. Stern had just completed a novel on concentration camp survivors of World War II, and the reading of Böll's book seemed like a metaphysical complement to his own thinking on the Holocaust. Böll, he wrote, was after bigger statistical game than post-Nazi German society or the social actions of the Catholic Church or of individual Catholics. In "a bitter and brilliant book" hard questions have been posed by an artist, he wrote, who has earned the right to ask them. "How can an honest man profess Christianity when Christian culture in the West failed to stem the rise of Nazism ... and when the Church thrives in a society that worships nothing but the values of the marketplace?" In three key reviews the existential dimension of the novel was emphasized. George Steiner in the *Reporter* wrote that Pope John and the clown stand for "the possibilities of love in a world in which these possibilities are embarrassing or ludicrously unrealistic. Schnier is, in certain obvious ways, the holy fool; his quest for grace leaves him a beggar in a city of stone. Or, more exactly, in a city built of lies." Also stressing the link to Pope John, Frank Warnke wrote in the *New Republic* that despite its criticism of the Church, the novel is, paradoxically, profoundly Catholic. "If society offers no vision of good, there remains the capacity for love within the individual — not only in Schnier's unreasoning belief in Marie's return, but also in the hopeless love for the very humanity he denounces. As the Clown phrases it, in language almost worthy of Swift, 'I would weep even at the grave of my mother,'" a mother described by the critic as "unspeakable." Bauke in the *Saturday Review* remarked that pensive self-pity, honesty, and a warm humanity make Schnier the best friend Holden Caulfield could have had. In Bauke's estimation, despite an exaggerated partisanship and a "pat assumption that the rich are bad and that goodness is limited to people with little money and an interest in socialism ... the writer triumphs over the novelist." Steiner, who in 1959 had written in one of the most salient essays on the development of the German language, "Everything forgets. But not a language. When it has been injected with falsehood, only the most drastic truth can cleanse it,"[6] emphasized the role of Böll's novel in revitalizing language corrupted by the Nazi experience. "*The Clown*," he wrote, "is one of the saddest, bitterest satires yet

---

[6] Georg Steiner, "The Hollow Miracle," in his *Language and Silence: Essays on Language, Literature, and the Inhuman* (New York: Athenaeum, 1967), 108.

written on the Germany of the Volkswagen and Christian Democracy." And he added, "I think Böll is right."

A minor publication comprising the title novella, *Absent without Leave (Entfernung von der Truppe)*, and a double novella, *When the War Broke Out, When the War Was Over (Als der Krieg ausbrach, Als der Krieg zu Ende war)*, followed in the wake of *The Clown* and its critical acclaim. Consequently the book received considerably more attention than its importance warranted and for the first time in Böll reception a majority of the reviewers were disappointed. No doubt the positive judgments were not uninfluenced by Böll's recently secured status. *Harper's* set the tone by referring to him as "a brilliantly serious and impressive novelist, author of that post–World War II classic, *The Clown*." The word "brilliant" cropped up in three other favorable reviews, this time in connection with the relative merits of the two novellas, so disparate in form: The *New York Times* called them both brilliant, *Saturday Review* the first, and *Commonweal* the second. The negative reviews were more negative than the positive reviews were positive. James Murray in *America* wrote that in *Absent without Leave* Böll's pace is much too slow, his symbols unconvincing, his aesthetic devices too subtle for his own good, and that the second novella is even less substantial than the first. What hurt considerably was that the two most prominent critics came down hard on *Absent without Leave*. The *New York Times Book Review* had selected as its reviewer the writer Kurt Vonnegut, a combat veteran of World War II (his most famous novel, *Slaughterhouse Five*, is based on his experience as a POW in Dresden when the city was senselessly obliterated by the American and British air forces in the final months of the war). Vonnegut found the novella "a royal pain, a mannered, pretentious, patronizing, junky sort of 'Notes from the Underground.'" In a long review in the *New Republic* that was also a professional assessment of Böll's strengths and weaknesses, Victor Lange, a pillar among American Germanists, apprised his lay readers that Böll, although a man of unquestionable integrity, has lost ground with the younger Germans because of his reluctance, and possibly inability, to emphasize "the radical resources of modern fiction." A born storyteller, Böll "may at times seem in danger of being swayed by his own compassion into melodrama and sentimentality."[7]

When a representative collection of Böll's short stories and satires entitled *18 Stories* appeared in 1966, the reviews were all favorable, a first in Böll reception. It was pointed out that despite their intensely local color they had a universal application and that the author's humane concern was a function of his style. By far the most-liked story was *Murke's Collected Silences (Doktor Murkes gesammeltes Schweigen)*, which D. J. Enright of the *New York Review of Books* regarded as on a par with Böll's best novels. The few "duds" in the collection were attributed to Böll's failure to keep his sympathy from spilling over into pathos. Among these stories: "In the Valley of the Thundering Hooves" ("Im Tal der donnernden Hufe"), "The Death of Elsa Baskoleit" ("Der Tod der Elsa Baskoleit"), and "The Adventure" ("Das Abenteuer"). Bauke in the *New York Times Book Review* did not particularly appreciate "the slightly smug attitude of Böll's non-heroes who feel good because they are good, because their hearts are in the right place, i.e., left of center. Where Böll's art is made to serve this vein, the result is a sermon, as in 'The Balek Scales' ["Die Waage der Baleks"]."

A second anthology of stories, entitled *Children Are Civilians Too* and published four years later, was downgraded by three of the six critics who reviewed it. These reviewers regarded the twenty-six very early stories it contained as quaintly sentimental vignettes and mood pieces, apprentice work, trial balloons for works completed later, as, in the words of Ernst Pawel in the *New York Times Book Review*, "no more than finger exercises by a talented novice, republished as an act of piety rather than for their intrinsic value." Among the three positive reviews one, by the Canadian Germanist William J. Schwarz, was quite singular. Böll, he wrote, is at his best as a true teller of tales, and his early work, including the present volume, is much more convincing than the ambitious novels, where literary appeal is all too often diminished by his "uncompromising hatred of the capitalist society in the Federal Republic." A third, very generous anthology, entitled *The Stories of*

---

[7] Lange's remark that the English translation of these novellas is "clumsy and embarrassingly unidiomatic" represents to my knowledge the only time Leila Vennewitz has ever been severely taken to task for not doing her job as Böll's translator.

Heinrich Böll, appeared in 1986. It comprised most of the stories in the previous collections plus an additional twenty-one, some of them recent, and all the novels prior to 1952. Regarded basically as a republication of earlier works, it received but two reviews worth mentioning, both of them favorable. D. J. Enright in the *New York Times Book Review* regarded the appearance of the book as a fitting memorial to the recently deceased Nobel Prize winner as well as "a tribute to Leila Vennewitz, his faithful English-language translator of more than 20 years." Sven Birkerts, who had just been cited for excellence in reviewing by the National Book Critics Circle, wrote in the *New Republic* that the collection honored "an ample achievement." Most memorable, he felt, was the fiction that treated "the immediate circumstances of war." For "Böll's strengths were those of a witness, not those of an inventor. His satiric eye was keen, but he had trouble sustaining plots that serve as credible vehicles."

A second anthology of fiction appearing posthumously, entitled *The Casualty* (*Die Verwundung und andere frühe Erzählungen*), comprised twenty-two stories written between 1946 and 1952 and not published in Germany until shortly before Böll's death. It was reviewed only in the *New York Times Book Review*. Russell Berman, a Stanford Germanist, felt that precisely because these stories lack the polish of the best of Böll's early fiction, they shed interesting light "on the emergence of the major voice in West German literature. One can watch Böll explore the several literary languages that suddenly become available after 1945: fragments of Expressionist prose from Weimar Germany, Surrealist turns of plot from the European avant-garde and some of the hard-nosed realism of the American short story. Usually he was read, with reference to that last component, only as the German heir to Faulkner and Hemingway, but this early work transforms one's understanding of the later, mature fiction in which moments of fantasy, the grotesque and the uncanny take on a new significance: the chronicler Böll turns out to be the modern E. T. A. Hoffmann." I might mention here three other works that received scant critical attention because they were retranslations into what one reviewer described as the "unobtrusive, responsible English"[8] of Vennewitz: *Adam, Where Art Thou?* and *The*

---

[8] G. W., *Newsweek*, 14 Sept. 1970, 118.

Train Was on Time, republished in 1970 in a single volume entitled *Adam and The Train*, and *Acquainted with the Night*, republished in 1978 with the new title *And Never Said a Word*. The same holds true more or less for works which were not current at the time they were translated into English. These comprise two novels, *The Bread of Those Early Years* (1977, *Das Brot der frühen Jahre*) and *A Soldier's Legacy* (1985, *Das Vermächtnis*), a collection entitled *Missing Persons and Other Essays* (1977, "Suchanzeigen"), as well as a travelogue, *Irish Journal* (1967, *Irisches Tagebuch*). Only the last of these books was received with major misgivings. *The Bread of Those Early Years* was cited by Pawel in the *New York Times Book Review* as a "powerful reminder of what Böll brought to postwar German writing, luminous decency and lucid prose, priceless gifts in 'those early years' when language itself had to be brought back to life." A highly favorable review by the noted novelist Saul Maloff in the *Nation* more than offset the apprehensions of Daniel Coogan in *America* about the credibility of Walter Fendrich's redemption and transformation. And Pawel's response to this question is certainly one of the more trenchant comments on how critics approach their Böll. The outcome is convincing enough, he wrote, "if you believe in fairy tales or people." Böll's "lost" novel, *A Soldier's Legacy*, written in 1947 and published in America in the year of his death, was reviewed five times, but two of the critiques were very short. It was dismissed by Joel Agee of the *New York Times Book Review* as a simple and affecting tale that reads like a draft for a first-rate novel, a sentiment shared by the novelist D. Keith Mano in the *National Review*. However, a fellow novelist, William Boyd, writing in the *New Republic*, considered it a remarkable achievement for a first novel despite certain defects typical of unpracticed authors: paradoxically, as a war novel it is very effective "for being more concerned about food than about fighting."

The reviewers of *Missing Persons*, Böll's first and, thus far, only general collection of essays published in America, were unanimous in their rejection of the book. But then, there was a total of only two reviewers (it is fairly safe to assume that as a writer of nonfiction Böll remains practically unknown among American readers). The in-house reviewer of the *New York Times*, Broyard, had absolutely nothing good to say, whereas Coogan in *America* felt that on rare occasions Böll did rise to his expected brilliance, for example, in "The Place was Incidental" ("Der Ort war zufällig"), and "The Moscow Shoeshiners" ("Die Moskauer Schuhputzer"), the latter of which Broyard, however, castigated as overly sentimental. Both reviewers were extremely disappointed with the literary address Böll gave at his reception of the Nobel Prize. Coogan called it "somewhat pretentious and turgid"; Broyard speculated that it must have tried even the legendary patience of the Swedish Academy.

Böll's description of the Ireland of the fifties, which appeared in America ten years after its publication in Germany, was accorded three polite reviews, two of them extremely short and perfunctory, the third by a benevolent Irish novelist, Sean O'Faolain in the *New York Times Book Review*. Unfortunately two other Irish reviewers of the book were anything but benevolent. The literary historian Kevin Sullivan in the *Nation* pronounced *Irish Journal* a vacuous and ponderous book whose Ireland exists only in the mind of Böll. "It is bad enough," Sullivan commented, "when a people sentimentalize themselves, as the Irish have been known to do, but it is insufferable when they are sentimentalized by foreigners." The Irish diplomat and cultural historian Conor Cruise O'Brien, writing in the *New York Review of Books*, added to Sullivan's charge of condescension that of callousness to the social plight of the Irish at the expense of creating an idealized foil for the revolting materialism of his fellow West Germans. "Wallowing" in the gentle resignation of the Irish, a characteristic due largely to the overriding influence of the Church, O'Brien contended, Böll laments any signs of progress. What follows in O'Brien's review is the sharpest attack in the New York press on the reputation of Böll, the moralist: "In the most abominable passage in his ghastly little book, this man actually deplores the introduction of 'the Pill' to Ireland. The untold misery that the Church's teaching on contraception, combined with an unquestioning faith and the poverty of the land have meant to so many thousands of Irish homes, means nothing to this literary tourist...."

In the eight years that intervened between the American publication of *The Clown* and of *Group Portrait with Lady* (*Gruppenbild mit Dame*), Böll wrote only one novel, if it can be called that. When it came to America in 1968, *End of a Mission* (*Ende einer Dienstfahrt*) gained the unique distinction of becoming the only one of Böll's works in English translation *not* to be reviewed by the *New York Times Book Review*. It received only two short and fairly ignorable reviews. In marked contrast, *Group Portrait* attained the ultimate place of honor in the New York press, page one of the *New York Times Book Review* — after all, Böll had just won the Nobel Prize. A second signal honor was assigning the review to one of its editors. Richard Locke began his critique with a few negative points: that among Americans the more aggressive and innovative Grass is often more admired than Böll; that *Group Portrait* is far from being a perfect work of art; that it is in fact not the literary equal of *The Tin Drum*, *One Hundred Years of Solitude*, and *The First Circle*. The rest was praise, first of all for its sheer humaneness, epitomized in Böll's mundane heroine, "who moves through a fallen world with something of the unselfconscious moral beauty of Faulkner's Negroes." What is especially attractive is that Böll's "secular story about the workings of grace in a venal society" is achieved without cant; "he does not wear his morality on his sleeve." The book is the epitome of his life work, reminding us of "the virtues and charms of old-fashioned European Catholic humanism, and it gives old-fashioned pleasures." Secondly, Locke reasoned, by his decision to make a woman the focal point of his novel, Böll has taken full advantage of his remarkable sensitivity to women, a gift which among American male writers only John Updike comes close to sharing. The more direct expression of his strong erotic and moral affection for women "seems to have released literary energy blocked by the anger he so often feels toward German men and masculine society." In this view Locke was strongly supported by C. L. Markmann in the *Nation*, who felt that Böll's turn to the feminine is the basis for the novel's finest artistic achievement. "One cannot recall any German novelist of any period," he wrote, "so sensitive to the truly erotic and so gifted in investing a whole novel with an erotic climate never dependent on or infused with the prurient or the clinical or the sheerly meretricious." Thirdly, Locke had praise for Böll's ability to evoke in Joycean fashion from his pseudodocumentary material the social life of a city and its people over half a century. Among the nine reviews of *Group Portrait* only two were negative, but they were totally so. Broyard began his review in the *New York Times* as follows: "Leni Pfeiffer, the heroine of *Group Portrait with Lady*, is described by some 60 people — yet they have not persuaded me that she exists." Geoffrey Wolff in *Time* proffered essentially the same criticism; what Leni is really like and why the fictional author has been compelled to document her story in painstaking fashion is "a riddle that remains after the novel ends." Broyard felt, too, that the novel failed badly in its ironical pretensions. "It is one thing to read a two-page parody of a popular author in the *New Yorker* magazine and quite another to read 405 pages that seem simultaneously to be parodying sociology, journalism, and literature itself." These criticisms notwithstanding, the impact the novel made on the New York press was, on the whole, very favorable. It can best be gauged by the conversion of Walter Clemons, hard-boiled in-house critic of *Newsweek*, to Böll's cause. "Böll," he wrote, "is an acerb, intelligent, unglamorous writer who inspires only muted respect in this country and a guilty feeling that we ought to read him but would rather read Günter Grass. *Group Portrait with Lady* may change this. It is in no way thrilling or enchanting, but it has a dry, stubborn attraction. One finally comes to like a novelist who so resolutely declines to charm us."

When *The Lost Honor of Katharina Blum* (*Die verlorene Ehre der Katharina Blum*) was published in America two years after *Group Portrait*, it too was discussed on the front page of the *New York Times Book Review*. The gist of Michael Wood's critique was that the novel may be minor Böll, but minor Böll is better than major nearly everybody else. The most interesting part of his review pertains to Böll's place in the history of postwar German literature. Emphasizing the structural identity of Böll's German with Kafka's, Wood said the point is not that Böll writes like Kafka but that "Kafka created a literary language that could contemplate enormities, and Böll, intentionally or not, avails himself of that language." According to Wood George Steiner was not quite correct when he theorized that the German language was one of Hitler's accomplices. Rather "it was a question of German experience having caught up with Kafka, so that German writers now inherit the unspeakable as a major subject. Kafka's voice is one of the very few voices they can still use." Bruce Cook in the *New Republic* stressed Böll's contribution to the development of the German novel toward realism as a "style," a "convention," and a "basic means of coming to grips with experience." No postwar German writer, he contended, has defied more successfully than Böll a literary tradition that saw the novel mainly as an august vehicle for philosophical speculation and discussion. Well into the 20th century German novelists were still dealing in "abstractions, puzzles, vast moral issues, vague religious matters — but seldom with the gritty dirt of everyday experience." Taking writers like Hemingway and Graham Greene as his models, Böll made a virtue of plain talk. The six positive reviewers (only one was negative) tended to stress Böll's steady and reliable workmanship — to cite Cook again: "a fine and conscientious worker with words, a craftsman as careful in his own way as his father, who happened to be a cabinet maker, must have been in his." They found the moral issue at the heart of the novel particularly relevant to the American scene — how to preserve, as Cook put it, "the precarious balance that exists in a free society between the rights of the individual to his privacy and that of the press to provide information for the public," and they were impressed with Böll's ability to "contain and present" the issue within the limits of a brief but by no means slight novel.

Of all of Böll's major novels the last of them to appear in America before his death, *The Safety Net* (*Fürsorgliche Belagerung*), unfortunately received the least hospitable reception by the New York press. Six reviews were strongly negative, one was very mixed, and three were fairly positive. John Leonard of the *New York Times* summed up in terse fashion nearly all of the complaints hurled at the novel, "Almost everything goes wrong in 'The Safety Net.'... It is so cluttered with characters that none can breathe. It is so dense with ideas that it sinks to the bottom of the mind. It broods on capitalism, without energy, and on terrorism, without suspense.... It is about guilt, and nobody is to blame. It needs a joke or two, but Mr. Böll, having won a Nobel Prize, is no longer permitted to be funny." Only two of the more forcefully made criticisms were missing from Leonard's list. It was generally felt that having rejected a callous capitalism and having repudiated terrorism for a number of reasons, Böll could have provided a meaningful basis for the solution proffered by the protagonist at the end of the novel, namely, that some form of socialism must prevail. This remark was felt to be unmotivated and strange, coming as it did from a pillar of the business community, and also unclear in light of the fact, as R. Z. Shepperd pointed out in *Time*, "that forms of socialism already prevail in most modern democracies." John Updike in the *New Yorker* actually took it to mean communism, which compounded his confusion. The second criticism had to do with the narrative structure of the novel, a series of interior monologues. The trouble with them, Anthony Burgess pointed out in the *Saturday Review*, "is that they all have the same vocabulary and rhythm, so that it is not always easy to know who is doing the thinking." Expatiating on this point of criticism, Richard Gilman in the *New York Times Book Review* argued that a major difficulty in Böll's fiction is "his distribution of themes and points of view among so large a number of characters." His best novels are those few "in which he does allow a single consciousness to provide a focus," namely, *The Train Was on Time*, *The Clown*, and *Katharina Blum*, and "much of his best writing is to be found in his short stories, almost all of which are told in the first person." The most compelling case for the novel was made by Robert Otter, who argued in the *New Republic* that it has two great strengths: it is pervaded by a profound nostalgia for "a humanly necessary sense of community in a world marked by class distinctions and ideological division"; and this "unsentimental nostalgia is accompanied by a persuasive novelistic representation of the old-fashioned virtue of love."

Böll's one and only venture into autobiography, *What's to Become of the Boy? or: Something to Do with Books* (*Was soll aus dem Jungen bloß werden? Oder: Irgendwas mit Büchern*) reached the American reading public less than a year before his death. A clear indication of the esteem in which Böll was held as a social critic was the fact that Gordon A. Craig, America's best-known historian of contemporary Germany, was asked by the *New York Times Book Review* to evaluate this slim volume covering but four teen age years of Böll's life. Of the six reviewers Craig and Phoebe-Lou Adams of the *Atlantic* were the only ones, in fact, not to be disappointed by what the historian called a "charming memoir." Among the criticisms leveled by the other reviewers: the memoir is self-indulgent and superficial; the scope of the book is dismayingly narrow; the author spends too much time telling us how much he does not remember; he limits himself to the externals of his story. Singled out a number of times for special mention were Böll's revelation that he and some other members of his family contemplated leaving the Catholic Church when the Vatican accorded the new Hitler government its first major international recognition, his confession that the family found it expedient to pick Böll's brother Alois by a drawing of straws to join the Storm Troops, and his contention that there was a direct connection between the chauvinism of his non-Nazi high school teachers on the one hand and Stalingrad and Auschwitz on the other. The most positive note among the negative reviewers was struck by Andrea Barnet in the *Saturday Review*. Böll may have failed to re-create the early Hitler years in a meaningful, historical sense, she wrote; nevertheless he was successful in a smaller way. "At the heart of this book is an impulse far more tender than the moral urgency of his more rigorous books: an adolescent's first, tentative recognition of the human potential for injustice."

When Böll died in 1985, works of his that could be described as current had not enjoyed any major critical acclaim at the hands of the New York press since the mid-seventies. With *Group Portrait* (1973) and *Katharina Blum* (1975), he had reached the pinnacle of recognition — front page in the *New York Times Book Review* and strongly laudatory critiques. In light of these successes his next novel, *The Safety Net* (1979), received more attention by the New York press than any of his other works since *The Clown* and the minor work that followed in its wake, *Absent without Leave* (both 1965). Having so much attention, as we have seen, proved to be unfortunate, for the novel was clobbered by the critics, as was Böll's next work and the last to appear in America before his death, the brief autobiography of his teens (1984). When his final novel, *Women in a River Landscape* (*Frauen vor Flußlandschaft*), did appear here, Böll had been gone for three years and had not scored big with the New York critics in thirteen, all of which may help account for the fact that the author seemed no longer to be news. The novel was reviewed only once, but this lack of attention turned out in all likelihood to be a good thing for Böll's reputation in America, since the book had been subjected to heavy attacks by some West German critics for being, as they saw it, among the weakest of his novels from the standpoint of form, plot content, and potential interest. It was also a good thing and, in a sort of metaphysical sense, a very apt thing that the person asked to review the novel for the *New York Times Book Review* was Vivian Gornick, a former staff writer of the *Village Voice* with decidedly progressive leanings, a feminist whose book on middle-class family life in Egypt praised a segment of society in which familial and personal relationships based on tenderness take precedence over worldly success and the acquisition of material goods, and a sociologist whose study of why American men and women of good will had been attracted to and ultimately rejected communism was permeated by a Camusian weltanschauung. Unlike some German critics, Gornick was not at all bothered by the apparently incongruous mixture of dramatic and prose forms. "Although the book is called a novel in dialogues and soliloquies," she wrote, "it in fact reads like a play script. It is almost as though Böll knew it was to be his final piece of work and, wasting no time, put what he had to say into the most economical form he could manage." The novel is "his stripped, and as it turned out, final statement in the matter of German worldliness" — the result of that pervasive moral indifference that made the new Germany just like the old. Böll's oeuvre, Gornick contended, rather than being descriptive or psychological, was "relentlessly social," a refusal to digest the evidence "that Hitler's incredible existence — in the world and as a German — had not made his countrymen and women see that they must make themselves anew from the inside out." It was precisely this refusal which made Böll "a powerful and influential writer, gave him his authority." In *Women in a River Landscape* Böll did away with investigative reporters and with the narration and dramatization of events. He boiled everything down to "people standing on a balcony, overlooking the flowing river (time and nature as backdrop), while they explain themselves endlessly, and to no avail, in a work depressingly reminiscent of a novel of the 1930's." "The writing," Gornick concluded epitaphically, "bears the stamp of one of the most genuinely high-minded men of letters this century has produced, and the words spoken on those terraces above the Rhine remain memorable long after the book has been laid down."

I began this paper on a personal note and I should like to end it on one. Of all the things said about Böll in the New York press over a period of more than thirty years there were three which struck me as particularly memorable. One was an editorial opinion in *America* written in the aftermath of President Reagan's Geneva summit meeting with Premier Gorbachev in November 1985. Entitled "When a President Went to Moscow," the editorial began as follows: "Once upon a time a president, backed neither by missile systems nor army divisions, a president who represented the most powerless group of people on the globe, went to the Soviet Union to negotiate on behalf of the human spirit. It sounds mythical but it really happened early in the winter of 1972. The man was the late Heinrich Böll and he had just been elected the international president of PEN, the worldwide association of writers."[9] The author of this tribute to Böll was fellow novelist Thomas Fleming, who went on to say that the American Center of PEN, of which he was the president, had strongly supported Böll for international president, not only because the Americans admired him as a writer but because they were even more impressed with the man they met at the International Congress held near Dublin in 1971. "In person, he emanated the inner spirit of his books — a stubborn faith in human goodness and God's mysterious mercy." The second was something fellow novelist Ernst Pawel wrote in a guest article printed in the *New York Times Book Review* shortly after Böll received the Nobel Prize; that the secret of Böll's appeal is "simple beyond understanding — integrity and a dash of genius; the utter, uncompromising integrity of the man coming through his work. He is both profound and eminently readable, a rare feat in the past and now all but outlawed."[10] And finally, in one of the last of the 127 reviews we have been surveying, fellow novelist, poet, and essayist D. J. Enright, the only one of our critics, by the way, to have reviewed Böll both for the *New York Times Book Review* and the *New York Review of Books*, emphasized in a very compelling way this inseparability of talent and integrity sensed by the majority of critics writing for the New York press. After giving a number of examples of how Böll's protagonists reflect his way of thinking and feeling, Enright pays him the ultimate compliment. "Böll's characters have the gift of always being in the wrong — which proves they are right.... In the novel *Billiards at Half-past Nine*, the anti-Nazi Schrella escapes to the Netherlands, where he is jailed for uttering threats against a Dutch politician who maintains

---

[9] Thomas Fleming, "When a President Went to Moscow," *America*, 1 February 1986, 62–64.

[10] Ernst Pawel, "Böll — Integrity and a Dash of Genius," *New York Times Book Review*, 5 November 1972, 47.

that all Germans should be killed. When the Germans enter the country they free him under the impression that he is a martyr. They soon discover their mistake, and he flees to England, where he is jailed for threatening a British politician who contends that nothing should be preserved of Germany but its works of art."[11]

---

[11] D. J. Enright, *New York Times Book Review*, 23 Feb. 1986, 42.

A Different Drummer:
The American Reception of Günter Grass

PATRICK O'NEILL

GÜNTER GRASS IS ALMOST certainly the best-known contemporary German writer in North America. He is certainly the only German writer ever to have been awarded what is probably the ultimate accolade of North American popular criticism, a cover story in *Time* magazine, which appeared as long ago as 1970. From the North American appearance of *The Tin Drum* in 1963 to the appearance of *The Rat* in 1987 and *Show Your Tongue* in 1989, each of his books has been immediately translated and promptly reviewed in the major reviewing organs. In comparative terms, his high-profile reception in Germany and in North America has been marked by one major similarity — namely, the polarization of response. But that surface similarity rests on two major differences. I shall commence with the similarity, continue with the differences, and conclude with one or two brief theoretical reflections on the role of similarity and difference in the reception of any translated text.

The German reception of Grass, as we may remember, was polarized from the beginning.[1] In 1958 the thirty-one-year-old Grass's literary

---

[1] I have already outlined this polarized reception in my *Critical Essays on Günter Grass* (Boston: G. K. Hall, 1987), drawing largely on the documentation assembled by Gert Loschütz, ed., *Von Buch zu Buch — Günter Grass in der Kritik: Eine Dokumentation* (Neuwied: Luchterhand, 1968). The present paper develops arguments first presented in my Introduction to *Critical Essays*. That volume also contains a selection of the reviews on which the arguments concerning the North American reception of Grass's work are based.

career was given a highly auspicious start in the form of a prepublication prize of the prestigious Gruppe 47 for the book that was soon to make Grass's name a household word, *Die Blechtrommel*. In 1959, in which year the novel appeared, he was awarded another major literary prize by a panel of critics in the north German city-state of Bremen, only to have the Bremen municipal government promptly refuse to present him with the award. He received the Berlin Critics' Prize in 1960, the French *Prix pour le meilleur livre étranger* in 1962, by which time *Katz und Maus* had appeared, and was elected a member of the German Academy of Arts in 1963, in which year *Hundejahre*, the third volume of what would later be called the "Danzig Trilogy," also appeared. In 1965 he received the prestigious Georg Büchner Prize — and in the same year *Die Blechtrommel* was publicly burned in Düsseldorf by a religious youth organization. By that time, we may remember, he was also the defendant in some forty legal actions — none of them successful — that had been launched against *Die Blechtrommel* and *Katz und Maus*.

The year that saw *Die Blechtrommel* burned in Germany saw Grass the recipient of an honorary doctorate from Kenyon College in Gambier, Ohio. The trilogy had reached North American readers in Ralph Manheim's translation over a much more concentrated period of time than had been the case in Germany, *The Tin Drum* appearing in the United States in February 1963 (though carrying a 1961 copyright date), *Cat and Mouse* only six months later in August 1963, and *Dog Years* in May 1965. They arrived, as Sigrid Mayer points out in her essay "Grüne Jahre für Grass," already preceded by Grass's European

---

Bibliographical information on many other reviews and articles in both German and English will be found in my *Günter Grass: A Bibliography 1955–1975* (Toronto: University of Toronto Press, 1976). For a critical analysis of German-language reviews of Grass's work from *Die Blechtrommel* to *Der Butt* see Franz Josef Görtz's article "Der Provokateur als Wahlhelfer: Kritisches zur Grass-Kritik," *Text + Kritik* 1/1a (1978): 162–74. For a more detailed analysis of the German reception of the earlier work see Görtz's *Günter Grass — Zur Pathogenese eines Markenbilds. Die Literaturkritik der Massenmedien 1959–1969. Eine Untersuchung mit Hilfe datenverarbeitender Methoden* (Meisenheim am Glan: Hain, 1978). For a compilation of extracts from early North American reviews of Grass's work see R. L. White's *Günter Grass in America: The Early Years* (Hildesheim: Olms, 1981). On the reception of Grass's work in the U.S. from *The Tin Drum* to *The Flounder* see Sigrid Mayer's article "Grüne Jahre für Grass: Die Rezeption in den Vereinigten Staaten," *Text + Kritik* 1/1a (1978): 151–61.

reputation, and *The Tin Drum* in particular unleashed a flood of reviews. Though opinions were by no means undivided, North American readers were obviously less predisposed than their German counterparts had been to be shocked by the historical and political implications of the three books, all of which deal grotesquely with the national shame of the Nazi years, and the general reaction of the reviewers was that it was a very good thing that at long last a German author was forcing German readers to come to grips, however uncomfortably, with the still-unresolved national past. As to the style, if I may permit myself the luxury of quoting something I have written elsewhere, "*The Tin Drum* was variously declared to be fantastic, romantic, expressionist, surreal, grotesque, absurd, realistic, and/or naturalistic, and to have more or less marked affinities with the work of Dante, Rabelais, Grimmelshausen, Bunyan, Swift, Sterne, Voltaire, Goethe, Melville, Proust, Thomas Mann, Joyce, Beckett, Faulkner, Camus, Dos Passos, Kafka, Döblin, Brecht, Böll, Johnson, Ionesco, Nabokov, and/or Heller."[2]

The Tin Drum was on the *New York Times* list of bestsellers for three months and sold some 400,000 copies in its first year, thus largely guaranteeing the instant success of *Cat and Mouse* and *Dog Years* as well. There was some disappointment expressed that *Cat and Mouse* was such a slim volume after what reviewers had delighted in describing as the baroque luxuriance of *The Tin Drum*; this perceived deficiency was more than made up for by the imposing bulk of *Dog Years*, which was praised as taking up the Danzig saga again along the lines laid down in *The Tin Drum*. This nostalgic reaction was to become a recurrent one both in Germany and in North America over the next decade or so, each novel in turn, for all the praise or condemnation that might also be lavished on it, being greeted in each case with more or less open disappointment that Grass had not chosen to rewrite *The Tin Drum*, had ceased to be the "drummer of Danzig," as he had early been dubbed.[3]

---

[2] *Critical Essays*, 4–5; this summation draws on the work of Sigrid Mayer ("Grüne Jahre") and of R. L. White.

[3] The phrase is John Simon's, who used it as the title of his review of *The Tin Drum*, "The Drummer of Danzig," *Partisan Review* 30 (1963): 446–53; repr. O'Neill, *Critical Essays*, 21–27.

Grass's work in the second half of the sixties, in fact, during which time he was actively engaged in West German politics, campaigning vigorously on behalf of the moderate reformist policies of the Social Democratic Party (SPD), moved markedly away from both the strongly foregrounded thematic concern with the Nazi past and the stylistic extravagance of the Danzig trilogy. The two most important texts of those years are the play *Die Plebejer proben den Aufstand* and the narrative *Örtlich betäubt* (1969), both, in another marked contrast to the trilogy, characterized by a severe clarity and economy of expression. *Die Plebejer* deals with a fictionalized version of events surrounding the East German workers' uprising of June 1953, focusing specifically on the role of the artist, and while the degree to which Grass may have intended the play as a personal attack on Brecht exercised a number of German critics considerably, the play was by no means the success that the trilogy had been. Its fate in North America, translated as *The Plebeians Rehearse the Uprising*, was no less lukewarm. In the case of *Örtlich betäubt*, however, translated as *Local Anaesthetic*, the divergence between the German and the North American reception is striking.

Örtlich betäubt is centered on the conflict between a German schoolboy, who intends to immolate his beloved dachshund as a protest against American involvement in Vietnam, and his middle-aged teacher, who espouses the wholly unexciting position that radical action is never as useful in the long run as reasoned democratic process. It was greeted in Germany with general disappointment, critics suggesting none too kindly that Grass, under the cover of writing a novel, had merely written a political tract extolling the virtues of an SPD-inspired moderate reformism. Especially the radical young, who had seized enthusiastically on Oskar, the drumming midget of *The Tin Drum*, as an emblem of anarchic disruption, now turned away disgustedly from what they perceived as the calcified neorationalist moralism of Grass's latest work. In the U.S., on the other hand, *Local Anaesthetic* fared very well indeed. Its appearance in early 1970 was greeted enthusiastically in the major reviewing organs, the seal of approval being most ostentatiously conferred when, as already mentioned, *Time* ran a cover story saluting the now forty-two-year-old Grass as possibly the world's greatest living novelist.[4]

Grass's literary output during the early seventies, still overshadowed by his continuing political involvement, was somewhat low-key, the main work of those years, *Aus dem Tagebuch einer Schnecke*, translated as *From the Diary of a Snail*, meeting with no more than a polite response both in Germany and in the U.S. There were, indeed, suggestions on both sides of the Atlantic at this time that Grass had by now clearly passed his prime and was essentially using the blend of fiction and nonfiction characteristic of the *Diary* (and, indeed, of all of his later works) to disguise that his narrative genius had in fact run dry. This was before *The Flounder*, however.

Heralded by a highly effective publicity campaign, *Der Butt* saw the light of day in July 1977, sold 450,000 copies within two years, and earned Grass, just about to turn fifty, some three million marks in royalties on its first edition alone. The critics were as enthusiastic as the book-buying public, almost every major journal and newspaper with any pretensions to literary interests devoting generous space and (although there were certainly strongly dissenting voices) in the main generous praise to the new Grass — and with almost every reviewer, be it said in passing, noting with satisfaction that *Der Butt* was far closer to the style of the Danzig trilogy than to that of his more recent texts. Critical reaction in North America, where *The Flounder* arrived in translation in 1978, was if anything even more clamorous. The scale was epic, the style robust, the narrative experimentation daring, the central concern — a feminist (or, as some readers would have it, an antifeminist) rereading of history — topical in the extreme. Reactions ranged from delight to fury — the latter largely on the part of readers who did not see feminism and humor as appropriate bedfellows — but one thing was clear: the tin drummer was back.[5] The following year saw another major international success for Grass and another reconfir-

---

[4] "The Dentist's Chair as an Allegory of Life," *Time*, 13 April 1970, 68–70; repr. O'Neill, *Critical Essays*, 38–49.

[5] See Sigrid Mayer's detailed study, "The Critical Reception of *The Flounder* in the United States: Epic and Graphic Aspects," in Siegfried Mews, ed. *"The Fisherman and His Wife": Günter Grass's 'The Flounder' in Critical Perspective* (New York: AMS Press, 1983), 179–95, also her listing of North American reviews of the novel in Mews, 214–16.

mation of the tin drummer image. Volker Schlöndorff's film version of *The Tin Drum* — made in collaboration with Grass — was released in 1979 to both popular and critical applause and won several prestigious awards, including an American Oscar for the best foreign film of the year.

Riding on the coattails of these two major successes, *Das Treffen in Telgte*, translated two years later as *The Meeting at Telgte*, an exploration of the world-historical role of writing — which it situates somewhere between vital importance and total impotence — was well received in both Germany and North America.[6] *Kopfgeburten oder Die Deutschen sterben aus* appeared in 1980, and in translation in 1982, to be greeted with the by now not unusual pattern of reaction to Grass's books in Germany, indignant rejection on the one hand, from those who saw only SPD-electioneering in the very thin disguise of narrative fiction, enthusiastic praise on the other, from those who saw another demonstration of Grass's consummate mastery of the art of narrative. American reaction, as in the case of most of Grass's books, tended to substitute at one end of the scale indifference for indignation, and at the other extreme even more lavish plaudits. Grass's next major work, *Die Rättin*, dealing with a doomsday scenario of total nuclear disaster and preceded by lengthy extracts in major German newspapers — and a 112-page prepublication parody by one Günter Ratte, entitled *Der Grass*[7] — was an instant best-seller in Germany and remained so for several months, impelling most reviewers to words of high praise, and some others to flat assertions that the book was simply not worth reading. While received with substantial interest in North America, however, *The Rat*, I think it fair to say, was greeted with no very great enthusiasm, certainly not with the furor caused first by *The Tin Drum* and again by *The Flounder*.[8] Grass's latest work to date, *Zunge zeigen*,

---

[6] Sigrid Mayer lists early North American reviews of *The Meeting at Telgte* in Mews, 216–17.

[7] Günter Ratte (pseud.), *Der Grass* (Frankfurt am Main: Eichborn, 1986).

[8] A handy synopsis of the conflict of opinions emerging from German-language reviews of *Die Rättin* can be found in *Fachdienst Germanistik* 4, no. 5 (1986): 12, 14. For the North American response see Jaroslaw Anders, "Floundering," *New Republic*, 13–20 July 1987, 29–32; Janette Turner Hospital, "Post Futurum Blues," *New York Times Book Review*, 5 July 1987; and the *Time* review, signed P. G., "Sinking Ship," *Time*, 20 July 1987.

focusing thematically on poverty in the third world, met with a marked lack of enthusiasm in Germany, and there does not seem to be any particular reason to assume that its recent translation, *Show Your Tongue*, will fare much better in North America.

Over the now more than twenty-five years of Grass's public literary career since *The Tin Drum*, the North American reaction to his work has for most of the time, as we have seen, largely paralleled the German reaction — and this might well seem a relatively meager conclusion for our survey to reach. What is more interesting are the reasons for that similarity, and these are different in at least two quite major ways. The major similarity of the North American and the German reception of his work has certainly been a very noticeable polarization of opinion. There has, however, been a clear qualitative difference in this polarization, German reaction varying from outrage — whether on the political Right or the political Left — to enthusiastic applause, the American reaction varying rather from outright indifference, if not boredom, to even more lavish praise. The difference is the result of two reasons, the first political, the second linguistic. These two factors will play a role in the reception of any translated author, of course, but in Grass's case their importance is a good deal more striking than usual.

As far as his German readers are concerned, Grass, quite naturally, is a German writer writing for Germans; for his American audience, however, he was very quickly elevated to the essentially depoliticized status of a "world author" — a status also achieved over the same period by such more or less overtly politically engaged writers as García Márquez, Pasternak, and even Solzhenitsyn. The implications of this elevation for political responses are obvious enough: while German readers react immediately and often passionately to Grass's presentation of the West German past and present, American readers can and do distance themselves from these "private" dynamics of the work's German reception. The American response, in this sense, and as is also quite natural, has consequently always been more the reaction to a conversation overheard than the response of a participant in that conversation. There has been one major and symptomatic exception to this; American reaction to *The Flounder* was if anything more extreme than the response to *Der Butt* in Germany, the political context of this particular novel far outreaching the limits of German local politics. The importance of those limits in general terms as a factor in the differential reception of Grass's work is, however, crucial. From being the bogeyman of the German political Right in the early sixties, Grass quickly became the bête noire of the radicalized Left — not instead, but as well — in the later sixties and has by and large continued to occupy this uncomfortable position between the two camps ever since. Most of this was of little or no importance to American readers, as can be seen particularly in the case of *Local Anaesthetic*. In Germany the reaction to this novel's apparently defeatist political attitude was generally very negative; in North America the political content naturally tended to be defused into an acceptably generalized and somewhat whimsical satire on bourgeois liberalism and its perceived impotence.

The second major differentiator between the German and the American responses is that of language. Obviously, most American readers deal with Grass in translation. Once again, that is to say, the conversation is to a degree one picked up by an eavesdropper, and the reader's reaction to Grass, as in the case of any translated author, is actually a reaction to Grass as mediated by his translator. Almost all of Grass's work to reach North American readers, including all of the fiction (with the very recent exception of *Show Your Tongue*), has been translated by Ralph Manheim — and Manheim's translations have from the very beginning been vigorously condemned by some critics and enthusiastically applauded by others. Such a response to a translator's work is not particularly unusual, of course. What distinguishes the reaction to Manheim's translations of Grass is its virulence — and its polarization. For every critic who deplores a long list of unpardonable blunders in Manheim's versions (and there are many of these critics), there is another who would agree with John Leonard that "when the gnomes of Stockholm get around to giving [Grass] his Nobel Prize, they should give one as well to his admirable translator, Ralph Manheim."[9]

To summarize, then: in both respects, political and linguistic, the American response to Grass's work can be characterized as a reaction to

---

[9] John Leonard, "Consider a Billion Germans," *New York Times Book Review*, 14 March 1982, 21. For a critical analysis of Manheim's translations from *The Tin Drum* to *From the Diary of a Snail* see Sigrid Mayer's article "Growing Grass in English," *Yearbook of Comparative and General Literature* 25 (1976): 64–69.

a conversation overheard; and in both respects it tends to polarize, just as the German response also tends to polarize (but for distinctly different reasons, as we have seen). In conclusion, it needs to be said that, however interesting the anecdotal details may be — and such details, we might remember, tend to increase in interest in direct proportion to the visibility of the author involved — the difference in theoretical terms between Grass's German reception and his reception in North America is in its essentials different only in degree rather than in kind from the differential reception of any writer at home and abroad. All writers, however great or small their individual talents may be, are received in one way by that receptive community whose values also produced those writers and in quite a different way by those other receptive communities whose values are shaped by having been produced precisely in different places, times, and contexts.[10] Grass read in German by a German is one thing, Grass read in English by an American (or an Irishman) is quite another — but then Grass read even in German by an Irishman or an American is essentially Grass of an entirely different color, and this is something we frequently overlook, although we would be well advised to keep it firmly in mind. Grass, of course, has absolutely no claim to any uniqueness in this. Any author read in his or her "native" receptive community is one thing and is quite another for readers in a "foreign" receptive community, even if those readers read the very same words in the very same language — and it may or may not need emphasizing at this point that this is no matter at all for any regret or attempted rectification. One of the most pertinent and necessary lessons of postformalist literary theory in its multiple shadings has surely been the lesson that reading texts in translation is essentially the only option the reader ever has. The drummer, in other words (and even if they are the same words), is always a different drummer.

---

[10] The concept of receptive communities here is based on Stanley Fish's notion of interpretive communities in his *Is There a Text in This Class? The Authority of Interpretive Communities* (Cambridge: Harvard University Press, 1980), 14.

The Economics of Literature: More Thoughts on the Reception of German Literature in the *New York Times*

VOLKMAR SANDER

EVER SINCE THE ECONOMICS of literature — as distinguished from aesthetic considerations of literary texts — has attracted our attention, we have had a lot to learn. On the one hand, there used to be Art and Culture, looked upon as being above mere trade, untouched by profit motives or political expediency, "expressing free and unconstrained subjectivity." On the other hand, there is all of a sudden also the "brute reality of ambition and calculation, of writing as commodity production," subject to the vagaries of the market place.[1]

We now know that Walter Benjamin's seminal essay on the relationship between the quasi-theological superstructure of aestheticism and the base and changing mode of mechanical reproduction of art products was only the beginning. The acceleration of technical innovation during our present phase of information explosion, including the production and dissemination of books, is seriously challenging beliefs, long held and fondly cherished, about the role of literature and literary critics. From what was called the "Gutenberg galaxy," the atmosphere of quiet contemplation, to the computerized, global transmission of data in seconds, which makes a fetish out of the

---

[1] Alan Trachtenberg, "Writers and the Market," *Nation*, 3 July 1989, 23.

newest craze, the development is about to overtake our capacity to absorb and retain knowledge in our accustomed fashion. This is not what post-Enlightenment thinkers had in mind when at the beginning of the last century they coined the slogan "Wissen ist Macht" (knowledge, or information, is power).

In a recent survey of the change in buying habits conducted by the West German Bookseller Organization we read, "More and more readers are concerned about the practical value to which their reading can be put." Especially younger people expect "that the time they spend reading somehow 'pays.'" They look upon books not as "Kulturträger" (repositories of culture) but primarily as sources for obtaining information.[2] From this state of affairs it is not very far to the belief that to read fiction is positively harmful to one's career. For the publishing houses — or rather printing concerns, since most publishers these days belong to one of the handful of media giants — this probably makes no difference. Following the laws of the market, they not only satisfy perceived desires but create new ones almost at will. Another recent report from the business section of a West German newspaper, the *Frankfurter Rundschau*, states, "Distribution firms urgently request publishers finally to draw the consequences from sales statistics and to withdraw titles that are hard or impossible to sell from retail stores." They of course mean us! A bit further on in the article this utilitarian verdict is sharpened to become an ax of moral execution: "It is not permissible to deny shelf space to titles that are selling well and to reserve that space to which they are entitled for a presentation of bad or unsalable objects."[3] This is the business section of the newspaper and

---

[2] Uwe Wittstock, "Geld gegen Geist oder Ab in die Nische," *Frankfurter Allgemeine Zeitung*, 20 Sept. 1989. Unless otherwise noted, all translations are my own.

[3] "Presse Grosso mahnt Verlage," *Frankfurter Rundschau*, 13 Sept. 1989. See also the decision of Random House to cut back on Pantheon Books, one of its subsidiaries, in "End of the Line," *Nation*, 5 March 1990; and ibid. "Newhoused," 19 March 1990. From the senior editors' letter of resignation: "The Pantheon we have all worked for is, we believe, ending. Good books may still be published here, but they will not be good *Pantheon* books. These, after all, were the books that involved risk — and not just the bottom line, but politically, socially, culturally" (p. 369). See also: Tom Engelhardt, "At Pantheon, Closed Books," *New York Times*, 8 March 1990, 25. Dough Ireland writes (in *Village Voice*, 13 March 1990, 38) of "unlettered greed" and quotes Pantheon authors like John Berger, "If publishing is run on the principles of supermarket accounting, on how much they brought in within the last 12 months, then literature is being destroyed," and Ariel Dorfman, "Even

hence this opinion is presented as a matter of fact, in all seriousness and without any touch of irony. We are supposedly dealing with a free market; there is much talk about "free choice," of existing "demand" and of satisfying real needs, and consequently this development, about which we cannot rejoice, is presented as inevitable and irreversible. The publishers no longer call upon us to give advice, but if we are asked at all, then we are asked to cope and adjust to the circumstances. One other caveat, self-evident but noteworthy nonetheless: we cannot hope to shed much light on the mechanics of the reception of anything unless we see it as imbedded in its overall social and political context. Books and information about them are, after all, only a small part of the overall problem of cultural transfer and news dissemination in general. In their study *Manufacturing Consent* Edward S. Herman and Noam Chomsky provide a devastating indictment of the notion of a "free press" and describe how the mass media are used to shape public opinion.[4] In their depiction of various "news filters," of what they call a "guided market system" and of self-imposed censorship, they show how the public is fed disinformation, not randomly but systematically. For this rather alarming development they coined the phrase "intentional ignorance," the consciously planned desire not to want to know certain things. For us, familiar with modern German literature, this is reminiscent of *Galileo*, Kipphardt's play on J. Robert Oppenheimer, or Dürrenmatt's quip about Brecht, of whom he said "er denkt so unerbittlich, weil er an vieles so unerbittlich nicht denkt" ("He thinks so relentlessly because there is so much he relentlessly ignores"). The ideological scissors in our own heads are far more effective than all external mechanisms of repression or censorship.

It is against this background that we have to ask ourselves about the role of literature. How and what is the reception of German literature in this country, especially as reflected in the *New York Times?* Over the

---

the dead are now being suppressed. The U.S. is becoming more and more closed — what's happening here is part of the growing self-censorship. The U.S. doesn't *want* to know what's happening in the world."

[4] Edward S. Herman and Noam Chomsky, *Manufacturing Consent: The Political Economy of the Mass Media* (New York: Pantheon, 1988). See also Philip Green's review (*Nation*, 15 May 1989), where he states, "Not to have read [Chomsky's essays] ... is to court genuine ignorance."

past fifteen years a number of dissertations have been written at my university, nine in all, that have tried to collect basic material to answer that question. They investigate a variety of sources, such as the *New York Herald Tribune*, *Saturday Review*, *Atlantic Monthly*, and the *Times Literary Supplement*. Four of them deal with the *New York Times*, three documenting the full century 1870 to 1970, and a fourth one, finished ten years later, which tries to combine and evaluate the collected data.[5] In addition, I have reported on the results in various articles elsewhere, so that it is not necessary to repeat myself here.[6] Let me summarize only the most general data: dealt with are the frequency of reviews, their scope, their relative number compared with other foreign language reviews, the genres and topics covered, the change in editorial attitude over the years, as well as dependence of critical fashions on extraliterary trends and conditions, including politics. Contrary to general opinion, there is no bias, let alone discrimination; the absolute number of reviews of foreign books is decreasing, but the relative distribution among reviews of works from German, French, Italian, Spanish, etc. has remained surprisingly constant over the years. It is the total number that gives cause for concern. In a typical year the progression from publication to review is about the following: of the 21,000 titles published in Germany, 750 (or 3.5 percent) are translated; 30 of these (or 0.1 percent) are reviewed. If it is true, as I think it is, that only what has been published can be reviewed, only what has been reviewed in the

---

[5] John Gordon, "The New York Herald Tribune 1935–1966," Ph.D. diss., 1974; Eva Schlesinger, "Atlantic Monthly 1919–1944," Ph.D. diss., 1976; Robert Granville, "Saturday Review 1945–1970," Ph.D. diss., 1975; Constance Hughes-Regn, "The Times Literary Supplement 1945–1960," Ph.D. diss., 1978. The three dissertations, all completed in 1973, cover the book-review section of the *New York Times* in various periods; Wolfgang Heinsohn's (1870–1918), Alice Carse's (1919–1944), and Doris Auerbach's (1945–1970). The last study is by Ursula Diezemann, "The Reception of German Literature in the American Press 1919–1970," Ph.D. diss., 1989.

[6] "Die 'New York Times Book Review': Zur Rezeption deutscher Literatur in den USA," *Basis* 4 (1973): 86–97; "Zur Rezeption der deutschen Literatur in Amerika," in S. Grünwald and B. A. Beatie, ed., *Theorie und Kritik* (Bern: Francke, 1974), 57–65; "Zur Rezeption der deutschen Literatur in der 'New York Times,'" in W. Paulsen, ed., *Die USA und Deutschland* (Bern: Francke, 1976), 160–73; "Zum deutschen Buch in Amerika: Produktion und Rezeption," *Deutsche Vierteljahrsschrift* 60, no. 3 (1986): 484–95. See also: "Der deutsche Bildungsroman in Amerika," *Deutsche Rundschau* 87 (1961): 1032–38; "Corviniana non leguntur: Gedanken zur Raabe-Rezeption in Amerika und England," *Jahrbuch der Raabe-Gesellschaft 1980*, 118–27.

Times can sell, and only what has been sold in appreciable numbers can have any effect — then our question about reception has to start with studying the rules and modes of selection. If only 0.1 percent is transmitted, how can there be any kind of comprehensive image? Does it not by definition have to be distorted? Just one extreme example of many: in a particular year 1.2 percent of the titles published in Germany fell into the category of "military books" (*Militär- und Wehrwesen*). Among the books translated this group constituted already 4.5 percent of the total; among those finally reviewed, 26 percent, or fully one in four. This example demonstrates what H. R. Jauss called the "Rückkoppelungseffekt rezeptionsästhetischer Prozesse" (feed-back effect of the process of reception aesthetics), a vicious cycle of self-fulfilling prophecy.[7] If one is convinced anyway that Germans have a predilection for the military, such selectively one-sided reviewing will serve to confirm this prejudice. The average American reader, who either has or wants no access to other information beside that in the *Times*, must get the impression that every German lieutenant, and certainly every general, is writing his memoirs — in short that nothing has changed.

Rather than repeating previous findings, I should like to extend the survey by reporting on the book reviewing of the *Times* from 1986 to 1988. Hans Winterberg of the Goethe Institute Boston, in cooperation with Inter Nationes / Bonn, has collected data for years. His survey of German-related reviews in British and American papers lists a total of 210 for the year 1986, 164 for 1987, 174 for 1988, or an average of about 180 per year. Of those, 27 (or 14.8 percent) per year, appeared in the *New York Times*, both in the weekend book reviews (23) and in the daily paper (4).

Divided by subject matter, the two largest categories by far deal with literature (24) and history (29), followed by psychology (5), philosophy (3), contemporary affairs (3), music (2), general essays (2), and one each on physics, art, photography, and film.

---

[7] Jauss, "Die interpretierende Rezeption eines Textes ... [setzt] den Erfahrungskontext einer ästhetischen Wahrnehmung immer schon voraus" (Reading and interpreting a text always presupposes the aesthetic perception which is determined by the reader's own context of experience). H. R. Jauss, *Literaturgeschichte als Provokation* (Frankfurt am Main: Suhrkamp, 1970), 175–77:

292   The Fortunes of German Writers in America

In the history group only 3 reviews are concerned with various questions of history,[8] whereas the large bulk, as is to be expected, deals more specifically with various aspects of contemporary affairs or recent Nazi history.[9] Included in this group are 8 studies or reflections on the Holocaust.[10]

Also perhaps included in this group should be 3 reviews on contemporary affairs, Willy Brandt's report on "Arms and Hunger," a history of the Baader-Meinhof group, and an account of the flop of the Hitler diaries.[11]

Of the 24 reviews discussing literature, 3 are concerned with older authors, (Rilke, Musil and Broch); all others review contemporary texts or, in the case of some older texts, new translations.[12] Three additional pieces, more in the nature of essays than reviews, deal with Karl May, Goethe's influence, and Peter Demetz's "After the Fires" on postwar German literature.[13] Three more are in a borderline category between

---

[8] Frederick the Great (2-2-86); Fritz Stern (10-6-89); Rosa Luxemburg (6-14-87).

[9] Berlin Olympics (6-15-87); White Rose (8-17-86); "Freicorps" (Theweleit: "Male Phantasies," 6-21-87); Daily life (1-16-87); Women in Germany (twice: 3-2-87, 1-3-88); Berlin Diaries 1940-45 (4-5-87); I. G. Farben (6-7-87); Weimar collapse (8-2-87); Caricatures (n.d.); Goebbels's Novel (8-28-87); U.S. recruitment of Nazis (n.d., 1988); "Operation Paperclip" (twice: 2-9-88, 2-14-88), Nazi-Soviet pact (11-20-88); Nazi medicine (n.d.); Nazi education (n.d.). One review deals with postwar history, "Two Germanies since '45" (n.d., 1988).

[10] The Holocaust (2-9-86; 6-22-86); Edith Stein (n.d., 1986); P. Sichrowsky (3-17-86); Nazi doctors (twice: 9-25-86, 10-5-86); Death Camps (n.d., 1987); Child in Auschwitz (2-21-88); Reflections on the Holocaust (n.d., 1988); Children's Books (n.d., 1988).

[11] Willy Brandt (n.d., 1986); Baader-Meinhof (1-3-88); Hitler diaries (4-13-86).

[12] R. M. Rilke (9-21-86); H. Broch (1-20-87), R. Musil (4-10-88). The other authors are: E. Canetti (two books: 7-1-86; 8-10-86); H. Böll (two books: 2-23-86; n.d., 1988); G. Hofmann (1-26-86); P. Süsskind (two books: 9-16-86 and again 9-21-86; 5-23-88); H. Chr. Buch, (n.d., 1986); P. Handke (two books: 7-27-86; 8-7-88); P. Celan (two books in one review: n.d. 1986); G. Grass (7-5-87); H. Bieneck (2-22-87); U. Johnson (11-8-87); M. Walser (11-1-87); I. Bachmann (11-29-87); F. Dürrenmatt (6-12-87); J. Becker (11-27-88); M. Maron (7-10-88); P. Härtling (8-28-88); W. Koeppen (12-18-88).

[13] F. Morton: "Tales of the Grand Teutons; Karl May among the Indians" (1-4-87); M. Walser: "Things Go Better with Goethe" (3-2-86); J. Ryan: "Compassion and the German Heart" (12-24-86).

The Economics of Literature 293

literature and psychology, reviews about the current reevaluation of fairy tales.[14]

Psychology proper is the subject of 5 reviews, 2 on Freud, 1 on his daughter Anna Freud, 1 on C. G. Jung, and 1 on Konrad Lorenz.[15] Philosophy is the topic of reviews of books by H. G. Gadamer, J. Habermas, and of *The Principle of Hope* by E. Bloch, which although written in the United States during Bloch's stay in the thirties and forties was not completely translated until 1985.[16]

All the remaining reviews must be grouped under "miscellaneous," since each subject is represented by only one review over these three years.[17]

Some books were deemed so important that they were reviewed twice, once in the back pages of the daily paper, usually by one of the regular book review editors, and once again more prominently in the *New York Times Sunday Book Review* by an outside reviewer. The five books thus treated twice during these three years are Robert Jay Lifton's *The Nazi Doctors* reviewed by Christopher Lehmann-Haupt (daily: 25 Sept. 1985) and by Bruno Bettelheim (Sunday: 5 Oct. 1986); Claudia Koonz's *Mothers in the Fatherland*, reviewed by Glenn Collins (daily: 2 March 1987) and Robert Jay Lifton (Sunday: 1 March 1988); Patrick Süskind's *Perfume*, reviewed by Chr. Lehmann-Haupt (daily: 16 Sept. 1986) and Peter Ackroyd (Sunday: 21 Sept. 1986); Tom Bower's "The Paperclip Conspiracy — the Hunt for Nazi Scientists," reviewed by John Gross (daily: 9 Feb. 1988) and David Wise (Sunday: 14 Feb. 1988); Maria Tatar's "The Hard Facts of the

---

[14] "The Hard Facts of the Grimms' Fairy Tales" (twice 11-15-87, 12-12-87); Salman Rushdie on a newly found letter by W. Grimm "Dear Mili" (11-13-88).

[15] "Freud and his Father" (n.d., 1986); Peter Gay: "Freud" (4-27-88), "Anna Freud" (10-16-88); "Jung" (2-14-88); "The Waning of Humaneness" (7-12-87).

[16] H. G. Gadamer (n. d., 1986); J. Habermas Interviews (n.d., 1986); E. Bloch: *The Principle of Hope* (11-23-86).

[17] On Art: "Kokoschka" (9-7-86); Film: Fassbinder (5-17-87); Music: Beethoven's "Changing Image" (n.d., 1987), Essays (7-8-88); Photography: A. Sander (n.d., 1986); Physics: Einstein papers (n.d., 1987).

Grimms' Fairy Tales," reviewed by Michiko Kakutani (daily: 12 Dec. 1987) and Humphrey Carpenter (Sunday: 15 Nov. 1987).[18]

Although Nazi history and contemporary political affairs were reported on extensively and comprise almost half of all reviews, some omissions seem noteworthy. While Willy Brandt's treatise on "Arms and Hunger" was represented, Helmut Schmidt's "Grand Strategy for the West" was not, which British papers like the *Times Literary Supplement* and the *Economist* covered. Even more surprising, given the *Times*'s propensity for history, is the absence of any mention of the "Historikerstreit" (debate among historians), a highly controversial subject in Europe and one dealt with frequently in the *Times Literary Supplement* and at least once in a thorough and lengthy essay by Gordon Craig in the rival *New York Review of Books*.[19]

Why should one source, the *Times*, be so important, if its book coverage comprises only a fraction of all news-reporting of books and is not really scholarly at that. The answer is obvious. Even after the establishment of a rival, the more thorough and scholarly but much smaller *New York Review of Books*,[20] the *Times* remains the most influential source of information on new publications for the general public. Once a serious book is published, its author and publisher are likely to look there first for a review. The influence of the daily reviews cannot be overestimated, not only because of their sheer numbers, about two hundred per year, but also because they are syndicated in this country and English-language papers abroad. In addition, the selection made by the *Times* editors serves as a screen for the many other newspapers outside New York City that have no regular book selections and who rely on the *Times*'s taste and expertise.[21] The worldwide circulation and the trend-setting appeal of the *Times* have their

---

[18] These reviews reinforce or balance each other. The one exception is the book by Maria Tatar, which was panned by both reviewers.

[19] *TLS* (11-7-86, 5-15-87, 2-2-87); Gordon Craig: "The War of the German Historians" (*NYRB*, 1-15-87).

[20] Founded in the early sixties, it is a semimonthly with a circulation (115,000) of less than 10 percent of that of the *Times*.

[21] L. A. Coser, Ch. Kadushin, W. Powell, *Books: The Culture and Commerce of Publishing* (Chicago: University of Chicago Press, 1985), 317.

repercussions on the standard of individual reviews. *Times* editors are acutely aware that they are serving a mass audience of well over one and one-half million, "many of whom would lose interest if the *Times* were to adhere to the high critical standards of, say, the [London] *Times Literary Supplement*, with its elite audience of some fifty thousand."[22] This at least partially explains why until recently the *Times* tended to put men in charge whose background was in general magazine editing rather than in book reviewing.

Apart from the decision whether to review a book at all, the length and location in the paper, whether on the front page or buried in the back, are also important. "A request for 400–800 words usually means that the book just qualifies for a notice; whereas 1000 words or more indicate that the editor or screening reader was impressed. In this way, as the literary critic Benjamin DeMott says, 'space allocation tends to prestructure opinion.'"[23] All this — selection, choice of reviewer, space — makes this process in the last analysis a political act. Undeniably, it makes a difference if, to cite an extreme example, the task of reviewing Ernst Bloch's *The Principle of Hope* is given to Leon Wieseltier, himself the literary editor of the *New Republic*, or to a philosopher academician, Marxist or otherwise. The main fact to keep in mind when speaking about mass reception is therefore that we are not dealing with scholarly reviews, written by peers of the author and members of a particular scholarly discipline, but by professional book reviewers. It should also be remembered that the daily reviewers of the *Times* write two, sometimes three, reviews a week. "They face limits of both time and space (750 words). It is no surprise that they may complain — as John Leonard did on the Dick Cavett show in 1980 — 'that they do not have the time to be a critic.'"[24]

---

[22] Ibid., 318.

[23] Ibid., 322.

[24] Ibid., 323. In their conclusion, the authors find U.S. newspaper reviewing "not particularly impressive" when compared to that of other countries. "In many European countries — Germany, France, and Switzerland for example — one can usually find distinguished book reviews in all the leading daily newspapers; and important books are brought to the attention of the reading public not only in the cities but across the provinces. In the United States, however, readers outside of New York and a few other metropolitan communities have to turn to media other than newspapers if they wish to keep

296   The Fortunes of German Writers in America

What about the size of initial printings of books? According to Elisabeth Sifton, then editor-in-chief of Viking, the absolute number of readers has remained fairly constant, even as the general population grows, and with it, the number of the first novels published.[25] Interestingly enough, this number — between 500 and 5000 — seems to apply everywhere, but this very sameness must be disconcerting to U.S. publishers. She states, "When a Swedish publisher tells an Italian or Brazilian or American publisher that he hasn't done as well as he had hoped with so-and-so's first book, he means just about what the other three would mean: he means he sold only a few thousand copies. But *he* sold his few thousand in a country of just a few million people, and America [in 1970] is a land of 220 million souls. The American publisher would have to sell 50,000 copies to reach the same pitiable proportion of the population reached routinely by his Swedish colleague."[26] Put another way: judged by the proportion of the population buying books, most books published in Europe, or at least a vastly greater number, would be best-sellers in U.S. terms.

The typical fate of a German translation on the American market is roughly the following: first the American publisher applies for reimbursement of all or part of the translation cost to Inter Nationes / Bonn. That granted, 2000 copies are produced. If the book is then reviewed by the *Times*, and only then, about 800 copies are sold the first year, 600 the second, perhaps 200 during the third and last year. The rest is then remaindered or, if the publisher is lucky, bought again by Inter Nationes to be given away through the consulates or Goethe Institutes as book prizes. In the fifth year after its first publication, it is as if the whole thing had never happened; the book is no longer available and considered out of print; often not even the publisher has retained a copy in his own archive. This is true not only of relatively

---

abreast of the publication and critical assessment of books of potential interest." Ibid., 325.

[25] Elisabeth Sifton, "What Reading Public?" *Nation*, 22 May 1982, 628–29.

[26] Ibid.; see also Stephen Graubard, ed., *Reading in the 1980s* (New York: R. R. Bowker, 1982), 77; making the same point is Mark J. Mirsky, *New York Times*, 16 April 1972. The same phenomenon has become known in some circles as the "Enzensberger-Konstante." H. M. Enzensberger facetiously stated that the number of readers of a particular book, say a volume of poetry, is constant. It will find the same number of readers, say 1256, regardless of the country of origin or distribution, whether in Denmark or in the U.S.

unknown authors but also of works by Handke, Weiss, Kipphardt, Enzensberger, Lenz, Hildesheimer, Bernhard, Peter Schneider, Christa Wolf, even Frisch and Dürrenmatt, in short all of contemporary literature. To cite one last example, Martin Walser's "The Runaway Horse." It had been a genuine runaway best-seller for several years not only in Germany but in other European countries as well before it was published by Holt, Rinehart, and Winston in 1980. Encouraged by the European record, the American house produced an unusually large first printing of 4500 copies, 1500 of which were destined for Great Britain and Canada. But it shared the fate of all other German translations, its first printing turned out also to be its last, and today the book is out of print. It is fairly obvious that if the shelf life of a book is so limited and if the initial printing is also largely identical with the total edition, one can hardly speak of any reception.

Speakers at a forum on "The Future for Publishing across Language Frontiers" held in Jerusalem in 1987 commented on what they called "the isolation of American culture." Whereas one of five books published in France is of foreign origin, as is one-third of the books published by most major French houses, with similar figures for Spain and Italy, the corresponding figure for the U.S. is one book in forty.[27] One of the causes seems to be the lack of foreign editors. One participant estimated that there are only three trade book editors in New York who read Italian and that the figure for those who read German is not much higher. In our case the fall from grace hurts even more because we had been spoiled for so long by the presence of the highly trained, committed, and articulate generation of emigrants from Hitler. Their mass exodus, comparable in size only to the fall of Constantinople that set the Renaissance in motion, had a powerful effect on all facets of

---

[27] *The Future for Publishing across Language Frontiers*, Report of a Forum in Jerusalem, April 7–9, 1987 (Gütersloh: Bertelsmann Foundation Publishers, 1988). Jonathan Galassi (Farrar, Straus & Giroux, N.Y.) said the scarcity of language expertise "is not just a problem of publishing; it's a problem in American culture in general. The root of the problem is our isolation" (190). Werner Linz (Crossroad, Continuum, Ungar, N.Y.) said "that the situation in the U.S. is growing worse, that American publishers produce a much smaller percentage of books in translation than the world average: 2.5 percent against 10 percent" (ibid.). Ulrich Wechsler's (Bertelsmann, Gütersloh) figures confirm this: "France and Germany 10%, Spain and Italy even higher, England 5% and the United States 2%" (ibid.).

cultural and academic life in this country, not the least of which was in the publishing industry.

Books and the ideas carried by them are, of course, only one aspect of culture-transfer. The exchange of Dallas soap operas, rock and roll and high tech for BMW's and recordings by Deutsche Grammophon seems to work quite well. Why are books the exception? In a *Times* review Judith Ryan says, "For the American reader, German literature remains stubbornly foreign, even when it appears readily accessible. This is particularly true in the case of postwar German writing."[28] Probably so, but why? I do not profess to know the answer but (in ending) would like to suggest ideas for your consideration. Like love, genuine appreciation and respect cannot develop simply because it is constantly demanded by one side. On the other hand, any kind of deeper understanding presupposes familiarity. As long as dissemination about facts of German life and thinking is haphazard and sporadic, such understanding will be very difficult to achieve. To get more information across is both a tall order and at the same time no new demand: we have been aware of this necessity all along. In the meantime, however, I think there is one thing we can do. One major obstacle of the American book market, we have seen, is the difficulty of keeping books in print. Not only to make information available but to keep it available is the task, and one which the so-called free market with its fast-changing demands is not interested, perhaps not equipped, to guarantee. As anybody can attest who has tried to teach a course in German literature in translation, it is almost impossible to repeat after only a couple of years because the English texts are no longer available. That is why some of us founded *The German Library*. Half of its planned one hundred volumes are out by now or under way, encompassing not only literature but also philosophy, history, music, essays in criticism, etc. The novelty of the series lies not so much in new translations or the fact that heretofore unknown texts are made public in English (although the series has both), as rather in the guarantee of the publisher to keep these books on the backlist and thus available for a long time. This is an expensive undertaking and would have been impossible without the strong commitment of Werner Mark Linz, the publisher, and the very

---

[28] Judith Ryan: "Compassion and the German Heart," *New York Times*, 24 Dec. 1986.

substantial subsidies from Bonn and especially German foundations and industry. If, beyond preaching to the already converted, we want to reach others — and that is what is meant by reception — the availability of a core canon of texts, perhaps to be expanded eventually, seems to be the first and indispensable step.

The Contributors

Clifford Albrecht Bernd (University of California, Davis)

Jürgen Born (Universität Wuppertal)

Thomas L. Buckley (University of Pennsylvania)

Bettina Cothran (Georgia Institute of Technology)

Donald G. Daviau (University of California, Riverside)

Wulf Koepke (Texas A&M University)

Ralph Ley (Rutgers University)

Warren R. Maurer (University of Kansas)

Siegfried Mews (University of North Carolina)

Patrick O'Neill (Queen's University)

Terry Reisch (Hillsdale College)

Jeffrey L. Sammons (Yale)

Volkmar Sander (NYU)

Guy Stern (Wayne State University)

Hans Rudolf Vaget (Smith College)

Hans Wagener (UCLA)

Index

A Soldier's Legacy, see Böll, works by: *Das Vermächtnis*
A Time to Love and a Time to Die, see Remarque, works by: *Zeit zu leben und Zeit zu sterben*
Absent without Leave, see Böll, works by: *Entfernung von der Truppe*
Acquainted with the Night, see Böll, works by: *Und sagte kein einziges Wort*
Adam, Where Art Thou?, see Böll, works by: *Wo warst du, Adam?*
"Adventure, The," see Böll, works by: "Das Abenteuer"
Adventure of My Youth, see Hauptmann, works by: *Abenteuer meiner Jugend*
Affairs of Anatol, The, see Schnitzler, works by: *Anatol*
Albee, Edward F., 170
All Quiet on the Western Front, see Remarque, works by: *Im Westen nichts Neues*
America, 250, 256, 261, 263, 266, 273

Annotated Arthur Schnitzler Bibliography, 158
Antifascism 131, 132, 134, 135, 136
Arch of Triumph, see Remarque, works by: *Arc de Triomphe*
Arendt, Hannah, 123, 127, 128, 129
Aristophanes, 31, 43
Armstrong, Louis, 234
Arnold, Matthew, 48, 50
Asch, Sholem, 199
Athenaeum, 55

Atlantic Monthly, 222, 251, 271, 290
Auden, W.H., 123
Audubon, John, 6
works by: *The Viviparous Quadrupeds of North America*, 6
Auerbach, Berthold, 58
Aufbau, 140

Bachmann, John, 6
"Balek Scales, The," see Böll, works by: "Die Waage der Baleks"
Bancroft, George, 31, 32
Banks, Maud, 108
Barker, Granville, 150
Bauke, Joseph, 259, 262, 264
Baum, Vicki, 95
Beaver Coat, The, see Hauptmann, works by: *Der Biberpelz*
Becher, Johannes R., 141
Becker, Godfrid, 43
Beckett, Samuel, 170, 279
Before Sunrise, see Hauptmann, works by: *Vor Sonnenaufgang*
Beharriell, Frederick J., 159
Benjamin, Walter, 126, 287
Benn, Gottfried, 88
Bentley, Eric, 205, 237, 240, 241, 242, 243, 245
Berlin, Jeffrey B., 158, 165
Bernstein, Leonard, 137
Between Heaven and Earth, see Werfel, works by: *Zwischen unten und oben*
Bieber, Hugo, 65
Billiards at Half-past Nine, see Böll, works by: *Billard um halb zehn*
Binding, Rudolf G., 93

Black Obelisk, The, see Remarque, works by: *Der schwarze Obelisk*
Blättermann, Georg, 28
Blei, Franz, 90
Bloch, E., 293, 295
Bloom, Allan, 234
Boas, Franz, 83
Bodenheim, Gretel, 209
Bodenheim, Hans, 209
Böll, Heinrich, i, vi, vii, 229, 249-275, 279
  works by: *Und sagte kein einziges Wort,* 255, 257, 266; *Wo warst du, Adam?,* 256, 257, 265; *Der Zug war pünktlich,* 257, 258, 266, 271; *Haus ohne Hüter,* 258; *Billard um halbzehn,* 259, 260, 261, 274; *Ansichten eines Clowns,* 261, 262, 263, 267, 270; *Entfernung von der Truppe,* 263, 272; *Als der Krieg ausbrach, Als der Krieg zu Ende war,* 263; *18 Stories,* 264; *Doktor Murkes gesammeltes Schweigen,* 264; "Im Tal der donnernden Hufe," 264; "Der Tod der Elsa Baskoleit," 264; "Das Abenteuer," 264; "Die Waage der Baleks," 264; *Children are Civilians, Too,* 264; *Das Brot der frühen Jahre,* 266; *Das Vermächtnis,* 266; "Suchanzeigen," 266; *Irisches Tagebuch,* 266, 267; "Der Ort war zufällig," 267; "Die Moskauer Schuhputzer," 267; *Gruppenbild mit Dame,* 267, 268, 269, 272; *Ende einer Dienstfahrt,* 267; *Die verlorene Ehre der Katharina Blum,* 269, 271, 272; *Fürsorgliche Belagerung,* 270, 272; *Was soll aus dem Jungen bloß werden? Oder: Irgendwas mit Büchern,* 271; 272; *Frauen vor Flußlandschaft,* 272, 273

Bogner, Fred, 255
Bonsels, Waldemar, 93
Booklist, 208
Booth, Brutus, 6
Börne, Ludwig, 43, 48, 57, 63
Boston Transcript, 214
Brahms, J., 204
Brassell, Jim, 169
Bread of Those Early Years, The, see Böll, works by: *Das Brot der frühen Jahre*
Brecht, Bertolt, i, vi, 93, 99, 102, 133, 139, 231-248, 279, 280, 289
  works by: *Caucasian Chalk Circle,* vi, 236-248; *The Threepenny Opera,* 234, 235, 244, 247; "Mack the Knife," 234, 235; "Dispute about the Valley," 240; *The Good Woman of Setzuan,* 241, 242; "Prologue," 240, 241, 242, 243
Broch, Hermann, 292
Brod, Max, 58, 66, 93, 127
Browne, Lewis, 60, 62
Burroughs, Edgar Rice, 204
Bury, Countess de, 51
Bury, Henri Blaze de, 51

Cabet, Etienne, 103
Call of Life, The, see Schnitzler, works by, *Der Ruf des Lebens*
Calvert, George H., 33

Campe, Julius, 43
Camus, Albert, 279
Canadian Forum, 126
Carlyle, Thomas, 18
Carpenter, Stephen Cullen, 7-11, 22, 24
Carroll, Lewis, 204
Causes of Germany's Moral Downfall, The, 82
Chaplin, Charlie, 136
Charleston, 1-3, 5-10, 13, 17, 21-25
Charleston Courier, 8, 11
Charvat, William, 12, 17
Chekhov, Anton, 100, 246
Chicago Sunday Times, 222
Chomsky, Noam, 289
Christian Examiner, ii, 28, 32, 33, 34, 37, 38, 39
Christian Science Monitor, 219, 222, 226
Churchill, Winston, 255
City Gazette, 10
Clapp, Henry A., 113
Clark, W.V., 221
Class Reunion, see Werfel, works by: *Der Abituriententag*
Clown, The, see Böll, works by: *Ansichten eines Clowns*
Coar, John Firman, 48, 50
Coleridge, Samuel T., 54
Colleague Crampton, see Hauptmann, works by: *Kollege Crampton*
Coming of Peace, The, see Hauptmann, works by: *Das Friedensfest*
Commonweal, 200, 250, 256, 260, 263
Columbia University, 70, 78, 117, 118, 119, 154
Conried, Heinrich, 112
Cooke, Alistair, 160
Cooper, James Fenimore, 103

Cooper, Thomas, 6
Cooperman, Stanley, 255
Copland, Aaron, 137
Cornell, J., 72
Critic, 111
Cronin, A.J., 199

Dante, 121, 279
Daily Worker, 137
Daybreak, see Schnitzler, works by: *Spiel im Morgengrauen*
Death in Venice, see Mann, Th., works by: *Der Tod in Venedig*
"Death of Elsa Baskoleit," see Böll, works by: "Der Tod der Elsa Baskoleit"
Decline of the West, The, see Spengler, works by: *Untergang des Abendlandes*
Dehmel, Richard, 87
Demetz, Peter, 54, 292
DeVoto, Bernhard, 217
Dial, The, ii, 29, 34, 35, 37
Diary, see Grass, works by: *Aus dem Tagebuch einer Schnecke*
Dickens, Charles, 126, 127
Döblin, Alfred, 92, 102, 279
  works by: *Wallenstein*, 92; *Berge, Meere und Giganten*, 92
Dog Years, see Grass, works by: *Hundejahre*
Dostoyevsky, Fyodor, 127, 256
Douglas, I.C., 199
Doyle, P.A., 226
Draper, Hal, 55, 57, 63
Drayman Henschel, see Hauptmann, works by: *Fuhrmann Henschel*
Dream Pad, The, see Remarque, works by: *Traumbude*
Dreiser, Theodore, 103, 118, 154
Dunlop, Geoffrey, 187
Dürrenmatt, Friedrich, i, 289, 297

Index

Economist, 294
Edel, Leon, 129
Edinburgh Review, 13
Edschmid, Kasimir, 90
Ehrenstein, Albert, 93
Eichthal, Wilhelm Baron von, 42
Einstein, Albert, 83, 85, 135, 136
Eisler, Hanns, 139
Eisner, Paul, 130
Ellet, Elizabeth F., 22
  works by: *The Characters of Schiller*, 22
Elliot, George, 48,
  works by: "German Wit," 48
Elliot, T.S., 170
Eloesser, Arthur, 84, 88
Embezzled Heaven, see Werfel, works by: *Der veruntreute Himmel*
Emerson, Ralph Waldo, 1, 13, 34-37, 103
Encyclopaedia Britannica, 153
End of a Mission, see Böll, works by: *Ende einer Dienstfahrt*
Engels, Friedrich, 74
Engle, Peter, 227
Enright, D.J., 261, 264, 265, 274
Enzensberger, Hans Magnus, 297
Esslin, Martin, 231, 232, 233, 237, 242, 244
Eternal Road, see Werfel, works by: *Weg der Verheißung*
Evans, Luther, 139
Everett, Alexander Hill, 31
Ewers, Hans, 94
Existentialism, 122, 123
Expressionism, 88

Fadiman, Clifton, 197, 205
Falke, Otto, 90
Fallada, Hans, 95
Faulkner, William, 216, 260, 265, 268, 279
Faust, Albert, 72

Fejtö, François, 66
Felton, Cornelius C., 32, 37
Feuchtwanger, Lion, i, 83, 87, 91, 92, 95, 96, 192
  works by: *Erfolg*, 83; *Jud Süß*, 87; *Power*, 91; *The Ugly Duchess*, 91;
Firda, Richard A., 211
Flagman Thiel, see Hauptmann, works by: *Bahnwärter Thiel*
Fleming, Thomas, 274
Flirtation, see Schnitzler, works by: *Liebelei*
Flotsam, see Remarque, works by: *Liebe deinen Nächsten*
Flounder, The, see Grass, works by: *Der Butt*
Follen, Carl, 28
Foltin, Lore, 208
Fontane, Theodor, 105, 171
  works by: *Effi Briest*, 171
Fool in Christo Emanuel Quint, The, see Hauptmann, works by: *Der Narr von Christo Emanuel Quint*
Forty Days of Musa Dagh, see Werfel, works by: *Vierzig Tage des Musa Dagh*
Forty-Eighters, 72-77, 79
Francke, Kuno, 45, 46
Frank, Bruno, 93, 94, 95
Frankfurter Rundschau, 288
Frenssen, Gustav, 89, 96
Freud, Sigmund, 85, 293
Friedrich, Otto, 234
Frisch, Max, 297
Frothingham, Nathaniel L., 31
Fuller, Margaret, 34, 36, 37, 40
Fülöp-Miller, René, 94
Furst, Lilian, 107

Gadamer, H.G., 293
García Márquez, Gabriel, 283
Gauss, Carl Friedrich, 16

Gazette and Daily Advertiser, 9
Geismar, Maxwell, 227
Genet, Jean, 170
George, Stefan, 88
German Express, 42
German Friendly Society, 5
Germanic Tribes and Romans, see Hauptmann, works by: *Germanen und Römer*
German Library, The, 298
Germany, A Winter Tale, see Heine, works by: *Deutschland: Ein Wintermärchen*
Gide, André, 96
Gilfert, Charles, 6
Gish, Lillian, 118
Goethe, Johann W. von, i, ii, iii, 2, 17, 18, 19, 21, 22, 25, 29, 30, 32, 33, 34, 100, 115, 117, 121, 279, 292
    works by: "Erlkönig," 19; "Gretchen am Spinnrad," 19; "The Song of Margaret," 19; "Der König von Thule," 19; *The Elective Affinities*, 19, 33, 37; *Wilhelm Meister*, 19, 20, 35, 39; *Wilhelm Meister's Apprenticeship and Travels*, 19; *Aus meinem Leben - Dichtung und Wahrheit*, 30; *Werther*, 30, 33; *Faust*, 2, 20, 32, 36, 39, 113; *Iphigenia*, 32, 37; *Egmont*, 37; *Hermann und Dorothea*, 71; *Götz von Berlichingen*, 33; *Tasso*, 32
Goethe, Ottilie von, 2
Gogol, Nicolai, 129
Goslar, Hans, 84
Graf, Oskar Maria, 93
Grass, Günter, i, vi, vii, 260, 261, 269, 277-285

    works by: *Die Blechtrommel*, 277, 278, 279, 280, 282, 283; *Show Your Tongue*, 277; *Katz und Maus*, 278, 279; *Hundejahre*, 278, 279; *Die Plebejer proben den Aufstand*, 280; *Örtlich betäubt*, 280, 284; *Aus dem Tagebuch einer Schnecke*, 281; *Der Butt*, 281, 283; *Das Treffen in Telgte*, 282; *Kopfgeburten oder Die Deutschen sterben aus*, 282; *Die Rättin*, 277 282; *Zunge zeigen*, 282, 284
Green Cockatoo, The, see Schnitzler, works by: *Der grüne Kakadu*
Greene, Graham, 270
Grillparzer, Franz, 31
Grimmelshausen, Hans J.C. von, 279
Group Portrait with Lady, see Böll, works by: *Gruppenbild mit Dame*
Grumbach, Doris, 256
Guthrie, William, 119

Habermas, J., 293
Halm, Friedrich, 7
    works by: *Ingomar, or the Son of the Wilderness*, 7
Handke, Peter, 297
Hands Around, see Schnitzler, works by: *Reigen*
Hansen, Harry, 199
Harper's Magazine, 251, 263
Harrison, J.G., 222
Harvard, 28, 32, 46, 53
Hauptmann, Carl, 103
Hauptmann, Gerhard, i, iv, 85, 99-108, 111-120, 152
    works by: *Anna*, 85; *Hannele*, 85, 108, 109, 111,112, 115,

116, 120; *Rose Bernd*, 88, 115, 117; *Die Insel der großen Mutter*, 90, 103; *Die Weber*, 99, 101, 104, 105, 109, 111, 112, 113, 114, 116, 117; *Die versunkene Glocke*, 99, 119; *Der Biberpelz*, 99, 104, 114, 115, 116, 117; *Germanen und Römer*, 103; *Abenteuer meiner Jugend*, 103; *Vor Sonnenaufgang*, 101, 104, 107, 109, 116, 117; *Einsame Menschen*, 104, 116; *Das Friedensfest*, 104; *Kollege Crampton*, 113, 114; *Fuhrmann Henschel*, 114, 117; *Der Narr in Christo Emanuel Quint*, 115, 116; *Atlantis*, 115, 116; *Bahnwärter Thiel*, 116; *Der Ketzer von Soana*, 116; *Veland*, 116

Haumer, Stephanie, 148
Havel, Vaclav, 182
Haven, George Wallis, 55
Hawthorne, Nathaniel, 127
Hayman, Ronald, 232
Hearken Unto the Voice, see Werfel, works by: *Jeremias-Höret die Stimme*
Heaven Has No Favorites, see Remarque, works by: *Der Himmel kennt keine Günstlinge*
Hedge, Frederic H., 33, 38, 39, 40, 50
    works by: *Prose Writers of Germany*, 38
Heine, Heinrich, iii, 21, 41-67, 85
    works by: *Die Götter im Exil*, 42; *Reisebilder*, 42, 49, 52, 56; *Buch der Lieder*, 43, 44, 49-51, 56, 60; *Deutschland: Ein Wintermärchen*, 45, 49, 50; *Memoirs*, 48; *Die Romantische Schule*, 49, 53, 55; *Atta Troll*, 49, 50, 53; *Neue Gedichte*, 49-50; *Lutetia*, 51; *Die schlesischen Weber*, 51; *Die Harzreise*, 52; *Ideen: Das Buch Le Grand*, 52 "Lorelei," 52; *Poems and Ballads*, 60; "Donna Clara," 60; "Hebrew Melodies," 64

Heinrich, Willi, 257
Heinzen, Karl, 45
Heller, Austin, 126
Heller, Erich, 126
Hellmann, Lillian, 137
Hemingway, Ernest, 216, 229, 256, 259, 265, 270
Henderson, Archibald, 152
Henry, Robert, 15, 17
    works by: "Romances of the Baron de la Motte Fouqué," 15
Heresch, Elisabeth, 159
Heretic of Soana, The, see Hauptmann, works by: *Der Ketzer von Soana*
Hermann, Edward S., 289
Hermann, Georg, 86
Hermann, Helene, 58
Herring, Herbert C., 83
Hesse, Heinrich, i, 88
    works by: *Steppenwolf*, 93
Heuser, Frederick W., 117, 119, 120
Hewett-Thayer, Harvey Waterman, 79
Hindenburg, Paul von, 82, 84
Hirsch, F.C., 223
Hitler, Adolf, v, 76, 82, 83, 182, 223, 226, 258, 260, 269, 271, 273, 297
Hoffmann, E.T.A., 265

Hofmannsthal, Hugo von, 87, 88
Holt, Henry, 119
Hoover, John E., 131, 135, 137, 138, 141
Hörth, Otto, 45
Hosmer, James K., 48
Howard, William Guild, 46
Howell, William Dean, 53, 57
Huch, Ricarda, 93
Huebsch, Ben, 84, 190
Hughes, Langston, 136
Hugo, Victor, 16
Humboldt, Wilhelm von, 6
Hunecker, James, 152
"Hungry Souls," see Mann, Th., works by: "Die Hungernden"
Hurlbut, William, 49
Huxley, Aldous, 204

Ibsen, Hendrik, 106, 152, 246
  works by: *Doll House*, 106
Iffland, August Wilhelm, 12
Ingarden, Roman, 4
International Arthur Schnitzler Research Association, 58
"In the Valley of the Thundering Hooves," see Böll, works by: "Im Tal der donnernden Hufe"
Irish Journal, see Böll, works by: *Irisches Tagebuch*
Iser, Wolfgang, 3, 4

Jackson, Donald L., 142
Jacobowsky and the Colonel, see Werfel, works by: *Jacobowsky und der Oberst*
Jarka, Horst, 156
Jauss, Hans Robert, 3, 291
Johnson, Uwe, 229, 260, 279
Jonas, Klaus, 119
Jones, James, 256
Joyce, James, 86, 100, 121, 279
  works by: *Ulysses*, 86
Jung, C.G., 96, 293

Junges Deutschland, 21

Kabinett des Dr. Caligari, 95
Kafka, Franz, i, iv, vi, 121-130, 208, 232, 259, 269, 279
  works by: *The Trial*, 122, 127; *America*, 123, 125, 126; *The Castle*, 122, 123, 124, 125, 126, 127; "The Metamorphosis," 122, 123; "The Judgement," 122
Kahler, Erich von, 190
Kaiser, Georg, 85, 87
Kalteisen, Michael, 5
Karpeles, Gustav, 58
Kauffmann, Stanley, 244
Keller, Gottfried, 83
Keller, Helene, 118
Kellermann, Bernhard, 86, 94
Kennebeck, Edwin, 256, 257, 259
Kipphardt, Heinar, 289, 297
Kirsch, Robert, 227
Klarmann, Adolf, 201
Klopstock, Friedrich, 32
Knopf, Alfred, 84, 125
Koestler, Arthur, 235
Koepke, Wulf, iv, 81-98
Kohut, George Alexander, 62, 63
Kolbenheyer, Erwin G., 89, 96
Kotzebue, August von, ii, 7-9, 12, 20, 106
  works by: *Der Spanier in Peru*, 8, 12; *Die Sonnenjungfrau*, 8; *Menschenhaß und Reue*, 8, 106; *Falsche Scham*, 9; *The Maid of Orleans*, 12
Krutch, Joseph Wood, 89-93

Lamprecht, Klaus, 218
Lang, Fritz, 95
Lange, Victor, 70
Last Masks, The, see Schnitzler, works by: *Die letzten Masken*
Lawrence, D.H., 223

Lazarus, Emma, 58, 60
  works by: "Don Pedrillo," 60; "Fra Pedro," 60; *Hiawatha*, 60
Legaré, Hugh Swinton, 2, 3
Leibnitz, Gottfried W., 16
Leland, Charles Godfrey, 56, 57
Lenz, Siegfried, 297
Lessing, Gotthold E., 7
  works by: *Minna von Barnhelm*, 7
Levin, Harry, 217
Lewes, G.H., 38
Lewis, C.S., 204
Lewis, Sinclair, 103, 118
Lewisohn, Ludwig, 87-90, 92, 93, 116, 153
  works by: *Mid-Channel*, 90, 92
Library Journal, 223
Life, 128, 136, 140, 142
Liliencron, Detlev von, 88
Lindley, Denver, 256, 258
Linz, Werner Mark, 298
Liptzin, Sol, 64, 154, 155, 157
Littell, Robert, 218
Loewenthal, Erich, 58
Lonely Lives, see Hauptmann, works by: *Einsame Menschen*
Longfellow, Henry W., 52, 73, 103
Lorenz, Konrad, 293
Los Angeles Times, 198, 227
Lovett, Robert M., 86, 92
Lowell, James Russell, 53
Luce, Henry R., 142
Ludendorff, E., 84
Ludwig, Emil, 90, 92-94
Luther, Martin, 18, 46
Lyon, James K., 133, 237

Mackie, J.M., 37
MacLeish, Archibald, 136
Maeterlinck, Maurice, 192
Magic Mountain, The, see Mann, Th., works by: *Der Zauberberg*
Magnolia, 14, 23
Maid of Orleans, The, see Schiller, works by: *Die Jungfrau von Orleans*
Mailer, Norman, 137, 256
Malraux, André, 223
Man and Masses, see Toller, works by: *Masse Mensch*
Manheim, Ralph, 246, 284
Mann, Heinrich, 93, 102, 192
  works by: *Diana*, 93; *Mother Mary*, 94
Mann, Klaus, 93, 123, 124, 125, 126, 128
Mann, Thomas, i, iv, v, 76, 86-89, 90, 94-95, 101, 102, 117, 124, 126, 133-144, 192, 229, 259, 279
  works by: *Buddenbrooks*, 76, 259; *Unordnung und frühes Leid*, 94; *Der Zauberberg*, 87, 89, 92, 97, 100, 224; *Herr und Hund*, 90; *Royal Highness*, 90; *Der Tod in Venedig*, 86, 90; *Jettchen Gebert*, 86; "Die Hungernden," 88
Marschalk, Margarethe, 107
Marsh, F.T., 223
Martens, Kurt, 90
Marxism, 129, 233, 235, 242
Matthews, T.S., 95
Maupassant, Guy de, 256
May, Karl, 292
Mayer, Sigrid, 278
McCarthy, Arthur, 142, 143
McCullough, D.W., 226
Meeting in Telgte, see Grass, works by: *Das Treffen in Telgte*
Meltzer, Henry, 107
Mencken, H.L., 83, 88, 154
Mendelssohn, Felix, 60
Mendelssohn, Moses, 60
Menzel, Wolfgang, 21, 22, 36, 56

works by: *Die deutsche Literatur*, 21
Metropolis, 90
Meyer, Agnes, 136, 139, 141, 143
Miller, Arthur, 137
Milton, John, 188
Mischel, Josef, 137
"Missing Persons and other Essays," see Böll, works by: "Suchanzeigen"
Molière, Jean-Baptiste, 246, 247
Moral Recovery of Germany, The, 82
Morgan, B.Q., 77, 152
Mörike, Eduard, 88
Morton, Frederic, 257, 258
"Moscow Shoeshiners, The," see Böll, works by: "Die Moskauer Schuhputzer"
Most, John, 112
Mozart, Wolfgang A., 178
Muller, K.O., 16
Muller, Siegfried, 119
Murke's Collected Silences, see Böll, works by: *Doktor Murkes gesammeltes Schweigen*
Musil, 292

Nation, 82, 83, 84, 87, 89, 91, 92, 93, 125, 215, 217, 220, 255, 257, 266, 267, 268
National Review, 251, 258, 261, 266
National Union Catalogue, iii, 70, 71
Naturalist, 106, 107, 113, 114
Nestroy, Johann, v, 166-181
works by: *Einen Jux will er sich machen*, 168, 177, 178, 179; *Posse*, 181
Neumann, Alfred, 91-95
works by: *Der Teufel*, 92
New Criticism, 127
New Leader, 251, 259

New Republic, 82, 84, 85, 86, 89, 91, 92, 94, 205, 218, 221, 251, 262, 263, 265, 266, 269, 271, 295
Newsweek, 220, 257, 269
New Yorker, The, 125, 197, 224, 251, 269, 271
New York Herald, 110
New York Herald Tribune Lively Arts, 224
New York Herald Tribune, 110, 114, 250, 290
New York Herald Tribune Book Review, 126, 223, 250, 256, 258, 260
New Yorker Staatszeitung und Herold, 156
New York Times, vii, 105, 110, 114, 115, 118, 219, 222, 225, 244, 249, 258, 259, 263, 268, 270, 271, 279, 289, 290, 291, 295, 296, 298
New York Times Book Review, 196, 203, 207, 225, 250, 255, 256, 257, 258, 259, 261, 263, 264, 265, 266, 267, 268, 269, 271, 272, 274
New York Review of Books, 250, 261, 264, 274, 294
New York University, 154
New York Volkszeitung, 112
Nicolai, Friedrich, 20
Nicolson, Herald, 143
Niebuhr, Reinhold, 16
Nietzsche, Friedrich, 85, 163
Night in Lisbon, The, see Remarque, works by: *Die Nacht von Lissabon*
North American Review, ii, 28-33, 37, 38
Nouvelle Revue, 105

"Observations on the War of Tomorrow," see Werfel, works by:

"Betrachtungen über den Krieg von morgen"
Oeller, Norbert, 12
O'Neill, Eugene, 100, 103, 118
  works by: *Mourning Becomes Electra*, 118
O'Neill, James, 109
Ophüls, Max, 149
Orwell, George, 223
Owen, C.R., 211, 217

Pachelbel, Carl Theodor, 6
Pachelbel, Johann, 6
Parker, A., 51
Parker, Dorothy, 137
Parker, Theodore, 36, 37
Pasternak, Boris L., 283
Paul, Jean, 16
Peabody, Andrew Preston, 37
Pisko, Ernest S., 226, 229
Pizaro, or the Death of Rolla, see Kotzebue, works by: *Der Spanier in Peru*
"Place was Incidental, The," see Böll, works by: "Der Ort war zufällig"
Plant, Richard, 223, 256
Platen, August Graf von, 43, 48
Plievier, Theodor, 257
Ploetz, Alfred, 103, 107, 111
Poe, Edgar A., 103, 122, 127, 129
Politzer, Heinz, 123, 124
Pollard, Percival, 152
Polyglot, 19
Poore, Charles, 219
Porterfield, Allen, 156
Pound, Ezra, 54
Prescott, Orville, 225
Price, Lawrence, 155
Priest, George Madison, 78
Princeton University, 78, 79
Proust, Marcel, 86, 96, 121, 127, 196, 279
Publisher's Weekly, 208

Punch, 177
Pure Heart, The, see Werfel, works by: *Barbara*
Puritanism, 95

Quincy, Josiah, 3
Quinn, Arthur H., 106

Rabelais, François, 223, 279
Rat, The, see Grass, works by: *Die Rättin*
Rathenau, Walter, 82
Rattermann, H.A., 44
Reagan, Ronald, 134
Reck-Mallesczewen, Fritz, 93
Redman, B.R., 218
Reichart, Walter A., 119
Reitzel, Robert, 45
Remarque, Erich Maria, i, vi, 95, 96, 211-230
  works by: *Im Westen nichts Neues*, vi, 87, 93, 94, 212, 213, 215, 216, 219, 222, 223, 225, 227, 228, 229, 256; *Die Traumbude*, 212; *Der Weg Zurück*, 215, 227, 228; *Drei Kameraden*, 216, 217, 227, 228; *Liebe deinen Nächsten*, 217, 218, 228; *Arc de Triomphe*, 218, 219, 220, 227, 228; *Der Funke Leben*, 220, 221, 228; *Zeit zu leben und Zeit zu sterben*, 212, 228; *Der schwarze Obelisk*, 223, 227, 228; *Der Himmel kennt keine Günstlinge*, 224, 229; *Die Nacht von Lissabon*, 225, 227, 229; *Schatten im Paradies*, 226, 227, 229
Renn, Ludwig, 94, 96,
  works by: *Krieg*, 94, 99
Reporter, 262

Index 311

Review of Reviews, 105
Revue de Deux Mondes, 13
Reynolds, Thomas Caute, 2
Rickenbacher, Eddie, 202
Riesser, Gabriel, 58
Rilke, Rainer Maria, 85, 87, 88, 208, 292
Ringelnatz, Joachim, 94
Road Back, The, see Remarque, works by: *Der Weg zurück*
Robbers, The, see Schiller, works by: *Die Räuber*
Robertson, J.G., 49
Robeson, Paul, 141
Robins, Natalie, 133
Rolo, C.J., 222
Romains, Jules, 192
Romanticism, 20, 55, 56, 85
Romantic School, see Heine, works by: *Die Romantische Schule*
Rose Bud, 13
Rosenfeld, Carl, 107, 109
Rosenfeld Theodor, 108
Russell's, 13, 20
Rutra, Arthur Ernst, 63

Safety Net, The, see Böll, works by: *Fürsorgliche Belagerung*
Salten, Felix, 93
San Francisco Chronicle, 224
Saturday Review, 217, 218, 224, 226, 250, 251, 255, 256, 259, 262, 263, 271, 272, 290
Savigny, Friedrich von, 16
Schell, Maximilian, 122
Sewanee Review, 119
Schermann, Harry, 203
Schickele, René, 93, 94, 95
Schiller, Friedrich von, i, ii, iii, 7, 9, 10, 12, 17, 21-23, 30-34, 38-42, 51, 71
 works by: *Die Räuber*, 7, 9, 10, 22, 23, 31, 33 *Fiesco*, 23; *Love and Intrigue*, 23; *Don Carlos*, 23; *Die Jungfrau von Orleans*, 23, 72; *Maria Stuart*, 23, 72; *Die Braut von Messina*, 23; *Wilhelm Tell*, iii, 23, 33, 71, 72, 74, 77; *Der Geisterseher*, 23; *Wallenstein*, 33
Schinnerer, Otto P., 154, 155

Schippers, J.G., 168
Schlegel, August Wilhelm, 2, 20, 24, 56
Schlegel, Friedrich, 20
Schleiermacher, Friedrich, 16
 works by: *Plato*, 16
Schneider, Peter, 297
Schnitzler, Arthur, i, v, 86, 93, 94, 145-182, 255
 works by: *Fräulein Else*, 90, 153, 157, 161; *Liebelei*, 145, 147, 149, 150, 152, 157, 159, 160, 161, 168, 174, 175, 176; *Freiwild*, 147, 164; *Das Vermächtnis*, 147; *Die letzten Masken*, 147, 156; *Der grüne Kakadu*, 147, 151, 156, 173; *Literatur*, 147, 156; *Das weite Land*, 147, 151, 168, 171, 173, 174, 180, 181; *The Gallant Cassian*, 147, 156; *Der Ruf des Lebens*, 147, 151; *Reigen*, 147, 149, 153, 159, 160; *Anatol*, 147, 148, 150, 153, 156, 157, 159, 160; *Spiel im Morgengrauen*, 148, 153, 161; *Rhapsody*, 153, 161; *Therese*, 153, 161; *None of the Brave*, 153, 161; *Beatrice*, 153, 161; *Flight into Darkness*, 153, 161; *Nachlaß*, 155, 158, 159; *Casanova's*

Homecoming, 153, 154, 161; *My Youth in Vienna*, 161; *The Mind in Words*, 161; *Some Day Peace Will Return*, 161, 164; *The Little Comedy and Other Stories*, 161; *Plays and Stories*, 161; *Little Novels*, 161; *Countess Mitzi*, 161; *The Highstrung Woman*, 162; *New Year's Eve*, 162; *Frau Berta Garlan*, 162; "Das Tagebuch der Redegonda," 173;
Schnitzler, Heinrich, 159
Schrumpf, Beatrice, 147, 154
Schulz-Behrend, George, 77
Schurz, Carl, 73, 74
Scott, Robert, 202
Seghers, Anna, 192
Shadows in Paradise, see Remarque, works by: *Schatten im Paradies*
Shakespeare, William, 31, 121, 170, 177
Sharp, William, 48
Shaw, Bernhard, 150, 152, 204
Show Your Tongue, see Grass, works by: *Zunge zeigen*
Siegfried, 90
Silone, Ignazio, 223
Slochower, Harry, 93
Socialism, 138
Solzhenitsyn, Aleksandr, 283
Sombart, Werner, 83
Song of Bernadette, see Werfel, works by: *Lied von Bernadette, Das*
Southern Literary Messenger, 13, 16-20, 22, 24
Southern Quarterly Review, 63
Southern Review, 2, 13, 14, 17, 20, 123, 126
Southern Rose, 13

Spark of Life, The, see Remarque, works by: *Der Funke Leben*
Spengler, Oswald, 90
works by; *Der Untergang des Abendlandes*, 90
Staël, Madame de, 14, 30
works by: *De l'Allemagne*, 14, 30
Stalin, Josef, 62, 242
Stanford University, 77
Star of the Unborn, see Werfel, works by: *Stern der Ungeborenen*
Steiman, Lionel B., 202, 208, 209
Steiner, Carl, 190
Sterne, Laurence, 279
Sternheim, Carl, 87
Stone, Jerome, 255
Stoppard, Tom, v, 147, 149, 160, 167-182
works by: *The Real Thing*, 172; *The Real Inspector Hound*, 173; *Dalliance*, 174, 180; *After Magritte*, 180; *Night and Day*, 180; *Travesties*, 180, 181; *On the Razzle*, 181, 182;
Storm, Theodor, i, iii, 69, 74-79
works by: *Immensee*, iii, 71, 74, 76, 77, 78
Stranger, The, see Kotzebue, works by: *Menschenhaß und Reue*
Strindberg, August, 106, 170
Sudermann, Hermann, 90, 93, 94, 106, 152
works by: *Der tolle Professor*, 93
Sunken Bell, see Hauptmann, works by: *Die versunkene Glocke*
Swift, Jonathan, 204, 262, 279

Taylor, Bayard, 73

Taylor, Harley U., 211
Tempo, 140
Teutone, Der, 5
Theatre Magazine, 112
Les *Thibaults, Les*, 96
Thienemann, Marie, 107
Thieß, Frank, 94, 95
Thomas, Calvin, 78, 79
Three Comrades, see Remarque, works by: *Drei Kameraden*

Ticknor, George, 73
Tidyman, Philip, 1
Tillinger, Eugene, 139, 140, 141, 142, 143
Time, vii, 142, 198, 218, 236, 251, 255, 256, 258, 260, 269, 270, 277, 280,
Times Literary Supplement, 290, 294, 295
Tin Drum, The, see Grass, works by: *Die Blechtrommel*
Toller, Ernst, 86, 93, 96
 works by: *Masse Mensch*, 86
Tomorrow and Yesterday, see Böll, works by: *Haus ohne Hüter*
Torberg, Friedrich, 185, 210
Toscanini, Arturo, 135
Train Was on Time, The, see Böll, works by: *Der Zug war pünktlich*
Trakl, Georg, 88
Transcendentalism, 29, 34, 35, 37, 40
Travel Pictures, see Heine, works by: *Reisebilder*
Tucholsky, Kurt, 84
Twain, Mark, 53, 103

Uhland, Ludwig, 54
Undiscovered Land, see Schnitzler, works by: *Das weite Land*
Ungar, Frederick, 159, 161

University of California, Los Angeles 159
University of Kentucky, 158
University of Michigan, 119
University of Texas, 55, 77
University of Virginia, 28
University of Wisconsin, 87
Unruh, Fritz von, 93, 95
Untermeyer, Louis, 63, 64
Untermeyer, Samuel, 108, 109
Updike, John, 268, 271
Urbach, Reinhard, 159
Urzidil, Johannes, 123, 124, 129, 130

Vallentin, Antonina, 66
Velben, Thorstein, 64
Viebig, Clara, 86
Viereck, George, 153
Viereck, Louis, 72
Village Voice, 272
Villard, Oswald Garrison, 82
Virgin of the Sun, The, see Kotzebue, works by: *Die Sonnenjungfrau*
Vodicka, Felix, 4, 146
Vogel, Margot, 159
Völker, Klaus, 239
Voltaire, 34, 279
Vring, Georg von der, 93

Wados, Harvey, 220
Wagener, John A., 5
Wagner, Richard, 85, 110
Wahr, Fred, 119
Waldinger, Ernst, 90
Walser, Martin, 297
Walz, John, 119
Ware, William, 34
Warren, Austin, 123, 126, 127
Washington, George, 38
Wassermann, Jacob, 85, 86, 87, 93
 works by: *Christian Wahnschaffe*, 85, 88; *The Goose*

Man, 86, 89; *Gold,* 86, 90; *Faber,* 90
Waugh, Arthur, 105
Weavers, The, see Hauptmann, works by: *Die Weber*
Wedekind, Frank, 87, 152
Weigand, Hermann, 100, 119
Weigel, Hans, 154
Weik, John, 42, 48
Weill, Kurt, 234
Weiss, Gerhard, 56
Weiss, Robert, 158
Wellek, René, 126
Welles, Orson, 122, 156
Wells, H.G., 204
Werfel, Alma, 209
Werfel, Franz, i, v, vi, 87, 88, 93, 95, 102, 185-210,
  works by:"God's Child and God's Singer," 185; *Das Lied von Bernadette,* vi, 186, 187, 188, 189, 189, 191, 192, 193, 194, 195, 198, 199, 200, 201, 203, 204, 205, 206, 207, 208, 209; *Stern der Ungeborenen,* vi, 186, 187, 188, 189,203, 204, 205, 206, 207, 208, 209; *Der Abituriententag,* 93, 195, 208; *Vierzig Tage des Musa Dagh,* 95, 187, 192, 193, 194, 195, 204, 207, 208; *Juarez und Maximilian,* 90; *Cella; or, The Survivor,* 186; *Der veruntreute Himmel,* 187, 188, 192, 194, 208; *Jeremias-Höret die Stimme,* 187, 188, 195; *Der Weg der Verheißung,* 188, 195; *Jacobowsky und der Oberst,* 188, 208; *Barbara,* 192, 195, 202; *Zwischen unten und oben,* 206; "Betrachtungen über den Krieg von morgen," 201; *Ella,* 209

What's to Become of the Boy? or: Something to Do with Books, see Böll, works by: *Was soll aus dem Jungen bloß werden?*
Whitman, Walt, 46, 53, 103
Wieland, Christoph M., 31, 32
Wilde, Oscar, 170
Wilder, Thornton, 156
William Tell, see Schiller, works by: *Wilhelm Tell*
Wilson, Edmund, 121, 123, 128, 129
Wolf, Christa, 297
Wolf, Theodor, 84
Women in a River Landscape, see Böll, works by: *Frauen vor Flußlandschaft*
Woolf, Virginia, 128
Wumberg, Gotthart, 146

Yale Review, 218
Young, Stark, 85, 86

Zschokke, Heinrich, 7
Zuckmayer, Carl, 93
Zweig, Arnold, 93, 95
  works by: *Streit um den Sergeanten Grischa,* 93, 94
Zweig, Stefan, 92
  works by: "Adepts in Self-Portraiture," 93